World-Views in Dialogue

*Towards renewal of the Golden Rule,
in understanding and in action*

Study and Anthology

by

Henk Bak

Reflection of an intercultural/interfaith 'walking meditation' project at
Evera, Trentham, Victoria – Australia

World-Views in Dialogue: Towards renewal of the Golden Rule, in understanding and in action.

Study and Anthology

By Henk Bak

Copyright © 2024 by Henk Bak

All rights reserved.

Layout and design, Archie Patel
Cover Design, Archie Patel

1st edition 2024

ISBN:
978-0-9756631-2-7 (paperback)
978-0-9756631-3-4 (hardback)

Published by :
Ludens Publishing
Trentham, Victoria, 3458, Australia
www.henkbak.com

Contents

Foreword *6*

Part One – Study *9*
   I. My Story   10
   II. Stages of Development of Human Consciousness   24
   III. Individual and Societal Consciousness and Lack Thereof   36
   IV. Note on Selection of Texts   55

Part Two - Anthology 62
   1. Dialogue and Language   63
   2. Concepts, doctrines and many ways of knowing   83
   3. Call for Renewal   172
   4. Experience   237
   5. The Golden Rule   276
   6. The Golden Rule in the Public Sphere   350
   7. Anthology Ceremonies, Rites & Practices   440

Epilogue *510*
    Acknowledgements   513

Foreword

This book began as a series of hand-outs for a meditative walk project in Trentham, Australia, as a contribution to the worldwide movement for intercultural and interfaith dialogue. Apart from an advertisement in a local newspaper and through some interfaith groups, there is no public reporting, and participants come as groups or individuals, not in any position of spiritual authority other than their own, be they layperson, scholar, nun, monk, rabbi, imam, elder, church minister or priest. It is designed to complement existing interfaith projects and practices, not to replace them. Instead of established places of worship, here it are groves or clusters of trees offering shadow and shelter, like shrines, 12 of them, which makes for a walk of more than half a mile, taking between one and a half and three hours imaginary pilgrimage: silent along the way, with readings and meditations at the sites.

As Trentham is a country town, ca 100 km NW of Melbourne, with towns and cities on distances between 25 and 140 away from here, a standard visit takes a day, with a 10am start and 4.30m ending: introduction, the walk itself, communal lunch and conversation. The place is a dedicated, permanent venue; it is available for the celebration of World Interfaith Harmony Week each day of this week, 1-7 February and at other times by appointment. The 'harmony' week falls in the bush-fire danger season, and not every day may be suitable.

The walk is supported by a hand-out, based on a particular theme and there is a booklet with texts taken from the different world-views, by which visitors can guide themselves on a walk. A dedicated library is available and at the occasion of the walk, I put a number of books on display, including two books that are the inspiration for this project: 1. 'Earth Celebration 1997', an extensive documentation of an interfaith project in Switzerland, under the motto: Many Rivers, One Ocean, initiated by Shin Gwydion Fontalba, Spiritual Teacher, in Switzerland, followed by 2 more celebrations in Switzerland, and one in India. 2. 'Walking Meditation' by Thich Nhat Hanh.

The meditative walk at Evera, Trentham, started in 2007 as a private observance, and became public in 2012, at the suggestion of a friend. In 2014 another friend suggested I write a book, which is based on the experience, practice and supporting study for this project, as an interfaith study, anthology and reader. The nature of the project, concentrating on the originating wellspring of each spiritual stream or religion, through meditation and conversation, doesn't lend itself to making photographs, media coverage and/or authoritative confirmation. And I forget to ask participants for a testimony on paper, probably because they have already expressed their appreciation by the intensity of their participation and their spontaneous comments.

The underlying theme of all walks and conversations is the 'Golden Rule', which can be considered as a crystallization of an age-long practice in all religions and in humanism, but in recent times has been constricted to people's private lives, whilst public life is often driven by other rules. The question then becomes, where in the religion's original impulse can religion and secular humanism be the inspiration for a revival of the golden rule in the public sphere: not a crystallization, but more like a seed, a new, living form, for times to come. The search for those seeds is part of the meditation and conversation, whether it is a new understanding of the Sabbath, of money, of education, of space.

A week before I sent it on its way for publication, I presented the manuscript of this book to three friends. One of them suggested that I bring the notion of the 'Golden Rule' forward, into the title. After some thought I was happy take up his suggestion. Expressions of the Golden Rule itself and renewal of its application form the dialogue's theme in the second half of the book. But the question 'who is my neighbour?' resonates as theme in the first half. There it is amplified to address all three elements of the Golden Rule: 'who is the Highest, most Sacred, who is God?'; 'who is my neighbour in a globalized world?' And: 'who am I, that the love for myself may be a worthy measure of my love for others.

The book's set-up in two distinct formats lends itself to a variety of uses:

> ▶ The study can be used as introduction and key to the selected texts of the anthology or as a stand-alone essay in the context of other studies. Similarly, the anthology can be used to illuminate the concepts and considerations presented in the study with a rich variety of expressions, reflective, poetic, practical and creative. It can also be used as a reader on its own, to be opened anywhere any time, for reflection and spiritual nourishment.

> ▶ The anthology is by itself also instructive for its intended concentric design: chapter 4, Experience is central to the whole, with the first three chapters dealing with past and present world-views and dialogue leading to the call for renewal; the last three chapters the actual embodiment of the Golden Rule in the past, in present public life and in the timeless realm of ritual and prayer.

Part One – Study

I. My Story

My first stories are those of my parents: a fight between Catholic boys of my father's village and Protestant boys of the neighbouring village. Both groups had ventured out through the paddocks in between the villages. After the clash the fight ended in lasting friendships. My mother grew up in Amsterdam and often mentioned her visits to the Jewish neighbours where she lit the candles for the Sabbath. During the war, living in The Hague, my mother had lengthy conversations with a Jewish shopkeeper in his modest stationary shop, who listened fascinated to the meditation on the passion, preached over the wireless by an exuberantly eloquent Franciscan priest. These stories were snippets of life in the Netherlands, when different religions and denominations had their own schools, their own newspapers, publishers, radio stations, with very little contact except in the street and shops.

For me, this story begins with memories of an imaginary walk with my mother and brother between seven churches representing the seven hills of Rome. That was done on Maundy Thursday in the Holy Week before Easter. In all Catholic churches of The Hague the Holy Sacrament was placed on the altar, surrounded with flowers and candlelight, for the faithful to worship and pray. It was like a city pilgrimage which ended not in the seventh church but in a tearoom instead. That's how my mother's father used to do it when she was a girl.

As a teenager I once participated in the "Stille Omgang", a silent walk at night through the streets of the centre of Amsterdam, to commemorate the miraculous re-appearance of the Holy Host over the wood fire, which had been thrown in there when a sick person who had received holy communion had not been able to keep it in. The miracle happened in the 14th Century; the silent walk stemming from the time that Catholic services in public were forbidden and were confined to private homes. What impressed me most in this nightly pilgrimage was the genuine devotion in which adult men were engaged in it. From these snippets it may have become clear how confined to his own Catholic environment this boy had been.

The first crack in this safe world came more as a wonder than a shock, when my piano teacher, Willem Hielkema, a young concert pianist, showed me his deep reverence for Beethoven's second last sonata, and for Bach: a religious reverence to the point that he told me that this music was, for him, enough: no need for any religion. My first experience of a shared reverence, without a need to share a particular form of religion itself. This crack opened wide when I went to study at the University of Leyden, where, just 4 years after the war, everything happened in the fresh new wind of what was called the "Doorbraak", the "Breakthrough": Protestants of different denominations, Catholics and Humanists started to take part in formerly exclusive organisations. Students from different backgrounds formed their traditional "Dispuuts" (Student Clubs). I remember an older student, preparing for the ministry in a protestant church asking me and a friend for a copy of the Imitatio Christi (following the footsteps of Christ), written by Thomas of Kempen, a Catholic brother, a century before the Protestant Reformation. I grew up a Catholic in a neighbourhood with many Protestant neighbours and in the last winter, elders of the local church organized soup kitchens for us, kids. But there was never talk about religious things. A senior Protestant theology student, talking about the Imitatio Christi with a junior Catholic Art History student like me, was a total new experience for me. So segregated were the different faith communities apparently till after the war. Each major faith community had its own schools, press, radio stations, political parties, the so-called "Zuilen" (columns), a vertical segregation based on "Sovereignty within one's own domain". This principle has been formulated by Dr Abraham Kuyper, who founded in Amsterdam the Vrije Universiteit based on Neocalvinist teachings. Kuyper has been a great statesman, responsible for much of the political culture in the Netherlands until today. (His broad world-view made him travel after he retired for 9 months through all the countries around the Mediterranean studying the rise of Islam in relation to Christian and Jewish traditions. In 2015, 110 years after his journey, a TV crew and a historian from the Vrije Universiteit followed his footsteps, interviewed people, scholars, journalists, activists, for a documentary which appeared in 2016, confirming the reminder in the Declaration of Marrakesh in that same year, that in those olden times Jews, Christians and Muslims lived peacefully together in 'countries with Muslim majorities'...Documentary: "Om the Oude Wereldzee", with subtitles and most interviews in English). What I experienced in a nutshell straight after the war was the beginning of a break-through indeed, but this vertical segregation is still there which enabled Muslim 'guest-workers' and migrants from North Africa and the Middle East to create a 'column' of their own, which provides security but also the isolation which the other segments of society are 'breaking through'.

It was in Leyden that I learned about the Dao and how the teaching of "doing nothing" can stifle a society, when wrongly understood. It was there that I first heard of Orwell and his 1984, through a visiting lecturer, Arnold Toynbee (also new to me), the historian who studied the rise, flourishing and fall of civilizations and distilled from there the notion of "creative minorities", which holds the key of youthful energy from which new civilizations arise. Then, in 1950, Toynbee was optimistic about our future. Later, I read parts of a summary of his 10 volumes, modestly called: "A Study of History", abridged by D.C. Somervell.

After a year I left Leyden, to join the Franciscan Order where one first lives a monastic life as a novice and a student in philosophy, psychology, church history, theology and bible studies. Later, one would work in communities or as a missionary somewhere overseas. I had missionary aspirations, which inspired me halfway through the 5 years I spent there, to help mount an exhibition on Christian Art in cultures as diverse as Chinese, Javanese, African, Melanesian, and Latin American. An experienced missionary and anthropologist gave a lecture with slides (images), in which he emphasized identifications of Christianity with indigenous motifs, notably the Madonna and universal Mother images.

Monastic life, with hours of chanting, prayer, meditation and study has enriched my life forever. Long walks in nature were a vital part of the experience and in the Catholic South and East of the Netherlands, traditional processions through the fields, in Spring and Autumn, praying for a good crop and thanking for a good harvest, were living connections with age old traditions. Every experience then was not just intellectual or informative, but soulful and sensory as well. Divine and sacred realities were not separated from earthly and secular conditions.

Halfway through my studies in theology I left the Franciscan way of life, when it had become obvious that the life was not healthy for me. A psychiatrist diagnosed me as suffering from 'frustration neurosis'. I learn now from Wikipedia, that she had identified wthis new syndrome which has since become part of the psychiatric discipline. Her name was Terruwe. She was a Catholic, who was treated with suspicion and criticism from Church authorities, because of her application of psycho-analysis in her practice: another example of religious isolationism. She became later recognized and was even consulted by popes. I later learned that Dr AnnaTerruwe had developed an understanding of social life as "bevestigend samenleven", i.e. a 'mutually affirming way of living together', an understanding based on a perceptive diagnosis of her time, which has proved more valid ever since. In 2011, at the centenary of her birth, a sculpture was erected on the theme of 'affirmative living together', in the town, Deurne, where she had spent her final years and a documentary film was produced, 'Generatie Nooit Genoeg/Generation

Unlimited' directed by Emma Westermann, focusing on the urgent need for 'affirmative living together', in a time when rampant consumerism leaves human beings continually dissatisfied and lonely. They may be in 'dialogue' with things, but not with one another...

After a 'gap year' I started my studies at the Catholic University of Nijmegen, "Raboud University" (the university where Dr Terruwe had studied, and where Henri Nouwen, the Catholic priest, who pioneered psychology in American Catholic spiritual life, had - at 'my' time there - been studying psychology. I did an all-round study in history, philosophy, art history and economic history. It was in my student years there, that I met my wife Helma, who was to become my life's companion for more than 50 years, until her death in 2014. In 1960, I was commissioned by the council of student faculties, of which I was a member, to research and report on a possible introduction of a "Studium Generale" as a foundation program for all students. In post-war Europe the universities were 'soul searching', addressing the embarrassing lack of intellectual and civic 'backbone' which university trained professionals, lawyers, doctors, philosophers, historians, teachers, etc. had shown regarding the rise of totalitarian regimes. In 1949/50 I had already experienced a new ferment and a "Studium Generale" in Leyden, where I learned of Hegel and his Dutch interpreter Gerard Bolland (1854-1922), and of the philosophical quandaries surrounding the physical notion of 'action over distance'. By 1959/60 there was a wealth of studies, reports, articles and books, proposals and experiments, converging attempts to broaden and deepen the intellectual and cultural world-view of students, to offset the limited and one sided vocational training offered by pre-war universities.

My report - partly representing the thinking and practice thus far - also contained some proposals placing professional training at the centre of wider contexts or circles, and deeper foundations or roots, a concept that was developed by the Dutch National Student Council. Instead of trying to emulate the Renaissance ideal of "Homo Universalis", I suggested "Homo Cardinalis" as the new ideal: the human being (homo) a pivot, a compass (cardo) able to turn in all directions in widening concentric circles of relevance and consequence. Two specific proposals stood out: the Catholic University should create professorial chairs for Islamic, Hindu, etc. studies and a chair for studies in women's ways of knowing. And the point was made, that in the world of science, including the humanities, there is not such a thing as a religious, (in this case catholic) mathematics, physics, psychology, anatomy or art etc., but that a religious/catholic world-view would offer a context and a stand point from which in all disciplines new possibilities of current 'blind spots' could be uncovered and new approaches to research and teaching encouraged. In hindsight I realize that universities like Nijmegen and e.g. the Free University in Amsterdam, with their religious foundation, had already a 'studium generale' built in. And universities like these have been pioneering a wider and deeper insight into the human constitution beyond any purely physical understanding: an insight through which the physical embodies life, soul and spirit. In Nijmegen the phenomenologist Buytendijk, the psychiatrist Prick, the psychologist Strasser and the art historian v.d. Meer were part of this broader movement, in which my wife Helma and I were educated.

The second proposal was, to create a chair and curriculum on 'women's ways of thinking', for which I got objections from my women friends who felt it was patronizing towards women. My father used to say 'women are realists'. My favourite thinkers of our time are Simone Weil and Hannah Arendt, and my wife Helma.

The report was accepted and sent to the University's Senate. I am not aware that the report was then accepted by the senate and acted upon. One professor had come to see me and questioned me on one sentence in my report: 'The university is on the one hand too scientific and on the other not scientific enough'. (In Dutch and German the word for science: 'wetenschap/Wissenschaft' denotes all forms of methodically acquired knowledge, not just so called 'hard science'.) I haven't followed it up but assume that in the long run some of the report has been implemented, probably fully independently of my report. Three years after this report I was instrumental in finding the title for our 1964 five-yearly interfaculty/international conference: Ecumene of Cultures.

The title, "Ecumene of Cultures", was inspired by a contemporary book: Vormkracht en Onmacht der Religie (Creative Power and Powerlessness of Religion) with chapter vii: Oecumene der Godsdiensten (Ecumene of Religions) by the philosopher, scholar, essayist and poet, Henri Bruning (1961). In that time "Ecumene" was still confined to interfaith relations between Christian denominations only. Apart from a positive response and extensive participation at the conference, I am not aware that either Henri Bruning's book or the conference itself found much response thereafter. They were obviously pioneering days, an observation recently confirmed for me by Professor Dr John Esposito, who, in a lecture on "Christianity and Islam" at the Australian Catholic University, Melbourne, reminisced about his own time back in the 1950's/60's when in the USA "Ecumene" was confined to Christian denominations and Islamic studies were something new (4 December

2015).

Personally, I was not involved in the conference itself, as I was busy teaching, finishing my doctoral degree and being engaged to be married to Helma Overmars, who became my lifelong teacher in women's ways of knowing. Through her nursing experience and doctor's training, as well as her pioneering spirit, she guided me into areas of spiritual awareness that I otherwise would never have explored or known: areas that are very pertinent to the choice of texts that constitute this anthology. Then, as a family, our children expanded our horizons outside our Dutch and Catholic world-views: towards African culture, healthy nutrition and Steiner Education.

What I gained from the 1964 conference, however, was an encounter with Friedrich Heer, Austrian historian, who had written a revealing book on that turning point in European history, ca 1200, when the previous openness between Judaic, Muslim and Christian world-views, with a rich exchange of scholarship of high quality, was rather abruptly closed: Roman law replaced prevailing Germanic law, inquisition replaced "hearing" and the Crusades replaced discourse. At the conference, Friedrich Heer gave a lecture entitled Homo Cosmonauta, exploring another turning point and the spiritual/cultural background of Russian, French. German and Anglo-Saxon aspirations towards space travel and its consequences for the future. Heer quoted from 10th century Russian Liturgy, to show how deeply this aspiration lived in the Russian psyche. After his lecture I had a lengthy conversation with Friedrich Heer over a glass of beer in the Student Society Club, which had a lifelong impact on me: he explained to me the difference between contradiction and polarity, not just in history but everywhere in life. With both there is opposition, but in contradiction the opposites exclude each other whilst in polarity the opposites include each other: the opposites are integral to forming a whole. I have never forgotten this distinction and started to apply it from the next day of teaching onwards. In the senior classes I could make sense between opposites like "essentialism" and "existentialism", between "expressionism" and "impressionism", "liberalism" and "socialism" etc. in all cases showing how both sides of the opposition are crucial for their transcendence into a higher harmony. An insight, too, that informs many of the choices in this anthology.

Through his books, Friedrich Heer also brought me into contact with the work of Gerhard Szczesny, who had written a bestseller, Die Zukunft des Unglaubens (the Future of Unbelief), which was followed by the publication of a correspondence between Friedrich Heer and Gerhard Szczesny: Glaube und

Unglaube (Belief and Unbelief). By the time of our conversation Szczesny had published another book, Die Antwort der Religionen (the Response of the Religions) – to 31 questions, each of which were answered by a leading Hindu, Buddhist, Jew, Catholic, Protestant and Muslim. It is still interesting reading after more than 50 years.

Meanwhile, I had developed a thematic approach to teaching history in my secondary school, which I called: "From History of Worlds to World History". Each year I added another theme:

- From tribe to world community – history of the world as "Dominion"
- From forest track to space travel – history of the world as "Horizon"
- From flint stone to nuclear power – history of the world as "Energy"
- From wilderness to landscape – history of the world as "Culture"
- From retaliation to international law – history of the world as "Tension"

The project was only half finished but what I had worked out in detail as study material for the students turned out to be a great preparation for my teaching after immigration with my family in 1978 to Australia.

In Melbourne, Australia, I taught for 18 years at what is now the Caulfield campus of Monash University, in the School of Art, Craft and Design. Especially in the courses for crafts people, I considered Australia a 'platform', from which to look out over the whole world, not just the Middle East and Europe, and present the crafts in the context of their cultures. It ranged from Japan, Korea and China in the East over Asia, Europe and Africa to the Americas in the West and Australia, New Zealand, Pacific region in the South. Not just history, but geography and anthropology as well. Eighteen years of living into those different cultures the world over: an ecumene of cultures, indeed.

My wife and I had – while still in Europe – discovered the work of Rudolf Steiner, through Steiner Education. There, I found stages of development in human history used as a thematic sequence year by year in primary school and an understanding of children's development as a reflection of the development of mankind (Inspired by Ernst Häckel's "ontogenesis following phylogenesis"). An education based on the insight that a five-year-old experiences the world differently to a nine year or twelve-year-old and that each age therefore thrives on different ways of learning.

The development of human consciousness in human evolution had been a constant theme throughout my teaching career. I never thought of nor spoke of aboriginal ways of thinking in my teaching as "primitive" or "inferior", or of Greek myths as "stories that are not true." I rather asked: 'what were the perceptions and the experiences that made those images and stories true for these peoples?' In this sense, Steiner's elaborations on the development of human consciousness confirmed, expanded and deepened what I already knew or had an inkling of, and Steiner's insights and teachings in spiritual matters and practices, confirmed, widened and deepened the spiritual outlook of my Catholic upbringing and Franciscan apprenticeship. Our children took to the Steiner School as fish to water, and Helma's medical practice and spiritual journey was equally enriched.

In 1994, I wrote an article in the Student Newsletter at the Caulfield Campus of Monash University about the benefit of meditation beyond relaxation: which I saw as a method to explore dimensions of our world, spiritual dimensions, that are not accessible to our everyday sense-perceptions. A professor of the medical school wrote to me afterwards, informing me that second year medical students had started 'meditation' as part of their course. I suspect that my article led to an invitation by 'Community Services' to conduct conversations between different religions on campus, especially with an eye to students from countries where religion is still the context of life, for whom a totally secular teaching, deprived of any spirituality, leaves them spiritually and culturally in a vacuum. I found a room and a reasonably suitable time, and advertised the project to run in eight weekly sessions, each with a question inspired by the Buddha's eightfold path. Chairs in a circle and a vase with flowers in the middle. No further ritual except a minute of silence at the beginning and at the close. Waiting with some participants before the start, Rabbi Jack Engel said: 'I can't help it, but here in Melbourne I breathe Christianity.' And then he added, 'But there is at least one thing, that we Jews have given the world: Halleluja!' Since that day I have made 'Halleluja' part of my morning meditation/prayer: speaking it through my body in eurythmic gestures, like a blessing or a dance.

The one question that remained unanswered by all participants in those conversations was addressing the seventh step on the eightfold path: how does a religion renew itself without losing the purity of its source? "Right Mindfulness" includes "Right Memory". Everyone seemed to agree, that the culture in which a religion arises or is adopted affects the purity of any tradition. It was a conclusion that I shared at the time, but had reason to reconsider when I started this current project.

In the first year the focus of the conversation was on the teachings of the different religions: truth, morality, sexuality, prayer, power, law, renewal, meditation and mysticism. In the second year the focus shifted to the ways religions express themselves in space: aesthetics, arts, forms, ceremonies, codes, creativity and collective manifestation. The form of the conversations in the third year shifted from discourse to stories on the themes of "Discovery", "Liberation", "Creation" etc. through to "Transformation" from Chassidic, Sufi, Christian traditions and life experiences. The Judaic contributions throughout the 3 years enlivened every session with stories, and in the third year Rabbi Hershi Worch co-convened the sessions and brought them even more to life with his guitar. I still play the tape of his songs that he gave me 24 years ago.

For the purpose of this story I insert here some of the introduction to my report to the Chaplaincy Committee of Management.

> *The Religions in Conversation project was thought of as a Chaplaincy contribution to the Caulfield campus, complementing the ongoing pastoral care. The idea was to place spirituality on the agenda of university discourse. This would enable participants to actually practise the openmindedness that the University's document on Education Policy preaches.*
>
> *That this does not seem to work in practice, however, may partly be due to the efficiency by which our culture has quarantined religion from public life, and to the conveyor-belt style of time-management that maximizes input-output teaching shifts, whilst minimizing interactive and interdisciplinary processes.*
>
> *The latter hindrance can be overcome by a more creative redesigning of the week, through which the Wednesday becomes the interactive and interdisciplinary hub of University discourse and teaching, ... Overcoming the former obstacle requires the effort it takes to realize that freedom of religion is just as little achieved by avoiding teaching spirituality as freedom of speech comes about by refusing to teach language.*

For the themes proposed for the conversations see: appendix 1 (Henkbak. com).

Looking back on those years I remember that I felt equipped and encouraged to take on this project by my study of Steiner's work, the practice of meditation based on his work and my participation in the Anthroposophical Society. Additionally, since 1990 Helma and I had been following the teaching of Gideon Fontalba, of Switzerland, and had become involved in his work, which was bringing Anthroposophy - and the work of other spiritual masters - to new levels of understanding, spiritual practice and relevance for our time and human society. Gideon was trained as a eurhythmist and had taught for ten years at the Waldorf School in Tübingen. [His biography, especially his spiritual journey the story of his transformation, under which he is now known as Shin Gwydion in Europe and Shin Shiva in India, is way beyond the scope of this, my life's story. Suffice to say, that for Helma, myself and others, as person and as teacher both Gideon and then Shin Gwydion brought new and urgently relevant insights into the human condition, the world situation and the spiritual resources to respond to them.]

In the middle of this transition, in September/October 1995, at a seminar in Bregenz, Austria, Shin Gwydion initiated a "Free and worldwide Movement for the Protection and Enhancement of Human Dignity." He presented Draft Statutes for this new "movement": three out of the 10 are directly relevant to this project:

> *6. The Movement points to new, deeper-reaching interconnections between the different peoples and nations, with respect to their ways of life, their tasks, and their traditions. It organises encounters accordingly.*
>
> *7. The Movement passes on a new understanding of the meaning of religions and the initiatic streams. It leads towards the common unity that lies above all differences and towards genuine conversation. The highest goal is the revelation of truth and actual union with the All-Godhead.*
>
> *8. The Movement advocates that all religious streams that have arisen out of genuine experiences of God and all living philosophy can, in the higher light-humanity of Christ, be received and brotherly/sisterly loved.*
>
> *(Unpublished transcript of seminar – 29 Sept-1 Oct 1995 Bregenz, Austria. For the full text see Henkbak.com)*

These draft statutes also promised to make new practices available; exercises, insights and meditations, to enable people to indeed protect and enhance the dignity of the human being. During the past two decades of patently ever greater onslaught on human rights and dignity worldwide, Shin Gwydion, the teacher of humanity who stepped into Gideon's place, brought about an avalanche of new 'material' through seminars, publications, initiatives, foundations etc., finally officially and publicly launching the movement in 2009. A movement, not an organization. Making practical, spiritual 'equipment' available for a movement that – in Shin's words – is already going on. What is meant by 'light-humanity of Christ'? one may ask, in a dialogue of world-views: for me it means that the one, whom Christians recognize as the 'Anointed One', has taught humanity to say 'I' and to 'be' it, regardless of any condition one is born in and lives, in Buber's word: unconditionally so.

Straight after presenting the Draft for the Movement, Shin initiated four Earth Celebrations, three in Switzerland and one in India (1997-2000). At the first Earth Celebration participants had been invited to bring some soil from their homeland, to be brought together in a special fire ceremony. The search for "common ground" in the conversations between religions found therewith its first and obvious answer: the Earth. This ceremony gained a touching poignancy for those from Australia as David Mowaljarlai had sent the ochre of his land in the Kimberley. David was a highly respected Elder in his Ngarinyin Aboriginal Community and in Australia's Aboriginal and non-aboriginal world and internationally, through his active engagement with the UNESCO etc. He had been invited and everything was organized for him to come with his fellow elders, but he had to cancel because of the death of his son. With the ochre he sent for the ceremony he included a letter which was read out during the ceremony. He explained the meaning and the use of ochre in his culture, expressed regret that he could not be there, and promised that he "would be there in spirit." Three days before the ceremony in Switzerland, back in Australia, David Mowaljarlai died. For Helma and for Monica Shalit, a friend from Melbourne, who had brought and read out David's letter to the people in Switzerland, it was clear: David Mowaljarlai was present there with them, indeed, in spirit! It was Helma who had invited David to participate in the Earth Celebration in 1997. We had been in a workshop with him at Melbourne University where Helma recognized him as the initiate and spiritual master he was. I attended only the third of the Earth Celebrations. It became the inspiration for the "World-views in Dialogue" project at Evera since 2007, that – in turn – became the inspiration for this study and anthology.

After having emigrated from Nederland, first to New Zealand (1976-8), then to Australia (1978) we had settled, lived and worked in Melbourne till the end of 1996. Helma practised as a healer, applying her training as a doctor in conventional medicine, anthroposophical medicine, homeopathy, other modalities and therapeutic painting. I had taught history, cultural anthropology and philosophy of craft, art and design in the School of Art & Design at Monash University. On my retirement we moved to Trentham, a small country town 100km NW of Melbourne, at the edge of mineral spring country and on the border of a forest. We settled on 15 acres of former farm/plantation land. Helma continued her practice with the intention to create an environment supporting the healing process and to heal nature as well. We called the place "Evera," (Bulgarian word for "Spring") and a name familiar to us through Peter Deunov's Paneurhythmy, a set of communal dances choreographed to re-connect oneself with nature and with the world of the spirit. These dances became part of our summer camps, one of the many activities, teachings, seminars, and festivals which Helma organised right from the beginning. With friends and working bees we planted gardens, orchards and about 150 trees and shrubs, including 7 clusters of natives in a wide circle at equal distances, so that the clusters became the points of a seven-pointed star. Helma had been inspired by the seven-armed candle holder of Judaism, the Menora. When these seven groves grew tall and offered shade to the wanderer, they inspired me to make them 'sacred sites', each representing one of the seven main world religions, all in the order in which Shin had arranged their tents, 10 years earlier, in Switzerland. The idea to turn this into a "Walking Meditation" project was inspired by the work of Thich Nhat Hanh: A Buddhist monk from Vietnam, activist against communist takeover, who – as a refugee – settled in France and founded Plum Village, where he practised and taught meditation and developed a way of walking meditation, which he brought to other places worldwide. He was also a poet and author of many books.

In 2006, Shin had stayed at Trentham for six days, giving a four-day intensive seminar, both deeply profound and deceptively simple: "The Secret of Renewal." It is the profound simplicity by which newborn children learn with the whole spectrum of their organism and with an appetite for learning. The centrepiece of the large tent were four stones which – together – represented the most ancient symbols of worship or sacred ritual. Two stones standing for "Law" and "Ancestors," common symbols in Aboriginal cultures, and two stones for "Mother Earth" and "Father Heaven," in Hinduism known as Shakti and Shiva, symbolised by Yoni and Linga. Shin explained the significance of these stones in a public lecture, after which they were honoured with a ceremony of songs, offerings, prayers and flowers. After the seminar we found a permanent place for those ceremonial stones on the land and this site became the beginning of the meditative walk along with the other seven sites, ending in the centre of the "star," representing the "Ocean of Life" i.e. where all spiritual streams come from and to where they all return.

After five years of walking this meditation by myself on most Sundays of the year, I was encouraged by a friend to introduce the project in the Trentham Neighbourhood Centre to a wider audience, which I did in May-June 2012 with lectures, conversations and a display of reading material and –at the end of which – the walking meditation itself.

Meanwhile I had also studied and gathered relevant texts to support my meditations and a theme arose as a guiding question: "How is it that all religious and humanist cultures teach the "Golden Rule" and billions of people practise this in their private lives, yet public life, and especially the economy, is in breach of this rule (now I would say: 'makes' people breach this rule) at every step on the road?" I began to realise that the Golden Rule is a crystallisation of laws and customs that have been part of people's public lives for thousands of years. This drew my attention to the positive role cultures must have played and still play in the handing over of religions during the ages. The role of culture is not necessarily distorting, as we had concluded at our Caulfield conversations. Their role is rather crucial. Cultures are the forms in which religions express and recognize themselves. I began to notice the differences in how the Golden Rule has been expressed and to get an inkling of what originally must have inspired the religions in which this rule had been "lived out." This anthology will highlight some of those differences.

The Dalai Lama warns against seeking unity by trying to fit those differences into one mould. Pierre Teilhard de Chardin realized: "Union, the true union in the spirit… differentiates." To which I might add: "union in matter…levels." Based on a mechanistic world-view, public life is increasingly levelling out differences, making the whole world dependent on, even addicted to the same gadgets, the same 'language traps'. Human beings are trapped as functions of the world's machinery, where there is less and less time for reflection. Where 'time is money' instead of – in Shin's words – 'time is life.'

I started to make notes immediately after each walk and to collect texts to be compiled for handouts. My wife Helma commented that those meditative walks made a difference to the land. After she had died, 29 October 2014, two new friends entered my life: Ron White, who told me to "write a book" and Alison O'Brien, 25, who encouraged me by saying: "wait 'til I have read the book!" I had been reluctant, but when I learned about Happold's book: Mysticism: Study and Anthology, I realized that my handouts were the nucleus of an anthology and that my introductions were my study, and that it might be possible to write that book. Here my story ends and – I hope – a door to other peoples' stories opens.

II. Stages of Development of Human Consciousness

There is still a tendency for contemporary historians, scholars and learned popularizers to imagine, evoke and describe the world-views and life experiences of bygone eras and past cultures in the terms of today: as if there is no difference in the kind, level and extent of human consciousness between then and now. In many respects this is most probably justified: hunger, thirst, procreative or erotic appetites, waking, sleeping, death and pregnancy must have been part of human consciousness from very early on. A skeleton, that allows and favours an upright posture, together with a position of the head sitting on the spine, rather than hanging from it, allowing a circular movement parallel to the ground, equips human beings to survey their surroundings and experience their boundaries in open space as horizon. Being equipped in this way might even be one of the steps in the evolution of consciousness which distinguishes human being from animal existence.

In a lecture at Evera in Trentham (2006), Shin Gwydion Fontalba pointed to the different ways animals and humans develop their consciousness over a lifetime: when animals grow old they do so in virtually every aspect of their existence. Humans, on the other hand, may grow old in some aspects and young in other. Old age takes its toll on the body, but doesn't necessarily prevent creative spirit and wisdom of soul to flourish if society allows and encourages it to happen (an observation many of us can confirm in our everyday experience and can find in traditions since times immemorial). Shin's remark complements the findings of anatomist Prof. Louis Bolk (1866-1930) and others in the early twenties of last century: that human bodily development is slow, 'retarded' as it were, compared with that of animals. Human anatomy and physiology develop at a relatively slow pace, whereas animals are born virtually complete, ready to go. Newborn children need a long time to mature. It is often said that children learn more in the first six months than in the rest of their lives. In a book that bears this title, Theodore Roszak characterizes the human being as "The Unfinished Animal". Dr Leen Mees's "Aangeklede Engel" (Angel in Clothes), was a response to Desmond Morris's Naked Ape. Children go through stages of development. Nine months pregnancy is much too short it seems. Old age seems to open up new possibilities for learning, development and even rejuvenation. At 82, Francesco Goya, father of modern art, portrayed himself leaning on two crutches and the words: 'I am still learning.' (In his seventies he had become a pioneer in a new technique, lithography).

Standing still to pay attention to "stages of development" in individual human biography may serve to alert us to the possibility that renewal of religion or spiritual culture implies and demands attention to the questions young children and young adults bring to us. It might be the answers or pointers in which they can "recognize" themselves, that provide humanity with the next step in the evolution of its consciousness. Spiritual cultures and religions failing the children's and young adults' aspirations and expectations hold humanity back, or, worse, allows it to dehumanize and to continue on the road to destruction.

The process of dehumanization might – in terms of consciousness – be most pronounced in the degradation of the senses. In urgent support of Hugo Kückelhaus' project, to revive awareness and redevelopment of the senses, Klaus-Michael Meyer Abbich notes: "Environmental degradation hits us only then, when it accelerates faster than the simultaneous degeneration of our senses." The "plein air" painters in Fontainebleau forest noticed pollution before the scientists took note; "landscape" was a painter's genre before it became an ecological concept. Mothers notice ill effects of medical treatments in their children earlier than the medical establishment, etc. Human culture from time immemorial was knowledge based, in the sense of functional interaction in the development of sensing and thinking. "Homo Sapiens" translates better as "tasting" or "savouring" than "thinking" human being. The Latin word for taste, to savour, 'sapere,' also means to be wise. "Sapientia" is wisdom. Age old crafts, recipes for paints, lacks, varnishes and remedies are testimony to this fruitful co-working of sensing and thinking, as are the visual and martial arts and the arts of music, dance, sculpture, architecture, etc.

The tendency in Plato's teaching to trust knowledge gained through thinking more than knowledge gained through the senses has persisted throughout the ages. It resurfaces after the Middle Ages when, pioneering ways of knowing no longer based on teachings of the past, the books of the philosophers or the scriptures, Descartes and Francis Bacon sought an independent "solid" foundation for knowledge in perception and reason. For Francis Bacon both remained foundational, but René Descartes chose reason over perception as basis for cognitive certainty. When René Descartes wanted to build up philosophy from scratch, i.e. independent from existing biblical and philosophical teachings, he looked for a foundation that is true as well as certain. He looked for a proposition that was clear, distinct and resistant to doubt.

When he came to the proposition 'I am doubting', he realized that he could not deny this proposition without at the same time affirming it. He experienced himself as the thinker of his thoughts. The French word 'penser' has many meanings, from thinking, to feeling, to doubting. Descartes himself repeatedly made clear, that his 'I think therefore I am' was not a syllogism, not a reasoning. It was a realization, a certainty, a truth, but one that was only grounded in the experience of his own thinking, not in the experience of anything else: not his body, not his senses. Hence the split between body and mind which in the (especially feminist) literature is known as the 'Cartesian split'.

After his proposition 'I think (therefore) I am', however, Descartes chose his thinking, not his experience as solid foundation for his philosophy. Over time reason became 'syllogism, reasoning', and experiment came to focus only on sense perceptions that can be 'harnessed, measured and counted' to fit mathematical formulae. Knowledge became equated with "certainty", competing with the alleged "certainty" of the ancients and the religions. The beginning of modern philosophy/science is also the beginning of insurance mathematics. Contemporary obsession with "security" and "control" turns the life of humanity into one gigantic, monstrous, dehumanizing experiment. In The Ethical Imagination, 2004, Margaret Somerville highlights "learning to live with uncertainty" as one of the urgent "virtues" required in our time…

The time of Newton and Descartes was also the time in Europe when the stream of printed words no longer confined itself to Bible and Philosophical /Scientific discourse, in Latin and in the mother tongue, but spilled over into something new: the novel. It was something that everyone could read, once Bible reading and school education had spread literacy wide and deep enough to reach the working classes. In his The Protestant Ethic and the Rise of Romanticism, Sociologist Collin Campbell notes that on Sundays after church and evenings after work, one cannot keep reading the Bible forever. The content of most novels, love stories in which lovers persist beyond boundaries of class, with tragic and happy endings, invites readers to imagine and live vicariously in parklike surroundings, mansions, stately city dwellings, with gentleman's/woman's ways of behaving and speaking, morals or lack of morals, furniture, clothing, china, cutlery to match. The industrial revolution with its mass production needed and found an eager market: the Queen's dinner service comes within reach. The culture of 'day-dreaming' started with the novel and began to drive markets to satisfy the unsatisfiable. Having acquired one's dream house or dream vehicle, the neighbours, [or the markets], come out with a better one. Collin Campbell compares the consumer of today with the ancient despot: the king or sultan who demands instant gratification of his every whim, no matter what the cost or suffering to others; "when we command the harp to play, it plays" (Sean Burke). This to the point, that today, every individual has the potential to become a despot, physically and virtually.

The same time spirit that produced the experiment and the novel also produced the "tabula rasa" theory and the distinction between primary and secondary senses: the theory that children come with a "clean slate," which needs to be "written" on by the senses: "No knowledge without sense experience." But only the perceptions that can be measured etc. give knowledge that is 'objective', presumably only sight and touch. All other experiences, including feelings, are considered to be subjective. This distinction lives on in the textbooks, but is no longer maintained except in all forms of consumerism, where the earth is acquired to be thrown away to waste, "consumed" without being "savoured." Children might be "tabula rasa", but with their "tabula", their senses, intellectual, practical and emotional capacities all open and eager to learn. They expect to be cared for and fed, but also to be able to unfold the full spectrum of their abilities, not restricted by an educational system that is run as a measurable experiment.

When Richard Dawkins held up his 2-year-old daughter to watch the comet Haley, he was aware that she was not able to see it, but he wanted her to be able to know later on, that she had been there. The father was eager for his daughter to see with a youthful appetite for seeing. I find this episode touching when I notice that as a scientist Dawkins has extensively and with awe written about the evolution of "eyes": more than 40 different evolutions, without ever mentioning the evolution of "seeing." He appears unaware of the possibility that appetite for seeing, for sensing, might be something like an inbuilt drive in nature, towards being able to see herself (and her comet), through more than 40 species of eyes, through the eye of a child.

If the evolution of life is often imagined as a tree or trees, from single or multiple beginnings branching out to the different species etc., the beginning of cosmic evolution is now commonly understood as a great explosion of concentrated energy into all the complexities of the physical universe or universes. This powerful image is perhaps not far off from the OM of Hindu and Buddhist understanding or from the "HASHEM spoke and it happened" of Genesis 1, Vandana Shiva's evocation of Shakti or Hildegard von Bingen's vision. "Big Bang" was a casual remark by a scientist in response when told of this new theory. I personally prefer to imagine this beginning as a "Deep Dive": Spirit entering into Matter as into an ocean, contracting with the limitations of space and streams of time, soul – life – physical and sub-physical existence. The ocean itself an expanse of pure energy, gradually concentrating into sub-physical, physical, living, ensouled existence. An image that might have more potential for understanding not only the complexity of the process but also the differentiation in the actual non- physical realities involved.

These observations and considerations thus far may serve to clarify the selection of many texts, especially in the middle parts of the first and of the following second section of this collection: the stage of consciousness which humanity is moving into and which informs a present-day 21st century dialogue between world-views. On the one hand, the relationship between art, science and religion as our ways of knowing, on the other hand the relation between economy, state and culture as functional domains in public life, where the Golden Rule needs to be reinstated and renewed. What in our time is becoming differentiated has in the past to various degrees been implicated in the ways that religions, theist or humanist, have embodied the Golden Rule in public life. This is evident most clearly at the stage of consciousness that is known as the "Axial Age." A consciousness through which humanity earlier or later over large areas of the earth – from China to Italy, from the Americas to Korea and Japan, from Norway to South Africa – changed from thinking in narratives and images to thinking in concepts and processes and from shaping communities out of natural, tribal traditions to articulating societies as rational organisations. When Karl Jaspers made the observations, which lead him to name this stage the 'axial age', he limited its time-frame to 800 – 200 BCE: the time of Lao Tze and Confucius, of Buddha, the Jewish wisdom books and the prophets, the Greek philosophers from Asia Minor to Italy. The time it took for this consciousness to spread around the globe might span from ca 1500 BCE to 1500 CE, at which point it began to be overruled by the Renaissance and Enlightenment in Europe and similar developments in India, China and Japan.

The beginning of the 'axial age consciousness' was characterized by a shift from mythological to conceptual world-views and from tribal to political organisation. The beginning of the European Middle Ages was characterized by the flourishing of new mythologies, narratives and images, without losing capacities of conceptual thinking and organization. Cathedrals in stone and philosophies in thought reached new heights in understanding and depths in life experience. It was a time in which Jewish, Muslim and Christian world-views and scholarship were in dialogue, until the Crusades, the introduction of the Inquisition and the last stage of the 'reconquering' of Spain by Christian rulers, put a drastic end to it. But even Ficino and his Plato Academy, Pica della Mirandola's Oratio on human dignity and Francesco Giorgi's Harmonia Mundi were still developed in dialogue with Jewish scholars, albeit under the watchful eye of the inquisition.

Going back in time makes it harder to find texts that fit the format of an anthology like this. Narratives need to be told and spun out, concepts demand definition and focus. I propose to limit myself to crucial moments in the transition between 'mythos' and 'logos.' The most telling and succinct example might be Rudolf Steiner's presentation of Pherekidos of Syros (ca 600BCE), who thinks in the concepts 'space', 'time' and 'matter' and speaks of Zeus, Chronos and Chton, i.e. mythical names to identify them. And, perhaps, the example of Krishna in the Bhagavad Gita: Arjuna hesitates to lead his brothers and their army into battle against his cousins. But Krishna admonishes him: 'fight!' i.e. break the limited understanding to attain the higher understanding, which is implicit in Krishna's teaching. Or Oedipus, the royal foundling, whose intellect is able to solve the riddle of the deadly Sphynx, but whose blood does not experience the bond that connects him with his parents: he – unknowingly – killed his father and – unknowingly – married his mother. (This is Robert Sardello's interpretation in a historic perspective that Freud's well-known interpretation lacks). The riddle of the Sphynx that terrorised Thebes: 'I go in the morning on fours, at midday on two and in the evening on three,' simple enough for a 5-year-old now, made sense as a dark riddle in a time when people experienced life as coming down from a higher, light-filled, existence, going through life as through a lower, darker place and leaving life as going to a higher place again. The new consciousness, that Oedipus represented, makes people experience life as clumsy in the beginning and again in the end, and strong and competent in the middle, and virtually oblivious of where they came from or will be going. This seems still the common feeling today, although I also noticed that people in my little town consoled me after Helma's death by saying: "she is on a journey," "she is in a good place" and mean it.

For me equivalents of the riddle of the Sphynx, just as serious and deadly when not solved, are the riddles that early childhood drawings and the art of old age, especially in some masters, confront us with. The freshness and dynamic vitality in lines, forms and colours arising from early childhood in many if not all cultures, which made them the envy of masters like Paul Klee and Picasso, come from children who arrive supposedly "tabula rasa." (i.e., with a cleaned slate.) Those works may point us to the light-filled dynamic existence where we come from. Many elderly people, when taking up creative art, blossom beyond expectation. On entering old age, master artists, such as Rembrandt or Beethoven, Michelangelo or Matisse, may embark on work that is no longer based on past experience or skill, but seems rather to be anticipating new and higher possibilities than their established mastery would allow or predict. Our society, especially in the West, so absorbed in reaching the highpoint in a career and using those highpoints as gauges by which life is measured and valued, fail to appreciate every stage of life as equally meaningful, fail thereby to do justice to childhood and to old age, in ways that dehumanize both. Not 'useful' yet or anymore, elderly and children are of secondary concern and their care is out-sourced for the sake of career or money as primary concerns. Hence my inclusion of texts relating especially to those stages of life in the sections dedicated to "renewal" and "ritual", implying not only renewal of appreciation and care, but also recognition of their unique role as sources of renewal itself. The same could and should be said of human beings who come to us with mental or physical disabilities.

Crafts and arts throughout the ages can be considered meaningful and effective signposts along the stages of consciousness: Signposts that increase in significance the further back in time they come from. Written documents and inscriptions disappear. In non-literate societies objects, sculptures, vessels, tools, buildings, cave dwellings etc. are part of spiritual, religious rituals and contexts as well as memory devices by which cultures maintain and accumulate the treasures of their wisdom and learning. Forcing ancient peoples away from their homelands cuts them off from their memory, the life-blood of their culture and their prosperity. Ancient economies were knowledge economies.

The stages of consciousness thus surveyed have been summed up in different ways by historians, sociologists, anthropologists, philosophers and spiritual masters, including August Comte, Sri Aurobindo, Jean Gebser and Claude Levi-Strauss. My own understanding has been mainly developed from Rudolf Steiner's work. A recent diagram by Dennis Kenny (as seen below) might

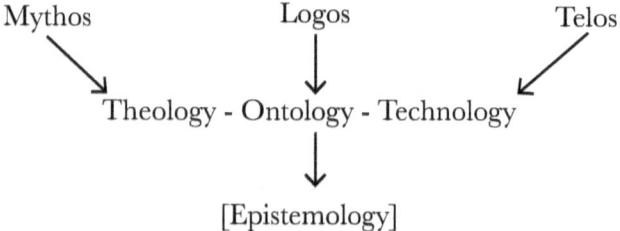

serve as a useful framework:

This is a simple diagram, suggestive of a step by step coming down from pre- and para- conceptual worlds into increasingly earth-bound, conceptualized world-views. The medieval and modern industrial revolutions led to a 'mechanisation' and then 'atomization' of our world-view. Denis Kenny (2003) suggested 'Telos' as the key to the present evolving stage of consciousness, aware of a 'value-free' technology in need of a sense of direction. Mythos is a Greek word for 'word,' 'narrative,' 'story,' especially story and narrative of creator beings, stories that explain how things came to be how they are. Telos is a Greek word for ideal or goal. As early as 1960 Jürgen Habermas expressed his concern with Technology and Science themselves acting as Ideology, i.e. as the telos to which all of society aspires, with no ethical or ontological context required. I added epistemology, the study of ways in which we know, as knowing anything with certainty became increasingly problematic as our awareness and application of "mediated knowledge" creates an ever increasing 'distance' between ourselves and the world we seem to know: printing press, graphics, photography, telescopes, microscopes, reading glasses, tele-hearing, -seeing, -speaking: there is hardly any form of knowing that is not mediated. All are extensions of our senses and our memory and are only to be trusted as far as our senses and memories are to be trusted. By replacing a training of the senses by training the use of media, we seek certainty and security in media, no longer in our own direct observations and recollection. This anthology presents some texts that resist this trend and restore confidence in our senses as primary sources of our knowing.

From the point of view of ancient cultures, which were much closer and more open to 'higher worlds,' this step by step increase in earthly mastery at the cost of spiritual competence must have been experienced as a process of darkening. The further back in time we go, the more impressive the formative power, vitality and intelligent grasp of natural forces and processes. The pyramids stand at the beginning of Egyptian civilization, not at the end. Like the Vedas in India and the Iliad and Odyssey in Greek literature, etc. The reluctance in ancient Egypt to introduce the art of writing for fear of weakening the art of memory, resonates in every age in which innovation replaces age old practices, from printing press to tablet computer, etc.

This 'darkening' was known in the East as Kali Yuga, i.e. 'dark epoch.' It began around 3000 BCE and according to Rudolf Steiner, Sri Aurobindo and others has been ending since the end of the nineteenth century. We are at a turning point in time, marvellously described by Robert Musil in his novel

Man Without Qualities (1930-1943) as a strong fresh wind blowing you over when walking from a quiet street you turn a corner... Since the 1880's there has been a storm of new developments, new beginnings in the arts, architecture, music, mathematics, science, technology, psychology/psychiatry as well as a wave of new experiences of a spiritual nature. The West has not had an up to date context available in terms of concepts to cope with this wave: western materialistic world-views offered no space for the deeply spiritual perceptions and experiences of a Vincent van Gogh, Friedrich Nietzsche, Kierkegaard and others. One way of coping was to learn from the East, from Indian gurus: the way of Helena Blavatsky; another way was to widen and deepen the scientific consciousness of the west itself, to trail-blaze a new, scientific and experiential way of having access, knowledge and understanding regarding spiritual realities as they come to light after centuries or millennia of darkness: the way of Sri Aurobindo, Beinza Dunov, Rudolf Steiner and others. There was a revival of spiritual knowledge and practices around the turn of the 19th/20th century and again – just as confusing – from the mid-fifties onward: the so-called "new age" phenomenon. It will be vital, for the renewal of all religions and spiritual philosophies, to sort the shallow, consumerist "spirituality" from the grounded, committed pathways to what I might call "spirit presence:" renewed contact with the being or beings and the realities from which our institutions originated and to which we return as the wellsprings of our renewal.

Looking back and surveying the vast expanse of time in which the stages of consciousness evolved might give a sense of standing on the shore of an ocean, watching the tide coming in. Fishing boats come sailing in: a metaphor for the texts collected in this anthology, like vessels or capsules carrying messages from different ages, reflecting the ups and downs of the waves in consciousness. Those 'capsules' or 'vessels' moving earlier or later with the same wave, independent of each other, like the cultures undergoing the same transitions independent of each other, not necessarily at the same time. I borrowed this metaphor from Rudolf Steiner, who called this method a "symptomatic" approach to world history. Especially when surveying world-views, characterizations are closer to the dynamic flow of historic time than static definitions. This chapter is greatly indebted to Steiner's "Riddles of Philosophy," partly for its content, as with the role of Hemsterhuis and Pherekides, but mostly for its method: itself a fruit of the consciousness of our time.

What then would, could or should be the "telos" of our currently evolving new stage of consciousness? We might become increasingly aware of what lingers on from a consciousness of the past that by now should have been overcome: science and technology in the role of ideologies that have come to haunt us: a once timely but then overdrawn claim on individual rights and rational judgement, finally at the cost of community and sensory as well emotional perception and experience. The terror of the French Revolution. The horrors of the American Civil War, recognized as the first instance of "modern warfare" and mass-destruction. The mechanization and then atomization of the way the world is conceptualized and understood has now torn people's lives, communities and natural environments apart in the name of 'systems integration' and globalisation.

The new awareness yearns for reconnection in all areas of existence, a religious aspiration, even if it be a secular one: re-connecting is another word for "re-ligare," from which the word religion is derived.

Jürgen Habermas has termed our time as 'post-secular,' aware that religions are emerging from societal irrelevance, from a time in which they had next to no impact on secular affairs. This is obviously no longer the case, even though their impact often continues or re-introduces an early stage of consciousness, in which the collective was valued higher than the individual. Fundamentalism and tribalism, not dissimilar to the regressive forms of patriotism and collectivism in national-socialist, fascist and communist regimes and even patriotism in democratic countries, displays a quasi-religious zeal, especially in times of war.

As I understand it, the new consciousness would aspire to restore and develop a kind of community and a sense of belonging in which the thriving of all its individual members is integral to the thriving of the communities themselves as wholes. And so, the recognition of individuals within communities within – and between nations: Mutual responsibilities in competence and in freedom instead of duty being imposed and denying individuals the chance and experience to ever live up to their full potential as mature and creative members of their communities.

For me, this aspiration would not make this new society a 'post-secular' society. On the contrary: the rise of the 'secular' has made it possible for religions and diverse spiritual cultures to meet in a social space that belongs to no one, not even to non-religious or non-spiritual people. Just as we share through the earth a same 'common ground,' we share a common time-frame as well, which – even though it developed out of ancient pre-Christian and Christian practices – is now a universal, neutral form of practical timekeeping, on top of which every religious or cultural institution can build its own. And, of course, no particular collective will claim summer and winter, rainy or dry seasons etc. as their own. I hope that the secular status of society is here to stay, not as a society devoid of sprit, but as a society aspiring to embody the spirit of humanity itself. Rather than 'post-secular' I would like to characterize the new society as: 'differentiated', i.e. a society in which the differences between its members, individually and collectively, are integral to its health and wholeness, where contradictions and uncertainties are part of life, left to be resolved when the time is ripe, rather than being used as justifications for conflict, and where polar oppositions are recognized as such and resolved in meditation and prayer, study and dialogue.

What I express as my understanding and hope reflects my reading and choice of pertinent texts in this anthology: e.g. Teilhard de Chardin's Unity towards the Spirit Differentiates in response to the rise of totalitarianism before the second world war, and e.g. Pope Pius XI 's succinct summary in 1931 of Pope Leo XIII's response to the rise of a collectivist socialism 40 years earlier: "No larger organization should take away tasks which smaller organizations can fulfil just as well or better." This was quoted by Schumacher in his Buddhist inspired Small is Beautiful (1970) and recently again – urgently – by Pope Francis in Laudate Si (2015).

As far as money is concerned, the telos of our time does not imply the abolition of money, but does require a total overhaul and transformation of the ways money is currently understood and is made to function in society. It is beyond the scope of this study to go into details. Some of the texts in the third part of this anthology should give some hints to the direction such a transformation might take. In a dialogue that wants to be conducted true to the evolving stage of today's consciousness, the misunderstanding, misdirection and misuse of one of the greatest achievements of the human spirit cannot be ignored: especially when money-power in the hands of religious and secular fundamentalists alike holds all of us to ransom. The scriptures don't avoid admonishing us about the right use of money. The word 'money' itself is derived from 'Juno moneta,' the 'admonishing' Goddess Juno, named after the abandoned temple in ancient Rome, where money was minted. It is by bringing our newest and brightest consciousness into money, that the money flow can be restored as the vital "life-blood" of human transactions: from the work with nature: forestry, agriculture, fishery, where natural surplus becomes a means for exchange, expressed in money, to the priceless work of cultural creativity and spiritual activity, where money enables what it cannot buy.

The most pregnant and at the same time comprehensive vision of humanity's 'telos' might be Simone Weil's response in 1943 to a request from a friend in England (in exile with the circle around General de Gaulle), to write down her vision for the world after World War II. Her essay begins with a shift in thinking from 'rights' to 'obligations.' The first and only universal obligation is "respect." The dignity of the human being - every human being - is based on individual destinies beyond our understanding and power. Our respect, therefore, can never be adequately expressed. We express it only indirectly by providing for everyone's physical needs (food, shelter, clothing etc.) and soul needs. The most sacred of the human soul's needs is the need for truth. The most fundamental soul need is the need for 'order.' Order is defined by her as a societal arrangement in which nobody is ever forced to sacrifice one essential obligation for another obligation that is just as essential. Hard to accomplish, perhaps never to be achieved, but necessary to strive for, if human dignity is, in deed and in effect, to become the rock on which a truly human society, and truly human communities, will be built.

III. Individual and Societal Consciousness and Lack Thereof

a. The Eightfold Path as a guide to dialogue

As far as today's consciousness is concerned, Kenny's (2003) "telos", aim or goal, calls for a sense of direction. When I was asked to convene 'religious conversations' I took Lord Buddha's Eightfold Path as a way to formulate my questions. I knew that Rudolf Steiner had, in at least two publications, extensively elaborated on the eightfold path and had suggested that what in the Buddha's time became available as esoteric knowledge, would – over time – become available for anyone who makes an effort to think this given teaching through. In the same way as, I assume, the wisdom of the Dao, of the Sabbath and other wisdoms, which were originally only available for the initiated, priests and rulers have, over time, become available to any serious and competent seeker. (In a democracy, every mature adult is a queen or king; likewise, in a time of 'self-responsibility,' everyone might be priest or priestess). When, in this anthology, the dialogue is extended and deepened beyond institutionalized doctrine, to include the so-called 'occult' or 'esoteric,' this might be appreciated in the light of the above. This move into an esoteric dimension is not restricted to religious world-views. Hidden realities, not immediately accessible to the senses, are often intimated in art, poetry, music and philosophical musings long before they are articulated in esoteric or exoteric teachings.

Since the time I used Lord Buddha's Eightfold Path for those conversations (1994-6, see appendix 1), it has continued over the years to make more and more sense to me. The Buddha taught the Eightfold Path, as the last of the 'four noble truths,' in a sutra called the 'turning of the wheel.' The wheel with eight spokes has become the signature of the Buddha's Way. The Wayfarer is led onto a path that is circular, but in the sense that it spirals upward: when the eighth step is done, the next first step begins at a higher level, unless one has learned nothing along the way. In this sense, the turning of the wheel represents a sense of direction. The 'right view' presents three choices: three paths are open: a downward spiral, an upward spiral and a going around in circles. Hence, the next step: 'right choice' ('right decision' or 'right thought'). When the paleolontogist and thinker Pierre Teilhard de Chardin struggled with the rise of totalitarianism in the 1920's, the crushing of the individual, he found an answer in 'differentiation,' not separation: i.e.

communality and individuality mutually including and strengthening each other. A middle way between fragmentation and collectivism, in short:

"Union in the spirit differentiates". A choice that implies the two alternatives:

> ▶ Unity towards matter, which erases, eradicates differences, and/or;

> ▶ Unity towards nothing, absolute indifference, signalled by Bernard-Henri Lévy, reporting and reflecting on the forgotten warzones of our time, festering on for years: meaningless wars, where none of the parties involved knows why they are fighting or for what – senseless, destructive for all involved. Paralysis, indifference, 'nobody cares' is perhaps the most formidable 'face' of faceless evil of our time.

'Right choice' becomes more critical day by day in a time in which 'right view' seems every day more problematic. Hence the urgent need for a dialogue between them, which brings us to 'right speech' as the third step on the path. How to express the inexpressible and how to translate and communicate the traditions and the current conversations in and between the participating faiths, philosophies, spiritual cultures? And if an esoteric dimension becomes part of the dialogue, right speech, right language etc. becomes more necessary even as it becomes more subtle. The same applies when the dialogue is extended in the direction of non-religious humanism or atheism.

Amongst the different translations of the fourth step I tend to prefer 'right attitude' over 'right action.' Right speech doesn't arise and happen in a vacuum, but in a 'space,' a 'sphere' or 'atmosphere' wherein the speaking takes place: Coleridge's "freedom that we have in common," Goethe's "respect and listening," Rabbi Zelman's "dialogic mentality." At Evera we practise 'listening conversation' and in Shin's teaching it is called 'synarchic' conversation: not monarchic, not oligarchic but synarchic: derived from the Greek word 'syn' as in 'together', 'archè' as in 'beginning,' 'initiating.'

A right attitude, then, requires silence – whatever words well up from thought, feelings and impulses may be put to rest, so that our feeling, intention and thinking are fully available in our listening to the thoughts, feelings and intentions of the other. The only way to perceive the thought of another person is to think that thought, putting one's own thought on hold, (not one's thinking). An open attitude – 'perceptive tact.' This then is also the basis for the next step on the path, the fifth: 'right position,' 'right livelihood.'

The first four steps did prepare us to find the right balance between aspiration and acceptance – between what one brings into the world by way of talent, disability, skill, handicap, training, education and what the world offers by way of opportunity and encouragement, to deploy those gifts and capacities, to make the most of the lack of them (handicaps, disabilities) and to develop them. E.F. Schumacher presents the Buddhist view on work as the means to sustenance, self-education and contribution to others. Right livelihood. Providing for someone's needs – cultivating one's character – making a difference to society. Which then leads to the sixth step: 'right endeavour,' also translated as 'right habit.' In both cases it is the way in which one is able to bring continuation in all of the above: a project, an initiative, a practice from smallest to largest, from modest beginnings to major movements. All spiritual cultures and religions began as 'right endeavours.' And at this stage of its development, or rather its stagnation, humanity is in urgent need of modest beginnings, modest but decisive: beginnings of renewal, wherever our established religions, or spiritual traditions – secular humanisms and atheisms included – are stagnant, stuck in the present, the past or going backwards. Or going forwards on the basis of irrational and/or ungrounded expectations…

A 'right mindfulness' is required, a living in the 'now,' and an attention to many realities at once, a new stage of consciousness, which Jean Gebser has named 'aperspectival' (i.e. beyond linear perspective). Something Rabbi Zelman has drawn our attention to: the need for a new cosmology, psychology, ecology; a new, esoteric dimension. To which I would add a new economy, sociology and anthropology. All big words and a tall order, which places us in the middle of a shift between two other big words: the first four steps on the eightfold path might be roughly summed up as 'right epistemology' i.e. right ways of knowing. One might sum up the last four steps as 'right ontology' i.e. right dealings with reality: the things one needs to be mindful of: livelihood, human constitution, societal needs and structures, past and future, right remembering and right looking ahead. In Peter Boghossian's 'Street Epistemology', the street is the ontological space in which the epistemological process happens. (A Manuel for Creating Atheists. Pitchstone Publishing Durham. NC 2013)

All of this requires 'right concentration and contemplation': Moments of slowing down and becoming still. A continuous and intermittent paying attention, which hopefully pays off with an enhanced, enriched and deepened 'right view' at the beginning of a second cycle on paths 'towards the spirit.'

b. Reclaiming the perceptual/experiential role in viewing the world

This first step on the eightfold path has been translated in various ways: right knowledge, right knowing, right insight, but as far as I know never as 'right concept.' 'Right view' strikes a balance between concept and percept, thinking and perceiving. A thinking that is not blind like a syllogism or an algorithm; a perceiving that is not meaningless like pure sensation or intoxication.

The texts selected for the anthology chapters 2 and 6 might be read as a search for what 'right view' might be, for now and for times to come. The selection is an attempt to provide the dialogue with pointers to the knowledge and insights now available to all, regardless of one's own view of the world. Access to many areas of knowledge that used to be the prerogative of religions and philosophies are now the domain of scientific expertise in the broadest sense of the world, not just physics and chemistry. Many professions now rely on advances in continuous 'academic' research relevant to their work.

Perhaps a short excursion is here in order. With the rise of science in the 16th -18th centuries, the question became acute: how can we justify universal laws based on limited numbers of observations? Future observations e.g. are not available. We 'induct' instead of 'deduce.' This was David Hume's problem, which Immanuel Kant solved by ascribing all generality of our 'natural laws' to the generality of human organs of perception and thinking: if we had been born with red eyes, we wouldn't be able to see the world other than red. We are born with a perceptual and intellectual equipment, that makes us see the world through the lenses of generality. The 'world itself' remains hidden from us. We cannot take off these inborn lenses. This – in a nutshell – was Kant's solution. Glasses were then still a rather new medium, but already part of a considerable technology of mediating perception: microscope, telescope, thermometers, etc. The philosopher's mistrust of the senses, from Plato to Descartes, became extended to include all mediated perception; and – indeed – this notion of a world, which is totally determined by the way our organs of knowing are built, still haunts much of modern discourse.

For Karl Marx this 'inbuilt lens' meant: how we see the world is determined by our relationship with the means of production, we own them or we don't. 'Ideology,' which used to be another word for philosophy, changed to mean the lens through which we 'know' the world. For feminism, the world becomes a 'male construct,' to be complemented by a feminine one. In the

20th century, linguists added language to the inbuilt ways in which we know the world. Nowadays we also seem to know that money makes us see the world through dollar-sign-eyes. I must add, that his 'critique of the pure intellect' didn't prevent Kant from moving on, from exploring other ways of knowing, especially 'aesthetic judgement' and the 'practical intellect,' that provides us with a moral compass. Goethe wished that Kant would have written a 'critique of the senses' as well, a project that in his time had been started by Kant's early contemporary Francois Hemsterhuis who estimated that human beings have at least 40 senses, but noted, that we don't even properly explore and train the 5 we traditionally refer to.

The notion of 'right view' seems strangely alien to our modern ways of thinking. In a modest, thoughtful little booklet, the Dutch philosopher R.C. Kwant has summed up the 'question of (this) medium determinism' in its title: Imprisoned in its own net, (Gevangen in eigen net. Samson Publisher. Alphen a/d Rijn, 1972). Which – in turn – inspired me to characterize modern, Western, epistemology as 'medium conscious.' Aquinas had already noticed that honey on a feverish tongue tastes bitter. Descartes's example, that to the eye a stick in the water appears broken, is hardly reason to distrust the senses, (something Descartes himself was aware of), as many other senses are available, even a look at the layer of water, to complete the observation. Recently, reading Francis Bacon's Novum Organon (1620), I came across the observation that tepid water appears warm to a hand coming from cold water, and cold to a warm hand: he doesn't say 'seems' as if to distrust the observation, but 'appears,' an observation that warrants further investigation. Had Bacon been able to use a thermometer, he would have noticed that the column moved up in the one and down in the other, and he could still have used the word 'appears,' but not 'seems.' This is why Goethe once commented that 'talking about optical illusions is blasphemy.' Instead of declaring optical effects 'illusions' he endeavoured to investigate them for 40 years before he published his findings in his Farbenlehre, (Colour Study) misleadingly translated as Colour Theory. Praised as an exemplary example of a thorough scientific investigator, a lesson for all scientists how to go about their work, Goethe refrained from considering his findings a 'theory,' i.e. a generalizing abstraction, no longer connected to the ongoing teaching (lehre) that conscious living with colour provided. For all its brilliance, Newton's theory is colourless, pure mathematics and his central, prismatic experiment, turned out to be an exception rather than the rule. Goethe published his colour studies with black and white and coloured cards, through which his readers could reproduce his main experiments by themselves. He redesigned Newtons' colour wheel into a practical device, by which now everyone can understand some of the basic relations between colours. Goethe didn't distrust his senses nor his intellect, he rather trained and used them to the full. To denigrate optical effects as illusions is blasphemy: one is apparently too lazy to properly use God-given, nature-provided, media.

Why this 'excursion' and dwelling on this apparent small historical detail? A colleague responded to my story 30 years ago: "So what?" My answer then was: "It is not honest!" When I showed Goethe's colour experiments in class, a student called out: "Why didn't they show this to us in high school?" Thirty years later I am not aware that they are shown even now. It was Goethe's experiments that made a systematic understanding of colours available, not just to artists, but to the general public as well. The explosion of colour in modern art and design stems partly from Goethe's research.

But there is more, two things more:

First: The current pace at which technology-driven science evolves, produces untruth at an enormous scale: for scientists to get funding and survive, they need to show what their findings might be worth, scientifically and/or financially, and – I suspect – ideologically. For that, they have to rush, to be ahead of the game. We get used to and probably immune to the pace in which scientific discoveries, often with adverse, even fatal consequences, are later found untrue. Especially, of course, in the medical and agricultural fields. Meanwhile, there is a growing movement to make our world slow down. At their core cultures, philosophies and religions are patient; perennial wisdom and a profound sense of belonging prevails over haste and rush. In the dialogue with scientist and educators an unhurried approach to science, with due attention to a whole spectrum of human experiences and natural phenomena, without imposing pre-conceived models onto them, would be very much in tune with what religious/humanist world-views have to offer.

Second: Goethe himself valued his colour studies above his literary masterwork Faust. In the scheme of things, colour seems to be so less urgent than the issues Faust is dealing with: modern man, a pact with evil, the emperor/developer's land-grab, the gamut of human experience from hell to heaven, constant striving, never resting. Colour seems so unimportant. And yet, his forty years of research was his training in 'right view' and Goethe ascribed his capacity to penetrate into human nature to his scientific work. In a remarkable book, Das Wort des Johannes, Hugo Kükelhaus places Goethe in one lineage from Lao Tze and Buddha to St John and presents his colour studies as a key to the understanding of their teachings. Why? Because of his striving for a 'right view.' Through colour, not unlike the Dao…

> *...in its natural state (it) appears to be unimportant,*
> *No one in heaven or earth dares to make it his subject.*
> *Were marquises and kings able to maintain it,*
> *The ten thousand things would submit to them on their own...*

And, not unlike the noble eightfold path as 'middle-course' between ascetism and ecstasy, prismatic colours arise and live out of the interaction of darkness and light, black and white, in Goethe's words: passivity ('suffering') and activity.

Kückelhaus (1900-1984) was a master craftsman, designer, philosopher, educator, best known for his pioneering design of children's toys and playground equipment. His dream, to create in the most industrialized area of Germany an oasis of sensory experiences, for which he designed the equipment, never happened because of security costs. But his insistence of the need for something like it has never lost its urgency.

c. Totalitarian legalism: 'linear logic' embodied in the 'nation state'

Anything cultural, and anything economic, that needs or wants to be done in our modern society has to be done through legislation and law-enforcement, i.e. through the state and a political process. Within the state the institutions most equipped and capable of getting things done are either corporate and/or ideological lobbyists, or the army and police...or in concert. It follows that any specifically economic objective, and any specifically cultural objective, is, in principle – and more often than not in practice – politicized and compromised by State legislation and power. Modern life is lived in a de facto totalitarian society, under a regime of 'totalitarian legalism' brutal or benevolent, mediated by a servile or serving public service, but economically and culturally dysfunctional.

Identification of state with society had been functional in times when both state and economy were embedded in a religious culture, and when the life, the breath and pulse of nature were the weave and the web that wove the fabric of society. The law gave shape and form to that which made society function: Hammurabi's law regulates building and healing professions with the authority of the Goddess; (The recent worry of the Chancellor of the Swiss Bundesrat Walter Thurnherr re: the impossibility to regulate the safely of cars and medical technology in a digital age mirrors the areas of Hammurabi's concern in Babylon more than 3760 years earlier), the story of Joseph in Egypt dramatizes a stage of economic management, under the guidance of Yahweh and the authority of a priest-king; Mosaic law, as later Islamic law, deals with issues of faith, philosophy, science, justice, finance and economy as expressions of God's will and human experience and common sense interwoven. Similar things can be said of middle eastern, eastern and pre-Columbian American regimes.

The European Middle Ages moved into the time of the Renaissance, i.e. the rise of the State as 'work of art', integrated, absolute, with prince, king or emperor as its God-given creator. The same time saw the rise of the individual. The individual religious reformer, artist, scientist, composer, poet, engineer/architect, philosopher, explorer and entrepreneur. Each as 'hero,' expert ruler in his or her own domain, competent and proud of it. Renaissance and Baroque rulers, popes, bishops, kings and the emperor himself displayed the grandeur of church and state by lavishly employing great artists and scientists in their service. The protestant reformers, inspired and legitimized by their readings of the Scriptures, translated in local languages, which the printing press made accessible to all, challenged the centralized nature of the early modern state. This could only be 'solved' by the principle that the ruler's religion becomes state religion, leading to a most devastating war of 30 years, massive persecutions and migrations. By the time democracy was born in the American and French revolutions, enlightenment had progressed far enough to proclaim bills of rights, freedom of religion and opportunity for pursuits of happiness or brotherhood, but not far enough to abandon the concept of the centralized state, a dominant culture and increasingly powerful industrialized economy, hungry like Ben Okri's Famished Road for natural resources and dehumanizing labour the world over.

The 18th Century Enlightenment in Europe, which spread around the world through colonial domination, had itself been dominated by the power of reasoning, not just reason. 'Light' become equated with 'intellect.' (For Goethe, conversation was more 'enlivening' than 'light.') The French terror had demonstrated how deadening sole reliance on the intellect could become. The whole 19th Century lived in a kind of schizophrenic dichotomy between cultural romanticism and economic materialism: crudely described as a cultivation of true feelings and refined sensitivities and beauty in novels, poetry, music, theatre and painting, etc. and unrelenting progress in mass-production, steam-driven transport, abject poverty and unprecedented squalor in living conditions. By the third half of the century, materialism had won out, old art forms became irrelevant and repetitive until the explosion of new art at the end of the century, an explosion that was also inspired by an influx and vitality of Asian, African, Polynesian, Melanesian and Pre-Columbian American art and spirituality. The 20th Century saw, economic, technological and corporate power harnessing emotional forces: such as revenge, patriotism, frustration, ideology and creating totalitarian regimes. These, – in their political guise as dictatorships – may have been in most cases dismantled but remain a latent condition in all western democracies. As Paul Riceour pointed out, "a democracy purely based on legality allows a freedom that creates inequality in the economy, which ultimately leads to war…" (Late night TV Interview, 1997). This insight became for me a definition of 'totalitarian legalism.'

This realization will be explored in Chapter 6 of this Anthology, as a most urgent theme for a dialogue between world-views, which – themselves – have too often aligned themselves with this totalitarian 'legalism,' which makes 'torture,' 'exploitation,' 'poisoning the environment' and 'outcome driven science' legal for those who can afford it. It is only in the area of obligations and rights, that all of us are 'born equal' and 'equal before the law.' In all other areas, cultural or economical, we are unequal, by nature and by condition: unequal in age, maturity, in talent, in limitation or handicap, social and cultural circumstance, family, faith, position etc. The notion of 'nation state' has thus far prevented a differentiation beyond legal equality.

The rise of electronic information technology has brought the opposition between contemporary totalitarian and democratic aspirations to a new level of sophistication, without a resolution in sight. The increasing 'intellectual' power of computers has meanwhile increased another mental condition beyond schizophrenia, autism: total disengagement with other people, inability to connect, to empathize. However useful electronic networks like the internet and Wikipedia are, they also create false illusions of individual or collective 'omniscience,' and facilitate all too real new forms of untruth, violence and domination. New levels of surveillance, intrusion and control, which – in the hands of a regime with authoritarian tendencies – strengthen a nation state's centralized power. At the same time, – under democratically inclined regimes – they challenge the identification of state with society and open, at least in principle, a way for the emancipation of the state from ideological or economic domination, from religious and secular ideologies on the one hand, and from corporate, unionized, scientific and religious powers on the other.

As embodiment of 'linear logic' the nation state doesn't tolerate 'contradiction,' nor does a legalistic concept of law. Within a legalistic framework, cultural freedom and economic solidarity don't only logically exclude each other, but also contradict the equality on which the law is based: as abstract concepts, solidarity excludes freedom - and freedom excludes solidarity. It is only outside the domain of linear logic, in the so-called real world, that apparent contradictions happen as a matter of course. The 'logic' operating in life is inclusive: 'polar', 'rhythmic', 'dynamic' like dark and light, day and night, summer and winter, dry and wet, heart beat (one moment utter tension, the other utterly at rest), breathing: oxygen in, carbon dioxide out, in a dance with nature where the plant world absorbs the carbon and breathes oxygen into the world of animals and humanity. In linear logic, opposite terms exclude each other: black or not-black, a mediating term is excluded. In life, black and white are mediated by a full spectrum grey and of colours, and in turn the opposition of the dark or blue side and the light or red side are mediated by the colours magenta or green, depending on which spectrum is considered. Young and old are mediated by maturity; even gender, masculinity and femininity are not without mediating expressions in between. Thus, in society, a solidarity with the natural world through ecology and economy can be understood as the polar (rather than contradictory) opposite of a freedom and creativity operating through cultural endeavours, like education, arts, healing, sciences and religions. Economy is frugal, whilst nature is lavish; cultural life is generous, its fruits are economical, distillations (largest number of essentials in the smallest amount of time and space). These are oppositions that are understood to be mediated by the equality which gives us a birth-right to both the creativity and the solidarity under the justice and protection of the state.

There is a lawfulness in both cultural and economic lives, that by its very nature i.e. being based on inequality, cannot be effectively found, defined and dealt with through the lawfulness of the state. Every one of us is 'citizen' in each of the three domains: in the economic domain we are unequal by age, physical condition, needs and capabilities. The relation to our livelihood varies from individual to individual and changes from time to time. The differences become very pronounced in times of calamities and wars. The same is true in the cultural domain, where everyone is born with different talents and limitations, mentally brilliant, competent, limited or disabled. And different circumstances enhance or limit opportunities for development. Only when we come together as human beings, without tag or discrimination, it is possible for us to meet as equals.

In a recent interview, the Chancellor of the Swiss Federal Council, Walter Thurnherr, has expressed his concern that the rapid development of electronic information technology makes regulating economic and cultural products and activities, e.g. the car industry and health, increasingly difficult if not impossible, which means that the state is increasingly less able to protect its citizens from faulty parts, dangerous procedures, etc. When asked: should we consult less? he answers: we should take longer. But he also asks himself: should we create new entities to deal with those issues increasingly out of reach of state power and authority? Turnherr is overseeing one of the oldest and most stable democracies in the world and finds that democracy is perhaps in need of institutions outside the framework of the nation-state. It seems time that the nation-state needs to place itself in a wider, societal context, where economic and cultural affairs are lawfully governed by their own, functional 'democracies'.

The recent revival of the Medina Charter, through the Declaration of Marrakesh, is testimony to the situation before the Ottoman Empire had been carved up into nation-states. The declaration refers to the time when Muslims, Jews and Christians could live in reasonable peace together, without referring to them as majorities versus minorities. It addresses the current nation states with Muslim majorities, urging them to treat non-Muslim minorities with justice and respect. Without economic and cultural democracies, merely economic and cultural powers (i.e. a religious or secular ideology), decide the fate of majorities and minorities alike.

The same can be said for the effect of carving up the Austrian-Hungarian Monarchy into nation-states, to a certain extent the falling apart of the Soviet Union, and the ongoing tendency of the European Economic Union to turn the whole of Europe into one nation-state, reviving old nationalisms and triggering resistance against the influx of non-Christian and non-European refugees.

This study is not intended to be a political treatise, but in my eyes a necessary, overdue critique of the societal environment in which a dialogue between world-views is taking place. On all societal levels, religious and humanist groups and leaders are up in arms against poverty, injustice, discrimination, violence and war. But as far as I can see, very little is done to address the underlying dynamics and structures that generate war, violence, discrimination, injustice and poverty by their very systems. This movement, in turn, would open a space for dialogues between world-views themselves, religious and secular, and dialogues between them and all other expressions of culture, on their own terms, not on terms imposed by political and/or economic powers.

Until recently, cognitive science has relied almost exclusively on brain research and neuro-physics. The brain became the ultimate key to everything cognitive. When a person had reached maturity, it was generally assumed that this person's brain would stop developing. It has been only in the last 40 years that the idea of neuro-plasticity, a brain capable of continuous development, has become accepted, since Norman Doidge's The Brain that Changes Itself (2007), became more widely known. Convincingly based on case-studies, Doidge's book refutes its own title: nowhere in those case-studies is it the brain itself, rather it is always people, actions, exercises and experiences that make it change. Neuroscientist Gerald Hüther, who together with his colleagues came to neuroplasticity via research on cockroaches, became a neuro-biologist. His realization of the enormous damage and stagnation the old theory has done and continues to do to people's potential to live a full life, enjoying the full development of their capacities, makes him work for a thorough reform of our education systems. He is not the first nor the only one, but for the purpose of this anthology, his clarity, enthusiasm and the sense of direction of his work may serve as a pointer to the need for rethinking epistemology as an urgent theme for a dialogue between world-views, religious and secular alike.

The relation between life, perception, experience and brain is no longer a concern for specialist or experts alone: any expert in one field is a layperson in any other. Religious and secularist humanist educators may be careful not to indoctrinate children and pupils in their care. A technology - driven and corporate-funded science nevertheless manages to get there first. Are educators, parents, teachers, preachers aware of the opposite directions in which brain and life's actions, experiences, senses and perceptions work on the development of a child? On the one hand actions feed and guide the brain, the brain connects and organizes: it is the integrating organ amongst the gathering of organs. Feeding and guiding the brain is called 'learning,' which can be a life-long journey. On the other hand: integrating the various organs into one organism, which happens in early childhood, can be done only once. Distracting the brain in early childhood from its constitutive function will affect a child's constitution for life. Any plasticity in the human constitution is inbuilt: size and proportions of bones and organs, glandular and circulatory systems become a given in a way the internal fabric of the brain is not: the more a human being is engaged in learning, the richer the fabric of the brain becomes. The brain's fabric becomes stagnant and fixated when it is deprived of life's ever buoyant appetite for learning. And the senses or brain are both instruments to the one who does the sensing and the thinking or fails to do so: the one who says "I" in the way, for example, Martin Buber hears it. Or the one who develops memory, imagination, ethics, intuition and common sense in equilibrium; John Ralston Saul's antidotes to linear thinking.

This might be how right view prepares for right direction: choice, decision. In this dialogue it might sometimes be the scientists, neurobiologist, anthropologist, psychologist, educator who informs their religious and philosophical partners in the conversation, and sometimes it might be the other way round, because philosophical and religious traditions have known this all along, and may now be encouraged to act on this 'new' insight with new confidence and enthusiasm. And a new language?

I leave the reader and possible partner in the dialogue, to continue their journey on the noble eightfold path, or any other noble path '…towards unity in spirit.'

d. Emancipate morality from legalistic ethics

Where there is a new right view, a new 'right' world might open itself up: after all, the search is for a 'common ground' corresponding with the 'common word.' The cosmos is such a ground, as is the human constitution. The interfaith movement is very much concerned with the environment as the present face of nature, of the earth, sacred, divine, mother. A new epistemology asks for a new, matching, ontology. Simultaneously on an individual, a cosmic and a societal level. Chapters 2 and 6 in this anthology offer some pointers in the direction of renewal on those levels.

Renewal of both the ontological and the epistemological aspects of renewal asks finally for a new morality, a new ethics. Long considered exclusively the realm of religion, ethical renewal is regaining its grounding in the sense of what it means to be human, to become human, to live and act humanly amongst ourselves, our fellow creatures and the cosmos. Human dignity is becoming the touch-stone for the renewal of morality, of lawfulness beyond legality. This, in turn, calls for a renewal of the virtues. As Margaret Somerville beautifully put it in her Ethical Imagination, 'Old virtues for a New World. Holding our Humanity in Trust,' and proceeds to add: 'living with uncertainly' to the more familiar virtues of old.

'Gratitude,' however, is not one of them, nor of the lists of others who have identified a number of virtues, such as Simone Weil and Rudolf Steiner. Perhaps gratitude is not traditionally considered a virtue because traditionally it was so natural that it didn't need effort or training to be grateful. Perhaps, rather than fear, gratitude might have been the primeval motivation for any religious expression. It is a suggestion that I leave to archaeologists, cultural anthropologists and historians of religion to investigate and – in the meantime – I propose gratitude as an urgent theme in our dialogue. 'Gratitude' is now anything but 'natural.' And if it was not classed as a virtue in the past, it most certainly must be classed so in the present. We take nature, life for granted: everything good, beautiful and true, that has been given to humanity and what humanity has given to our generation and beyond. But taking this for granted is beneath the standard of human dignity, the touch stone of our ethics or morality, past and present. One place where gratitude is commonly expressed is in non-fiction books, where the author thanks family, close friends, editor and contributors to the work in various ways. Margaret Somerville takes it one step further when she thanks her in-house connection with nature, her two cats Ozone and Didgeri-don't, which I am tempted to identify with the two major streams of ethics: one based in virtue and one based on rules.

That the Ten Commandments of the Jewish Bible were written in stone was the outer sign of them being written in the human heart. Even those who have forgotten or never known the divine lawgiver can read those precepts in their hearts: the negatives in all modulations of "Thou shall not kill", the positives in modulations of "Respect and honour what is most sacred to you" ... and dedicate the effort, time and space to do so. The virtues involved to fulfil the positives are not spelled out, those involved in the negatives are hinted at: if one cannot legislate courage, one might punish lack of it, not legislate honesty, but punish lies, etc. And – of course – the number of negatives, of prohibitions grows with the number of possibilities: forgery of banknotes became a nineteenth century crime, computer hacking a 21st century phenomenon. The 20th century developed indoctrination into an 'art.'

The 18th Century Enlightenment was, amongst other things, an attempt to develop an ethics without legislator, but still based on rules. One which made it possible to reason from general principles to particular situations. The 'reasonable' became the 'reasoned', the outcome of syllogisms with the consequent erosion of 'common sense', sense of justice, sense of balance, 'ratio' = sense of proportion. As long as the spirit of the law was informed by a sense of justice, this reasoning was and is a meaningful contribution to achieving justice, but when and where the sense of justice was replaced by a sense of expedience, of domination etc., a rule-based ethics alone is no longer functional or tenable. A contemporary dialogue between world-views might contribute to a renewal of the appreciation, understanding, training and practice of virtues as the underpinnings of rules and the foundation of their effectiveness. Obedience itself is a virtue and slavish following of rules is not obedience. Since the Nuremberg Trials after the second World War it has become recognized that "command is command" (Befehl ist Befehl) is not a valid defence in court. And since the 19th century, especially in response to the ill-effects of the industrial revolution in England, "duty of care" has become (again) a legal obligation, the roots of which go back to Hammurabi's law in Babylonia, more than ca 3772 years ago.

The re-introduction of a virtue-based ethics in philosophical discourse by Elisabeth Anscombe in the 1960's has been welcomed, but – to my knowledge – not widely followed up. The ethicist Margaret Somerville brings 'old virtues' back for a 'new world', without directly linking them to her rule-based approach to bio-ethics.

Outside mainstream philosophy, especially outside its 'analytical' branch, virtue ethics has continued to be explored. My own knowledge in this area is rather scant, and a few examples might have to serve. In the first half of the 19th century, Coleridge and Carlyle; in the second half, John Ruskin and the Art-and-Craft movement come to mind. In the beginning of the 20th century the theosophical and anthroposophical movements developed a new, articulate insight in the virtues, not only as given and acquired qualities of character but also – through their practice – as sources of new, lasting forms of moral strength.

Some of these insights date back to the Middle Ages, where there was a sense that virtues formed a kind of moral organism or harmony: practising one and not offending against any other, means having them all. When in our time Martin Buber in his 'I and Thou' invites us to listen to the way the other says 'I', it is only the 'I' that speaks with integrity, i.e. where the just, the truthful, the compassionate, etc. resonate in his or her speaking, that is the true 'other' in any real encounter. Any other way of speaking 'I' sounds false and out of harmony. In a time of 'post-truth' and 'tribal epistemology' (Jonathan Freedland, 'Guardian Weekly' 27 April-4 May 2018), our world has become a screaming dissonant.

Even though non-Western cultures have now become ensnared in this tangled web of a morality based on expedience and power, I get the impression that they did not develop the equivalent of a Western rule-based ethics code of ethic replacing their traditional reliance on virtue. The Sanskrit origin of the word 'virtue' is 'vira,' which means 'hero', the accomplished human being. In Latin 'vis' means force or power, 'vir' means 'man' and 'strength.' The German 'Tugend' and the Dutch 'deugd' means something strong, reliable, lasting, something that still resonates with the English 'tough,' when pronounced with the original 'g' instead of 'f'. A 'Tugenichts' is a 'good-for-nothing', an 'ondeugd' is a vice. I remember watching with my students a documentary of a ceramic factory, its production of tableware totally mechanized, except the final stage: each item was checked for its sound, and if it didn't ring or resonate, the item was rejected: an apt metaphor for the virtue that rings through in a virtuous person. It is a robust reliability, which is not to be found in any reasoning, right or wrong. The seven gods of happiness in Shinto arrive by ship on New Year, six men and one-woman, deified sages from Hindu, Dao and Buddhist origin. The woman in the middle with a lute representing harmony, the others: peacefulness, loyalty, compassion and wakefulness, industriousness and righteousness. Again, a certain structure in their relationship, and solidity in their appearance.

It is, in this context, pertinent to note that 'economy' and 'charity' were denoting virtues before they became institutionialized. The Rijksmuseum in Amsterdam has a 16th century altarpiece, consisting of 7 panels depicting the 'seven works of mercy' as described in the Gospel of St Matthew: feeding the hungry, quenching the thirsty, clothing the naked, welcoming strangers, visiting the sick and the prisoners with - in the centre - caring for the dead. They are large panels, which let you look into the streets of a 16th century town in the North of Holland, presumably Alkmaar. In four of the pictures (from left to right) people gather in front of a house waiting to be fed, etc. The last two pictures open a view into a hospital and a prison. What first touched me in those paintings was the modest presence of the Christ in each of them, hardly noticeable, waiting in the queue like everyone else. The seventh panel in the middle depicts a burial below, and the Christ in heaven as the judge who at the last judgement speaks: "...I was hungry and you gave me food...". More recently I began to see this image differently: The people queuing in the first four scenes suggest a beginning of institutionalising charity, and in the last two, hospital and prison have become institutions already.

And economy? Before the 15th century, economy meant a measured allocation of the resources of the house or estate. 'Nomos' from the Greek 'nemein', (as in astronomy); 'ecos' from the Greek 'oikos' = house (but also inhabited region as in 'ecumene'). The term was also used for the allocation of grace or salvation. The 'nomos' has the connotation of 'measured' (as in astronomy), which gets a moral meaning when applied to the wealth to be shared. Before it became the designation of a discipline and domain of society, 'economy' had a moral meaning, more like a virtue: the accomplished woman praised in Proverbs of the Jewish bible: Frugal. Good husbandry, industrious. No waste. By the time economy became a societal domain and a discipline in its own right, its meaning as 'virtue' was taken over by aesthetics as a new branch of philosophy. One of the first thinkers in this new field of study was Francois Hemsterhuis, who was best known for his definition of a work of art as 'the greatest number of ideas in the shortest time and space,' a kind of economy of means, a definition that is still in use today.

With the rise of the centralized nation-state, rulers treated their country as their income generating business, to finance their conspicuous status and their professional armies. They were 'trader-kings,' their economy was known as 'mercantilist.' The emphasis on monopoly, control and taxes stifled what used to be a naturally functional economic life. The founding fathers of economy as a discipline and branch of science insisted on freeing the economy from this stifling regime: in France by returning to nature and farming as the source of all prosperity, in England by concentrating of manufacturing and trade as the new sources of wealth, relying on the colonies as source of their raw materials. The leading pioneering economist in France was Francois Quesnay, a doctor, physician to the king, Louis XV. Familiar with the organic circulation in the human body, Quesnay understood economic life as naturally cyclic. Adam Smith, the second founder of economy as a science, shared the mechanical world-view of his time and understood economic activities as subject to physical laws like gravity, action and reaction. As a professor in ethics he developed a separate ethics as a guide for dealing humanely with the economic mechanisms, which by themselves were considered 'value-free'. In Quesnay's understanding, 'economy' had still retained its status as a virtue. With Adam Smith, economy and ethics became two separate systems, one based on ethical rules, the other on mechanical laws: the dilemma effectively summed up in the term: 'enlightened self-interest.'

In a time when farmers are driven from their lands and forced to join the growing army of the unemployed, and while the industrialized world is choking the rivers and oceans with waste, it is high time that Francois Quesnay be remembered and the notion of economy as a virtue be reconsidered. Unemployment and poverty are the systemic fall-out of booming business: charities and social welfare are doing overtime, re-distributing some of the wealth which a functional economy would have distributed fairly and effectively in the first place. Instead of breaking this vicious circle and working towards a charitable and functional economy, religious and humanist charities and state welfare agencies seem resigned to this perpetuation of a dysfunctional economy.

The major religions have something to say about fair wages and honest measures. They have fought and are fighting against slavery, even though the 'labour market' is slavery in a different key: it implies that work is a commodity, which can be sold and bought in a market place: this makes the worker a slave, every worker: the highest paid employer as well as the lowest paid employee. Instead of an 'invisible hand' that makes the system work well for all, there are 'invisible shackles' that makes bosses slaves of their overrated 'market value' and their workers slaves of a market that drives their income down.

It is at this point that a dialogue between worldviews needs to include a dialogue between religious/humanist organizations and sociological/economic disciplines. When it comes to find some stability in a world at drift, Nassim Nicholas Taleb makes a helpful distinction between things that are fragile, others that are robust and things that gain from disorder, which he calls 'antifragile.' In his book, Antifragile, he describes those 'three different types of exposure' extensively and sums them up in a table in three columns, over four pages, under the headings fragile – robust – antifragile: many of those triads are relevant for our dialogue, but I mention only three:

- Economic life: econophasters, cults – anthropologists – religion
- Political systems: nation state; centralized - ... – collective of city-states; decentralized
- Regulation: rules – principles – virtue

According to Taleb's understanding, (amongst many things Taleb is a philosopher and an expert in risk management), virtue, decentralized political systems and religion are antifragile, i.e. growing strong through adversity. I am tempted to fill the gap in Taleb's diagram, i.e. between nation state and city states with empires like the Ottoman Sultanate and the Austrian-Hungarian Monarchy. And a functionally differentiated society, (Niklas Luhmann's style), would decentralize power away from domination by state or any other domain within society as a whole, i.e. a collective of domains instead of city states, but with a similar effect: a nation as a commonwealth over which the leadership serves to represent the whole, to uphold the constitution as a societal, not only a legal document. This idea was foreshadowed by social historian Ferdinand Tönnies, proposed by leading Soviet intellectual Alexander Bogdanov in Russia and by spiritual teacher and innovator Rudolf Steiner in the West. Tönnies is best known for his distinction between society (Gesellschaft) and community (Gemeinschaft), Bogdanov for his founding of the first blood transfusion service in the world, and Steiner for the way he developed several areas of social life, by making spiritual insights into the human being, nature and society very practical and productive e.g. in education, health, agriculture and the arts. A similar idea appears also to be implied in Pierre Teilhard de Chardin's elaboration of his 'union differentiates', ultimately leading to what Teilhard has named a 'Point Omega', but on less lofty levels might mean an 'overarching authority'. The notion that spiritual insights can lead to practical methods and results may open the possibility that a dialogue between religions and spiritual movements forms a substantial contribution to societal transformation for the better.

IV. Note on Selection of Texts

The word 'anthology' itself, from Greek: 'anthos' = 'flower' and 'legein' = 'glean, gather', suggests something creative, poetic, like a 'bouquet', a flower arrangement. In this project the chapters appearing as a botanical garden, with plants hand-picked from a diversity of gardens, meadows, forests… a kind of scio-diversity, a variety of experiences, perceptions, ways of thinking, gems of wisdom… a variety not only between world-views but also within shared world-views. The Latin word for anthology: 'rosarium', a 'rose-garden' might even be a more appropriate metaphor for this project: on the one hand the common genus: 'world-views', on the other the variety in species: single-petals, multi-petals, smooth and thorny, beautiful in sight or scent, or both… This metaphor has an added philosophical flavour: the name 'rose' was at the centre of the 13th century debate between realism and nominalism, the question whether our universal words, rose, human, rock, etc. denote a real, existing universality or are they only names, convenient labels, without any corresponding reality.

Are world-views, spiritual cultures, religions, named (say) Islam, Buddhism, Christianity, Judaism, Hinduism, Humanism just 'labels' without a common reality or do they refer to real, existing entities, something one might call the 'spirit' of this or that culture, a being? Discussing a similar question with a young friend recently, we both agreed that the suffix '-ism' was too abstract and that we would rather think and speak of 'the way of the Buddha', 'the way of Israel or Juda', 'the way of the Hindus'. Names like Islam, Shinto, Baha'i suggest something concrete, something of an entity rather than an abstraction. The suffix –ism also seems to suggest something absolute, closed off in itself, without room for internal diversity. The suffix '-ity', as in 'Christianity' still suggests an entity, or –at least – a social space, something like what in the German language is distinguished as 'Gesellschaft' = 'society' from 'Gemeinschaft' = 'community'. Margaret Thatcher's statement quoted as: 'there is no society, only individuals' was her justification of rather supporting individuals who were actually building communities, no longer individually dependent on government hand-outs. This distinction arising in the public sphere is now also more and more part of the way that spiritual cultures, religious and secular, identify themselves: as communities rather than societies. This is something that gets lost in an anthology like this. Some texts might reflect the world-view of a society, a rather impersonal social space, official doctrine or practice, but I guess that most of the selected texts originated in actual communities, letters, sermons, personal reflections, prayers… And interfaith activities are mostly community activities, with larger organisations, functioning nationally or internationally as frameworks and forums for communities and individuals to 'compare notes', to share experiences, insights, resources etc.

This anthology is intended to become such resource, an instrument for entering the 'dialogical space' not totally unprepared, and - for a younger generation - a kind of orientation into this world of possible ways of making sense of our world as a 'world in becoming', where new perspectives reflect ancient wisdoms, new experiences and new insights bring new life into old traditions which leads to new forms. It might also serve as an instrument to follow up on the Dalai Lama's suggestion: how to further mutual understanding and respect between different religions: from conversations between religious leaders, between scholars, undertaking a pilgrimage together and sharing prayers and ceremonies. An anthology like this might also be instrumental in the communication between lay-people and those who are ordained, members of monastic orders, teachers and students, scholars and leaders: thus traversing the 'dialogical space' not only horizontally, but also vertically.

Communities themselves have their own, 'flatter' hierarchies: such as schools, communities in and around places of worship, temples, synagogues mosques, churches, meeting-places, conference centres, etc. and within world-views: denominations. An atheist worldview for example might from the outside appear quite uniform, due to a strong consensus in arguments against religion, but becomes quite diverse on a closer look into individual atheists' approaches towards everything else. I quote the biologist Richard Dawkins for the enthusiasm with which he explores and describes nature – the everyday new wonder and for the way he is at pains to distinguish an ontological from an epistemological approach to the evolution of life, not for the way he promotes his brand of atheism. I include philosopher Alain de Botton for his appreciation for what religions create in terms of beauty, meaningful practices and – indeed – community. I quote the philosopher Peter Boghossian for the care, honesty and empathy by which he assists recidivist criminals in lifting the spell of their certainties, which drives the recurrence of their crimes, for his outspoken humanism, even though I find his tough technique problematic. I don't think one finds 'evidence' by questions aimed at destroying 'from the outside' the 'epistemic landscape' people are living in, the ground they stand on and the coherence that comes from life's experience, etc. Still, Boghossian's 'Street Epistemology', - where it pays attention to context, and where it is backed up by its great wealth of source material, - offers a great deal to learn from in the context of a dialogue, in which other 'thoroughfares' like the Eightfold Path and the Dao are long time partners. His book is incredibly well researched and supported by evidence this way or other, but this anthology is not meant to dissuade or convince anyone about anything and certainly not to 'help' or 'treat' others in the conversation. The atheist authors mentioned above have been drawn into this dialogue from the outside. Jürgen Habermas has made himself a partner in the dialogue on his own accord. His contributions to this dialogue speak for themselves.

In the age of enlightenment (18th century) Francois Hemsterhuis has been described as the 'Dutch Plato' or the 'Socrates of The Hague' because he developed his philosophy in dialogue and correspondence, not as a system. He and his friend Gottlob Ephraim Lessing broke the spell of the 17th century 'Cartesian split' between body and mind. In the 20th century Gregory Bateson alerts his university colleagues, that this split is still haunting us and to the consequences this implies for society, not just for religion.

Some of the quotations are rather lengthy, to do justice to context. That a tiny text is picked out of the weave or texture of a larger, organised whole is bad enough, and sometimes I feel that in our hasty time it is not a bad idea to every now and then stand or sit still and pay attention and respect to the thought process and considerations that makes the writer write what she or he writes. Considerate, a word derived from the Latin 'con' = 'with' and 'sider'= 'star'. One would meet under higher auspices, in this case under certain constellations. In our case, perhaps, under certain rather complex circumstances. Paying attention to the etymology of words and to the cultural contexts they come from, is part of an intercultural dialogue, where common ground is sometimes found in the histories of words themselves, and not only in the dialogue between Indo-Germanic languages. [A dialogue is not an academic discourse, but academic insights might occasionally bring new dimensions to one's awareness.]

As an historian I have always been interested in turning points, in moments when a new way begins to break through existing patterns of the time. Archimedes 'eureka' realisation that the volume of the water replaced by an irregular, virtually unmeasurable object, like a king's crown, was equal to the volume of that object itself, was a next step in quantification of the physical world. Or e. g. Bishop Ambrose of Milan reading his book in silence. Augustine of Africa, who had come to consult him was surprised. In his time books were read aloud: a next step in interiorising the spiritual world, etc. A sense of what was there before the thing we take for granted, the 'age of enlightenment' brought certainly new insights and new social arrangements, but an awareness of what went missing of an infinitely richer culture and social fabric, might help to realise why our world is now dangerously uncertain, full of the false certainties that hold it to ransom. I sometime felt that this occupation with old texts turned me in a kind of dinosaur in the eyes of a younger generation, but when I emailed this sentiment to my young friend, she told me to not say this anymore: "wait till I have read the book!" So, I refrain from thinking that, and when I notice that a person like Hildegard of Bingen of the 10th century features sometimes in the Top Ten, I feel encouraged. And to find her quoted by a prominent Hindu scientist, scholar and activist like Vandana Shiva, encourages me even more.

Even though I quoted the Dalai Lama sometimes, I have refrained from quoting him extensively, because that might fill half the book. The same with Rudolf Steiner and others. Valentin Tomberg has been quoted extensively, because his few publications are little known, and not everything is published in English: notably his work on the foundation of justice as studied at universities, but also his 'philosophia perennis' as Dom Bede Griffith characterized his major work on Christian Hermeticism, which is available in English.

I have quoted the Australian Aboriginal Elderand Lawman David Mowaljarlai from three sources, one of which I would like to mention for its importance: the book Gwion Gwion, a monumental work of international significance. It was the fruit of David Mowaljarlai's initiative and action and moving power, to engage people, institutions, governments, in Australia and overseas, the UNESCO, to create a work in texts and images that documents a spirituality and a culture, written and inscribed in the land, the rock paintings, the stories, concepts, customs and laws reaching back in time over more than 20,000 years, in order to preserve and protect them, as 'world heritage' against the inroads of exploitation and 'modern' development. And this before the ones who still were bearers of the knowledge and competent in the practices involved would have passed on. Under the auspices of the UNESCO Gwion Gwion Dulman Mamaa - Secret and Sacred Pathways of the Ngarinyin Aboriginal People of Australia was published in four languages: English, German and French, and Ngarinyin, as well as the original English in transcript of what the elders themselves had to say. Apart from those literal transcriptions, it contains also elaborate further explanations in the three languages. The esoteric nature of the book becomes clear through a statement on its cover, that the book contains knowledge to which not all Aboriginal People are allowed access.

Even though I have quoted Fettullah Gülen's words from two of his books, I was unsure of their context. Gülen is the initiator and leader of a widespread educational movement in Turkey and the world, he is also a very controversial figure and here I was confronted with a (for me) new phenomenon: I appreciate Wikipedia as a great resource, but I would not be able to check out all the information it publishes about Fettullah Gülen and his movement on its website. When I had an opportunity to ask Salih Yücel about this, his response was rather relaxed: Gülen has been in controversies his whole life. Yücel teaches Islamic studies as associate professor at two universities in Australia and has recently published an in depth study on Gülen's life and work, from which I have been able to quote just before finalising this book. These quotes may shed light on Gülen's teachings and intentions, but may, perhaps, also suggest why his work is controversial as well…Yücel recognises him as 'one of the leading revivalists of our time'.

There is one significant study and anthology of religious texts: Hindu, Zoroastrian, Hebrew, Buddhist, Christian, Islamic and Sikh, issued by the Council of the Theosophical Society, under the title: Universal Text-Book of Religion and Morals Volumes 1 and 2. First published in 1910 and now out of print, but available on the internet for free. A wealth of wisdom which I discovered only recently, but still find worth quoting from. Its underlying structure of 'concepts' and 'virtues' seems to have come naturally to both anthologies more than a century apart.

Over sixty years ago Penguin Books published 'a companion-book to comparative religion' by A.C. Bouquet under the title: Sacred Books of the World 1954, still a rich resource, standing on its own, from which I only borrowed two quotes, viz. Justin Martyr and Rhys Davis' translation of the Buddha's Eightfold Path.

In the same year, in which I thought to have completed this book and in which Dzavid Haverick had suggested to highlight the Golden Rule in its subtitle, Justin Parrott received his PhD from the University of Wales, Trinity Saint David with a dissertation entitled: The Golden Rule Islam: Ethics of Reciprocity in Islamic Traditions. 2018. Revisiting this book in May 2020, mainly to pay more attention to an element of the Golden Rule, which somehow seems to have disappeared from the public dialogue, the "-as yourself", I asked Dr Haverick whether in Islam there is place for "love yourself", apparently implied in this third element in the Golden Rule. He referred me to Justin Parrott's thesis, which offered me not only guidance through the wealth and wisdom of Islamic traditions and interpretations, convincingly confirming not only my expectation, but also sharing my understanding, that without the "-as yourself" the "love your neighbour" would have no measure, criterion or 'anchor' as it were. His dissertation reflects also the evolutionary shifts in consciousness referred to in the second chapter of this book.

Another late addition, Mustafa Chérif's 'Islam and the West' (2007), reporting on his conversation with Jacques Derrida, in Paris four years earlier, served to turn the section on international law into meaningful reaffirmation of the Golden Rule as its time honoured foundation worldwide. .

Finalising the text of this chapter, after some late inclusions, I begin to realize that I have somehow become part of the dialogue itself. Selecting texts required some sense for what would be part of the intended dialogue and what not…In the beginning those choices came naturally, they felt right, the dialogue itself emitted its own resonance, but the later choices were not so straightforward, required some discernment. There is a difference between a debate/polemic and a dialogue. In a dialogue, contributions are addressed to an imaginary centre, the actual issue or theme at hand, not to the one who spoke before, rather co-creating a resonance rather than generating reactions or responses…

Hence, notwithstanding the linear format of a book, the texts are loosely arranged in different ways: sometimes like a theme with variations, sometimes in contrasting pairs, sometimes in a logical sequence, a process. The book form itself forces a linear structure: text after text, section after section. The reader might wander along with them, stand back and choose, gain an overview and connect texts from different sections or chapters of the book. Or he or she might do the opposite: let the book fall open and begin to read from where it lands. The format and the economy of a book also tends to make it crowded, where one would love to give individual texts more space for contemplation. The more the reader will be familiar with the book as a whole, the more she or he may be able to 'enter' it as a space, the dialogical space as it has been intended.

Part Two – Anthology

1. Dialogue and Language

*Where I raise the staff,
the land is limitless,
and truth is ground and goal
for all destiny-paths of man.*

Gideon Fontalba
The New Word

Introduction

Entering a space of ongoing dialogue.

In the few years that I have walked the imaginary pilgrims route from site to site at Evera, from spiritual culture to spiritual culture, I gradually got a sense of entering a dialogue that has been going on for centuries. It is this sense of space as well as time that informs the arrangement of texts in this first chapter. First a focus on 'dialogue', the need for it and its nature. Then a focus on 'space', the ground we walk on, nature, earth and cosmos, our common home land that we share from the beginning, before shrines, temples, sacred buildings: on this point there is no need to search for this common ground, we walk on it, but there is every need to start paying attention – together – to share perceptions, experience and to give thanks.

The way this project has evolved, 'dialogue as pilgrimage', happens to reflect the four suggestions the Dalai Lama quoted in the opening text as ways to deflect conflict. It also opens room for interaction between leaders, scholars, practitioners and pilgrims. Fundamentalism, fanaticism and violence may be a reaction partly to internal loss of connectedness with one's original impulse and unity, partly to oppression and dispossession from the outside. But also, the consequence of an alarming gap between highly developed spiritual wisdom and scholarship on the one hand, and the rampant ignorance that feeds narrowmindedness and violence on the other.

Dialogue between equals like scholars and leaders is important, and as human beings we are all equals; but in the face of fanaticism and ignorance, there is an urgent need for an educative dialogue, a dialogue between the educated and less or not educated, an "asymmetrical relationship" (Martin Buber), in which teachers learn to develop a sense for hidden and never expressed needs and hidden and never asked questions. And where leaders may learn to encourage and enable mullahs and imams, rabbis, priests and other 'shepherds' in their local communities to translate the message and wisdom of their faith, their openness to diversity of interpretation and potential for development and for transcending fixations which hold back their truth as source of renewal within their own communities and beyond. Scholars might learn from the experience and insights of genuine practitioners, and both scholars and practitioners might learn from a new generation, what and why some of the old ways do not work for them anymore and to search together with them for the original freshness and openness of their world-views. The language of the scriptures and traditional wisdom is a sanctuary in a rapidly changing world of communication and their continuation is therefore more vitally necessary than ever. Similarly with sacred buildings. They are time honoured expressions of faith and world-views, often even symbolic evocations of a spiritual cosmos. Both language and building are like an umbilicus cord, connecting our present day with earlier times without buildings and without scriptures.

Hence a pilgrimage between sacred sites in nature instead of sacred buildings might therefore serve as an opportunity to create a distance and allow a perspective for scholars, 'shepherds', practitioners, newcomers from within or without their own communities, to reconnect with these origins and to activate their potential for renewal in our own time.

There was a time that one naturally belonged to a religion or spiritual culture. Then, with the rise of a new, more individualised consciousness, one would have a religion or world-view as a matter of choice. The consciousness of our time, however, demands more and more that we be religion, (Gideon Fontalba) i.e. religion or a spiritual culture would no longer be like a spiritual/cultural interior design or style of costume that suits me best, but rather to live out of the original inspiration, the "divine goodness" (anonymous internet message from Storm of Love) or "source of transcendence" (John Esposito). To be this source, this divine goodness. Notice Martin Buber's concern with the way we say "I". The word "I" as the 'shibboleth of humanity'. Which also means: the "I" as the common ground. No religion or spiritual culture will ultimately go for less. Practitioners and preachers 'applying' a religion without 'being' it, without living it, causes a lot of resentment against religion itself. (The Dalai Lama speaks of 'genuine' practitioners.)

The texts are chosen and arranged in an order that suggests a step by step unfolding of an idea, mostly flowing and expanding, as from Coleridge to Goethe to Habermas, from a religious, natural to a rational context. Sometimes conflicting or puzzling juxtapositions as with Justin Martyr, Qur'an: Victory (48:29) next to Pope Francis and Dzavid Haverick: from a certain closed-ness to a decided openness. Read within their own contexts, their positions might not be so closed, after all, as they look for us now. For example: "Logos" in Justin's time and culture was common ground. In the time of Mohammed 'believers' included Jews and Christians, a status they had in common.

I could not resist including Shin Gwydion Fontalba's visionary evocation of the common space and time in which our dialogue ultimately takes place. What is not a shrine? (Shinto), what is mosque, synagogue, temple? (Sufism) What is eye without the sun? (Goethe) – gradually moving from the visionary to the earth-bound experience, the ultimate presence – here and now (Thich Nhat Hanh), as our true home (David Mowaljarlai), the ultimate as common destination (H Bak); the Way beyond rules (Lao Tzi). The technocrat's way to destruction versus the shepherd's way to redemption (Heidegger); going back to the time before the mosque (Qur'an 24: Light).

And in between: about entering a space of ongoing dialogue – set in the past (Umberto Eco) and set in the future (Ben Okri) and – with Li-Tai-Po's "The Mysterious Flute" – set in a poetic, timeless now. Language of flute and language of birds: Do birds speak? Does nature speak? Nietzsche, Guido Gezelle and Richard Rorty. There seems to be a listening in all three: the rocks in Nietzsche's 'philosophers poem' might not make a sound, but Nietzsche still sensed their search for loneliness. In another context Rorty will listen to discern between words that "have become a nuisance and a half-formed new vocabulary which vaguely promises great things" (See Chapter 2). In Camus' conversation with intellectual leaders of his time, those present preferred not to listen. In chapter 6 it may become clear, that the responsibility for intellectuals to engage in 'listening conversation' right across the spiritual/cultural domain, not only religions and philosophies, gains in relevance, the more our world sinks into intellectual confusion and a moral morass. It is the poet Gezelle, who places 'listening' at the heart of dialogue. In Dutch we have a proverb: 'speaking is silver, silence is gold'. To borrow a Dao way of saying: 'to speak is necessary, to listen is essential'.

This sequence of texts ends where it began: Kakkib li'Dtia Warrawee'a's ancient aboriginal sense of 'varied perspectives' as a key to understanding, returns in Jean Gebser's concept of today's 'aperspectival consciousness', beyond the 'linear perspective' of an earlier, rationalist age… A fitting opening towards the theme of Chapter 2.

Texts

*What can we do to ensure that the differences between religions do not
continue to give birth to division and conflicts in human society?
Dialogue between scholars of religion on the academic level.
Dialogue between genuine practitioners.
Meetings between the leaders of the faith.
Joint pilgrimage to holy places.*

The Dalai Lama
Towards the True Kinships of Faith
2010, p. 131

An Australian Aboriginal Tradition in Conversation

Dialogue to get to know each other

*O mankind, We created you male and female, and made you into nations and
tribes that you may come to know one another.
The noblest among you in God's sight are the most
pious. God is all-Knowing, All-Experienced.*

Qur'an The Chambers. 49:1

"Blessed are the dialoguers!

*Rabbi Zalman insists that form, not only substance, is
important because each other's form ..." helps one to really
get to see the out- and in-lines of one's own cogitations.*

*So, as the structural strokes of this presentation are appreciative of the
beatitude of the peacemakers, the substantive issue calls for a new beatitude:*

*Dt*ondryen is to seek and see truth by perception, in perspective and from
varied points of view. This is the third tenet of Kirridt Yordtharrnba.*

*A varied perspective is the key to perception
Perception is the key to understanding
Understanding is the key to respect
Respect is the key to harmony
Harmony is the key to joy*

Joy is the key to enlightenment.

[ ]

One of the most important events during this time* was the exchange of new philosophical ideas. Why? Aboriginal people had considerable free time on their hands – philosophical exploration and discussion were an important pastime in Aboriginal life.

[ ]

The greatest insult one can possibly express in Ya-idt'midtung is to say that someone is droong-karla: unable to see things in perspective and from different points of view.

Kakkib li'Dtia Warrawee'a
There once was a tree called Deru
2002, pp. 29,31
[Aboriginal understanding of dialogue, Ya-idt'midtung language group]

Blessed are the dialoguers, for in their concerned sharing they fulfil what is written

Then did those who respect God (more than their own creeds) talk with one another and YHVH attended and listened in and wrote it in the book before Him titled: THOSE WHO FEAR YHVH AND RECKON WITH HIS NAME. (Malachi 3:16)

Amen, Alhamdullilah, Shanti, Om
Rabbi Zalman Schachter-Shalomi
The Dialogical Mentality
1981, pp. 11-13

Form arising out of freedom

The medium by which spirits understand each other is not the surrounding air, but the freedom, which they possess in common.

S.T. Coleridge
Biographia Literaria XII
1815, p. 140

---

* Yearly gathering of the four political groups of the Ya-idt'midtung, to collect the moths at Mount Bogong, trade, ceremonies and exchange.

More enlivening than light

No sooner had the Snake beheld this reverend figure, than the King began to speak and asked: "Wence comest thou?" – "From the chasm where the gold dwells." Said the Snake. – "What is grander than gold" inquired the King. – "Light," replied the Snake. – What is more enlivening than light?" said he. – "Conversation."

J.W. von Goethe, Thomas Carlyle (Translator)
Fairy Tale of the Green Snake and the Beautiful Lilly
1832

The public sphere a dialogical space.

If religiously justified stances are accorded a legitimate place in the public sphere, however, the political community officially recognizes that religious utterances can make a meaningful contribution to clarify controversial questions of principle.

Jürgen Habermas
An Awareness of What is Missing
2011, pp. 21-22

There is no social bond without faith

... when someone is speaking to us, he or she is asking to be believed. And that belief assures both the exchange of words and financial credit, social credit, and all forms of credit and legitimacy in society. This faith is the social bond itself. There is no social bond without faith. Now I believe that one can radicalize the secularization of the political while maintaining this necessity for faith in the general sense that I have just defined and then, on the foundation of this universal faith, this shared faith, this faith without which there is no social bond, one can and must respect strictly defined religious affiliations. And I am persuaded that authentic believers, those who are truly Jewish, Christian, or Muslim, those who are truly living their religious beliefs and not simply endorsing the dogma of those religions, are more ready to understand the religion of the other and to accede to that faith, whose universal structure I have just described, than others. Consequently, I believe there is no contradiction between political secularization and a relationship to what you call the Mystery of life, that is the fact of living together in faith. The act of faith is not a miraculous thing: it is the air we breathe.

Mustafa Chérif, Theresa Lavender Fagan (Translator)
Islam and the West: A conversation with Jacques Derrida
2008, pp. 57-58

Logos as Reason beyond the Christian – Non-Christian divide

We have shown that Christ is the Word (Logos) of whom human race are partakers, and those who lived according to reason (logos) are Christians, even though accounted atheists.

Justin Martyr (ca 100 – 165 C.E.) Apology I in: A.C Bouquet:
Sacred books of the world: a companion source-book to comparative religion
1954, cover page

Jews and Christians are believers, too

Muhammed, the Messenger of God, and those who are with him, are adamant against the unbelievers but merciful towards one another.

You see them bowing in like prostration, seeking God's favour and good will. Their marks are upon their foreheads from the traces of prostration. Such is their description in the Torah and their description in the Gospel: like a sown field that sends forth its shoots, then braces it so thickens and rests firmly in its stalk – a sight pleasant to farmers, but thereby to mortify unbelievers.

God promises those amongst them who believe and do righteous deeds forgiveness and glorious reward.

Qur'an
Victory 48:29

Recent call for dialogue

Whether on the world stage or in their communities, religious and cultural leaders have a responsibility to speak the language of tolerance and respect. This is a central message of World Interfaith Harmony Week.

Ban Ki-moon
Press Conference by Secretary-General Ban Ki-moon at United Nations Headquarters
2014

Dialogue: mutual openness, especially in conflict

…the best way to deal with conflict. It is the willingness to face conflict head on, to resolve it and to make a link in the chain of new process. "Blessed are the peacemakers!" (Mt 5:9)

> *An attitude of openness in truth and in love must characterise the dialogue with the followers of non-Christian religions, in spite of various obstacles and difficulties, especially fundamentalisms on both sides. Interreligious dialogue is a necessary condition for peace in the world.*
>
> [ ]
>
> *This dialogue is in the first place a conversation about human existence or simply, as the bishops of India have put it, a matter of "being open to them, sharing their joys and sorrows".*
>
> [ ]
>
> *A dialogue which seeks social peace and justice is in itself, beyond all merely practical considerations, an ethical commitment which brings about a new social situation. Efforts made in dealing with a specific theme can become a process in which, by mutual listening, both parts can be purified and enriched.*
>
> Pope Francis
Gaudium Evangelii
2013, pp. 164; 176-7

A culture of peace: also a culture of dialogue

> *In constructing and fostering a culture of peace, an important and genuine insight is: 'to be religious is to be interreligious'. Accordingly we need to have reflective inter-religious identities with a global vision, which will be able not only to promote our own cultural-religious uniqueness and to reflect on the essential nature of religious practice and expression, but to desire to talk and participate with followers of other faiths and their religious rituals and/or ceremonies. It will, then, create a climate of interreligious harmony, social cohesion and a human rights observance. By fostering a culture of peace, people also promote a culture of dialogue. Each aspect of such a culture would contribute to people's mutual learning, building sophisticated relationships with each other and the surrounding natural environment, and developing a better projection for their shared future.*
>
> Dzavid Haveric
Islam and pluralism within the West: A collection of essays
2014. p.130

To be partner in a dialogue one needs to be fully oneself

How much of a person a man is depends on how strong the I of the basic word I-You is in the human duality of his I.

The way he says I – what he means when he says I – decides where a man belongs and where he goes. The word "I" is the shibboleth of humanity.

Listen to it!

[ ]

How beautiful and legitimate the full I of Goethe sounds! It is the I of pure intercourse with nature. Nature yields to it and speaks ceaselessly with it, she reveals her mysteries to it and yet doesn't betray her mystery…

Martin Buber in: Walter Kaufmann's
I and Thou
1970, pp. 115-16

Light

God is the Light of the heavens and the earth.
His Light is like a niche in which there is a lantern,
The lantern in a glass,
The glass like a shimmering star,
Kindled from a blessed tree,
An olive, neither of the East nor of the West,
Its oil almost aglow, though untouched by fire.
Light upon Light
God guides His light whomever He wills,
And God strikes parables for mankind.
God has knowledge of all things.
In houses which God permits to be raised,
And His Name to be mentioned therein,
there He is glorified, morning and evening,
By men whom neither commerce nor trade
Distracts from the remembrance of God,
From constant prayer, and from giving alms.

The Qur'an
24 Light [35-39]
Translation: Tarif Khalidi

About: Entering a conversation as if entering a dialogue that is already happening...

Adso: "True" I said, amazed. Until then I had thought each book spoke of the things, human or divine, that lie outside books. Now I realized that not infrequently books speak of books: it is as if they spoke amongst themselves. In the light of this reflection, the library seemed all the more disturbing to me. It was then a place of a long, centuries-old murmuring, an imperceptible dialogue between one parchment and another, a living thing, a receptacle of powers not to be ruled by a human mind, a treasure of secrets emanated by many minds, surviving the death of those who had produced them or had been their conveyors.

Umberto Eco
The Name of the Rose / Conversation in a library between novice and master
2001, pp. 277

Invisible presences 1

That was when he first became aware that the vast hall was crowded. It was crowded with invisible presences... Their collective presence electrified the hall...

[ ]

When he sat, he felt the masters all around him. He heard their murmurs and their muted conversations...

Ben Okri
Astonishing the Gods
2000, pp. 135-6

Invisible presences 2

A person kneels before a tree and to reflect on the troubles and joys of life. The person imagines mornings and evenings in a great forest of prayers, swarming and teeming with life.

A person is learning how to pray.

Michael Leunig
The Prayer Tree / Introduction
1994

The mysterious flute

One evening, when flowers and all the leaves of trees
Filled the world with perfume, the wind carried the song
of a mysterious flute to me. At once I cut
from the shrub a willow twig and
My song flew responding through the blooming night.

Since that evening the birds hear - the earth asleep -
A conversation in their common sound of song.

Li-Tai-Po in: Hans Bethge's
Die Chinesische Flöte: Nachdichtungen Chinesesche Lyrik
(1905) 6th edition, p. 35
[Translated by Henk Bak]

'Invisible presences' in an interrogation room: haunting rather than uplifting

It is a room where questions are asked – suspicious questions, friendly questions, clever questions, and a few stupid questions. And it is a room where answers are given to those questions – suspicious answers, friendly answers, clever answers, and a few stupid answers. A very plain room, as I say, but God knows how much heartache and pain and despair and sometimes joy those bare walls have witnessed. In this room, hope comes up like the sun, or sinks behind the mountains forever.

[ ]

'Now he wants to know, where you come from,' says Amin.

'Where I come from? Mazar-e Sharif.' What a crazy question. It's written right there on the document in front of Mr Johnson.

'And is Mazar-e-Sharif a small town or a big town or a small city or a big city?"

Crazier and crazier.

'It's is a big city,' I say. Then I think of the Australian cities I've seen and those I've heard about, such as Sydney, which is so big that its

buildings crowd each other out and people have to build higher and higher into the air. I say, 'In Afghanistan, it's big, here may be not so big.'

'And what famous buildings are found in the city of Mazar-e-Sharif?'

Okay. I'm beginning to get it now. Mr Johnson is giving me a test. Why doesn't he just say so? He can ask me anything. I know the names of half the shops in Mazar-e-Sharif. I can tell him where I bought Coca-Cola, and where I bought bread, and where my friends and I used to buy sweets when we had a little bit of money, and where we played cops-and-robbers – everything.

'Lots of famous buildings,' I say. 'The hospital. The government buildings where all the offices are kept. The police barracks. The bazaar, many famous buildings around the bazaar.'

'One building is very famous.'

'Very famous?' I try to think. Is this a trick? What does he mean when he says, 'very famous'? I look at the representative, Petra, but he just shrugs.

'Very famous in what way?'

'A very famous shrine.'

'Oh. Okay, now I know what you mean. The shrine of Ali.'

The problem was, that we Afghanis don't think of a mosque as a famous place. Somebody coming to Mazar-e-Sharif to visit the Shrine of Ali would not say, 'Can you tell me where the famous shrine of Ali is to be found?' He would say, 'Where is the Holy Shrine of Ali?' If something is holy, we don't call it famous, because it is too holy to be famous.

Najaf Mazari & Robert Hillman
The Rugmaker of Mazar-e-Sharif
2008, pp. 45-46/49-51

Silence as absence of speech becomes oppressive, dehumanizing

In the great silence. Here is the sea. Here we can forget the city. Even though its bells there still sound just now the Ave Maria – this dark and wicked but sweet noise at the cross roads between day and night – but only for a moment still! Now all the world is silent. The sea lies there pale and shiny, she can not speak. The heaven plays his eternal mute evening game with red, yellow, green colours, it can not speak. The little cliffs and the strips of rocks that run into the sea as if to find the spot where it is the loneliest, none of them can speak. This uncanny dumbness, that suddenly overwhelms us, is beautiful and horrendous, the heart expands in it. – Oh, the hypocrisy of this mute beauty! How well would she be able to speak, and how evil, too, if she wanted to! Her bound tongue and her suffering happiness in the face is a trick to mock your sympathy! Even so, let it be! The mockery of such a might doesn't embarrass me. But I pity you, nature, because you must be silent, even though it is only your malice that binds your tongue, yes, I pity you because of your malice! – Ah, it gets stiller still, and my heart swells one more time: it is frightened by a new truth, it can not speak either, it joins in with the mocking when the mouth calls out into this beauty, it relishes in its sweet malice of being silent. Speaking, yes thinking becomes hateful to me: do I not hear behind every word the error, the illusion, the madness laughing? Should I not mock my compassion? Mock my mocking? – Oh sea! Oh evening! You are bad teachers! You teach the human being to cease being human! Should he yield to you? Should he become what you are now: something pale, shiny, dumb, overpowerful, at rest above itself, elevated above itself?

Friedrich Nietzsche
Morgenröthe (Dawn)
1918
Translated by Henk Bak, Set to music by Alphons Diepenbrock as symphonic poem for baritone and orchestra.

The world does not speak. Only we do.

Richard Rorty
Contingency, irony and solidarity
1989, p. 6

Language cannot awaken in us the mechanism of comprehension unless it has already realized a sort of organic complicity with the object.

Mikel Dufrenne
Phenomenology of the Aesthetic Experience
1973, p. 128

When the soul doth listen
all the world speaks in ways that live,
even in the softest, finest whisper
language, tongue and token give.
Leaves with leaves on trees
Chatter in the wind,

Rapids in the streams
talk aloud like friends;
whirring winds and rumbling clouds,
where God's holy feet did tread,
evoke and tell and speak
the hidden word – both deep and sweet...
when the soul does listen!

Guido Gezelle (1830-1899)
1859
[Translated from the Flemish by Henk Bak]

... isn't sad to go to your grave without even wondering why you are
born? Who, with such thought, would not spring from bed, eager
to resume discovering the world and rejoicing to be part of it?

Richard Dawkins
Unweaving the Rainbow
1998, p. 6

From the showing of a single stalk of bracken, a fern, to the image of a divine and cosmic tree

...There is a special element [expressed in] this kind of plant—
(bracken, silver wattle). This is another very old plant. You see they have
similarities and the similarity is based on the principle of the tree or of
the plant. That is, again and again, the same principle grows from the
stem in a smaller form—from the branch, then from the little stem. You
can see that when I hold it [horizontally] it is like a landscape with
a lot of trees standing on the one branch, on the one root, on the one
stream of energy, because at the same time it is also stream of energy.

It is only the law where each next branch leaves the main branch that
is different with this plant or that plant. And then, as we come closer
we can see that the leaves follow the same principle: the little leaves
of these trees which you can recognize—some needle trees also have
this principle—you can see they are yet more refined, especially when
there are good outer conditions. A tree on a tree on a tree on a tree.

This is a very living and very important law, which has not
really been seen by a lot of people, [except] by some friends of
science who are very interested in plants. But mostly it is the
various old traditions which speak about these laws.

Now imagine that this tree—perhaps not exactly in this form, but according to this principle—were to be only fire and light. Think that it is only fire and light: not green plant, not such physicality, more energy stream, looking like fire and looking like light. And think and imagine that such a tree—as the old traditions all over the world said—such a fiery and light-filled tree might grow through all the universes, all the cosmoses, all the galaxies, in a form of energy-stream, feeding all the worlds hanging like fruits on this tree.

Shin Gwydion Fontalba
Secret of Renewal
Trentham, 2006

*There is no place,
on this wide earth –
from ocean's boundless space
to mountain's highest peak
where nature's power is not divine
and nature's presence not a shrine.*

From the Shinto tradition

The Light

*What are "I" and "You"?
Just lattices
In the niches of a lamp
Through which the One Light radiates.*

*"I" and "You" are the veil
between heaven and earth;
lift this veil and you will see
How all sects and religions are one.*

*Lift this veil and you will ask-
When "I" and "You" do not exist
What is mosque?
What is synagogue?
What is fire temple?*

Shabistari in: Andrew Harvey and Eryk Hanut's
Perfume of the Desert: Inspirations from Sufi Wisdom
1999

Walk together and be in touch with life

According to the Buddha, life is available only in the present moment, in the here and the now. And when you go back to the present moment, you have a chance to touch life, to encounter life, to become fully alive and fully present. That is why every step brings us back to the present moment, so that we can touch the wonders of life that are available.

Thich Nhat Hanh
Moving with presence: A walking meditation

I have arrived
I am home
In the here
And the now
I am solid
I am free
In the ultimate
I dwell

Thich Nhat Hanh
The Long Road Turns To Joy: A Guide To Walking Meditation

Seeking refuge – being solid

When we were in our mother's womb, we felt secure – protected from heat, cold, and hunger. But the moment we were born and came into contact with the world's suffering, we began to cry. Since then, we have yearned to return to the security of our mother's womb. We long for permanence, but everything is changing. We desire an absolute, but even what we call our "self" is changing. ...When we touch the ground, we feel the stability of the earth and feel confident. When we observe the steadiness of the sunshine, the air and the trees, we know we can count on the sun to rise each day and the air and the trees to be there tomorrow. When we build a house, we build it on ground that is solid. Before putting our trust in others, we need to choose friends who are stable, on whom we can rely. "Taking refuge" is not based on blind faith or wistful thinking. It is gauged by our real experience.

[ ]

When our five skandhas – form, feelings, perceptions, mental states and consciousness – are in harmony, there will be naturally the right action and peace. Conscious breathing brings about calmness and harmony. Aware that practicing in this way is the best thing we can do, we will feel solid within and we will be a true vehicle for helping others.

Thich Nhat Hanh
Living Buddha, Living Christ
1995, pp. 119,122

Wandjina can't walk in jails

Fire is the spirit of life, love, family,
all those kind of things are tied up with that.

In the womb, we are in a little world.
When we are born to the larger world, the first things we see are
the sun, the family and the fire, these three important things.

We grow up with that spirit of caring and warmth of the sun, fire and love
from our family. Those are the growth elements, the elements of Wandjina.
Wandjina can't walk in jails.

When Aborigines are cut off from that, they want to kill
themselves. They just die then and go to Dulugun. There
is only that channel. And they are all coming back.

David Mowaljarlai
Yorro Yorro: Aboriginal Creation and the Renewal of Nature
1993

I walk the earth
Drink in the light
From the old
Towards the new
I am spirit
I aspire
To the ultimate
I strive.

Henk Bak
World views in Dialogue
Trentham 2014

Dao is the Way

The Way constantly takes no action.

....

*[If] Marquises and kings can maintain it,
[then] the ten thousand things transform on their own.*

*Once they have transformed, should desires arise,
You must quell them using the nameless natural state [pu].
You must also know when you have enough.
Knowing [when you have enough], you will be tranquil,
And the ten thousand things will be stable all on their own.*

Robert G Henricks
***Lao Tzu's Tao Te Ching: A Translation of the Startling New
Documents Found at Guodian / Chapter 32***
2000, p. 53

An imaginary walk back in time the origin of life

...Not only is life on this planet amazing, and deeply satisfying, to all whose senses have not become dulled by familiarity: the very fact that we have evolved the brain power to understand our evolutionary genesis redoubles the amazement and compounds the satisfaction.

'Pilgrimage' implies piety and reverence. I have not had occasion here to mention my impatience with traditional piety, and my disdain for reverence where the reverence is anything supernatural. But I make no secret of them. It is not that I wish to limit or circumscribe reverence; not because I want to reduce or downgrade the true reverence with which we are moved to celebrate the universe, once we understand it properly. 'On the contrary' would be an understatement. My objection to supernatural beliefs is precisely that they miserably fail to do justice to the sublime grandeur of the real world. They represent a narrowing-down from reality, an impoverishment of what the real world has to offer.

*I suspect that many who call themselves religious
would find themselves agreeing with me.*

Richard Dawkins
The Ancestor's Tale: A Pilgrimage to the Dawn of Evolution
2004, p. 506

Technology as ideology – the tyranny of the possible

Shepherds live invisibly and outside of the desert of the desolated earth, which is only supposed to be of use for the guarantee of the dominance of man whose effects are limited to judging whether something is important or unimportant for life. As the will to will, this life demands in advance that all knowledge move in the manner of guaranteeing calculation and valuation.

The unnoticeable law of the earth preserves the earth in the sufficiency of the emerging and perishing of all things in the allotted sphere of the possible which everything follows, and yet nothing knows. The birch tree never oversteps its possibility. The colony of bees dwells in its possibility. It is first the will which arranges itself everywhere in technology that devours the earth in the exhaustion and consumption and change of what is artificial. Technology drives the earth beyond the developed sphere of its possibility into such things which are no longer a possibility and are thus the impossible. The fact that technological plans and measures succeed a great deal in inventions and novelties, piling upon each other, by no means yields the proof that the conquests of technology even make the impossible possible.

The realism and moralism of chronicled history are the last steps of the completed identification of nature and spirit with the being of technology. Nature and spirit are objects of self-consciousness. The unconditional dominance of self-consciousness forces both in advance into a uniformity out of which there is metaphysically no escape.

It is one thing just to use the earth, another to receive the blessing of the earth and to become at home in the law of this reception in order to shepherd the mystery of Being and watch over the inviolability of the possible.

Martin Heidegger
The End of Philosophy/part 4
1975

Truth: a special responsibility and challenge for intellectuals

Don't you think that we all are responsible for the lack of values? And if we, who come from Nietzschean thought, nihilism, or historical materialism, were to openly declare that we were wrong, that moral values do exist, and that from now on we will do all that is necessary to establish and clarify them, don't you think that this will offer a beginning of some hope?

Albert Camus in conversation with Koestler, Sartre and Malraux
29-10-1946
From Camus' notes, in Rob Riemen's
Nobility of Spirit: A Forgotten Ideal

Kakkib li'Dtia Warrawee'a ancient aboriginal wisdom resonates in Gebser's 'aperspectival' structure

While rationalists regard everything non-rational as being merely objectionable irrationality, irrationalists regard the rational as merely irrational – as irrational as our spatial world is in the eyes of Indians who regard it a "Maya" (appearance). We are not speaking in favour of this antithetical negation and rejection, but we called attention to their respective deficient manifestations. Indeed we have even gone beyond this and shown that even the pre-rational was not just valid at one time but rather that its structure continues to be effective in us as one of our co-constituents. And further, that the archaic structure is ineradicable and remains ever-present even today as a consequence of its originary present.

Just as the magic structure cannot be represented but only lived, the mythical structure not represented but only experienced, and the rational structure neither lived nor experienced but only represented and conceptualized, so the aperspectival structure cannot be represented but only be "awared-in-truth".

Jean Gebser, Noel Barstad and Algis Mickunas (Translators)
The Ever-Present Origin / Part One: The Foundations of the A perspectival World.
1989, p. 267

2. Concepts, doctrines and many ways of knowing

Thinking without experience is empty,

Experience without thinking is blind.

Immanuel Kant

Introduction

With this chapter we move from preparation to involvement. After preparing for entering a dialogical space with openness, we now come to face realities, each other's realities and face to face with one another: a space that defies definition but may hold an intimation of a 'Thou', in Martin Buber's sense or a 'Sun that shines through all realities as Truth' (as Shin Gwydion Fontalba expressed it). The range of questions, that open this chapter, reaches wider and deeper than the range of tentative responses in the following texts. Some questions reflect back on chapter 1 and others foreshadow chapters 3 and 4, where questions of renewal and individual experience are addressed. The broad structure of the chapter reflects the structure of the Golden Rule itself: Who is my neighbour – who is God – who am I? Followed by 'how do I know?' and 'how to find meaning?'

In a dialogical space texts that appear on paper the one after the other, may draw us into spaces as wide and far apart as galaxies. A cursory reading may give a sense of conversation overheard from a distance; close reading of two or three texts together may invite us in as witness, as mediator, someone who concentrates on what is central to this particular dialogue, or, in Gregory Bateson's words: on the 'pattern that connects'.

World-View

Those two words denote two of the three main concerns in the history of human thinking, common sense, philosophy and theology: reflecting on the question what the world is and how we know the world. The third question being: what is a good life or 'how should one live'? Where and when human consciousness moved on from thinking in images and narrative to thinking in ideas and concepts, the search for answers to the first question, i.e. 'what is…?' dominated the discourse. The second question: 'how do we know?' became urgent after people started to search knowledge through their own efforts, no longer by consulting the scriptures or the philosophers of the past. The third question has always been asked and answers sought first via an understanding of what the reality actually is, i.e. via concepts and definitions: 'what is justice', 'what is good', 'what is love' etc. and later via one's own experiences, perceptions, assessments, following one's own moral compass. This third question, the question of morality, ethics, attitude and virtue will be addressed in chapters 5 and 6, which deal with the Golden Rule, as the essence of any ethics.

The dialogue itself between these world-views takes place between individuals and groups, stand-points from which they view – realities in which they live etc. and the perceptual, experiential, intellectual consciousness their viewing of the world amounts to. In this selection an attempt is made to capture as much as possible what might be relevant both epistemologically and ontologically, taken from traditional treasures and from the newest realizations of our own time: what is to found in contemporary anthropology (study of human being) and contemporary theology (study of divine being) and contemporary philosophy in the background of both.

Aesthetics is in many ways integral to all three: it uncovers lawfulness in the development of forms, all forms, including ways in which we shape society and organizations therein, thus including religious institutions as well; it pays attention to the way reality, existence, beings appear, show up, revealing their face… and, thirdly, how perception in the broadest spectrum of sensing, physiologically and beyond, is integral to any formation of a world-view, without which a world-view is not a 'view', not grounded in the reality in which we all live. The reader will therefore find statements on aesthetics not only in the section on ways of knowing, but also on forms of existence and especially later on, on its role in education. One task of the historian is to restore that part of a dialogue that has been suppressed, Habermas, 1961: 'The unity between knowledge and interest shows itself in a dialectics, that restores out of the historical traces of the suppressed dialogue that what has been suppressed'. Hence the inclusion of the texts by Hemsterhuis and Merleau-Ponty, which both represent that part of the enlightenment, that has been suppressed up to this time: Hemsterhuis during the enlightenment, Merleau-Ponty more than a century after. Both Hemsterhuis and Merleau-Ponty have been part of an undercurrent, that since the 'Rosicrucian Renaissance' (Dame Frances Yates) has maintained an appreciation for the role of feeling, imagination, intuition and sense perception, that mainstream thinking has overruled as merely subjective.

The subject matter is as vast, wide and deep as the ocean. The texts are scooped as it were out of this ocean, selected with an eye for the contexts, occasions, times and places where dialogues might actually take place: continually or intermittently, in communities, interfaith groups, senior high school and first year university courses, conferences, pilgrimages, study groups; in individual – internal – ponderings and dialogues as well. Within the limitations of this project I hope the selection is sufficiently diverse and relevant, to function as an inspiration and instrument to get the conversation going and unfolding, opening up new territories to discover and explore, as well as revisiting familiar grounds and seeing them with new eyes.

The main themes of this dialogue are the 'Divine' and the 'human': The human being considered with its most common understanding as (physical) body, being alive, soul and spirit. The Divine considered as the most High and Sacred, Purest Consciousness, God known and unknown by many names. The most common understanding of what is beyond understanding may be Its 'inwardness' and 'openness'. Hinduism knows this Being by 108 names, Islam by 99 names. Being all-knowing, all-merciful, all powerful doesn't make Allah three gods, just as being Father, Son and Holy Spirit doesn't make the Christian God three gods. It may be in 'divine inwardness' that our different world-views find a horizon beyond which they converge. The texts selected range between 'personal' and 'impersonal' concepts of the Divine, and concepts that transcend the divide between feminine and masculine. God as God-and-Goddess understood as One.

In Western understanding I notice two blind spots when considering the way the human being is constituted: on the one hand a 'scientific' view is often blind to the distinction between the human body alive and the human body lifeless: all life is then often explained by merely physical and sub-physical means and mechanisms. On the other hand a 'spiritual' view is often blind to the distinction between spirit and soul. The latter blind spot leads to a rather fuzzy kind of spirituality, thriving on 'experiences', beautiful or dark, soulful but without grounding in discernment. The former leads to a puzzling kind of materialism, where matters of life, soul and spirit live in another world, experienced and acted upon in real life, without recognizing them as other than effects of physical/chemical processes. In the most advanced scientific explorations in Astro-physics and Quantum Dynamics physical matter appears to be dissolved into pure energy and thereby to approach ancient cosmologies. Spiritual masters like Rudolf Steiner and the Dalai Lama have seen in quantum mechanics/dynamics an opening towards a spiritual understanding of the universe, and so does Shin Gwydion.

In between sections on the human and the Divine: a section on beginnings, origins, stories of creation and accounts of conceptual understanding, from ancient to modern. For an Australian Aboriginal story, see the Ngarinyin people's story of the beginning of the Law. Hints of how the Jaara Jaara people of the Dja Dja Wurrung language group tell their story of the beginning, can be found in notes that the late Uncle Gene Roberts had passed on to Reverend Mel Clark, the Anglican vicar of Woodend –Trentham, the area where I live.

With his Climbing Mount Improbable and An Ancestor's Tale Richard Dawkins has given two modern, highly informative accounts of the evolution of life: the first from the perspective from the beginning onwards, whereby every next step in evolution appears 'improbable' on the basis of the knowledge available at the step before; the second from the perspective of today, tracing back the steps, now established by competent research, appearing no longer 'improbable' but very probable or even certain. Having arrived at the beginning, Dawkins refrains from turning back, because his return to the present would have been another 'Mount Improbable', just as unpredictable as the first. 'Improbability', however, itself has never been understood as a property of plants and animals themselves, only as the way they might have shown up for those who traced the process of evolution, from the known to the not yet known. They would only appear 'improbable' as long as the earlier stage in the process is not sufficiently understood.

I think that Dawkins would probably agree with me, when I note, that his central argument in his 'The God Delusion' (Chapter 4), is based on the assumption that – with God – 'improbable' is thought of as a property, whilst with plants, animals and humans it is not. All the steps on the way back in evolution are probable, if not certain: why would one step further back, suddenly become improbable? Incomprehensible yes, especially when one realizes that the God of Jews, Hindus, Christians and Muslims, Sikhs, Bahá'í and others, is thought of as ever present, ever sustaining, not only present before beginnings, but present now, and still present when all has passed. If 'improbable' means 'unforeseeable' on the basis of now available knowledge, then every genuine work of art, poetry, music, scientific writing would be 'improbable', but it never makes the existence of the scientist, musician, poet or artist improbable. Every new born child is a wonder. And for Dawkins every day is a wonder, too.

Dawkins' 'argument' for atheism may be flawed, but I suspect his 'motive' is not. It is rather to be found in the later chapters of his 'God Delusion', driven by indignation for every horror perpetrated in name of religion and of God. As a historian I know there is more to that, of course, but from my experience as a Catholic, I know no fiercer and more perceptive critics of the church than Catholics themselves. And Marilynne Robinson has pointed out, that all the horrors of the Old Testament are known to us, because the people of Israel were "talking to themselves".

Peter Boghossian's 'Manuel for Creating Atheists' is strong in the direction of destroying belief-systems as one destroys a house. A Street Epistemologist aims at its foundations. This to liberate the believer from falsehoods and illusions, to make place for a humanistic vision based on honesty and truth. It doesn't tell the 'born again atheist' how to (re)build his or her house. And wisely so. Humanist world-views have a long and worldwide tradition to draw on. The terms 'foundationist' and 'coherentism' are 'absolutes' for the purpose of demolition. Boghossian uses the term 'deconstruct', a word coined by Jacques Derrida in the context of literary criticism. It means that one attempts to interpret a text not by pulling the text apart, i.e. by analysizing, but by identifying in a text its constituent parts, whilst maintaining one's attention for the whole. Prosper Mallarmé wrote a number of versions of a poem on poverty and a poor man. In his book 'Glas' (ringing, resonance) Derrida comments that in the latest versions the earlier versions are still resonating. To destroy a house is not to deconstruct but to demolish. It may be in coherence, not coherentism, and grounding that evidence can be found, not only in building a new humanism, but also in deconstructing rather than demolishing the house that believers are living in. There is more potential for resonance in Boghossians method than his book gives credit for.

Jean Gebser's way of characterizing our current stage of consciousness as 'aperspectival', i.e. the need to transcend the 'rational' consciousness with its reliance on linear perspective, will 'resonate' throughout the remainder of this work. It places 'world-view' itself in a new light. It reminds me of the story Gideon told of the famous Sufi sage Nashruddin: When the master, who was everywhere considered a fool, entered an inn, some scholars interrupted their conversation and asked Nashruddin: "what is superior: the sun or the moon?" He answered: "the moon of course, because she lights up the night. The day is already light, so the sun is less important". Vision is more than perspective, listening is more than hearing: silence is part of the world of sound, darkness is for vision what silence is for sound, and all our senses live and work in a world each in the 'space' of their own 'silence'. A worldview transcending its own 'linear' perspective, becomes 'vision' again in the full sense of the word, and the word of its teaching can 'resonate' beyond its own direct participants. What Martin Buber says of the word of Socrates or Jesus, can be said of the word of anyone who speaks his or her world-view in the way one says "I Am": not 'about' it, but 'being' it. In that full humanity out of which we speak as individuals in dialogue, ultimately a "We Are" may arise, a "WE" in which all of us as individuals would recognize ourselves and in which all world-views would resonate with one another, without obscuring or muffling one's own. Rather they would enrich and enhance each other…

In the next chapter and in chapter 6 there will be some direct references to this 'aperspectival' approach, but a drastic evocation of what happens and actually has happened, especially in the Western culture, can be found immediately after Jean Gebser's text. Romanyshyn's book is a fascinating history of how linear perspective, with its 'vanishing point', has led to a culture of disembodiment, pathological and destructive, which in this anthology is one reason and motive more to emphasise the vital significance of a training and education of the senses as integral to any path of human development, in life, soul and spirit: individually and collectively. Hence, I assume, Rabbi Zalman's insistence that the form of our dialogue is just as important as its content.

An adequate grounding of a spiritual understanding of the world requires another opening: a reappraisal of age-old traditions, which – especially since the Age of Enlightenment – have been suppressed in Western intellectual and academic discourse, traditions known as 'occult' or 'esoteric'.

For the consideration of the questions raised in this and the following chapters, it is high time that the 'unfinished project' of the Enlightenment (Habermas) gets finished and the dialogue gains competence in those areas of perception and the heart, that have been undernourished for too long. Which also means that it is time that all participants in the dialogue, religious or secular/humanist, become familiar and competent in the teachings of the so called 'esoteric' schools, that – by themselves – are not religions, but offer teachings beyond the dominant 'exoteric' styles of understanding, i.e. religious dogma and scientific doctrine.

The term 'supernatural' might have become obsolete (Rorty/Pigliuzzi), not so much because there is no longer a spiritual dimension to 'contemporary' reality, but because the spiritual dimension is (again) considered a natural part of contemporary reality. I refer to the work of the historian Frances Yates, who pioneered the study into this area, via Scotus Erigena, Raymond Lull, Giordano Bruno, Francesco Giorgi and others. She suggested the term "Rosicrucian" for the nature of the 'Elizabethan Renaissance' in 16th and early 17th century England, in which advances in science were meant to be matched with advances in morality, an ideal that got lost in the 'Age of Enlightenment'. It is the cultural historian Wouter Hanegraaf who in the last 25 years has put the study of 'esotericism' back into the academic discourse. As I have not (yet) managed to read and study his books, I include, instead, a lengthy quotation from Wikipedia about his work in this selection.

Different religious, spiritual and secular world-views have their own esoteric traditions, which may need to become part of our dialogue, if only for the possibility referred to by Rabbi Zalman Schachter-Shalome, that those world-views are esoterically closer to each other than exoterically. Rabbi Zalman himself seems ambivalent in his appreciation of the avalanche of esoteric literature that the younger generation seems to prefer above the scriptures and classical texts. He would have been pleased, I guess, that Wouter Hanegraaf treats the "New Age" movement and esotericism as two different historical phenomena (two different books).

Integral to a grounded esoteric training is also a training in being at home in all areas of human existence: not only psychological and physical, but also sensory. Hence some texts, old and new, about the role and importance of the senses and their relationship to the brain. Insights in the development of the human being from conception onwards and education enhance this development... It is important to note, that - on the one hand - during about the first seven years of a child's development, the brain is especially engaged in guiding the development of the child's physical constitution, growth and inner organs. This process takes place only once. On the other hand it are the senses and active engagement with the world in all its aspects, that feed the brain: this learning may last a life time, even to the end (Audrey E. McAllen. Reading Children's Drawings. Rudolf Steiner College Press. Fair Oaks, USA.2004. p 2).

A cursory look at traditional Jewish and Muslim education tells me, that children wisely were not too early taught 'religion' in any intellectual way. In early childhood children learn both by play and from example, the brain allowed to be engaged in the child's bodily development, the child allowed to be a child. The introduction of the Catechism in the Catholic Church, to instil church teaching in children, in the 16th century, seems, at least in hindsight, ill advised.

Some contemporary considerations of evil which escape the grasp of our rational, philosophical understandings and concepts may be yet another grounding in preparation of our dialogue. The chosen texts speak for themselves, but I draw attention to Henri Bruning's thoughts. Part of his texts could also have been placed in another section of this chapter or in chapter 6: his notion of being a 'sourdough', 'ferment' in the bread of humanity might be the responsibility for all of us in our different world-views. His hunch, in 1961, that the fundamentalisms of our time are degenerated, distorted expressions of this noble responsibility, sounds prophetic: the tyranny of the 'known good' an almost 'satanic' attack on 'good will'.

To end this chapter with some texts on hope is to foreshadow and connect with what in chapter 3 will be addressed as calls for renewal.

Texts

Prelude: from wonder to questions, from traditional answers to new challenges

In wonder all philosophy began; in wonder it ends: and admiration fills up the interspace. But the first wonder is the offspring of ignorance: the last is the parent of adoration. The first is the birth-throe of our knowledge: the last is its euthanasy and apotheosis.

Coleridge, Aphorism IX

How can we meet each other as human beings?

How do different streams understand:
the essential nature of the human being, the true I and the false selves?
the genuine WE: what is a gathering of many people, what is community?

What do you see as central in your stream or religion, and how is the way to God?
What is regarded an important practice?
What are the virtues that need to be developed?

How is the viewpoint: God as Redeemer, Healer, Judge, Saviour (one who sets things right)
How would an image, an imagination be that could help us to approach God?
How do you approach God and the helping beings?

How does your stream regard the Holy Ones?
How do you look at birth, life, death, the overcoming of death, existence before birth and after death?
What reveals itself to you as the aim of development?

Shin Gwydiion Fontalba
The word 'stream' resonates with the event's theme: Many Rivers – One Ocean
Leaflet circulated at the Earth Celebration, Switzerland 1999

Aboriginal Culture Central Australia

Kanyini = connectedness of all, all is one spiritually, psychic, life, physical

At 40,00 years the oldest living culture on earth…, guided by a discipline: 'don't take more than you need and don't destroy…' Four principles:

1. Tjukurpa = belief system
2. Kurumpa = spirituality
3. Lori = land; being at home wherever I am
4. Wultja = family; all is family: rocks, water, air, fire, plants and animals as well as human beings are my family. The Earth is our Mother. That makes you and me brother and sister.

A Film by Melanie Hogan
Kanyini Over 40.000 years of culture. One philosophy that connects us all

Buddha's Teaching

Now by the wayfarer… a middle course has been thoroughly understood…

And what is that middle course…?

Just this noble eightfold way, namely,

-right view
-right purpose
-right speech
-right action
-right livelihood
-right endeavour
-right mindfulness
-right concentration

This is that middle course which has been thoroughly understood, making vision, making knowledge, which conduces to calm after toil, to thorough knowledge, to understanding, to nirvana.

A Muslim tale: a path through seven valleys

Hoopoe said: 'We have seven valleys to cross and only after we have crossed them shall we discover the Simurgh. No one has ever come back into the world who has made this journey, and it is impossible to say how many parasanges there are in front of us. Be patient, O fearful one, since all those who went by this road were in your state.

The first valley is the Valley of the Quest, the second the Valley of Love, third is the valley of Understanding, the fourth is the Valley of Independence and detachment, the fifth of Pure Unity, the sixth is the Valley of Astonishment, and the seventh is the valley of Poverty and Nothingness beyond which one can go no further.'

Farīd al-Dīn 'Aṭṭār, C. S. Nott (Translator)
Conference of the Birds
2000

There is small chance of truth at the goal where there is not a child-like humility at the starting-point.

Samuel Taylor Coleridge
Aids to Reflection
1843

The philosophical enlightened self-understanding of modernity stands in particular dialectical relationship to the theological self-understanding of the major religions, which intrude into this modernity as the most awkward element of its past.

It is not a question of an unstable compromise between irreconcilable elements. We should not dodge the alternative between an anthropocentric orientation and the view from afar of theocentric or cosmocentric thinking. However, it makes a difference whether we speak with another or merely about one another. If we want to avoid the latter, two presuppositions must be fulfilled: the religious side must accept the basic principles of universalistic egalitarianism in law and morality. Conversely, the secular reason may not set itself up as judge concerning truths of faith, even though in the end it can accept as reasonable only what it can translate into its own, in principle universally accessible discourses.

Juergen Habermas
An Awareness of What is Missing: Faith and Reason in a Post-secular Age
2010

What gives the human being his true being, his dignity, his destiny, is the very fact, that the cosmos, the universe doesn't treat him as an under-aged child, that gets the truth without further ado thrown in its lap, but assumes that he acquires the truth through his own work, work of his whole life.

Rudolf Steiner

Life between Death and Rebirth - Sixteen lectures by RUDOLF
STEINER / Dornach 2 February 1915
1975, p. 10

Who is my neighbour?

Stories of Origin:

> *... the more I contemplate this in and out of itself living cosmos, the more I experience God – out of whom all has become – as the absolute Unknowable, and the more God "manifests" himself as such. I don't have a different experience when I listen to the perfect singing of a woman's voice or listen to Mozart, Bach; or when I read Shakespeare or Sophocles, Hölderlin, Goethe, or the Vedas, the Edda etc. My awe doesn't only concern what I read or hear, but the human being, the human capacities, the nobility thereof, that realised these great creations of humanity. I am confronted with the (sublime) "Phenomenon of Man", the unfathomable wonder of it and I experience a glimmer of God as Majestic and Unknowable.*

Henri Bruning
Vormkracht en Onmacht der Religie: Missionair Christendom (By way of introduction: The Second Commandment)
1961, p. 24

Maori Culture

> *...Rangi and Papa, or Heaven and Earth, were the source from which, in the beginning, all things originated. Darkness then rested upon the heaven and upon the earth, and they still clave together, for they had not yet been rent apart...Hence these sayings....:" There was darkness from the first division of time, unto the tenth, to the hundredth, to the thousandth." ...*

> *At last the beings who had been begotten by Heaven and Earth, worn out by the continued darkness, consulted by themselves, saying," Let us now determine what we should do with Rangi and Papa, whether it would be better to slay them or to rend them apart.*

[ ]

> *At length their plans having been agreed upon, (to rend them apart) lo, Rongo-ma-tane, the god father of the cultivated food of man, rises up, that he may rend apart the heavens and the earth: he struggles but he rends them not apart.*

[After three other gods have tried in vain]

Then, at last, slowly uprises Tane-mahuta, the god and father, of forests, of birds, and of insects, and he struggles with his parents, in vain he strives to rend them apart with his hands and arms. Lo, he pauses; his head is now firmly planted on his mother, the earth, his feet he raises up and rests against his father the skies, he strains his back and limbs with mighty effort. Now are rent apart Rangi and Papa, and with cries and groans of woe they shriek aloud," wherefore slay you thus your parents? Why commit you so dreadful a crime to slay us, as to rend your parents apart?" ...

No sooner was heaven rent from earth than the multitude of human beings were discovered whom they had begotten, and who had hitherto lain concealed between the bodies of Rangi and Papa.

Then, also, there arose in the breast of Tawhiri-ma-tea, the god and father of winds and storms, a fierce desire to wage war with his brothers, because they had rent apart their common parents...it was his brothers alone that wished for this separation, and desired that Papa-tu-a-nuku, or the earth alone should be left as a parent to them.

The god of hurricanes and storms dreads also that the world should become too fair and beautiful, so he rises, follows his father to the realms above, and hurries to the sheltered hollows in the boundless skies; there he hides and clings, and nestling in this place of rest he consults with his parent, and as the vast Heaven listens to the suggestions of Tawhiri-ma-tea, the thoughts and plans are formed in his breast, and Tawhiri-ma-tea also understands what he should do.

Sir George Grey "The Children of Heaven and Earth"
Polynesian Mythology and Ancient Traditional History
Auckland H. Brett 1885. Quoted in: Barbara C. Sproul's
Primal myths: Creation myths around the world
1979, pp. 340-1

Creation

From the conception the increase.
From the increase the thought.
From the thought the remembrance.
From the remembrance the consciousness.
From the consciousness the desire.

The world becomes fruitful;
It dwelt with the feeble glimmering;

It brought forth night:
The great night, the long night,
The lowest night, the loftiest night,
The thick night to be felt,
The night to be touched,
The night not to be seen,
The night of death.

From the nothing the begetting,
From the nothing the increase,
From the nothing the abundance,
The power of increasing
The living breath;
It dwelt with the empty space,
And produced the atmosphere which is above us,
The atmosphere which floats above the earth;
The great firmament above us dwelt with the earthly dawn,
And the moon sprung forth;
The atmosphere above us dwelt with the heat,
And hence produced the sun;
They were thrown up above,
As the chief eyes of Heaven:
Then the heavens became light,
The earthly dawn, the early day,
The mid-day.
The blaze of day from the sky.

Richard Taylor Te Ika a Maui London 1855 in: Barbara C. Sproul's
Primal myths: Creation myths around the world
1979, pp. 338-339

Creation: places where the god did stop.

Everything as it moves, now and then, here and there, makes stops. The bird as it flies stops in one place to make its nest, and another to rest on its flight. A man when he goes forth stops when he wills. So the god has stopped. The sun, which is so bright is one place where he stopped. The moon, the stars, the winds, he has been with. The trees, the animals, are all where he has stopped, and the Indian thinks of these places and sends his prayers there to reach the place where the god has stopped and win help and a blessing.

Claude Lévi-Strauss
Totemism

1962, p. 28

Ancient Iran

As the Holy One I did recognize You, Wise Lord (Ahura Mazda), when I have witnessed You in my vision by the creation of life, that – at the last turning point of creation – You will reward the works and the words – evil with evil and good with good destiny – through Your noble sense.

At which turning point You will appear with Your Holy Spirit, with Kshathra (realm) and Vohumano (benevolence), through the work of which the people of Asha (the good law) are empowered. These good people are nominated by Armaiti (the goddess of the earth) as the ones who proclaim of Your judgement, that no one can circumvent.

Bücherei, Fischer
Die Nichtchristlichen Religionen. Verfaßt und herausgegeben von Helmuth von Glaseanapp
1964, pp. 293
[Translated by Henk Bak]

Ancient China

Heaven and earth were jumbled together in a cosmic egg for eighteen thousand years, and Pan Gu lived in the midst of it. The heavens and the earth split apart. The pure Yang essence became the heavens, the heavy Yin essence was the earth. Pan Gu was between them, nine changes in a day, a god in the heavens and a sage on the earth. Every day the heavens rose higher by ten feet, the earth grew thicker by ten feet, and Pan Gu became ten feet taller. When he reached eighteen years of age, the heavens were infinitely high, the earth was infinitely deep, and Pan Gu was infinitely tall.

…heaven and earth split apart, not in the way that a solid body splits in two with a crack, but rather as a gradual separation of two essences; the light, pure yang essence rose up and became the heavens, the heavy yin essence sank and became the earth.

But that was not the end of the separation of heaven and earth. The process had only just begun.

Notice how Chinese people pay a lot of attention to changes…

[ ]

For the Chinese, this idea of mastery in both realms is an ideal way of being, one to which we should all aspire: a heaven where idealism can spread its wings and fly freely, with no need to compromise with all the rules and obstacles of the real world; and the ability to keep our feet planted firmly on the ground, so that we can make our way in the real world.

[ ]

Idealism and realism are our heaven and earth.

{]

…humankind is equal to the heavens and the earth: heaven, earth and people are referred to together as the Three Realms – the three equally great and important things from which the world is made.

Yu Dan
Confucius from the Heart Ancient Wisdom for Today's World / The San Wu Li Ancient Creation Story retold with comment
2006/7, pp. 13-15

The New Rule

It's the old rule that drunks have to argue and get into fights.
The lover is just as bad. He falls into a hole.
But down in that hole he finds something shining,
Worth more than any amount of money or power.

Last night the moon came dropping its clothes in the street.
I took it as a sign to start singing,
Falling up into the bowl of the sky.
The bowl breaks. Everywhere is falling everywhere.
Nothing else to do.

Here's the new rule: break the wineglass,
And fall toward the glassblower's breath.

Jalal al-Din Muhammad Rumi in: Coleman Barks (Translator)'s
The Essential Rumi
1985

'Source of Being' in the world of forms, of bodies, of spirits…

It is not even possible to speak about Absolute Being, but that is why the word 'Hu' when it is used in that way does not stand for a being. It stands for that Source from which Being comes. It is the same as that which in Buddhism is called Nirvana. Nirvana means the state which is beyond Being. Therefore looked at from the side of Being it appears empty nothingness – just as from our side silence appears as the absence of sound…if you enter into silence, you become aware that sound is an intrusion. You realise how much greater silence is than sound. The same way that you realise that the emptiness that has no attributes is very much greater than any attribute. These things one can have some kind of acceptance of, and it is at this point that all religions, all teachings unite. This is the transcendental source of all religions.

In the world of forms religions differ from one another. In the world of bodies, they can conflict with one another and one teaching can exclude another and everything can be seen only relatively. In the second world, in the world of spirits, religions have the same form, because the forms have no longer that fixedness. This means, for example, that two saints who meet in the world of spirits would not have any question such as 'Are you a Christian, are you a Muslim, are you a Jew? And so on. They would recognise one another and would not be concerned with form. In the third world certainly all religions are one, but in another sense. They are all manifestations of the power of God. But in the fourth world they are all one in another sense, that they all lost in the same source. Their differences are not merely from the same manifestation of God, but they disappear altogether.

Intimations Talks with J.G. Bennet at Beshara.
1975, p. 74

A Buddhist View: the principle of interdependence

The Dalai Lama: The entire Buddhist worldview is based on a philosophical standpoint in which the central thought is the principle of interdependence, how all things and events come into being purely as a result of interactions between causes and conditions. Within that worldview it is almost impossible to have any room for an atemporal, eternal, absolute truth. Nor is it possible to accommodate the concept of a divine Creation. Similarly, for a Christian whose entire metaphysical worldview is based on a belief in the Creation and a divine Creator, the idea that all things and events arise out of mere interaction between causes and conditions has no place within that worldview. So in the realm of metaphysics it becomes problematic at a certain point, and the two traditions must diverge.

[ ]

Sister Eileen: My question is simple, I think…If a meeting between Your Holiness and Jesus could be arranged, would you like that? And what do you think you would ask or discuss during your time together?

The Dalai Lama: For a Buddhist, whose main object of refuge is the Buddha. When coming into contact with someone like Jesus Christ – whose life clearly demonstrates a being who has affected millions of people in a spiritual way, bringing about their liberation and freedom from suffering – the feeling that one would have toward such a person would be that of reverence toward a fully enlightened being or a bodhisattva.

Sister Eileen: Would Your Holiness have certain questions you would like to ask him?

The Dalai Lama: The first question I would ask is, "Could you describe the nature of the Father?" Because our lack of understanding concerning the exact nature of the father is leading to so much confusion here.

Sister Eileen: Well, now we think it's both Father and Mother! pp. 82-83

[ ]

In Buddhism, especially in Madhyakama Buddhism, the principle of interdependence is understood in three ways. The first is in terms of cause and effect. In this case, interdependence is linear: certain causes and conditions bring out certain results. This interdependence of causes and conditions is common to all Buddhist schools. There is a second level of understanding in which interdependence is understood more in terms of mutual dependence, in which the existence of certain phenomena is mutually dependent upon other phenomena. There is a kind of interconnectedness. This is very clearly reflected in the idea of "whole" and "parts". Without parts there cannot be a whole; without a whole there cannot be parts. There is a mutual dependence. A third understanding of the principle of interdependence is more in terms of identity: the identity of a particular event or object is dependent upon a context or its environment. In some sense identity is regarded as emergent: it is not absolute, it is relative. Certain things and events possess identity in relation to other things and events. These are the three levels, or three different ways, in which the principle of interdependence is understood. p.104

His Holiness the Dalai Lama explores the heart of Christianity - and
of humanity
The Good Heart: John Main Seminar London 1994

A local Australian Aboriginal view of the origin and beyond (2015)

Good morning, my name is Gene Roberts and I am a proud Jaara Jaara man of the Dja Dja Wurrung language group. It is with pride that I appear here today on behalf of my dear Elder, Uncle Brien Nelson. Also I would take this time to announce my respect to all of my Elders, both past and present and all Elders that may be with us for this rather special day on many fronts.

The Jaara Jaara have been the traditional custodians of this land where we are gathered for in excess of 60,000 years and we are but a small part of, the oldest living race upon this planet. We have cared for, protected and nurtured this beautiful country. Throughout those 60,000 years, we have also formed ceremony, recognising our creation spirits such as the Rainbow Serpent who constructed the beautiful life-giving waterways and our ancient land. We honoured and still continue to honour Bunjil, our creator and Waah our protector within our ancient song-lines.

We as a people never saw these creation spirits as gods. They were separate, self-contained identities that were the existences of something that contrasted with their attributes. They basically exist that we, as aboriginal people can identify with our environment, our reason for being and provide a foundation for our societal stability. This belief system served us well for those 60,000 years and guided our actions as to how we would respect and honour all things, living and inanimate.

In the year 1788 A.D, rightly or wrongly, the first settlers and convicts began arriving on our shores. The human cargo of those sailing vessels, brought their hopes, dreams and aspirations for a new life for themselves. The colonists also wisely brought their belief system, their religion along also, for everyone is in need of spiritual guidance.

The Anglican faith was a leading representation of that spiritual and moral necessity and continues to be today. Here in our beautiful Woodend, I am proud to say the Anglican Church is an integral part of our small spirited community. Anglicans first worshipped on the site of the current church in a small wooden building from 1859.

[ ]

> The Anglican Church has cooperated alongside my Jaara Jaara people with a most benevolent understanding of our cultural practices, a beautiful symbiosis if you will. Indeed your own Indigenous deacon, the Reverend Robyn Davis has displayed this amicable association on many occasions.
>
> That tradition is still evident today as I respectfully appear here for two special occasions today. As many here may already be aware, our wonderful Vicar, Melissa Clark has been ordained a Reverend and I sincerely congratulate my friend for her achievement. Secondly, I have the pleasure of offering our dear friend, The Rt. Reverend Andrew W. Curnow - Bishop of Bendigo and friends, a "Wominjeka", a "Welcome to Country."
>
> Welcome to Jaara Jaara country, and whilst you are here please enjoy the land, where tens of thousands of generations of my people have performed sacred ceremonies, raised families, successfully farmed, cared for the environment and welcomed strangers that are now our friends. With a welcome being issued, it is understood that whilst one is a visitor to our country, you would respect all others that are also on our country as we have done so for millennia.
>
> Wominjeka to everyone gathered here today and especially my new friend Melissa Clark and her beautiful family.
>
> Thank you.

Text provided by the Reverend Melissa Clark, December 2018

Creative energy: like footsteps in the sand

> A great current of creative energy gushes forth through matter, to obtain from it what it can. At most points it stopped; these stops are transmuted, in our eyes, into the appearance of so many species, i.e. of organisms in which our perception, being essentially analytical and synthetic, distinguishes a multitude of elements combining to fulfil a multitude of functions, but the process of organization was only the stop itself, a simple act analogous to the impress of a foot which instantaneously causes thousands of grains of sand to contrive to form a pattern.

Henri Bergson quoted in Patricia E. Kaplan, Susan Manso's
Major European Art Movements, 1900-1945: A Critical Anthology
1977, p. 351

Evolution 1

The Western idea of evolution is the statement of a process of formation, not an explanation of our being. Limited to the physical and biological data of Nature, it does not attempt except in a summary or superficial fashion to discover its own meaning, but is content to announce itself as the great law of a quite mysterious and inexplicable energy. Evolution becomes a problem in motion which is satisfied to work up with an automatic regularity its own puzzle, but not to work it out, because, since it is only a process, it has no understanding of itself, and, since it is a blind perpetual automatism of mechanical energy, it has neither an origin nor an issue.

[ ]

The ancient idea of evolution was the fruit of a philosophical intuition, the modern is an effort of scientific observation. Each as enounced misses something, but the ancient got all the spirit of the movement where the modern is content with the form and the most external machinery.

[ ]

We know that an evolution there is, but not what evolution is; that remains still one of the initial mysteries of nature.

For evolution, as is the habit with the human reason's accounts and solutions of the deep and unfathomable way of the Spirit in things, raises more questions than it solves; it does not do away with the problem of creation for all its appearance of solid orderly fact, any more than the religious affirmation of an external omnipotent Creator could do it or the illusionist's mystic Maya…

[ ]

The way man sees and experiences the universe, imposes on his reason the necessity of a one original eternal substance of which all things are the forms and a one original energy of which all movement of action and consequence is the variation. But the whole question is, what is the reality of this substance and what is the essential nature of this energy?

The word evolution carries with it in its intrinsic sense, in the idea at its root the necessity of a previous involution. We must, if a hidden spiritual being is the secret of all the action of Nature, give its full power to that latent value of the idea. We are bound then to suppose that all that evolves already existed involved, passive or otherwise active, but in either case concealed from us in the shell of material Nature. The Spirit which, manifests itself here in a body, must be involved from the beginning in the whole of matter and in every knot,

formation and particle of matter; life, mind and whatever is above mind must be latent, inactive or concealed active powers in all the operations of material energy.

[ ]

East and West have two ways of looking at life which are opposite sides of one reality. Between the pragmatic truth on which the vital thought of modern Europe enamoured of the vigour of life, all the dance of God in nature, puts so vehement and exclusive a stress and the immutable Truth to which the Indian mind enamoured of calm and poise loves to turn with an equal passion for an exclusive finding, there is no such divorce and quarrel as is now declared by the partisan mind, the separating reason, the absorbing passion of an excessive will of realization. The one eternal immutable Truth is the Spirit and without the Spirit the pragmatic truth of a self-creating universe would have no origin or foundation; it would be barren of significance, empty of inner guidance, lost in its end, a firework display shooting up into the void only to fall away and perish in mid-air. But neither is the pragmatic a dream of the non-existent, an illusion or a lapse into some futile delirium of creative imagination; that would make the eternal Spirit a drunkard or a dreamer, the fool of his own gigantic self-hallucinations.

[ ]

Because this infinite Spirit and eternal Divinity is here concealed in the process of material Nature, the evolution of a power beyond Mind is not only possible, but inevitable. ...since the Divinity is involved here and is emerging, it is inevitable that all his powers or degrees of power should energy one after the other till the whole glory is embodied and visible.

Robert Mc Dermott, Inner Traditions (Editor)
The Essential Aurobindo
1987, pp. 70-73;79-80;82

Evolution 2: (ontology) Ancestor's Tale, the way backwards.

The genial host, having guided Chaucer and the other pilgrims from London to Canterbury and stood impresario to their tales, turned around and led them straight back to London.

If I now return to the present, it must be alone, for to presume upon evolution's following the same forward course twice would be to deny the rationale of our backward journey. Evolution was never aimed at any particular endpoint...If we turn around and move forward now, we cannot retrace our steps. That would imply that evolution, were it to be a rerun, would follow the same course, putting those same mergers into reverse gear in the form of splits...p. 48

Richard Dawkins
The Ancestor's Tale: A Pilgrimage to the Dawn of Evolution
2004, p.13

Evolution 3: (Epistemology) Climbing Mount Improbable, the way forwards.

On our route we shall have occasion to look at spider webs – at the bewildering, though unconscious, ingenuity with which they are made and how they work. We shall reconstruct the slow, gradual evolution of wings and of elephant trunks. We shall see that 'the' eye, legendarily difficult though its evolution sometimes seems, has actually evolved at least forty and probably sixty times independently all around the animal kingdom.

Richard Dawkins
Climbing Mount Improbable
1996, p. 2

The street as the ontological 'landscape' in which epistemological enquiry happens...

Street Epistemology harks back to the values of the ancient philosophers – individuals who were tough-minded, plain-speaking, known for self-defence, committed to truth, unyielding in the face of danger, and fearless in calling out falsehoods, contradictions, inconsistencies, and nonsense.

[ ]

The Street Epistemologist is a philosopher and a fighter. She is savvy and street smarts that come from the school of hard knocks. She relentlessly helps others by tearing down falsehoods about whatever enshrined "truths" enslave us.

But the Street Epistemologist doesn't just tear down fairytales, comforting delusions, and imagined entities. She offers a humanistic vision. Let's be blunt, direct, and honest with ourselves and with others. Let's help people develop a trustfulness of reason and a willingness to reconsider, and let's place rationality in the service of humanity. Street Epistemology offers a humanism that's taken some hits and gained from experience...

Peter Boghossian
A Manuel for Creating Atheists
2013, pp. 16-17

Emergence

.... The laws of physics and chemistry include no conception of sentience, and any system wholly determined by these laws must be insentient. ...the fact that the study of life must ultimately reveal some principles additional to those manifested by inanimate matter...

[Here follows a description of several stages of "emergence", from sentience to comprehension...Then the text continues:]

Engineering and physics are two different sciences. Engineering includes the operational principles of machines and some knowledge of physics bearing on these principles. Physics and chemistry, on the other hand, include no knowledge of the operational principles of machines. Hence a complete physical and chemical topography of an object would not tell us whether it is a machine, and if so, how it works and for what purpose...(But) only the physical-chemical structure of a machine can explain its failures. Liability to failure is, as it were, the price paid for embodying operational principles in a material the laws of which ignore these principles.

Such a material will eventually cast off the yoke of such foreign control.

[ ]

The operational principles of machines are embodied in matter by ... artificial shaping. These principles might be said to govern the boundary conditions of an inanimate system – a set of conditions that is explicitly left undetermined by the laws of nature.

We may call the control exercised by the organizational principle of a higher level on the particulars forming its lower level the principle of marginal control. ...

[ ]

Inanimate nature is self-contained, achieving nothing, relying on nothing and, hence, unerring. This fact defines the most essential innovation achieved by the emergence of life from the inanimate. A living function has a result which it may achieve or fail to achieve. Processes that are expected to achieve something have a value that is inexplicable in terms of processes having no such value. The logical impossibility of such explanation may be affiliated to the dictum that nothing that ought to be, can be determined by knowing what is.

Michael Polanyi
The Tacit Dimension
1967, pp. 38-44

About the Blue that wanted more...

Imagine the blue that you see here wishing dearly that God add still more from his paint-pot, so that it becomes even more blue.

God says: "I don't have any blue left to make you still more blue than you are. You have got all my blue already. Nonetheless, I can strengthen your blue and make it more luminous than it is now."

"You want to increase me without giving me anything? I have to stay stuck in my poverty?"

"That is exactly what you must, for I have nothing to give. Everything has been given. But I can make it so, that every seeing eye sees you more blue and radiant. You must only give up the wish, that I give you something. I have nothing."

"If you have already nothing to give me, then just take the little blue that you gave me. Then I also don't want to have or be this anymore. All or nothing, that is my pride."

God felt sorry for the blue's unhappiness. And he did what is God's way and made the blue more blue, without adding anything to it or taking from it.

All eyes, however, that since then saw it, noticed that it was more blue than before. And what happened then, happens always: you can see it.

Here you see it where the old and the new are placed next to each other. In both cases it is the same blue. Only, one of the two blues shows itself markedly more blue and luminous.

When you look closer into it and reflect on your experience, you can even notice, that the blue in the orange coloured field moves beyond itself, transcends itself, extends and stretches itself. At the border between the blue and yellow-red areas a play of rays appears. To be sure, all this happens only in the eye that is seeing. And what God has actually done is, that by embedding the blue in the yellow-red, he has at the same time made innumerable people open their eyes. Or, also this: God looked at what he had done. He saw it and let it be seen. He brought it before the eyes.

Hugo Kükelhaus
Das Wort des Johannes / Alfred Metzner Verlag – Frankfurt am Main
1958, p. 1-3
[The two kinds of blue mentioned in the text on page 1 appear on the next page as examples of 'simultaneus contrast'
Translated by Henk Bak]

In dialogue 'perspectival' world-views approach their 'a-perspectival' – ever present – origin on a new level of consciousness.

One difficulty which to some may seem insurmountable is the difficulty of "representing" the aperspectival world. This world goes beyond our conceptualization. By the same token, the mental world once went beyond the experiential capability of mythical man, and yet the world of the mind became reality. Anyone who objects that the aperspectival is, in spatial terms, unimaginable, incomprehensible, impalpable, inconclusive, and unthinkable – and there will be no end to such objections – falls victim to his own limitations of comprehension and to the visual representation imposed by the world. Some will also undoubtedly be irritated by the talk of arational possibilities which are not to be confused by the irrational or pre-rational.

[ ]

Just as the magic structure cannot be represented but only lived, the mythical structure not represented but only experienced, and the rational structure neither lived nor experienced but only represented and conceptualized, so the aperspectival structure cannot be represented but only be "awared-in-truth".

Jean Gebser, Noel Barstad and Algis Mickunas (Translators)
The Ever-Present Origin / Part One: The Foundations of the A perspectival World.
1989, p. 267

Through linear perspective, 'neither lived nor experienced': body vanishes – corpse appears...

In the space of the world opened up by linear perspective there is reason and motive to abandon the body. A spectator self ensconced behind its window has no need for the body, and indeed, in dispensing with the body the spectator with his or her eye upon the world can rid himself or herself of all those extraneous odors and sounds, textures and tastes, temperatures and rhythms which compose the world. In leaving the body behind, the self behind the window can better realize its vision of the world, a vision purified of the flesh, sterilized, if you will, a vision we might say without taste.

There is also reason and motive to abandon the body for a spectator self, whose vision of the world is fixed upon an infinite horizon. A body whose eyes are drawn out and into a sensuous world, an e-motional body sensitive to the allure of things, lingering over them, would be a hindrance to the realization of this fixed and infinite vision. Such a body, whose eyes would find fulfilment of their vision in a movement toward the world, a body whose also be feet and hands, and nose, and ears, and skin, would be an obstacle. In much the same way, there is reason and motive to abandon the body for a self which, as it approaches the horizon, must shrink from the bottom up towards the head in order to fit within the space opened up by linear perspective vision. The hegemony of the head leaves no room for the pantomimic body, for that body with its power to generate spaces, to create situations. Within the linear, and homogeneous space of explanation, within that grid where all space has become equal and the same, the heterogeneous pantomimic body has no place.

It is a body, therefore, which we no longer need, a body which has become an obstacle; a body for which there is no place is a body ready to be abandoned. It is also, on the other side of this abandonment, a body ready to be reinvented. The corpse is the most visible image of the abandoned body. It what the human body becomes in our increasing distance from it. It is what the pantomimic, e-motional body becomes for a spectator self behind a window with heady vision fixed upon an infinite horizon. The corpse, whose destiny is the astronautic body of technological functioning, is also the most dramatic and historically accurate first step in our reinvention of the body. It is an invention which begins with a certain way of looking at the body, with the anatomical gaze.

Robert D. Romanyshyn
Technology as Symptom & Dream / Chapter 4 Body as specimen
1989, pp. 114-5

B. Who is God

Grasping the unconceivable in concepts and words.

An attempt to grasp a millennia old aboriginal spirituality of Australia

> *One of the distinguished visitors to Ngarinyin Bush University was the Right Reverend Dr. Peter Carnley, Anglican archbishop of Perth, whose visit was the subject of an Australian Broadcasting Corporation documentary film for their Compass program. After a week's saturation in Ngarinyin philosophy, beliefs, visits to rock art sites, and participation in secret Men's Business and sacred ceremony, he stated that prior to Bush University he thought that Aboriginal spirituality was probably rooted in a kind of pantheistic mythology and doctrine. He now recognized that their spiritual practice was far more complex and inspiring. He called it "panentheistic". He said this was different from pantheism, a doctrine that identifies the deity with the universe. Here was a philosophy in which the Divine is the source and the spirit of Creation, with an added dimension of "beyond our understanding". What Mowaljarlai described as the energy cord that unites everything is also the energy supply that enlivens everything, and gives Creation its texture and shape. This is Wunggud, the blueprint of Creation. It manifests first as idea. Then, with the energy of its own intent, it projects the idea into a physical form. Through this means Wunggud imprints itself on rock walls in the form of a painting. It is the glue of Creation as well as the resonance, the life force. The nature and essence of Wunggud that is comprehensible is always manifest in relationship, the primary universal governing law of nature.*
>
> Hanna Rachel Bell
> **Men's Business-Women's Business: The Spiritual Role of gender in the World's Oldest Culture**
> 1998, p. 124

Seven gods of happiness.

> *Shinto: Gods as deified humans, sages. They arrive in a ship on Japanese New Year.*

1. Fotesan (Hotei)
- *Originally a Chinese Buddhist Saint*
- *Carries a little Buddha inside him.*
- *Rewards peacefulness*

2. Fukurokujisan
- *A Dao deity*
- *Spirit of the South Pole Star*
- *Rewards faithfulness with happiness, promotion, high rank, longevity*
- *Faithfulness to Shinto, Buddha and Konfutze*

3. Juryoojin
- *A Chinese philosopher deified after his death as a Dao deity*
- *Carries a round fan that he waves to fend off evil.*
- *Is followed by a deer that lives 3000 years.*
- *Rewards compassion with fortune, health, long life, many healthy children*

4. Benzaiten (Benten)
Identified with Sarasvati, Hindu goddess of streams, wealth, eloquence
The only female god; god of study, dance and prayer, music, chants and language.
Rewards care

5. Bishanmontensan
Identified with Hindu god Vaisravana
Originally the guardian of the North Gate
Rewards working with talents, creativity, integrity
with happiness and prosperity.

6. Daikokutensan
Carries a hammer (tsuchi) which produces a coin, a sack full of gold or produce.
Loved by the merchants
Rewards perseverance, industriousness and love for parents

7 Ebisusan
God of prosperity and safety.
Rewards righteousness with luck bestowed on generations without end.

'Sosha' is the name of one shrine for all deities

Bhartrhari: a grammarian's doctrine of revelation – The True Word

Perhaps the best way to begin to understand Bhartrhari's view of Vedic revelation is to begin as he does, with the ultimate ground of revelation, the absolute Brahman, which he characterizes as Word, Sabda. In the opening verses of the Brahmakanda, which is the first book of his major work, the Vakyapadiya, the 'Treatise on Sentences and Words', Bhartrhari introduces us to the basic themes of his metaphysics:

Brahman, the True Word, which is without beginning or end, which is imperishable Syllable, manifests itself in the form of objects; from it the production of the world [proceeds]. Although it is proclaimed to be one, it is divided through having recourse to its powers. Although it is not different from its powers, it exists as if it were different from them. The six transformations, beginning with birth, which are the source of the differentiation of beings, are dependent on its power of time, to which parts have been attributed. Of that One, which is the seed of all things, there is this state of multiplicity, having the form of the enjoyer, the object to be enjoyed, and the enjoyment.

[ ]

"Those who know the Veda know that this universe is a transformation [parinama] of the Word. This universe came forth from the hymns (of the Veda)."

... for Bhartrhari the world order is a dynamic system of interconnecting forces or actions that are the actualizations and self-manifestations of Brahman's own intrinsic capacities. The changing world as we experience it is the condition [sthiti] that Brahman assumes through its power of self-veiling [avidyasakti] and its power of Time [kalasakti]. The world is less understood as a world of substantial things than as a process of action and experience, having a dynamic, triadic structure. Rather than a world of things, the world is primarily a world of actions and relations, the realization, the actualization of Brahman's expressive potentialities.

David Carpenter
Revelation History and the Dialogue of Religions: A study of Bhargtrhari and Bonaventure
1995, pp. 35-38

Overflowing Being – Manifest in the Book of Scripture and of Nature

Bonaventure's discussion of God presents us with a God who is supremely self-communicative. From all eternity, the Father's plenitude of being naturally overflows in the generation of a Son, his Word and Image, together with whom he further breathes forth the Holy Spirit, in an eternal act of perfect mutual love. p 92

[ ]

In Bonaventure's view reality itself is characterized by its tendency to communicate or express itself. This is true of all things, and the divine being is no exception. Indeed it is the most true of the divine:

"We must admit that there is generation in the divine Being. And I believe that the most important reason for this is the fact, that every nature is communicable." pp. 93-4

[ ]

...It is the emanation of the Holy Spirit as free and generous love that provides the foundation in God for revelatory activity of the Word as inspired, as a divine gift of grace.

[ ]

...although Bonaventure's theology of revelation is essentially Trinitarian, i.e. involves all three Persons of the Trinity, we noted above that the second Person as Word holds a privileged place. We must now consider this Word more closely, and specifically in its relationship to creation, redemption, and revelation as the threefold Word, the verbum increatum, incarnatum, and inspiratum, always keeping in mind, however, their common Trinitarian background. p. 96

[ ]

...The created order is understood as text, as the liber naturae, in which the divine Word is to be read...It is God's Word, the verbum increatum spoken ad extra in the act of creation which is equally an act of self-disclosure...Against the backdrop of this book of nature, the drama of human freedom will be played out, under the guidance of the verbum

inspiratum, and centered on the verbum incarnatum, the Word as incarnate in Jesus of Nazareth. It is this drama that will provide the subject matter of the book of scripture. The schema of the threefold Word is thus a powerful unifying theme in Bonaventure's thought. p. 98

David Carpenter
Revelation History and the Dialogue of Religions: A study of Bhargtrhari and Bonaventure
1995

Creation – manifestation of God's Word and Presence

With Thy Word creates Thou creation, and after making Thou pervades it.

Sikh Religion
Var-Maru, Guru V
Annie Besant
The Universal Text Book of Religion and Morals. Volume 1 & 2
1910, p. 60

When he Himself created the form of the universe, in three qualities He manifested Himself.

Sukhmani, Guru V
As above, p. 50

Nature: a book of amazement and wonder

Nature in its entirety is an exhibition of wonderful things. But we prefer to call it a "book". It is because we hear it like a book, read it like a book, just as if we were watching the gilded lines and decorations of a book in all colors, and we watch it in great admiration. Every morning we see it painted anew, decorated in front of us with its dazzling heights and gaze at it losing ourselves in amazement and wonder.

Dogu, Ergil
"Fettullah Gülen and the Gülen Mlovement in 100 Questions"
Islamiccenter.org/environment-and-natural-living/retrieved
9.12.2016,
Quoted by: Salih Yücel
A Life in Tears Understanding Fettullah Gülen and his Call to Service
2018, p. 39

Our own nature reveals the Tao

*We need not talk about empty and far-away things: if we know
the reality of the Tao we must seek it within our own nature.*

*Love itself is the original substance of love; reverence
is love in graceful expression; righteousness is love in
judgement; and wisdom is love in discriminating.*

In the process of world-becoming, Love is the older

*In the Argonautica, when Orpheus, in the presence of Chiron and the
heroes, sang about the beginning of things, following the theology of Hermes
Trismegistus, he placed Chaos before the World, and located Love in the
bosom of that Chaos, before Saturn, Jove, and the other gods, and he
praised Love in these words: Love is the older, perfect in himself, and best
counselled. Hesiod, in his Theology, Parmenides the Pythagorean, in his
book On nature, and Acusilaus the poet agreed with Orpheus and Hermes.
Plato, in the Timaeus, describes Chaos in a similar way, and places
Love in it. And in the Symposium Phaedrus recounted the same thing.*

*The Platonists define chaos as an unformed world, and world as a formed
chaos. According to them there are three worlds, and likewise there will
be three chaoses. The first of all things is God, the author of all things,
whom we call "the Good" itself. He creates first the Angelic Mind,
then the World Soul, as Plato calls it, and last the World Body. That
supreme God we do not call a world, because world means ornament,
composed of many, whereas God must be completely simple. But we
do declare Him to be the beginning and the end of all the worlds...*

Marsilio Ficino, Sears Jayne (Translator)
Commentary on Plato's Symposium on Love (1469)
1985, pp. 37-38

God loves and God is Love

*God speaks of the great reality of love many times in the Holy Qur'an. He
mentions those whom He loves, such as, for example, those who rely on Him:
And when you are resolved, rely on God; for God loves
those who rely [upon Him]. (Aal 'Imran, 3:159)*

> *However, God's Love is not merely one of God's acts or actions, but one of God's very Own Divine Qualities or Names. This can be seen by the many Divine Names in the Holy Qur'an which denote God's loving qualities (such as 'the Gentle'——'Al-Latif';*
> *'the Kind'—'Al-Raouf';*
> *'the Generous'—'Al-Kareem';*
> *'the Forbearing'—'Al-Haleem';*
> *'the Absolutely Reliable'—'Al-Wakil';*
> *'the Friend'—'Al-Wali';*
> *'the Good'—'Al-Barr';*
> *'the Forgiving'—'Al-Ghafur';*
> *'the Forgiver'—'Al-Ghaffar';*
> *'the Granter and Accepter of Repentance'—'Al-Tawwab'; and*
> *'the Pardoner'—'Al-Afu')*
> *and in particular His Name 'the Loving' (Al-Wadud), which occurs twice in the Holy Qur'an.*
>
> **Ghazi Love in the Holy Qur'an**
p. 15

The universe an expression of Shakti

> *Energy is Shakti – the primordial power of creation, the self-organizing, self-generative, self-renewing creative force of the universe in feminine form. Shakti comes from the root "sak", meaning "the capacity to do", "to have power". Shakti is power. Shakti is force. Shakti is the personification of primordial energy and the source of all divine and cosmic evolution and also the source and controller of all forces and potentialities of nature. The universe is an expression of Shakti and an infinite reservoir of power.*
>
> Vandana Shiva
Soil Not Oil: Climate Change, Peak Oil, and Food Insecurity
2009, pp. 186,188

Intellect connected to faith

> *...how could I make visible those intangible aspects of Muslim culture that in mitigating power relations, bring distinction to Islam and its female believers: hospitality, generosity, respect for elders, adoration of children, a strong sense of community, enduring social ties, and family loyalty? How could I give texture to the way Muslim cultures engender a sense of pride in a woman, especially as a mother? How could I make tangible that powerful sense of belonging, of identity that only culture can endow? How*

could I explain the role that faith has played in the lives of women who find inspiration in Islam as a way to redress their personal challenges?

The Qur'an does not speak only to men. It speaks, quite explicitly to women. I knew this at a young age, not because I read the Qur'an, but because I talked to God all the time. I knew with certainty that He responded. May be this spiritual consciousness was a result of my Sufi ancestry; my grandfather and father were Sufis of the popular Tijaniyyah order in Sudan. Sufism has historically welcomed women's spiritual connection to God. Or maybe it was because it never occurred to me that my gender could impede a relationship with God. These conversations taught me that intellect was connected to faith. As an adult, I found it unreasonable that God would prefer men to women in anything, but especially in terms of worshipping Him.

Hibba Abugideiri
George Washington University

Not male nor female

I could feel God all through me, that he was so majestic and beautiful. His creation made me curious and made me want to commit to him and find out more about him.

Allah is not considered male or female. Of the two parts of the word – Al and lah – one is masculine and one is feminine, so together they point to the fact that God is beyond gender.

Ayesha in: Lana Dalberg's
Birthing God: Women's Experiences of the Divine
2013

Sabbath and Shekinah

In the Jewish mystical world, the Sabbath is identified with the Shekinah, the Divine Feminine. It's a sense of being held and embraced. It could be an embrace of a gentle male, too... It's just a sense of protection and belonging, a sense of oneness with community and other people around you.

SaraLeya Schley, Rabbi of Chocmat Halev Under the Wings of
Shekhinah in: Lana Dalberg's
Birthing God: Women's Experiences of the Divine
2013, pp. 187-191

The Face of God 1.

You have screened Yourself off with a cloud, so that no prayer can pass through," we read in the book of Lamentations. And yet it is told that Reb Azriel David Fastag, a disciple of the Hasidic Rebbe of Modzhitz, spontaneously composed and began to sing what has become the best known melody to Maimonides Twelfth Principle of Jewish Faith while in a cattle car from the Warsaw Ghetto to the Treblinka death camp: "I believe with perfect faith in the coming of the Messiah, and even though he may tarry, nevertheless I will wait every day for him to come".

A young man managed to escape from the Treblinka-bound train, taking with him the niggun, the melody of reb Azriel David Fastag's "Ani Ma'amin." Eventually the melody reached the Modzhitzer Rebbe, who is said to have exclaimed, "With this niggun the Jewish people went to the gas chambers, and with this niggun, the Jews will march to greet the Messiah.

[ ]

Could it be that God, the true God, did not hide His face from Reb Azriel David Fastag in the cattle car to Treblinka but instead gave him inspiration and strength to compose his niggun?

Menachem Z. Rosensaft
God, Faith & Identity from the Ashes: Reflections of Children and Grandchildren of Holocaust Survivors
2015, pp. 74,75

The Face of God 2,

*And GOD wanders over the world
and all the world shines in fine luminous light,
as from the sun and from the moon. -
And in all the trees there are faces,
and every being shows its countenance,
and every countenance dwells in the human being,
and every human being carries within himself all faces of all beings,
to enable him to recognize them and himself in their mirror.*

Shin Gwydion Fontalba

Lord Buddha facing the Universe and God

He (the Buddha) by Himself thoroughly understands, as he sees, as it were, face to face, this universe – the world below with all the spirits, and the world above, of Mára and of Brahmā and all creatures, Samanas and Brahmanas, Shining Ones and men, and He makes His knowledge known to others.

Tevija Sutta in Annie Besant's
The Universal Text Book of Religion and Morals
1910, p. 74

The nature of being 'One' 1.

...the doctrine of the Trinity. How if this doctrine should at last, after endless errors, right and left, only bring men on the road to recognise that God cannot possibly be One in the sense in which finite things are one, that even His unity must be a transcendental unity, which does not exclude a sort of plurality? Must not God at least have the most perfect conception of Himself, i.e., a conception in which is found everything which is in Him? But would everything be found in it which is in Him, if a mere conception, a mere possibility, were found even of his necessary Reality as well as of His other qualities? This possibility exhausts the being of His other qualities. Does it that of His necessary Reality? I think not. Consequently God can either have no perfect conception of himself at all, or this perfect conception is just as necessarily real, i.e., actually existent, as He Himself is... When I believe that I recognise in God a familiar reduplication, I perhaps do not so much err, as that my language is insufficient for my ideas: and so much at least for ever incontrovertible, that they who wish to make the idea thereof popular for comprehension, could scarcely have expressed themselves more intelligibly and suitably than by giving the name of a Son begotten from Eternity.

Gotthold Ephraim Lessing
The Education of the Human Race
1780, p. 74

The nature of being 'One' 2.

God shows Himself in three Aspects, as three fundamental Modes, as three essential Qualities, as discharging three primary functions in relation to His Universe. This fact has give rise to the Trinities in many religions, ancient and modern, and the Musilman objection to the idea of a Divine Trinity is due to the crude and anthromorphic presentations of it on the one hand, and, on the other, to the supreme necessity in the time and country of the Prophet Muhammad, to emphasize the Unity of God as against the chaos of deities in which the Unity had been lost. Stated rationally, no one can objection to the truth of the Triplicity. Stated emotionally, its conception by the ignorant, though loving, worshipper, may often affront the philosopher.

[ ]

A well instructed Zoroastrian writer: "Ahura, the Life-Giver, Mazda, the Great Thinker, and Spenta-Angra, the twin forces of evolution and involution, may be looked upon as the three Aspects of the deity in Mazdism." So also the Hebrew declared that man is made in the divine image, and in his inner teaching —concealed from the populace for the same reason which swayed the Prophet of Arabia – speaks of Ainsuph, the One: manifesting as Kepher, the Crown, the Bliss-aspect of Deity, root of the Will in man: as Binah, Intelligence, the Consciousness-aspect of Deity, root of cognition in man; as Cochmah, Universal Mind, the Existence-aspect Deity, root of Activity in man. This is the root truth underlying all Trinities...

[ ]

...the Mighty, the Wise, and the Merciful of the Musilman; the variously named Trinities of the Egyptian, Chaldean and other dead religions; all proclaim with one voice this inner triplicity of consciousness in the universe in which He manifests. The three Aspects of Divinity revealing themselves in a universe become, for the dwellers in that universe, three Beings; in the words of the famous Christian creed: "Three Persons, but One God"

[ ]

In this doctrine of the three divine Aspects – of God in relation to His universe – we have the primary truth of the divine Unity made concrete, and applied to the primary functions of Divinity in His worlds. ...He is the Father of our Spirits, the Protector of our lives, the Source of our activities; we come into these close relations with Him as individuals, while in His own nature we know Him as our innermost-Self.

Annie Besant
Universal Textbook of Religion and Morals
1910, pp. 38-41, 44

The one only God, Janārdana, takes the designation of Brahmá, Vishnu and Shíva, accordingly as HE creates, preserves, or destroys... He is the cause of creation, preservation and destruction.

Vishnu Purāna, I.ii.62 in: Annie Besant's

Universal Textbook of Religion and Morals
1910, p. 47

God's inwardness seen as impersonal One Being and as three Persons interrelating.

As the Hindus say, God is at the same time personal and impersonal. He is impersonal in the sense that his infinitely mysterious manner of being a Person is infinitely different from the human manner. It is only possible to grasp this mystery by employing at the same time, like two pincers these two contrary notions, incompatible here on earth, compatible only in God. (The same applies to many other contraries, as the Pythagoreans had realized.)
[ ]

Saints of a very lofty spirituality, like St John of the Cross, have simultaneously and with equal force both the personal and the impersonal aspects of God. Less developed souls concentrate their attention and their faith on one or the other of these two aspects. Thus little St Theresa of Lisieux only represented to herself a personal God.

Simone Weil In: Letter to a Priest section 12, Published in: David Rapier's
Gateway to God
1982, pp. 117-8

Ahûra Mazda says: (I) am Life-giver and Nourisher, (I) am Knower and the most spiritual Evolver....I am of the name Ahûra (Bestower of Life) and am of the name of Mazda (Most Wise)

Yasht, I. 1.2 in: Annie Besant's
Universal Textbook of Religion and Morals
1910, p.4 8

O Ahûra Mazda! On account of Thy just royalty Thou livest in one and the same dwelling with Asha (Truth), and with Vohû-Mano (Good Mind).

Ushtarad Gâthâ, xliv.9. in: Annie Besant's
Universal Textbook of Religion and Morals
1910, p. 49

Divine Creator Fire

... I, the fiery life of divine essence, am aflame beyond the beauty of the meadows, I gleam in the waters, and burn in the sun, moon, and stars. With every breeze, as with invisible life that contains everything, I awaken everything to life. The air lives by turning

green and being in bloom. The waters flow as if they were alive. The sun lives in its light, and the moon is enkindled, after its disappearance, once again by the light of the sun so that the moon is again revived. The stars, too, give a clear light with their beaming.

[ ]

And thus I remain hidden in every kind of reality as a fiery power. Everything burns because of me in such a way as our breath constantly moves us, like the wind-tossed flame in a fire. All of this lives in its essence, and there is no death in it. For I am life. I am also Reason, which bears within itself the breath of the resounding Word, through which the whole creation is made. I breathe life into everything so that nothing is mortal in respect to its species. For I am life.

[ ]

Since God is Reason, how could it be that God, who causes all divine actions to come to fruition through human beings, is not active! God created men and women in the divine image and likeness, and marked each of these creatures according to fixed standard in human beings. From eternity it was in the mind of God to wish to create humanity. God's own handiwork. And when God completed this action, God gave over to act with it just as God had formed the divine handiwork, humanity.

And this I serve by helping. For all life lights up out of me. I am life that remains ever the same., without beginning and without end. For this life is God., who is always in motion and constantly in action and yet this life is manifest in a threefold power. For eternity is called the "Father", the Word is called the "Son", and the breath that binds both of them together is called the Holy Spirit. And God has likewise marked humanity, in human beings there are body, soul and reason.

Matthew Fox (Editor)
Hildegard van Bingen's Book of Divine Works: With Letters and Songs
1978, pp. 8, 10-11

The relation between female and male constitutes, pervades and enlivens All

The hexagram is not at all the symbol of good and evil, but rather it is that of the threefold pure act or "fire" and the threefold pure reaction (mihi fiat secundum verbum tuum) or "light of fire", i.e. "water". "Fire" and "water" signify that which acts spontaneously and creatively on the one hand, and that reacts reflectively on the other hand – the latter being the conscious "yes" or light of mihi fiat secundum verbum tuum (let what you have said to me be done to me). This is the elementary meaning of the "seal of Solomon" – elementary in the sense of the elements "fire" and "water' on their higher level.

But the still higher meaning that this symbol hides – or rather reveals – is that of the luminous Holy Trinity i.e. that of understanding of the Holy Trinity. Then it is the hexagram comprising the two triangles. Father-Son-Holy Spirit; Mother-Daughter-Soul (see figure). And these three triangles of the luminous Holy Trinity are revealed in the work of redemption accomplished through Jesus Christ and conceived through Mary-Sophia. Jesus Christ is the agent, Mary Sophia is its luminous reaction. The two triangles reveal the luminous Holy Trinity in the work of creation accomplished by the creative Word and animated by the "yes" of Wisdom Sophia. The luminous Holy Trinity is therefore the unity of the triune Creator and the triune natura naturans ('the world pregnant with new life'), i.e. the unity of the threefold Fiat and the threefold mihi fiat secundum verbum tuum, which reveal itself in natura naturata (the world as new life'), in the world before the Fall, and it is the triune divine spirit and the triune divine soul of the world manifesting in the body of the world – in natura naturata.

Anonymous [Valentin Tomberg], Robert A. Powell (Translator)
Meditations on the Tarot: A Journey into Christian Hermeticism / Nineteenth Major Arcanum The Sun Le Soleil
1991, pp. 547-8

Personhood as inwardness?

The concept of personhood is not in the least capable to declare the essential nature of God, but it is valid and needed to say, God is also a person.

Martin Buber's I and Thou, Quoted in: Martin Schleske's
Klang Munich
2014, pp. 2048-9
[Translated by Henk Bak]

Concept of God, the Highest, the most Sacred, Stream of Energy and Consciousness...

One could be justified in saying, the main person in the Bible is God. Can one then seriously believe in a personal God?

[ ]

A psalm can provide a point to start from. The psalm word says: "The One who planted the ear, should he not hear? The One who made the eye, should he not see?" (94:9) I want to speak further along these lines: The One who has created the human being as a person, should he not at least be a person? I am convinced that God cannot be less than what I am: active, working, willing, thinking capable to suffer and to love. God is the love that makes us persons. Above all, that's why he is a personal God. To know God therefore means, to become more like him, i.e. to become someone who loves. Herewith the question concerning God himself has not been answered, but only the one concerning our relation to him. About what else, however, speak apart from our relation with him?

Martin Schleske
Der Klang. Vom unerhörten Sinn des Lebens (Sound. About the Meaning of Life in a Way not Heard of)
2014, pp. 247-8

God exists beyond human grasp.

A case of contradictories which are true. God exists. God does not. Where is the problem? I am quite sure that there is a God in the sense that I am quite sure that my love is not illusory. I am quite sure that there is no God in the sense that I am quite sure that nothing can be anything like what I am able to conceive when I pronounce this word. But that which I can not conceive is not illusory.

Simone Weil
Gravity and Grace
1997, pp. 167-8

Meditation on the one and the many

Is the mind a single thing?
Or is it a plural thing?
If it is a single thing, how doth it come to such,
seeing that it manifests itself variously?

If it is a number of things, how can it be so. Since all of them must necessarily be inseparably one in their true nature?

Observing this, one findeth the mind not to be a number of things; and as it is free of the extremes [of singleness and plurality', it is called The Great Symbol', that which doth not abide in absolute rest [or finality].

In the quiescent state of Samadhi of the yogin who attaineth realization, the All-Discriminating Wisdom of the Transcendental Intellect alone dawneth, and nothing else. Therefore, the Great Symbol, the Reality, is called 'That which is devoid of characteristics.

Walter Evans-Wentz
Tibetan Yoga and Secret Doctrines: Or, Seven Books of Wisdom of the Great Path, according to the Late Lama Kazi Dawa-Samdup's English Rendering
1970, p. 145

Difference is intrinsic to relationship

......Individuality and relationship are not mutually exclusive. It is immediately apparent, that only that what is not identical can be related, that difference is intrinsic to relationship. Physical and psychic differences between forms allow the currents of dynamic tension to pass between them...

Carla Needleman
The Work of Craft
1993

A true sign is its own evidence 1.

...Doubt has to be distinguished from discrimination. Discrimination is necessary. Freedom from doubt does not mean freedom from discrimination, or the ability to recognise what is acceptable and what is not acceptable. Doubt is something else. It is based on the wrong and egoistic demand, that one has the right to have evidence, that one has to have things proved to one. If one sees how doubt has its roots in egoism, then one can see that putting away doubt means the putting away of a demand.

[ ]

Jesus says, 'the wicked and adulterous generation seeketh after a sign, but there shall no sign be given, save the sign of the Prophet Jonas.' If you understand that answer, you understand how one works against doubt. Were they entitled to ask for a sign? Was He not giving signs left and right? ... You have to see just what it is in you that asks for a sign, that says, 'prove it to me; give me evidence of this'. When you see this in yourself, you are actually able to let it go and accept what is in front of you. 'I can see the step in front of me, I don't need more; I have confidence that there is a beneficent power in this universe, in this creation. I do not want to know what I am not ready to know. I do not ask signs; proofs of anything'.

J.G.Bennett
Intimations: Talks with J.G. Bennett at Beshara
1975, p. 65

A true sign is its own evidence 2.

*In fact, they (the blasphemers) cried lies to the Truth
when it came to them, and are thus in perplexity.*

*Have they not observed the sky above them and how We
erected it and decked it out, how free of cracks it is?*

*And the earth, how We spread it out and placed in it towering
mountains, and caused it to sprout forth of every lovely species?*

*An eye-opener is this, and a remembrance to every
servant turning to God in repentance.*

*From the sky We sent down blessed water,
Wherewith We caused gardens to flower and grains for the harvest,
Soaring palm trees bearing serried clusters – sustenance to mankind.
With it We revived a region that was dead.
Likewise shall be the Resurrection.
[ ]*

Did the first creation make us weary? Yet they doubt a new creation.

We created man and know what his soul murmurs to him,
But I am nearer to him than his jugular vein.

The Qur'an /verses 50:5 – 50:11; 50:12-5016

Hindu view

Seated equally in all beings, the Supreme Lord,
unperishing within the perishing

- he who thus sees, he sees.

(Sri Aurobindo's comment: "...That is the true seeing, the
seeing of that in us which is eternal and immortal...")

Sri Aurobindo
Bhagavad Gita and Its Message: With Text, Translation and
Sri Aurobindo's Commentary
1995, p. 208

New times need to grow new words, like seeds

Usually it (philosophy) is implicitly or explicitly, a contest between
an entrenched vocabulary which has become a nuisance and a half-
formed new vocabulary which vaguely promises great things.

Richard Rorty
Contingency, irony and solidarity.
1989, p. 9

The word 'supernatural' still relevant for questions like morality and free will.

These days, I would guess that most philosophers consider themselves
naturalists. [ ] The N-word, in their case, may mean anything from
the minimalist statement that no supernatural realm is allowed in
philosophizing (...) to the more nuanced, quasi- Quinean position
that philosophy needs to take science on board to make progress..."

"Three main ideas emerged from this unusual gathering: (i) there
is no (sensible) philosophy that is not a naturalistic philosophy.
(ii) there is disagreement on the issue of reductionism; (iii) there is
disagreement on the implications of naturalism for crucial philosophical

questions, particularly concerning morality and free will.

On Naturalism, Massimo Pigliucci reports on a recent workshop:
In: Philosophy Now
96 May/June 2013

Mystery beyond words

Two enigmatic concluding words: Heraclitus fragments and Mark Gospel

"Heraclitus of Ephese used to say: 'The enduring measure (logos) of existence keeps eluding humans, whatever measure we apply or where-ever we stand.'

This is not a discouraging message, not an arrogant attitude or obscure teaching, this is an effective way to say that all our knowing remains unknowing, our wisdom unwise and our hope hopeless, unless we know that we know nothing. Wisdom is to be aware of our ignorance."

"Mark 16:8: 'And the women came out and ran away from the tomb not telling anyone as they were overawed.'

Did the women really have nothing to say and had they then seen, heard or understood nothing? On the contrary! They were the first witnesses of the resurrection, they had seen the angel, had heard his words, the empty grave had been pointed out to them. Why then didn't they say anything to anyone? Not because they thought that their testimony, belief or thoughts would not be understood or shared anyhow. Also not because what they had learnt couldn't in any way be put into words. The mystery of the resurrection found in their awe its most excellent expression and their reluctance to speak and their retreat into silence was the best homage to what they had seen. Their reticence was the only way to announce the resurrection."

Charles Vergeer
Boek en Wijsheid (Book and Wisdom) / Een zin (One sentence)
1999, pp. 240-1,
[Translated by Henk Bak]

C. Who am I?

Human Being

Wonders are many on earth, and the greatest of these
Is man, who rides the ocean and takes his way
Through the deep, through wind-swept valleys of perilous seas
That surge and sway.

He is master of ageless Earth, to his own will bending
The immortal mother of gods by the sweat of his brow,
As year succeeds to year, with toil unending
Of mule and plough.

He is lord of all things living: birds of the air,
Beasts of the field, all creatures of sea and land
He taketh, cunning to capture and ensnare
With sleight of hand.

Hunting the savage beasts from the upland rocks,
Taming the mountain monarch in his lair,
Teaching the wild horse and the roaming ox
His yoke to bear.

The use of language, the wind-swift motion of brain
He learnt; found out the laws of living together
In cities, building him shelter against the rain
And wintry weather.

There is nothing beyond his power. His subtlety

Meeteth all chance, all danger conquereth.
For every ill he hath found it remedy,
Save only death.

O wondrous subtlety of man, that draws
To good or evil ways! Great honour is given
And power to him who upholdeth his country's laws
And the justice of heaven.

But he, that too rashly daring, walks in sin
In solitary pride to his life's end.

At door of mine shall never enter in
To call me friend.

Sophocles
Antigone: The Theban Plays
1980, pp. 135-6

Buddha: the awakened man

It is a incontestable fact that Sakyamuni, the historical Buddha, never declared the identity of his human being with divine being... The Dishanikaya, a long collection of Buddha's discourses in Pali, contradicts it on each page and uses a multitude of arguments and facts to the sole end of persuading the reader (or the listener to the Buddha's discourses), that Buddha was the awakened man, i.e. he became completely conscious of the common and ordinary human experience on earth — that of birth, sickness, old age and death — and drew from it practical and moral conclusions which are summarized in his eightfold path.

[ ]

It was a man — and not a messenger from heaven — who awoke from the sleep of passive acceptance, habit, the stupefying influence of transitory desires, and the hypnotic force of the totality of human conventions.

Anonymous [Valentin Tomberg], Robert A. Powell (Translator)
Meditations on the Tarot: A Journey into Christian Hermeticism
1991, p. 612

On Human Dignity 1.

On the last day of creating the world, God created the human being: so that he may know the laws of the universe, love its beauty and admire its grandeur.

He did not tie him to any fixed place nor to a set pattern of behaviour or any inevitable necessities, but He gave him mobility and free will.

"I have placed you in the middle of the world" — the Creator says to Adam — "so that you are better placed to look around and see all that is in it.

I created you as a being that is not just only heavenly, mortal or immortal, so that you may be your own free maker and conqueror. You can degenerate to animal or you can raise yourself to divine being.

What animals bring out of their mothers' body is what they shall have. The higher spirits are, from the very beginning or soon after, what they will remain in eternity. Only you have been given the ability to evolve, to grow out of free will. You have the germ of all kinds of life within you."

From: Pico della Mirandola (1463-1494)'s De Dignitate Hominis
English translation by Henk Bak from Valentin Tomberg's German transcript.

On Human Dignity 2.

And remember when God said to the angels: 'I shall appoint a deputy on earth', and they answered 'Will you place therein one who sows discord and sheds blood while we chant Your praises and proclaim Your holiness?'

God said: 'I know what you do not.'

He taught Adam the names of all things. Then he displayed them to the angels and said: 'Tell me the names of these things, if you are truthful.'

They said: 'Glory to You! We have no knowledge except what You taught us. You! You are All-Knowing, All-Wise".

God said:' O Adam, reveal to them their names.' When Adam revealed their names, God said:' Didn't I tell you that I know the unseen of the heavens and the earth? That I know what you make public and what you hide?'

And remember when God said to the angels: 'Kneel before Adam'; they knelt, all except Satan, who disdained, grew proud and became an unbeliever.

Tarif Khalidi
The Qur'an / The Cow 2: 29-31
2009, pp. 6,7

On Human Dignity 3.

Having created the world and all that liveth and moveth therein, He, through the direct operation of His unconstrained and sovereign Will, chose to confer upon man the unique distinction and capacity to know Him and love Him - a capacity that must needs be regarded as the generating impulse and primary purpose underlying the whole of creation...Upon the inmost reality of each and every created thing He hath shed the light of one of His names, and made it a recipient of the glory of one of His attributes. Upon the reality of man, however, He hath focused the radiance of all His names and attributes, and made it a mirror of His own Self. Alone of all created things man hath been singled out for so great a favour, so enduring a bounty.

Bahá u 'lláh Gleanings XXVII p.65 In: Artemus Lam's
The Odyssey of the Soul
1995, p. 14

On Human Dignity 4:

Human dignity is given into your hands. Guard it! It sinks with you, with you it will be uplifted.

J. Friedrich Schiller
The Artists
1789

Human Being between Sprit and Matter 1.

When I saw truly, I knew that all was primeval.
Nanak, the subtle (spirit) and the gross (material) are, in fact, identical.

Guru Granth Sahib in *The Times World Religions*
2002, p. 193

Human Being between Spirit and Matter 2.

We have now been led to the concept of such an alternating working between the two drives, where the working of the one grounds and at the same time limits the working of the other, and where each single one attains the highest expression through the other being active.

It is only in the light of reason, surely, that this alternating relationship of both drives enables the human being to fulfil his existence. It is in the most proper meaning of the word The Idea of his Humanity, therefore something infinite, which he in the course of time can come ever more close to, without ever attaining it, however. He shall not strive to form at the expense of his reality, and not strive to reality at the expense of form; he shall rather seek absolute being through something limited and search for limited being through seeking without end. He shall position himself opposite a world, because he is person, and shall be person, because a world stands in opposition to him.

[ ]

Would there be occasions, however, where he makes these experiences simultaneously, where he became conscious of his freedom at the same time as of his existence, where he felt himself as matter and got to recognize himself as spirit – assuming that such occasions can actually be experienced – then they would awaken a new drive in him. This would happen exactly because the other two drives – which, considered on their own, would oppose each other - now have joined in working together and therefore rightly would count as a new drive.

The sensory drive wills that change occurs, that time has content; the form drive wills, that time be suspended, that there be no change. This other drive, therefore, in which both drives work together (I may for the moment be allowed to call it drive-to-play, till I will have justified this name), the drive to play would thus be intend to suspend time within time, to unite becoming with absolute being, change with identity…Letter 14 pp. 330-1

[ ]

…For, to put it finally into words, the human being plays only, when he is a human being in the full meaning of the word, and he is only there a human being, where he plays. This statement, that at the moment perhaps seems paradoxical, will acquire a great and deep significance, when we first have come to apply this to the double earnestness of duty and destiny; it will, I promise you, carry the total edifice of the aesthetic art and - even more consequential - the art of life.

But it is only for science that this proposition may come as a surprise; it lived and worked a long time already in the art, and in the feelings of the Greek, their most important masters – life becomes more indifferent, as soon as dignity is involved, and duty loses it urgency, as soon as inclination begins to pull. Similarly: the mind takes the reality of things, the physical truth, freer and quieter, as soon as this truth comes to meet the formal truth, the law of necessity, and the mind feels no longer strained by the abstraction, as soon as it can immediately be turned into something visible. In one word: by coming into contact with ideas all reality loses its seriousness, because it becomes small, and by meeting up with the experience, the necessary leaves behind its seriousness, as it becomes light.

But what does just play mean, now we know that that under all human conditions, it is precisely play, only play, that makes him complete, and unfolds his double nature. What you, according to your understanding call: limiting, I call after mine: the opposite expanding and this justified by proof.

The human being takes what is only pleasant, good, perfect seriously, but with what is beautiful he plays.

J. Friedrich Schiller
Über die Ästethische Erziehung des Menschen (On the Aesthetic Education of Man) / 15th Letter
1793, pp. 335-6
[Translated by Henk Bak]

Understanding the human constitution, a common ground.

In order to understand what falling in love is, we must first understand what human beings as such are, as falling in love is something that occurs within – and to – human beings. Indeed, it is illogical to seek to understand the actions of something without first understanding the thing itself.

Human beings are composed of three main parts: the body, the soul, and the spirit. The body is individual and physical; the soul is individual but subtle (supra-physical); and the spirit is supra-individual and supra-physical.

[ ]

*And bodies have senses, such as hearing and sight. God says:
The lightning well-nigh snatches away their sight; whensoever it gives them light, they walk in it; and when the darkness is over them, they stop; had God willed, He would have taken away their hearing and their sight; Truly, God has power over all things. (Al-Baqarah, 2:20)*

[ ]

God alludes to the other bodily senses, namely taste, smell and touch.

[ ]

*And God alludes to smell in the following verse:
And grain with husk, and fragrant herb (Al-Rah-man, 55:12)*

[ ]

God speaks of three 'kinds' or 'parts' of the soul, namely: the soul which incites to evil' ('al-nafs al-ammarah bil-su'), the 'self-reproaching soul' ('al-nafs al-lawammah') and the soul at peace ('al-nafs al-mutma 'innah').

[ ]

And God speaks of the human soul's faculties: ...the intelligence (aql)...the human capacity to learn (ta'lim)...the human faculty of speech (kalam)...And God speaks of human beings' will (iradah)...(...iradah is a kind of love).

[ ]

And God speaks of human sentiments ('atifah)

[ ]

...memory (dhakirah)...imagination... intuition...feelings...sense...insight...

[ ]

The Spirit (al-Ruh)

God says that He breathed of His Spirit into the first man.

> *Then He proportioned him, and breathed into him of His Spirit. And He made for you hearing, and sight and hearts. Little thanks do you give.*

(Al-Sajdah, 32-9)

However, one cannot hope to mentally know very much about the spirit, because God says:

> *And they will question you concerning the Spirit. Say: 'The Spirit is of*
>
> *the command of my Lord. And of knowledge you have not been given but*
>
> *a little.*

(Al-Isra, 17:85)
Gazi Love in the Holy Qur'an
2010, pp. 269-274

Between (physical) body and soul: life in seven life processes

Although Rudolf Steiner merely enumerated the seven life processes, and said a few words about them in his book Anthroposophie. Ein Fragment, you will understand that it is a vast subject, a tremendous subject, because it concerns more or less the whole of what we call 'life'.

[ ]

...translations of the German terms used by Rudolf Steiner:
Breathing – Warming - Nourishing
Secreting
Maintaining – Growing – Regenerating (Reproducing)

This translation indicates the living forces of these
processes, not so much their anatomical foundation.

[ ]

I tried to show how breathing is naturally the first of the seven life processes. It is the first because in breathing we communicate with the world. It is essentially what we call 'rhythm'; the giving and taking, the coming and going that connects us like an umbilical cord to the world. There is not something outside and something inside, like two separate entities which communicate with one another, but both are inside as well as outside. It is living, it 'breathes' in the arms of the world...

[ ]

The second step is warming. What has been inhaled is now permeated by warmth...in warming the breathing process is brought into a kind of form, a gestalt. It is warmed through and thereby starts to form itself. Following this warmth-permeated entity, which is now separated from the outside world and created, starts to take in nourishment; the process of nourishing arises. These are the first three processes and they are intimately connected with the surrounding world.

As soon as they are established, a response arises from within, namely secreting. Secreting works together with breathing, warming and nourishing. It transforms what is taken in and maintaining makes it into its own. As soon as this is done the individualized substance maintains its existence out of which growth can begin. Once it has reached a certain size it is able to regenerate, reproduce.

Karl König
A Living Physiology Lectures and Essays /The Seven Life
Processes II 1960 pp. 70-71
1999

The word 'Soul': an inwardness integral to the human constitution

Modern consciousness is not really comfortable with the word "soul" and in my opinion the loss of the word has been disabling, not only to religion but to literature and political thought and to every human pursuit. In contemporary religious circles souls, if they are mentioned at all, tend to be spoken of as saved or lost, having answered some set of divine expectations or failed to answer them, having arrived at some crucial realization or failed to arrive at it. So the soul, the masterpiece of creation is more or less reduced to a token signifying cosmic acceptance or rejection, having little or nothing to do that miraculous thing, the felt experience of life, except insofar life offers distractions or temptations.

Marilynne Robinson
When I was a Child I read books
2012, p. 8

The word 'I' (1): the shibboleth of humanity.

How much of a person a man is depends on how strong the I of the basic word I-You is in the human duality of his I.
The way he says I – what he means when he says I – decides where a man belongs and where he goes. The word "I" is the shibboleth of humanity.
Listen to it!
How dissonant the I of the ego sounds!...

[ ]

But how beautiful and legitimate the vivid and emphatic I of Socrates sounds! It is the I of infinite conversation, and the air of conversation is present on all its ways, even before his judges, in in the final hour in prison. This I lived in that relation to man which is embodied in conversation...

[ ]

How beautiful and legitimate the full I of Goethe sounds! It is the I of pure intercourse with nature. Nature yields to it and speaks ceaselessly with it, she reveals her mysteries to it and yet doesn't betray her mystery...

[ ]

And to anticipate and choose an image from the realm of unconditional relation: how powerful even overpowering, is Jesus' I-saying, and how legitimate to the point of being a matter of course!

Martin Buber, Walter Kaufmann (Translator)
I and Thou: New translation by Walter Kaufmann
1970, pp. 115,116

The word 'I' (2): I AM understood as meaning "the 'I'

Jesus' characteristic mode of speech about God and the rule of God was indirect, articulated in parables. What then of the seemingly direct 'I am' sayings of St John's Gospel? In Greek, these words would be heard as "'I am' is the good shepherd" – a statement which, taken at surface value, no Jew would question, though it could (and often did) raise suspicion.

Charles Sherlock
WORDS and The WORD – case studies in using scripture
2013, p. 15

The word 'I' (3): the spirit that embodies itself in soul, life and body

...here we are, a gaudy efflorescence of consciousness, staggeringly improbable in light of everything we know about the reality that contains us. There are physicists and philosophers who would correct me. They would say, if there are an infinite number of universes, as in theory there could be, then creatures like us would be very likely to emerge at some time in one of them. But to say this is only stating the fact of our improbability in other terms.

Then there is the odd privilege of existence as a coherent self, the ability to speak the word "I" and mean by it a richly individual history of experience, perception and thought. For the religious, the sense of the soul may have as a final redoubt, not as argument but as experience that haunting I who wakes us in the night wondering where time has gone, the I we wake to, sharply aware that we have been unfaithful to ourselves, that a life lived otherwise would have acknowledged a yearning more our own than any of the day-lit motives whose behests we answer to so diligently. Our religious traditions give us as the name of God two deeply mysterious words, one deeply mysterious utterance: I AM. Putting to one side the question of their meaning as the name and character by which the God of Moses would be known, these are words that every human being can say about herself, and does say, though always with a modifier of some kind. I am hungry, I am comfortable, I am a singer, I am a cook. The abrupt descent into particularity in every statement of this kind, Being itself made an auxiliary to some momentary accident of being, may only startle in the dark of night, when the intuition comes that there is no proportion between the great given of existence and the narrow vessel of circumstance into which it is inevitably forced. "I am Ozymandias, king of kings. Look at my works, ye mighty; and despair.

Marilynne Robinson
Absence of Mind: The dispelling of inwardness from the modern myth of self
2010, pp. 109-111

The word 'I' (4): the 'being' that one 'is'

Philosophy, precisely as "Being speaking within us", expression of the mute experience by itself, is creation.
Being is what requires creation of us for us to experience it.

Maurice Merleau-Ponty
The Visible and the Invisible / Ch 4 The Intertwining – the Chiasm
/ Working Notes
1992, p. 197

The word 'I' (5): perception rooted in imagination, imagination rooted in the 'I'

The primary imagination I hold to be the living power and prime agent of all human perception, and as a repetition in the finite mind of the eternal act of creation in the infinite I AM.

Samuel Taylor Coleridge
Biographia Literaria / Chapter 13
1960, p. 167

To be or to have...evidence

I don't identify as an atheist because nothing extra-epistemological is entailed by the fact that I do my best to believe on the basis of evidence. Neither my reasoning nor my conclusion about the probability of a divine creator means I am a good guy, or I'm kind to my dog, or I am a patient father...If "good critical thinker" were to be substituted with "atheist", then perhaps it would be clear that atheism entails nothing beyond the fact that one doesn't believe there's sufficient evidence to warrant belief in God.

[ ]

Atheism is not about racism, homophobia, or not practicing tai chi; it's simply about not having enough evidence to warrant a belief in God. Atheism is about epistemology, evidence, honesty, sincerity, reason, and inquiry.

Finally perhaps because I don't view atheism as an immutable characteristic, like eye color, I don't consider it an identity. I am willing to change my mind if I am presented with compelling evidence for the existence of a God or gods. I can understand why many theists consider belief a part of their identity, as they often claim that they are unwilling to change their minds. One may be more likely to consider something a part of one's identity if it's not subject to change.'

Peter Boghossian
A Manual for Creating Atheists
2013, pp. 37-8

An Avatar declares himself...

The Avatar comes as the manifestation of the divine nature in the human nature, the apocalypse of its Christhood, Krishnahood, Buddhahood, in order that the human nature may, by moulding its principle, thought, feeling, action, being on the lines of that Christhood,, Krishnahood, Buddhahood, transfigure itself into the divine, The law, the Dharma which the Avatar establishes is given for that purpose chiefly......each incarnation (Avatar) holds before men his own example and declares himself that he is the way and the gate; he declares too the openness of his humanity with the divine being, declares that the Son of man and the father above from whom he has descended are one and that Krishna in the human body...and the supreme Lord and Friend of all creatures are but two revelations of the same divine Purushottama revealed here in his own being: revealed here in the type of humanity.

Sri Aurobindo in: Essays of the Gita, Madras 1922, pp. 190-1,
Quoted by
Anonymous [Valentin Tomberg], Robert A. Powell (Translator)
Meditations on the Tarot: A Journey into Christian Hermeticism/ Letter XXI: The Fool
1991, p. 610

The Secular sacred 1

So the counsellor commits himself humbly to his task, entering in the reality that has found form in another human being, thoughtfully aware of the word: take your shoes from your feet, for you stand on sacred ground.

Jaap van Praag
Founder of the Humanistic Fellowship, Nederland (1953)

The Secular sacred 2

For people who are not religious in the orthodox sense, the authentically sacred, in the form of the secular sacred, can be found in the essence of being human – the search for morality exercising the power to become fully oneself, undertaking the search for meaning in life. The authentically sacred might also be experienced, and as a result identified, in a sense of wonder and awe.

Margaret Somerville
The Ethical Imagination: Journeys of the Human Spirit
2006, p. 55

When does human life begin 1: A Ngarinyin view

White men think they only have to have sex with women that's all they have to do to have a baby. For Aboriginal people, God puts the baby into the womb.

An Aboriginal man, who has had sex with his wife, goes along the place where he himself was created, where the reflection and image of God is. The Aboriginal man gets his children from the spiritside, not just from himself.

David Mowaljarlai
Yorro Yorro: Aboriginal Creation and the Renewal of Nature
1993, p. 86

[ ]

David Mowarjarlai: "These things (all the elements of the land: rocks, water courses, waterholes, trees, animals) recognize you. They give their wisdom and their understanding to you when they come close to you ...It's pulling you".

What is above is mirrored in what is below. Form above – Idea/ Power below; Wandjina above – his image imprinted below. Water is both substance (below?) and form (?). Songs are enacting the relationships between above and below.

Something experienced below with some element

of the land announces conception.

Place of conception or birth determines your belonging. E.g
"He is Hibiscus Man and Mountain Man..."

Hannah Rachel Bell: "The land reflects itself in where you
are born...tree...mountain. The land names us..."

Notes by Henk Bak at
An Evening on Australian Spirituality with David Mowarjarlai,
Michael Leunig, Hannah Rachel Bell organized and moderated by
David J. Tacey at Melbourne University in 1996

When does human life begin 2: A Jewish view

Most often in Jewish sacred literature, a fetus in the womb is considered a human life "under construction." The soul is usually described as arriving when the first breath of life is taken at birth. The primary Jewish imagery for the beginning of life comes from Genesis 1:2, where breath hovers above the waters of earth before life emerges from that cosmic womb. Then, in Genesis 2:7, after the body of Adam is fashioned from the clay of the earth, G*d is described as breathing life into him. These stories frame the basis for the Jewish view that the fetus gains full human rights and status only once the baby's head has emerged from the birth canal [Ohalot 7:6].

There is one Talmudic passage in which a Greek philosopher presses a rabbi on this issue until--probably for the sake of peace with the Greek occupiers of the Land of Israel--the rabbi accedes to the prevailing view in Greek culture that the soul is present from conception. This concession did not, however, change the Jewish perspective that the activation of the fetus's status as a human with full human rights still occurs upon birth.

The Designated Soul

The soul a baby will receive is traditionally understood to be pre-destined. The combining of the particular soul with the particular body it enters results in a human. An often-cited commentary relates that all the souls that will ever exist were "created during the six days of Creation, and were in the Garden of Eden, and all were present at the giving of the Torah [at Sinai]". [Tanhuma, Pekudei 3]. This perspective is reflected in Jeremiah 1:5: "I knew you, before I formed you in the belly, before you left the womb." Or as sometimes friends or family are known to say to small children, "We knew you before you were even a twinkle in *your parents' eyes". In the Talmud the distinction between body and soul is particularly clear in this passage: "When the time arrives for a person to depart from this world, G*d takes G*d's portion back and leaves the portions contributed by the parents". [T. Niddah 31a]*

There are many terms for soul and soul qualities in Jewish sacred literature such as reasoning, curiosity, innovation, intuition, emotion and awe – all of which become possible once a child has been born. (To learn the five primary Hebrew terms for soul and more about each dimension of soul they represent, please see Meaning & Mitzvah by Rabbi Milgram, pages 26-29.)

The Torah confounds our senses by offering us an impossible paradox: that humans are created b'tzelem elohim, "in the image of G*d". [Genesis 11:7]. G*d in Judaism has no image, that's foundational. So what kind of koan or, spiritual brain puzzle is this? Rabbi Harold Schulweis, teaches a helpful midrash:

"The angels, having heard that God planned to create the human being in His image, grew jealous. What does mere mortal man have to deserve such a gift? The angels plotted to hide the image of God from the human being. One angel suggested that it be hid on the tallest mountain. Another suggested that it be sunk into the deep of the sea. But the shrewdest angel demurred. "Man", he said, "is an adventurer. He will climb the highest mountain. He will plumb the deepest ocean. But if we want to hide it from him, let us hide the image in himself. It is the last place in the world that he will seek it".

Another popular midrash also emphasizes this notion of not making it easy to uncover our connection to the Big Picture. This story also accords the fetus cognitive ability while in the womb. It goes like this: While the fetus is gestating, an angel is teaching it Torah, all of Torah. When the child is about to be born, the angel flicks the child just above the lip, causing everything that was learned to be forgotten. [Niddah 30b] Just enough residual memory remains for the human to experience the urge to seek, savor, and believe we can find and connect again to that sweet, deep learning in our lives.

At the burning bush Moses asks how to name the source of his realization that slavery does not have to be a forever thing, that he has the contacts and training to attempt redeeming the Israelites. The answer, described as coming from G*d, is: Ehyeh. "I Am Becoming". Moses asks again, and the idea is then elaborated: ehyeh asher ehyeh, "I am becoming what I am becoming". According to this exchange we are all very much *created in the image of G*d. As parents, we foster the great unfolding of potential within creation by how we raise our children. We are part of the research and development team creating the future. In this way each human arrives in service of the Infinite Potential for Change inherent within creation. From this we experience joy, awe, challenge, and trembling before the awesome responsibility of becoming a parent.*

Rabbi Goldie Milgram
When Does Life Begin? A Jewish View

When does human life begin 3: the Sikh religion's view

Life begins.

Union and separation: our destiny is preordained.

Shortly after conception -, the embryo forms. Life begins with the five elements and the intricate body parts and organs are formed. Then infused with the soul, the vulnerable life is nourished and protected from the harmful elements. All the while the unborn meditates. - In the heat of the womb, life thrives and upside down indeed (the final position of the fetus in the last few weeks of labor and delivery). In the womb the creation survives by meditating upon the creator's name, with every breath. Finally one is born and eventually forgets one's origin and becomes engrossed with the material world. After leaving the womb, one interacts with the conscious world and forgets God. Growing up is certainly not easy, especially when reincarnation hovers just around the corner unless one meditates upon the name of the primal lord.

First comes the body: the process described.

-The structure is made from the five elements. p.1007

*-From egg and sperm, you were conceived, and
placed in the fire of the womb. p.706*

-From the blood of mother and the semen of father the human body was created and the Lord accomplished this wonderful feat.

-The human body was kept in the well of the womb. Then life was infused in it and its grandeur further enhanced.

-Mouth, eyes, nose, ears hands, teeth, hair etc. were bestowed upon it.

*-Man was given sight, speech, power of listening and
consciousness of security in the Word. For his ears, eyes,
tongue, and skin, the form, joy, smell etc. were created.*

*-By giving the best family (of human beings) and birth in
it, the lord god gave shape to one and all organs.*

Then enters the soul.

*-In the mother's womb, life was enshrined and cherished
[ ] You were blessed with body and soul.*

-The unborn life is nourished and protected.

-The unborn meditates

*-Within each and every breath, he contemplated the True
Name, deep within himself, within the womb.*

Birth

-The womb of the great mother earth gives birth to all.

Growing up

*-During infancy the mother pours milk into the mouth
and makes the baby expend its bodily waste.*

*-When grown up, the individual leaves aside the creator Lord,
becomes engrossed with the world around (maya).*

-Without the perfect Guru, man goes on to be engrossed in the web of maya.

SikhWomen.com
Empowered - Mind, Body, Spirit - Empowered

When does human life begin 4: Embryological view

*Every stage (in embryonic development) realizes its own equilibrium, namely
as transition out of earlier to later differentiation. The not-yet-seeing eye
lives in other functions. The eyes transmit warmth radiation. They steer
hormones in the direction of the kidneys. They develop themselves towards
seeing exactly in these functions and continue to stay in connection with them.*

Whilst therefore nothing is being shaped purely for its later function, nevertheless is everything from the beginning orientated towards the state of differentiation and complexity, which is later possible.

Every time the human race realizes itself anew in the individual. The inherited information is diffuse and becomes precise only in the flow of the processes of formation.

[ ]

Human individuals show already in their earliest formation recognizable signs of an "incomparable uniqueness", by which it distinguishes itself from hundreds of other embryos. The "high degree of form-differentiation" in comparison with embryos of other mammals leads to two conclusions:

The human being does develop itself not towards becoming human, but as human being, and shows itself as an individual, that sustains itself as such throughout the processes of its development. For these the motherly and fatherly chromosomes are only one of the material forms, in which the sustaining of the individual finds its anchor.

Therewith every human being is 'person' from the beginning. To describe even the earliest human life-processes, they must be understood as "spirit-related".

This spiritual element is to be assumed from the beginning, because nothing essentially new gets added to the movements of the ontogenesis. Already in the germ, therefore, everything is – whilst at the time only that is being developed in the process which is able to actually be.

Rudolf zur Lippe
Sinnenbewustsein: Grundlegung einer anthropologischen Aesthetik (Sensory Consciousness Foundation of an Anthropological Aesthetic) / Chapter on Embryological Foundations with input from Erich Blechschmidt
1987, pp. 184-5

D. How do I know?

Feeling, Sensing, Perceiving: against the dominant tendency to trust reasoning more than sensing, here are some significant steps in the movement towards recognition of the vital role the senses play in any effective way of knowing. A thinking that doesn't engage the senses might be compelled to ask: 'Why is there something rather than nothing?' As soon as one has engaged oneself thoughtfully in a range of sense experiences and perceptions, this question might be followed by: 'why is this 'something' immeasurably manyfold, multifaceted, dynamic? And why does it happen in an environment where there is apparently unlimited space for more…?'

The term 'aesthetics' derived from the Greek 'aisthesis' meaning sensory experience/perception, started to be used in the 18th century not just in the context of art and music. Hüther's interview is printed in full because of its definitive rejection of the illusion that neuro-physics can teach us how we learn. This may bring any dialogue between world-views up to date as a learning process, for ourselves and the generations to come…

Hemsterhuis on feeling as an organ of perception

The relation between the moral and the visible face of the universe is not less commeasurable than that between the visible and the audible or between the audible and tangible etc. and all the different faces of the universe we perceive through these different organs are equally and distinctly subjected to the contemplative and active faculties of the human being.

Love, hate, envy, respect are words that express experiences just as distinct as those of tree-star- tower; of ut-re-mi; of sweet-bitter- sour; of the scent of a rose, of jasmine or poppy; of cold-hot; of major-minor key.

If there happens to be a difference in the precision or purity of our perceptions of these different faces, one has to consider either lack of practice in the organ concerned, or a possible modifying constraint given in society.

In the actual modification of society, our organs of sight and hearing are the most practised and the least constrained; and those of taste, smell, touch and the heart, are more constrained and less practised; and as a consequence, we have clearer perceptions of the visible and audible faces of the universe than of its moral, tangible etc. ones.

[ ]

But this organ, this heart, that lets me experience the face of the universe, differs in principle from our other organs, in that it lets us experience a face of which our soul, our me are part; thus for this organ my own me becomes an object of contemplation, and therefore gives this organ us not only, like the other organs, experiences of relations that things outside us have with us, but also those relations that we have with those things, from which we gain an initial sense of responsibility.

The human individual, as we have considered him above, in all the perfection of his intellectual power, arrives even at a notion of the Divine; but he would not have any experience of responsibility, not toward God nor toward anything whatever...pp 115-6

Francois Hemsterhuis
Lettre sur l'Homme et ses Rapports 1772
Ed. Meyboom 1846-1850, pp. 113-4
[Translated by Henk Bak]

S.T. Coleridge on 'Reason' as distinct from 'formal logic' and 'sensing'.

I should have no objection to define reason with Jacobi, and with his friend Hemsterhuis, as an organ bearing the same relation to spiritual objects, the universal, the eternal, and the necessary, as the eye bears to material and contingent phaenomena. But then it must be added, that it is an organ identical with its appropriate objects.

Thus God, the soul, eternal truth, &ct are the objects of reason; but are themselves reason. We name God the Supreme Reason; and Milton says, "whence the soul reason receives, and reason is her being".

Whatever is self-conscious knowledge is reason; and in this sense it may be safely defined as the organ of the super-sensuous; even as the understanding whenever it does not possess or use the reason as another and inward eye, may be defined the conception of the sensuous, or the faculty by which we generalize and arrange the phenomena of perception: that faculty the functions of which contain the rules and constitute the possibility of outward experience.

In short, the understanding supposes something that is understood. This may be only its own sets of forms, that is, formal logic; but real objects, the materials of substantial knowledge, must be furnished, we might safely say revealed, to it by organs of sense.

[ ]

Again, the understanding and experience may exist without reason. But reason cannot exist without understanding; nor does it or can it manifest itself but in and through the understanding, which in our elder writers is often called discourse, or the discursive faculty, as by Hooker, Lord Bacon and Hobbes: and an understanding enlightened by reason Shakespeare gives us as contradistinguishing character of man, under the name ""discourse of reason".

In short, the human understanding possesses two distinct organs, the outward sense, and "the mind's eye" which is reason: whenever we use that phrase (the mind's eye) in its proper sense, and not as a mere synonym of the memory or the fancy. In this we may reconcile the promise of revelation, that the "blessed will see God", with the declamation of St John, "God hath no one seen at any time".

Samuel Taylor Coleridge
The Friend A Series of Essays / Essay 5
1986, pp. 96-97

Primacy of continuity 1

The phenomena succeed each other in time, bound by causality because your coloured view wants this regularity, but right through the walls of causality 'miracles' glide and flow continually, visible only to the free, the enlightened.

L.E.J. Brouwer
Life, Art and Mysticism
1905

Primacy of continuity 2: Basic intuition of every intellectual activity, including mathematics

In the following chapters we shall go further into the basic intuition of mathematics and of every intellectual activity as the substratum, divested of all quality, of any perception of change, a unity of continuity and discreteness, a possibility of thinking together several entities, connected by a 'between', which is never exhausted by the insertion of new entities. Since continuity and discreteness occur as inseparable complements, both having equal rights and being equally clear, it is impossible to avoid one of them as a primitive entity, trying to construe it from the other one, the latter being put forward as self-sufficient; in fact it is impossible to consider it as self-sufficient. Having recognised that the intuition of continuity, of 'fluidity', is as primitive as that of several

> *things considered as forming together a unit, the latter being at the basis of every mathematical construction, we are able to state properties of the continuum as a 'matrix of points to be thought as a whole'.*
>
> L.E.J. Brouwer
> ***Dissertation 1907 Collected Works.***
> 1975, p. 17

Primacy of continuity 3: thinking in 'things' and 'shocks': an 'epistemological monstrosity'

> *Parallel with the problem of thing-ism (chosism) one should further more pose the similar problem of shockism (choquism). With the notion of shock we are faced with a kind of epistemological monstrosity. One presents it as simple and it has an initial complexity, because it synthesizes geometrical and materialistic notions. In this way one builds science and philosophy on a collection of crude and naïve images. What would Hume's philosophy have been if people had not played billiards! A cannon (Fr: carambolage = billiard cue) was sufficient to create a philosophy of the whole of nature!*
>
> Gaston Bachelard
> ***Epistemologie***
> 1971, p. 57
> [Translation from the French by Henk Bak]

The primacy of continuity 4: the 'pattern that connects'

> *I hold to the presupposition that our loss of the sense of aesthetic unity was, quite simply, an epistemological mistake.*
> *[ ]*
>
> *We have been trained to think of patterns, with the exception of those of music, as fixed affairs. It is easier and lazier that way but, of course, all nonsense. In truth, the right way to begin to think about the pattern which connects is to think of it as primarily (whatever that means) a dance of interacting parts and only secondarily pegged down by various sorts of physical limits and by those limits which organisms characteristically impose.*
>
> Gregory Bateson
> ***Mind and Nature: A Necessary Unity***
> 1980

The primacy of continuity 5: The 'flesh of the world'

Each "sense" is a "world," i.e. absolutely incommunicable for the other senses, and yet constructing a something which, through its structure, is from the first open upon the world of the other senses, and with them forms one sole Being.   *Working Notes p. 117*

We have to reject the age-old assumptions that put the body in the world and the seer in the body, or, conversely, the world and the body in the seer as in a box. Where are we to put the limit between the body and the world, since the world is flesh? Working Notes p. 138

Flesh of the world, described (apropos of time, space, movement) as segregation, dimensionality, continuation, latency, encroachment---

Then interrogate once again these phenomena-questions: they refer us to the perceiving/perceived Einfuehlung, for we are already in the being thus described, that we are of it, that between it and us there is Einfuehlung. (Sensing what is inside the other, inside the 'object' of sensing, empathy)

That means that my body is made of the same flesh as the world (it is perceived), and moreover that this flesh of this body is shared by the world, the world reflects it, encroaches upon it and it encroaches upon the world. (the felt [senti] at the same time the culmination of subjectivity and the culmination of materiality), they are in a relation of transgression or overlapping. Working Notes p. 248

Maurice Merleau-Ponty
The Visible and the Invisible / Ch 4 The Intertwining – the Chiasm
1992

Primacy of continuity 6: Tacit Dimension

I have described how we learn to feel the end of a tool or a probe hitting things outside. We may regard this as the transformation of the tool or probe into a sentient extension of our body, as Samuel Butler has said. But our awareness of our body for attending to things outside it suggests a wider generalization of the feeling we have of our body. Whenever we use certain things for attending from them to other things, in the way we always use our own body, these things change their appearance. They appear to us now in terms of the entities to which we are attending from them, just as we feel our own body in terms of the things outside to which we are attending from our body. In this sense we can say that when we make a thing function as the proximal term of tacit knowing, we incorporate it in our body – or extend our body to include it – so that we come to dwell in it.

Michael Polanyi
The Tacit Dimension
1967, pp. 16

A layperson: an expert on everyday life...

True, artistic production is bound to become semantically stunted if it is not carried out as a specialised approach to problems that are meaningful in themselves, as something purely for experts which pays no regard to esoteric needs. Everyone, including the critic, (the trained recipient) agrees to sort out the problems in question under just one abstract aspect of application. However, this sharp differentiation, this exclusive concentration on one dimension, is lost as soon as the aesthetic experience is assimilated into the life-history of the individual or incorporated in collective experience. Reception by the layman (who ought rather be called the expert on everyday life) acquires a different direction from the one it is given by the professional critic, whose attention is taken up with purely artistic developments. [ ] As soon as it is used exploratively to throw light on a real-life situation and related to real-life problems, it becomes involved in a word-game that is no longer that of aesthetic criticism. The aesthetic experience then not only alters the way we interpret those needs which inform our perception of the world: it also enters into cognitive interpretations and normative expectations and changes the way in which all these factors interrelate.

Juergen Habermas
Modernism – an unfinished Project** / **Lecture on reception of the Adorno Prize
1980

Time Is Out of Joint

...While much that universities teach today is new and up to date, the presuppositions or premises of thought upon which all our teaching is based are ancient and, I assert, obsolete.

I refer to such notions as:

a. The Cartesian dualism separating 'mind' and 'matter'.

b. The strange physicalism of the metaphors which we use to describe and explain mental phenomena – 'power', 'tension', 'energy', 'social forces', etc.

c. Our anti-aesthetic assumption, borrowed from the emphasis which Bacon, Locke and Newton long ago gave to the physical sciences, viz., that all phenomena (including the mental) can and shall be studied and evaluated in quantitative terms.

The view of the world – the latent and partly unconscious epistemology – which such ideas together generate is out of date in three different ways:

a. Pragmatically, it is clear that these premises and their corollaries lead to greed, monstrous overgrowth, war, tyranny, and pollution. In this sense our premises are daily demonstrated false, and the students are half aware of this.

b. Intellectually, the premises are obsolete in that systems theory, cybernetics, holistic medicine, ecology, and gestalt psychology offer demonstrably better ways of understanding the world of biology and behaviour.

c. As a base for religion, such premises as I have mentioned became clearly intolerable and therefore obsolete about 100 years ago. In the aftermath of Darwinian evolution, this was stated rather clearly by such thinkers as Samuel Butler and Prince Kropotkin. But already in the eighteenth century, William Blake saw that the philosophy of Locke and Newton could only generate 'dark Satanic mills'.

Necessarily every aspect of our civilization is split wide open.

In the field of economics, we face two overdrawn caricatures of life – the capitalist or the communist – and we are told that we must take sides in the struggle between these two monstrous ideologies.

In the business of thinking, we are torn between various extremes of affectless-ness and the strong currents of anti-intellectual fanaticism.

As in religion, the constitutional guarantees of 'religious freedom' seem to promote similar exaggerations: a strange, totally secular Protestantism, a wide spectrum of magical cults, and total religious ignorance. It is not accident that simultaneously the Roman Catholic Church is giving up the use of Latin, while the rising generation is learning to chant in Sanskrit!

> A memorandum circulated by Gregory Bateson to the Regents of
> the University of California, August 1978 in: Mind and Nature: A
> Necessary Unity
> 1980, pp. 231-232

Street Epistemology as break down strategy

> *Foundationalists argue that specific beliefs are justified if they're inferred from other beliefs. Descartes is a good example of a foundationalist. He starts with the fact that he exist as the foundation for his beliefs. "I think therefore I am". Descartes constructs additional propositions based upon this proposition. For example, once he establishes the reliability of his senses, he then constructs propositions about the accuracy of his perceptions of the world – when he perceives something clearly and distinctly he's not deceived. For example, once he establishes the reliability of his senses, he then constructs propositions about the accuracy of his perceptions of the world – when he perceives something clearly and distinctly he's not deceived. Descartes and other foundationalists come to know the world by basing their beliefs on fundamental and often irreducible propositions.*

> *Coherentism doesn't work in the context of a belief intervention because artefacts in one's epistemic landscape (an ancient text, one's feelings, one's experiences) are used to refer to each other. For example, subjects will emphatically state that their personal experiences confirm 'The Urania Book is true', and that their feelings are also confirmatory evidence. Using a coherentist model, it's impossible to break through and meaningfully engage. ...because of the circular nature of justification. That is, each artefact is justified by other artefacts, yet does not receive justification from any outside source. Thus from the inside a coherentist system everything makes sense – exactly as if one were in the matrix.*

> *Street Epistemologists should use a foundationalist paradigm when deconstructing a subject's faith.*

> Peter Boghossian
> ***A Manuel for Creating Atheists***
> 2013, pp. 74-5

To deconstruct is to find resonance in the constituent parts of a text

The poem is always also the active "translation"
of another poem that rings within it.

Jacques Derrida
Glas (ringing, resonance)
1974, p. 153
Derrida's comment on Stéphane Mallarmé's four poems on
the theme of poverty, where earlier versions resonate in the
later ones

Reclaiming the notion of a 'third reformation'.

I should like to try to persuade sensible historians to use the word 'Rosicrucian'. ...The word could, I suggest, be used of a certain style of thinking which is historically recognizable without raising the question of whether a Rosicrucian style of thinker belonged to a secret society. p. 264

[ ]

The Rosicrucian enlightenment included a vision of the necessity for a reform of society, particularly of education, for a third reformation of religion, embracing all sides of man's activity – and saw this as a necessary accompaniment of the new science. Rosicrucian thinkers were aware of the dangers of the new science, of its diabolical as well as its angelical possibilities, and they saw that its arrival should be accompanied by a general reformation of the whole wide world. This side of the message was perhaps best understood in parliamentarian England, though circumstances prevented its application, and after the Restoration, science was allowed to develop in isolation from utopia, and apart from the idea of a reformed society, educated to receive it. The comparative disregard of the social and educational possibilities of the movement was surely unfortunate for the future. pp. 277-8

Frances A. Yates
The Rosicrucian Enlightenment
1975

Bacon's New Atlantis: arts, science and technology in a moral context. (1627)

But now to come to our present purpose. When the king had forbidden to all his people navigation into any part that was not under his crown, he made nevertheless this ordinance; that every twelve years there should be set forth, out of his kingdom two ships, appointed to several voyages; That in either of these ships there should be a mission of three of the Fellows or Brethern of Salomon's House; whose errand was only to give us knowledge of the affairs and state of those countries to which they were designed, and especially of the sciences and the arts, manufacturers, and inventions of all the world; and withal to bring unto us books, instruments, and patterns of every kind; That the ships, after they had landed the brethren, should return, and that the brethren should stay abroad till the next mission. These ships are not otherwise fraught, than with the store of victuals, and good quantity of treasure to remain with the brethren, for the buying of such things and rewarding of such persons as they should think fit. ...thus you see we maintain a trade not for gold, silver, or jewels; not for silks; nor for spices, not any other commodity of matter; but only for God's first creature, which was Light: to have light (I say) of the growth of all parts of the world. p. 89

[ ]

For our ordinances and rites: we have two very long and fair galleries: in one of these we place patterns and samples of all manner of the more rare and excellent inventions, in the other we place the statues of all principal inventors. There we have a statue of your Columbus, that discovered the West Indies: also the inventor of ships: your monk that was the inventor of ordinance and of gunpowder: the inventor of music: the inventor of letters: the inventor of printing: the inventor of observations of astronomy: the inventor of works in metal: the inventor of glass: the inventor of silk of the worm: the inventor of wine: the inventor of corn and bread: the inventor of sugars: and all these, by more certain tradition than you have. Then we have divers inventors of our own, of excellent works; which you have not seen, it were too long to make descriptions of them; and besides, in the right understanding of those descriptions you may easily err. For upon every invention of value, we erect a statue to the inventor, and give him a liberal and honourable reward....

We have certain hymns and services, which we say daily, of Lord and thanks to God for his marvellous works: and forms of prayers, imploring his aid and blessings for the illumination of our labours, and the turning of them into good and holy uses.

Lastly, we have circuits or visits of divers principal cities of the kingdom; where, as it cometh to pass, we do publish such new profitable inventions as we think good. And we declare also natural divinations of diseases, plagues swarms of hurtful creatures, scarcity, tempests, earthquakes, great inundations, comets, temperature of the year, and divers other things; and we give counsel thereupon, what the people shall do for the prevention and remedy of them. pp. 105-106

Francis Bacon
New Atlantis: A Work Unfinished
2015

Varela: Unruly conversational interaction allows for moments of cognition

A classic illustration of the perceptual guidance of action is the 1958 study by Richard Held and Alan Hein, who raised kittens in the dark and exposed them to light only under controlled conditions. A first group of animals was allowed to move around normally while harnassed to a yoke: their gross movements were transferred mechanically to a second group of animals conveyed in gondolas. The two groups shared the same visual experience, but the second group was entirely passive. When the animals were released after a few weeks of treatment, the first group behaved normally, but those who had been carried around behaved as if they were blind (my emphasis).: they bumped into objects and fell over edges. This marvellous study supports the enactive view that the objects are not seen by the visual extraction of features, but rather by the visual guidance of action. Similar results have been obtained under various other circumstances and studied even at a single-cell level.

Unless the reader feels that this example is fine for cats, but removed from human experience, let us consider another case. In 1962, Paul Bahy Rita designed a video camera for blind persons that can stimulate multiple points in the skin by electrically activated vibration. Using this technique, images formed with the camera were made to correspond with patterns of skin stimulation, thereby substituting for the visual loss. Patterns projected onto the skin have no "visual" content unless the individual is behaviourally active by directing the camera using head, hand or body movements. When the blind person does actively behave in this way, after a few hours of experience a remarkable effect emerges: the person no longer interprets the skin sensations as body-related, but rather as images projected into space being explored by the bodily directed "gaze" of the video camera. Thus, in order to experience "real objects out there", the person must actively direct the camera (using his or her head, hand). pp. 331-332

Conclusion.

I have argued that perception does not exist of the recovery of a pre-given world, but rather of the perceptual guidance of action in a world that is inseparable from our sensorimotor capacities. Cognitive structures emerge from recurrent patterns of perceptually guided action. I can summarize, then, by saying that cognition consists not of representations but of embodied action.

[ ]

It is, therefore, the very contemporary input in cognitive science for the understanding that points in a direction which I consider Post-Cartesian in two important ways.

First, knowledge appears more and more as built from small domains, that is, microworlds....

Second, such microworlds are not coherent or integrated into some enormous totality regulating the veracity of the smaller parts. It is more like an unruly conversational interaction: the very presence of this unruliness allows a cognitive moment to come into being according to the system's constitution and history. The very heart of this autonomy, the rapidity of the agent's selection, is forever lost to the cognitive system itself. Thus, what we traditionally call the "irrational" and the "nonconscious" does not contradict what appears as rational and purposeful: it is its very underpinning. p. 336

Francisco J Varela
Incorporations / The Reenchantment of the Concrete, Knowledge as enaction
1992

Steiner: On the vital importance of an education of the senses, all the senses.

Official science of the present day (1919) does not rise to an observation so fine as to distinguish between the seeing of colour, and the perception of form with the help of the sense of movement, rather it mixes everything up. But in the future it will be impossible to educate through such confusion. For how is it possible to educate a child to use his sense of sight without knowing that the whole human being pours himself into the act of seeing by way of the sense of movement? This leads us to another point: You are dealing with the act of seeing when you perceive coloured forms.

This act of seeing is a complicated act. But since you are a unity you can re-unite in yourself what you have perceived in the two ways, through the eye and through the sense of movement. You would look at a red circle in a dull and blank way if you could not perceive the red in one way and the form of the circle in quite a different way. But you do not look upon it in a blank way because you look at it from two sides, the colour through the eye and the form with the help of the sense of movement, and life compels you to join the two together inwardly. There you form a judgement.

And now you understand judgement as a living process in your own body, which comes about through the fact that the senses bring the world to you analysed into members. The world brings to you what you experience divided into twelve separate members, and in your judgement you join the things together again because the separate parts do not want to continue as separate parts. The form of the circle is not content to remain mere form as it is to the sense of movement, neither is colour content to remain mere colour as it is perceived by the eye. Thus the function of judgement becomes an expression of your whole being.

Now you see the deep meaning of our connection with the world. If we had not twelve senses we should look at our environment like dullards, we should not be able to experience an inward judgement. But since we have twelve senses we have a fair number of possibilities of uniting what is separate. What the ego sense* experiences we can connect with the other eleven senses, and that is true of each sense. In this way we get a large number of permutations in the combinations of the senses. Besides that we have a great many possibilities through the fact that we can connect the ego sense for example with the thought sense and the speech sense and so on. There we see in what mysterious way the human being is connected with the world. Through his twelve senses things are separated into their component parts and the human being must attain the power to reunite these component parts. In this way he participates in the inner life of the things. From this you will understand how infinitely important it is that man should be so educated that one sense should be developed with the same care as another, for then the connections between the senses, between the perceptions, will be sought quite consciously and systematically.

Rudolf Steiner
Study of Man
1919, pp. 122-123

---

*   In Steiner's description of the senses, the sense of ego or 'I' refers to our perception of the 'I' of the other person; and the sense of thought refers to the thought of the other person. This reference resonates with Martin Buber's 'I and Thou'...

Gerald Hüther: Learning enthusiastically

Interview 2012

How do people learn?
Generally speaking, we think "learning" means cognitive, formal learning. We tend to associate "learning" with studying and memorizing vocabulary, factual information of all kinds, mathematical formulae and so on. From a neurobiological point of view, however, this is only the least little bit of what we learn. Every learning experience involves emotions.
The most important learning experiences come to us, essentially, by way of our bodies – which means that learning is always an experience of the whole body. At the same time, every learning experience involves emotions. We are only able to learn when the so-called emotional centres in the brain are activated. These centres release neuroplastic messenger substances enabling what has been learned to become anchored in the brain. In other words, whatever the learning experience, if it is to be successful there has to be emotional activation. The most enjoyable activation we know of is "enthusiasm".

What do you mean by "enthusiasm"?
Enthusiasm is an emotion that went missing in our contemporary functionalized society. Picture yourself how you felt as a small child when, after trying many times, you eventually managed to haul yourself up by the table leg – or the first time you stood upright on your 2 feet. That feeling is enthusiasm. It is a very deep sensation that seizes the whole body – unless, like most adults today, a person is completely blocked and no longer has access to his or her emotions. Enthusiasm activates the emotional centres. The state of enthusiasm goes along with activation of the emotional centres in the brain. You can think of the emotional centres as resembling a watering-can. As soon as you tip the watering-can, the neuroplastic messenger substances pour out of the spout and flow all over the brain.

[ ]

Can we humans make ourselves smarter, or dumber?
Neuroscientists have found children are not born with too few neuronal links – meaning we would have to produce more for them through education and culture – but on the contrary with too many networks. This means: It is up to us how many of these excess networks children will actually use in life, or more specific it's up to the life environment in which a child grows up. A rich life environment for a child poses the maximum number of problems

and challenges – such as a world in which you have to climb trees, or build a house for yourself, or cook your own food. What is not used withers away again.
In a "pet" or "zoo animal" environment in which everything that people need in life is put in front of them, these potentials could not be developed. The excess networks would only wither away again. This is what neuroscientists call "experience-dependent plasticity". Inside the brain, too much is provided at the outset; then comes the question: "What will the child actually need in this world that he or she grows up in?" What is used will remain in place, and what is not used will wither away. Children living in the Amazonian rainforest learn 120 different shades of green and can name them all, using 120 different terms. Potential of that kind is either used in practice or little used. Children here can at best distinguish light green, green and dark green. How far a potential is actually used depends on how important it is. If in a given culture something is pointless and unimportant, it will not be used. The result is that what was once a possibility, this potential, this over-provision in the brain, and is not used, will just wither away.

What determines what will be learnt?
The keyword we need for understanding this is "significance". What is significant and what is not is determined by cultural differences. If something matters to a child, it will be learnt. This poses a challenge at the moment, because anything connected with the classic idea of "learning" is insignificant to children. Young people growing up today think it is more significant and more interesting to learn how a person becomes famous. 100 years ago, what mattered was being a soldier. 200 years ago it was important to be a seafarer and an adventurer, and so on. Every culture, every society has its own idea of what matters most to it, and then invites its children to conform to this idea. As a society, and with regard to the media, we need to ask ourselves: do we really want our children's priorities to be set for them by the media, given that the media's interests are primarily commercial?

Shortened version of a conversation with Prof. Dr. Gerald Hüther 2012
conducted by Dr. Maya Götz (IZI).
Gerald Hüther was at the time Professor of Neurobiology and Head of the Center for Neurobio-logical Prevention research at the university of Göttingen (Psychiatric Clinic) and the university of Mannheim/Heidelberg (Institute of Public Health).

When thinking gets fully engaged in sensing...

Two things fill my mind with ever increasing wonder and awe, the more often and persistent perceptive thinking engages itself with it: the starry heavens above me and the moral law within me. I see both in front of me and connect them immediately with the consciousness of my existence.

Immanuel Kant
Kritik der praktischen Vernunft / Conclusion
1788

The nature of the hermetic tradition

Now Hermeticism, the living Hermetic tradition, guards the communal soul of all true culture. I must add: hermeticists listen to — and now and then they hear — the beating of the heart of the spiritual life of humanity. They cannot do otherwise than live as guardians of the life and communal soul of religion, science and art. They do not have any privilege in any of these domains: saints, true scientists, and artists of genius are their superiors. But they live for the mystery of the communal heart which beats within all religions, all philosophies, all arts and all sciences — past, present and future. And inspired by the example of John, the beloved disciple, they do not pretend, and never will pretend, to play a directing role in religion, science, art, in social or political life: but they are constantly attentive so as not to miss any occasion to serve religion, philosophy, science, art, the social and political life of humanity, and so to infuse the breath of life of their communal soul — analogous to the administration of the sacrament of Holy Communion. Hermeticism is — and is only — a stimulant, a "ferment" or an "enzyme" in the organism of the spiritual life of humanity. In this sense it is itself an Arcanum — that is to say the antecedent of the Mystery of the Second Birth or the Great Initiation.

[ ]

The first Arcanum — the principle underlying all the other twenty-one Major Arcana of the Tarot — is that of the rapport of personal effort and of spiritual reality. It occupies the first place in the series because if one does not understand it (i.e. take hold of it in cognitive and actual practice), one would not know what to do with all the other Arcana. For it is the magician who is called to reveal the practical method relating to all the Arcana. He is the "Arcanum of the Arcana", in the sense that he reveals that which it is necessary to know and to will in order to enter the school of spiritual exercises whose totality comprises the game of Tarot, in order to be able to derive some benefit therefrom. In fact, the first and fundamental principle of esotericism (i.e. of the way of experience of the reality of the spirit) can be rendered by the formula:

Learn at first concentration without effort;
transform work into play;
make every yoke that you have accepted easy
and every burden that you carry
light!

Anonymous [Valentin Tomberg], Robert A. Powell (Translator)
Meditations on the Tarot: A Journey into Christian Hermeticism/ Letter I
1991, p. 6,7

On Wouter Hanegraaff: Study of esotericism, a work in progress

His dissertation New Age Religion and Western Culture: Esotericism in the Mirror of Secular Thought was published by Brill in 1996. Two years later a USA paperback version was published by State University of New York Press. This work constitutes one of the first non-polemical academic reviews of the New Age movement, presenting an analysis on the basis of its important texts. It covers important authors, themes, aspects of New Age belief, and finally looks at the New Age in the context of traditional Western esotericism. It has helped pave the way for a number of further studies that have appeared in various journals, concerning the New Age phenomenon.

Hanegraaff's second book-length publication was Lodovico Lazzarelli (1447-1500): The Hermetic Writings and Related Documents (Tempe 2005; with Ruud M. Bouthoorn). Lazzarelli was treated by Frances A. Yates as a secondary figure, but the Hanegraaff-Bouthoorn book argues that Yates's "grand narrative" of the Hermetic Tradition needs to be revised. It seeks to restore Lazzarelli's place in the history of Renaissance hermetism and contains critical annotated editions and translations of Lazzarelli's hermetic writings, plus several related documents such as the previously unpublished biography of Lazzarelli by his brother, and texts by his spiritual master Giovanni da Correggio.

Hanegraaff's small volume Swedenborg, Oetinger, Kant: Three Perspectives on the Secrets of Heaven (West Chester 2007), is an expanded version of the introduction he wrote for the New Century Edition of Swedenborg's "Arcana Coelestia". It analyzes Swedenborg's worldview as expounded in his main work, and discusses the early German reception history by Friedrich Christoph Oetinger and Immanuel Kant. Oetinger originally saw Swedenborg as an ally but eventually criticized his idealist philosophy as the antithesis of his own incarnational theosophy. Kant took Swedenborg much more seriously than is commonly assumed, and their basic ontological and epistemological perspectives are remarkably compatible.

Hanegraaff's second full-scale monograph Esotericism and the Academy: Rejected Knowledge in Western Culture was published by Cambridge University Press in 2012. It tells "the neglected story of how intellectuals since the Renaissance have tried to come to terms with a cluster of 'pagan' ideas from late antiquity that challenged the foundations of biblical religion and Greek rationality". "Expelled from the academy on the basis of Protestant and Enlightenment politics", Hanegraaff argues that "these traditions have come to be perceived as the Other by which academics define their identity to the present day". He argues that our common perspectives on Western intellectual and cultural history are based upon a highly selective "eclecticist" historiography grounded in Enlightenment ideologies.

One year later, Hanegraaff published an introductory textbook, Western Esotericism: A Guide for the Perplexed (Bloomsbury 2013). It gives a systematic overview of Western esotericism as a field of academic research, focusing on questions of definition and demarcation, main historical currents, polemical and apologetic discourse, worldviews, ideas about knowledge, and practices, as well as the impact of modernization and the interdisciplinarity of the field. The book ends with an annotated bibliography.

Apart from these books, Hanegraaff has published numerous articles in academic journals and collective volumes. He is the (co-)editor of seven volumes in the study of religion and Western esotericism, including the two-volume Dictionary of Gnosis and Western Esotericism (Brill: Leiden 2005), and "Hidden Intercourse: Eros and Sexuality in the History of Western Esotericism (with Jeffrey J. Kripal)". He is a former (and founding) editor of Aries: Journal for the Study of Western Esotericism (now edited by Peter J. Forshaw) and the "Aries Book Series: Texts and Studies in Western Esotericism" (now edited by Marco Pasi; both Brill). He is member of the editorial board of the journals Religion, Numen, Religion Compass and Esoterica, and is on the advisory board of Journal of Contemporary Religion and Nova Religio.

Wikipedia /Wouter Hanegraaff
https://en.wikipedia.org/wiki/Wouter_Hanegraaff

E. The existential struggle for meaning

Between Evil and Hope:

The first and the last contribution is from Susan Neiman who refuses to 'domesticate' the reality of evil through any 'reasonable' system. Forty years before her, Bruning prophetically senses the 'nearly satanic' power by which the 'known good' turns 'good will' into what we now know as fundamentalist terrorism. Journalist and philosopher Bernard-Henri Lévy chooses to live for a significant time in places of senseless war, forgotten by the world for years on end and reflects on the experience. For Schiller the human being still had a choice, which for Marilynne Robinson 200 years later got lost. Four texts on hope: the rationalist Grayling, the ethicist Somerville, the hermeticist Tomberg, and Albert Camus who speaks his truth unqualified. A last thought is for the children, our hope for any renewal, beyond the 'tyranny of the known good' (Bruning) and refusing to stop seeking reason where adults might give up (Neiman.)

At the beginning (of creaton?) both good and evil as beings. Zoroastrian world-view

And in the beginning both Spirits were there, the twins, who by their own word are named the good and the evil in thinking, speaking and doing. Between them the ones who act well have chosen rightly, not the ones that act badly. And when these Spirits came together for the first time, they determined life and death, and that in the end the worst shall be for those whose belief is false, but the best reward for those who belief rightly.

Under both these Spirits, the one whose belief was false chose the worst in his doing, but the Holy Spirit that which is right, He Who dresses Himself with the most solid heaven as His garment, (and with Him) all those who through pure deeds want to bring gratitude to the Lord, openly professing their faith in Mazda.

Fischer Bücherei
Die Nichtchristlichen Religionen. Verfaßt und herausgegeben von Helmuth von Glaseanapp
1964, pp. 293
[Translated by Henk Bak]

Evil: no longer a phenomenon that fits in systematic understanding

> *...the problem of evil is the guiding force of modern thought. Most contemporary versions of the history of philosophy will find this claim to be less false than incomprehensible. For the problem of evil is thought to be a theological one. Classically it's formulated as the question: how could a good God create a world full of innocent suffering? Such questions have been off-limits to philosophy since Immanuel Kant argued that God, along with many other subjects of classical metaphysics, exceeded the limits of human knowledge. If one thing seems to unite philosophers on both sides of the Atlantic, it's the conviction that Kant's work proscribes not just future philosophical references to God but most other sorts of foundation as well. From this perspective, comparing Lisbon with Auschwitz is merely mistaken. The mistake seems to lie in accepting the eighteenth century's use of the word evil to refer to both acts of human cruelty and instances of human suffering. That mistake might come naturally to a group of theists, who were willing to give God the responsibility for both, but it shouldn't confuse the rest of us. On this view Lisbon and Auschwitz are two completely different kinds of events. Lisbon denotes the sort of thing insurance companies call natural disasters, to remove them from the sphere of human action...Earthquakes and volcanoes, famines and floods inhabit the borders of human meaning. We want to understand just so much about them as might help us to gain control. Only traditional – that is, premodern – theists will seek in them significance. Auschwitz, by contrast stands for all that is meant when we use the word evil today: absolute wrongdoing that leaves no room for account or expiation.*

>> ...how can human beings behave in ways that so thoroughly violate both reasonable and rational norms? The sharp distinction between natural and moral evil that now seems self-evident was born around the Lisbon earthquake (1705)...
>> Susan Neiman
>> ***Evil in Modern Thought an alternative history of philosophy***
>> 2003, p. 9

Evil: the tyranny of the known good

> *Sourdough is a substance mixed in with another substance which is totally, in every particle, prepared to undergo the working of the sourdough itself. And the sourdough is with everything of itself prepared to totally permeate the substance in which it finds itself...*

> *[ ]*

> *I believe, that these aspects are essential and uncover a fundamental*

attitude and fundamental way of relating. They seem to make understandable that the human being, due to its nature lives for nothing else than to receive God's word – and that God's word can, due to its nature, be nothing else a full response to that longing...

[ ]

It then seems as if the whole religious history of humanity despite ( ) its most disconcerting aberrations, has in essence been one vehement struggle to bring forth this word. All degeneration can perhaps in origin be explained by people's inability to bring forth this word, this word of human goodness, or by the very absence of this word. One senses that this is the case, when the love as taught by Christ, is not being recognized as the actual, creative principle. The reign of the known good as ordering principle brings nearly always compulsion, deception, misleading, violence with it, generating a reality with all the depraved passion which calls for violence and feeds on it. The tyranny of the known good (which is not the real human goodness) is a frustrated will to truth as well, a frustrated conscience, a sense of responsibility driven into a corner, this also has its origin in the humiliating inability to fully know the good. One may consider this a nearly satanic humiliation of humanity's good will.

Henri Bruning
Vormkracht en Onmacht der Religie: Missionair Christendom
1961, pp. 196-8

No place for inwardness

... Now that the mystery of motive is solved – there are only self-seeking and aggressive, and the illusions that conceal them from us – there is no place for the soul or even for the self. Moral behaviour has little real meaning, and inwardness, in the traditional sense, is not necessary or possible. We use analysts and therapists to discover the content of our experience.

Marilynne Robinson
The Death of Adam: Essays on Modern Thought
2005, pp. 74,128

Meaninglessness: the face of evil in our time

Reflections

5. A nostalgia for war

...eight years ago, in Bosnia, where it's this lack of nostalgia, this incapacity to regret, thus to imagine, the old notion of anti-fascist war – in short, the failure to make a claim for even the idea of a just war – that was responsible for the non-intervention of the West and, thus, for the prolongation of the siege of Sarajevo, and for its rows of murdered civilians. Have things changed with the era of "suicide attacks"? And did the West have to be struck in its heart to regain consciousness, as well as its ability to defend its own values? We shall see. The only thing we can say, for now, is that the disappearance of meaning is not an idea, but a fact, and that, for this fact, for this actively experienced nihilism, we are already paying the price.

6. On the meaningless
But that too is an idea. The disappearance of meaning is a fact but it is, still, an idea. And I am not even sure if this idea, this envisioning of war capable, without the least sense or reason, without anything at stake, of producing an infinite amount of devastation, is very easy to conceive of...Anti everything that Hegelianism has taught us about the economy of Evil in the world...

It is also anti-Kantian ... "There is no science of the individual," Kant insists...in view of which he appeals to a "new Kepler able to explain the universal laws of the historical evolution of humanity", in other words to give a meaning to what, at first sight had none...

Finally it is anti-Christian ...Doesn't the heart of the Christian revolution lie in the idea that there is no unhappiness, misery, suffering, war, that, if only you look carefully, doesn't turn out to be ad majorem Dei gloriam?...Wasn't hope given to men so they could have, in the words of Saint Irenaeus, the strength to wait for that moment of "divine pedagogy" where what one has known forever, which doesn't need, as in Hegel, to be revealed via work, labor, or dialectics, will be expressed that we never suffer in vain, since "God treats us like his son"?

It's an idea that goes counter to the essential part of the philosophical, theological, and political tradition of the West. It's a perspective that attacks from the rear the whole sedimentation of beliefs, conviction, self-evident facts, and instincts that, necessarily make up "common sense". And that's why it is at the very limit of the thinkable –that's why we find it so difficult to imagine this idea of a war for nothing.

Bernard-Henri Levy
War, Evil and the End of History.
2004, pp. 128-129

Hope 1.

Hope, however, is one of the strongest of motivating emotions. As a non-rational sentiment it has no interest in weighing the likelihood of success; it just adds more hope, that things will work out as hoped; that 'this time things will be different', that at the very strength of hope will itself surmount obstacles and alter realities.

A.C. Grayling
Thinking of Answers. Questions in the Philosophy of Everyday Life
2010, p. 65

Hope 2.

Hope is a human good. It is real, but it is not a physical reality, not a scientific fact, and not necessarily based on reason (although it is not antithetical to reason). It simply belongs to a different order of realities. We can argue that it is inherently wrong to intentionally destroy hope – which is what torture does. Torture makes the present reality of pain the only reality for the tortured person – the person becomes the pain. Consequently, no matter how much 'good' might be done by torturing a person, it is inherently wrong to do so. It's worth noting that we reach the conclusion of inherent wrongness by agreeing on a common 'good' – hope – and by agreeing that it is inherently wrong to destroy that 'good', and not by basing our arguments on moral relativity, nor by relying on an appeal to a moral authority such as God or religion.

Margaret Somerville
The Ethical Imagination: Journeys of the Human Spirit
2006, p. 236

Hope 3: Contemplating the essence of biological and spiritual growth.

Hope is for spiritual evolution what the instinct of reproduction is for biological evolution. It is the force and the light of the final cause of the world or, if wish, the force and the light of the ideal of the world – the magical radiation of the "Omega point", according to Teilhard de Chardin. This "Omega point" to which spiritual evolution is tending ... is the central point of the "personalising world". It is the point of complete unity of the outer and inner, of nature and spirit, i.e. the God-man, the resurrected Jesus Christ, just as the "Alpha point", the prime mover or the effective cause, is the Word which set in motion electrons, atoms, molecules, i.e. movement directed towards their association into planet, organisms, families, races, kingdoms.

[ ]

Now, the spiritual exercise of the seventeenth Arcanum is that of the endeavour to see together – "to contemplate" – the essence of biological growth (the agent of growth) and the essence of spiritual growth (hope), in order to find, or rather re-find, their analogy their intrinsic kinship and, lastly, their fundamental identity. For it is a matter of grasping the essence of the water which flows both in the obscure process of growth, multiplication and continuity in biological reproduction and in the clarity of the serene heights of hope. It is a matter, therefore, of coming to an intuition of water such as it is understood in Moses' account of the second day of creation, where God "separated the waters which were under the firmament from the waters that were above the firmament" (Genesis I, 7), and of understanding ("understanding") that the light which flows above consciousness and the instinctive drive which flows beneath consciousness are fundamentally the same thing – separated to act according to two different modes – namely water, which is the principle of growth and evolution, both biological and spiritual.

Anonymous [Valentin Tomberg], Robert A. Powell (Translator)
Meditations on the Tarot: A Journey into Christian Hermeticism
1991, pp. 472

A child refuses to stop seeking meaning

In rejecting Kant's account of reason as systematic, I do not reject his picture of reason as uncompromising. The adamant child who wants every question answered expresses something about the nature of reason...Reason's tendency to keep going until all its demands are met is relentless. Some will dismiss it as childish; others will shrink from it as potentially totalitarian. Caution is always in order, for all the alternatives are worse. The smaller the expectations of the rational, the less its demands of the real. Where reason's demands are too humble, it concedes all the terms to reality before the struggle begins.

The picture of reason as inherently systematic is fatal to any form of philosophy we will want to preserve. If the events that determined the twentieth century left contemporary experience fractured, any conception of reason that can be salvaged must reflect fracture itself... The analytic division of philosophy into areas of specialization...reflect a will to system grown embarrassed, not a rejection of it. Where experience was truly shattered, the pieces will never be neatly ordered again. They are pieces of a whole which reflects the fact that reason, if not a system, is still a unity. Ethics and metaphysics are not accidentally connected. Whatever attempts we make to live rightly are attempts to live in the world.

[ ]

Meaning is a human category, and must be won against a background. A life that was inevitably meaningful would defeat itself from the start. Between the adult who knows she won't find reason in the world and the child who refuses to stop seeking it, lies the difference between resignation and humility.

Susan Neiman
Evil in Modern Thought: an alternative history of philosophy
2003, p. 327,328

For study, reflection and conversation.

As I intend this anthology to become a resource for teachers, senior students and anyone interested in widening and deepening one's own world-view and the dialogue between us, I re-introduce the eightfold path of the Buddha, in a different translation, one of the many to be found. Perhaps a means to measure of what one has learned in the meantime and a preparation for a next round in the 'turning of the 'wheel' on the way to renewal.

right view
right choice
right speech
right attitude
right livelihood
right endeavour
right mindfulness
right contemplation

[Translated by Henk Bak, based on different sources]

3. Call for Renewal

Religion is a source of transcendence

John Esposito

Introduction

After the need for dialogue (Ch.1) and attention to difference as integral to religions' and spiritual philosophy's function as 'source of transcendence' (J. Esposito), (Ch.2), the call for renewal sounds well founded in thought, even if less audible in practice. An anthology like this seems to lend itself less to descriptive case-studies of actual instances of renewal, than to discursive considerations of what renewal would and should look like – i.e. in which areas, under which conditions, etc. The material gathered to highlight practical approaches in the areas of culture, economics and politics will be presented in the later chapters of this anthology.

There is, however, one area of renewal to be considered, that is essential and a common concern to all religious and spiritual cultures: the ways in which children are welcomed and received when they come to this earth with all the gifts of renewal they bring with them from where they come from.

Here a few texts that bring a new understanding of the nature of childhood, especially the human nature of its embryonic development, right from the moment of conception. Please note: texts on actual forms of welcoming and receiving children into this world, prayers, ceremonies, rites and education are to be found in Chapter 7.

New generations come with new gifts but also with new expectations, hence the lengthy quotations from Rabbi Zalman's passionate and articulate call for a new cosmology and a whole range of established disciplines of research, study and education and Jürgen Habermas's recognition of a lasting role for religions in modern society, amidst secularization, as a necessary context for any genuine and fruitful interaction and dialogue between secular and religious/spiritual world-views. On the strength of his appraisal I would suggest, that the term 'post-secular' doesn't do justice to Habermas's own diagnosis: the dynamics of renewal he suggests works both ways: as world-views both rationalism and religions need to play a role, without domination of either. As soon as rationalistic and religious approaches fight for domination (as now is happening in the Middle East and elsewhere), both become ideologies, fundamentalisms, i.e. thought-systems based on power and power interests.

Despite his positive appreciation and wealth of inspiring examples which Alain de Botton has gathered in his Religion for Atheists, the tone of his introduction betrays a sense of belligerence, in short: Christianity stole from tribal, Greek and Roman spiritual cultures, we atheists should steal them back. Aside from a lack of historical finesse, the claim has much to say for it and seems to point to a deeper level of spiritual resources, of study, knowledge and practice, that belongs to nobody but humanity as a whole. "C'est le ton qui fait la musique": a French saying that roughly translates as: "It is the tone that turns a tune into a melody', e.g. the tone of voice in speaking, or the tone of one's writing in a letter or book. A kind of 'resonance', for which arguing is deaf and blind.

I got the same feeling when reading Ulrich Libbrecht's Introduction to Comparative Philosophy. The English version, under the title Within the Four Seas (2007) is a condensation in one volume of what has been published in Dutch in four. When it comes to his philosophy of life's understanding of religion, the tone is perhaps a little terse, but the book as a whole is the result of a life's work, study and teaching at the Universities of Antwerp and Utrecht, a priceless wealth of knowledge, understanding and insight, pioneering a field of study that to my knowledge has seldom been explored so extensively and in depth. Reading Libbrecht's book, I realize that my approach to world-views as a philosopher has never been "comparative", but rather conversational or dialogical. I select and place texts next to text not to compare but to imagine and invite dialogue. And as an historian I invite readers also to pay attention to the dates of publication, which may suggest cultural contexts and may reflect stages in the development of consciousness. Libbrecht's warning against an economic development that makes us comfortable has an early pre-cursor in Ronald Knox's premonition of the consequences of the bomb on Hiroshima, shockingly quickly followed the one on Nagasaki.

A number of the selected texts in this chapter suggests that our time demands an uncovering of these hidden resources or deep structures. They might not anymore be the sole prerogative of religions and spiritual cultures, and were often – even within those religions – withheld from common access, hence the term 'esoteric' or 'occult', which then often identified with forbidden, dark, evil forces. And just as specialist areas of science require specialist training and degrees of mastery, so did and do those forms of hidden knowledge require specific training and degrees of initiation. In this respect modern science mirrors the much older esoteric training etc. Not in the sense of copying, but following the deeper underlying measure of any form of developing consciousness and skill. Like apprenticeships in crafts, arts and martial arts. As long as the term 'science' is commonly understood as 'physical science', based on number and measurement under controlled – 'purely' physical – conditions alone, I would prefer to call this deeper form of knowledge 'spirit knowledge'.

Rabbi Zalman explained to Margaret Crosby in an ABC radio interview, that religions are exoterically often in conflict, but esoterically very close. The difference being: that 'exoterically' one is told how to live, 'esoterically' one is shaper of one's own destiny. In Rabbi Zalman's colourful language: 'exoterically someone else is the boss, esoterically you are the boss'. This I understand to be a reference to our 'I Am', the Christ word that after 2000 years still hasn't been fully grasped as the core of being human, as 'spirit knowledge' and the wellspring of all ethics and morality, not confined to any religious/ spiritual/ humanist doctrine or command. The Ten Commandments and the Sermon on the Mount or the Sermon of the Turning of the Wheel, are written in the human heart, not just on stone or in books. It becomes increasingly likely that – from Rudolf Steiner's Ethical Individualism to Margaret Somerville's Ethical Imagination, from the Dalai Lama's call for an extra-religious foundation for universal ethics to the Blechsmidt/ zur Lippe finding that what is conceived in human conception is a human individual from the beginning – spirit knowledge outside the domains of religions or philosophies is here to stay.

Rationalists and atheist have access to this knowledge too, if they are prepared to practice what it takes in terms of respect, attitude and method. Without such training, people's judgements on spirit knowledge are based on the same kind of ignorance as judgements on the intricacies of –say – nuclear science, by people not trained in that field. And in both cases it is through the fruits that one recognizes the tree, whether one is a biologist or not.

Echoed by Marilynne Robinson's cry: "I miss civilization, and I want it back," Aboriginal cultures around the world, marginalized and disconnected, would still be able to play a crucial role in re-connecting humanity with its spiritual origin and nature as ever-present wellsprings of renewal. The short set of texts from David Mowaljarlai selected for this chapter does no justice to the depth and breadth of the spirit knowledge he has given and has had published as elder of the Ngarinjyn people in the Kimberley, Western Australia. Not only for Australia, but for the world. In this sense Mowaljarjai belonged in the same league with Rabinadrath Tagore, Mohandas Gandhi and Sri Aurobindo in India and Senghor and Wole Soyinka in Africa.

Where Aboriginal and Indigenous traditions have been broken and marginalized everywhere around the globe, especially the Hindu tradition and Shaivism in India must be the oldest unbroken traditions on earth. And their vitality and potential for renewal, which we also see in some forms of Buddhism, Judaism and Christianity, especially the Celtic ones, may confirm Habermas's sense, that religions are here to stay, especially as the only repositories of formative power inherent in their rituals, music, poetry and art.

Against the end of the 18th century 'Enlightenment' period, the philosopher Gotthold Ephraim Lessing confronted the 'positive' religions with their lack of enthusiasm for renewal through a universally accessible kind of knowledge. From a rationalist point of view. Lessing is best known for his Nathan the Wise, a play in which the claims of three monotheistic religions, as if only one of them has the truth, are challenged. A father gives each of his three sons a ring, giving each the impression that he is the only one to receive this ring with the power to make one loved. When after his death they start to fight over it, Nathan the Wise explains to them, that their fight proves that the original ring must be lost.

A century after Lessing, after an – arguably – intensely materialistic age, a fresh wind of spiritual, artistic and scientific renewal, blew through Western culture. In his novel The Man without Qualities, Robert Musil lets the protagonist look back from 1913, and marvel how twenty years ago it was as if one walking a quiet street turned a corner and was blown away by a strong wind, a new spirit that created new, unheard of, never seen, new forms in painting, architecture, dance, music, theatre, etc. as well is new access to spiritual experience and knowledge. Much of the latter was derived from contacts with the East, despite the fact that it was in the West that most pioneers of this spiritual renewal and universal knowledge were building on their own spiritual traditions and were bringing spirit knowledge up to the level of consciousness of our time through their own research. Masters like Peter Deunov in Bulgaria, Michael Aivanhov in France, Rudolf Steiner and Valentin Tomberg in Central and Western Europe were contemporaries of Rabindranath Tagore, Mohandas Gandhi, Krishnamurti and Sri Aurobindo in the East. And the East had been generously represented at the beginning of the first Parliament of World's Religions, held in Chicago 1893.

Mainstream culture and institutional religions have still to catch up and recognize, that with the rise of the individualized consciousness, the ultimate source of spiritual understanding and renewal is no longer the sole domain of institutionalized authority, scientific, religious, humanist or otherwise. Individuals, on the other hand, have now to equip themselves in what is required to carry and develop this individual consciousness and responsibility through education and self-education, exercise and practise, skills and virtues, alone and with others. Musil's human being 'without qualities' can no longer define and identify him/herself with what she or he 'has'. It is the being that one 'is' who counts. Whatever qualities one brings to this life or acquires in this life matter only so long as the one who says 'I' is in charge.

Digitalisation has taken over the world, removing humanity further and further away from the actual, un-(broken down and then)-reconstituted experiences of life. Virtual sensation has taken over from actual perception at a rate, that makes the environmental philosopher Klaus Michael Meyer Abbich note that: "we only notice the degradation of our environment when this happens at a faster rate than the degradation of our senses".

How far are our spiritual and religious cultures removed from actual, first hand sense experience? Not even the five commonly named senses are fully activated and developed, let alone the much wider range of senses that has actually been identified and the many more waiting to be discovered or re-discovered, a perceptiveness not only for physical realities, but realities of life, soul and spirit as well.

It seems now the task of religions and spiritual cultures, to uncover their overgrown wellsprings of originating truth, love and wisdom and speak again that language that resonates in all.

There is already a great deal of emphasis on 'deeds' rather than 'doctrine' and on many issues of social justice and environmental health religious and secular organizations work side by side for the common cause. Their underlying motive is more and more expressed in terms of "dignity" rather than "justice": against the dominant shift from the 'professional' to the 'managerial' approach - which is discrete, legal and which lends itself towards manipulation in the hands of professionals-in-power – towards the primordial, continual, inviolable, which connects all humans on a deeper, 'archaic', experiential level. "Dignity" does not only inspire us to bring each and all of us on the same level of respect and life conditions, but makes us also re-connect with higher and deeper levels of existence in ourselves and in the world of life, soul and spirit, ultimately to what is most sacred for us.

It is from the (re)discovery of those higher and deeper levels that new insights and new energies may arise, which may assist in transcending many, if not all, of the obstacles in the way of a humane, just and creative society, thriving on "natural prosperity" rather than struggling for "sustainable development".

This also means a shift from the dominant role of 'professionals' in our religious/spiritual cultures, to a more serving role, where the continuity of everyday life, experience and practice of all people resumes its primal, enlivening, leavening, renewing functions.

All life wants to renew itself and this happens in and through encounter. Thus, encounters within and between world-views may generate renewal (this chapter), and Simone Weil finds in nature's wisdom an example of finding order in a society, where nobody would ever be forced to 'sacrifice one essential obligation to fulfil another obligation that is just as essential'. (Chapter 6). The difference being, that what happens in nature on a certain level of consciousness, will have to happen in humanity on a much higher, perhaps yet unknown level of consciousness.

The notion of 'consciousness' itself seems to be stretched to the limit: 'scire' = to know and 'con-' = with: a knowing that knows its knowing, witness like in the old English word for con-science = 'inwit', an inner knowing, a being present to the knowing itself... Living memory, living awareness...even there 'encounter'. One faces oneself or not...How far are we removed from humanity facing itself as humanity? Nations facing nations, races facing races, cultures to cultures, states to states, economies to economies and – again – within nations and worldwide: facing economies, facing states facing cultures etc. right down to the tiny pockets of social life: encounters requiring an intelligence and wisdom on the level of a humanity that matches the intelligence and wisdom of nature's ecosystem: eco-sophy.

> *O mankind, We created you male and female, and made you into nations and tribes that you may come to know each other.*
>
> **Qur'an The Chambers. 49:1**

It is – perhaps – not too far off the mark, when in our time this 'that you may come to know each other' is extended to include humanity's recent development into economic, cultural and political domains: that they indeed may come to know each other, too. The living God may have guided humanity's evolution to a point where we may hear Him continue His Word saying: We have guided your evolution to a maturity, which allows you get to know each other as sisters, brothers, partners in nature, as equals and citizens of the world, and as fellow travellers on the way toward one's true self.

These considerations form the background of a very specific meditation at an ever-deeper level, when I meditate on renewal in the sacred site dedicated to Islam. Rather than meditating on a list of the 99 names of Allah, I like to encounter those names in the contexts where they arise in the Holy Qur'an itself, i.e. in encounters: God knows when humans cheat on orphans and widows, or in measuring their wares at the market; he gives his laws, especially for the protection of the poor, because he is merciful; and he demonstrates his superiority over all 'gods' through his creation. He is all-powerful. And following Prince Gazi's example, where he in his "Love in the Holy Qur'an" gathers all the names of God which speak of his love, so do I like to gather those names that speak of his power, his mercy and his knowing. And I meditate especially on a Sura that presents Allah as Light. For this verse has become for me a prime example of how an ancient word has the power to generate ever new understanding for every new generation to come.

An anecdote: In March 2016 a group of 25 people travelled from Trentham to three suburbs in North Melbourne. The first visit was to the new mosque in Brimbank, impressive, sober, modern and very welcoming. We received a detailed explanation of the way a building like this functions, and why. At question time a participant of the group asked: 'do you ever renew yourself?' To which the spokesman said: 'No. We have all that we need: the Qur'an, the Hadith, the 5 commandments'. This answer made me spontaneously get up and ask the question again: 'Is not the Qur'an' rich and powerful enough to bring new insights to new times?' or words to that effect. To which he answered: 'Yes. But I don't understand the young people of today. We have youth groups on Saturdays and we do try'.

Only much later I realized what made me get up and say what I said: it was this part of the sura 'Light' (24:35-39; translation Tarif Khalid):

> *The glass like a shimmering star:*
> *Kindled from a blessed tree,*
> *An olive, neither of the East nor of the West,*
> *Its oil almost aglow, though untouched by fire.*
> *Light upon Light*
> *God guides His light whomever He wills,...*

For years now, my meditation at the Islamic sacred site at Evera, in Trentham, has been focused on Allah as the One and Only God, convinced that the nature of this oneness is not akin to the nature of a monolith or solid rock. His infinite power, mercy and knowledge must be alive, not only towards the world and humanity but also within Himself, masculine nor feminine or – perhaps – divinely feminine and masculine as One: Oneness alive in an eternal, self-renewing – self-loving – self-knowing dialogue, inner life overflowing into creation, manifesting Itself as All-Knowing – All-Merciful – All-Powerful to humanity and the world.

This is not Islamic teaching, but a non-Muslim's tentative and hesitant intimation of how renewal might come about: the Holy Qur'an as an inexhaustible source of renewal, for me embodied in this 'shimmering star', this 'oil almost aglow', this 'Light upon Light', like a stammering expression of divine inner 'light, love and life'.

Similar and other experiences and intimations are to be gained likewise at other sites. And interfaith conversations may enrich them and bring new life to the institutions in which world-views are embodied. In a second set of three chapters dealing with the Golden Rule (Ch5), the relation between religious, spiritual ideals and economic, ecological realities (Ch6) and –in chapter 7, a selection of texts on some of the many integrating issues, such as stages of life, childhood, food and gratitude. But in between those two sets of chapters, there is a chapter that places experience, perception, observation at the centre of the collection.

The selection of texts is based on relevance for the theme, not on personal opinion, although it remains a personal choice. There is always a question of discernment, first for author/compiler who makes the choice and then for the reader to consider…For example my decision to include two texts by Fetullah Gülen, who was introduced to me as a poet and a mystic. Having included in chapter 6 the Declaration of Marrakesh of 2016, an authorative call for clarity from Muslim scholars gathered in Morrocco, I feel it's only fair to include some of Fettullah's writing as well. Perhaps less a scholar than an eloquent preacher, he has a large and influential audience, mainly through schools. This chapter 3 is about renewal and in this respect I feel Gülen's is either problematic or at least enigmatic in a way that the Declaration of Marrakesh is not. Recently I had the chance to check with Assoc. Prof Salih Yucel, who teaches Islamic Studies at several Universities and has written a book on Gülen. He assured me that Gülen had always been controversial, but that there is apparently nothing to worry about. Here I have made my choice and leave it to my readers to consider…

Even though science is based on 'observation' and 'thought', our modern sciences are driven by thought, controlled experiments, and statistics rather than full live experience and a comprehensive developed 'sensorium'. Our common universally human – integral – science doesn't only need dialogue in intellectual, academic and scholarly terms, but in experiential terms as well: involving all our senses, not just the ones that lend themselves to calculations and formulas and not just the physical ones. Life, soul and spirit, feet, hands and heart have their own ways of knowing and renewing. This middle section turns out to be the shortest chapter in the book but is in fact underlying all other selections in as far as they are genuine and not just abstract theories.

And by far the greatest expression of experience is to be found outside the scope of this book: King David played the harp and danced his heart out before the arc of the covenant, Lord Shiva is the great cosmic dancer. Nietzsche thought that humans should become great dancers, if they aspired to create a star. I don't know whether the prophet himself was a dancer, but the Sufis certainly are. Jeshua danced with his disciples and Christian churches still maintain some forms of inspired and inspiring movement in processions, especially in the South of Europe and America, and even in places like Echternach in Luxemburg. These and other forms of spiritual and religious art need to be remembered and re-appraised when we move in our dialogue to include religious, spiritual and mystical experience as a primal source of renewal.

Another opening towards renewal is the notion of 'repeated earth lives' as a possibility outside any form of argument or teaching. As Tomberg puts it: one doesn't teach that the person who wakes next morning is the same as the one who went to sleep the night before. One knows from experience. When people know from experience that they have been here before, they know. They can be deluded by their experiences, but so can people who wake up and take their dream world with them into the new day. A reality check is always in order; by suppressing genuine experiences of past lives, established religions and scientific disciplines have reduced the potential human life span to the duration of a physical embodiment, which – perhaps for good reason – has interrupted an age-old sense of continuation beyond conception and death. It might be time to make this possibility a theme of our conversations. In his book 'Give Judas a Chance' Pietro Archiati gives in the chapter that bears the books title a lively description of the way – when teaching in South Africa – his African students spontaneously improvised a play in which God Father was challenged by Mother Mary on behalf of Judas:" having only one chance was honestly not fair". The rest of the book is full of arguments set in stories, imagined or told out the author's own experience (Spiritual Science Publication 1999). Perhaps one needs imagination to overcome the century long suppression of what people, especially children, have experienced all along, but were not allowed to tell or quickly learned to keep silent. And that, when one of the clearest thinker of the Age of Enlightenment had already claimed: "is not eternity mine!" Lessing was writing this on the basis that the human being's potential for evolving is much too strong and versatile to be exhausted within the span of a single life on earth. To come to where we are now we must have gone through many times and places, and have learnt from them, other than just this one. Even after the time spent in this life, the human being can be aware of his or her own potential for further learning and development in a future life. Lessing doesn't base his conviction on experiences from a past life, but on the experience of the overflowing potential that this one life has to offer. His perspective is oriented towards the future, not the past. The 'education of humanity' wants to continue into the future. And he is resolved to once again be part of it. There is no way to 'prove' individual existence before conception and after death, just as there is no 'proof' that the one who wakes up is the same as the one that went to sleep. The continuity is carried by the one who says 'I'. Body, life and soul is what one has, spirit is what one is.

I find myself elaborating on this subject, wondering whether I am the 'convener' or 'participant' in this part of the dialogue. In my – limited – experience as convener, I have found that the theme is easily brushed aside, presumably because it doesn't fit in our modern world-view, religious or otherwise. At one occasion I made the mistake to suggest – apparently prematurely – that the possibility of pre-existence before conception would help us to adequately receive a child into this world, it was rejected out of hand, without a moment of even considering the thought. Hence, perhaps, my concern that such a theme be sufficiently elaborated upon, before being introduced into the dialogue. Where the need and call is for renewal, this theme would need to be addressed rather than brushed away.

Something radically new asks for a new language, words, grammar, semantics, etc. In the last chapter we saw Jean Gebser introduce the word 'aperspectival' and differentiate it from a range of similar terms. We need old language to create the new. In this chapter on renewal I continue to quote him, to show how he considers this asperspectival consciousness as underlying most, if not all, of the processes of renewal in our time. It challenges the very notion encapsulated in the words 'world-view'. Since the Renaissance

Western culture has placed the individual as the point from which to view the world: visually as the point from where our vision vanishes in space, i.e. where all the lines in a three-dimensional picture come together, metaphorically as our 'view-point', logically as the 'premise' of our syllogism etc. Gebser pointed out that the earlier stages of consciousness: magical, mythical and rational don't disappear with this new, aperspectival, stage. And each chapter is full of examples of those different stages forming a rich mosaic of world-views, or rather glimpses of them, and a mosaic is richer the more its little fragments are catching the light differently…In this sense chapter 2 is an exercise in this new consciousness. 'Comparative philosophy' or 'comparative religion' would be 'perspectival': every element would be measured against a scale of 'less and more', or 'further and closer' etc. Chapter 3 would be an apersectival consciousness in action: in a dialogue, world-views do not lose their perspectival (rational), mythical, or magical primal structures, but they now function in a space wide and deep enough for them to resonate with other world-views. It takes courage to enter a dialogical space and it takes a generosity of spirit to generate a harmony for humanity at large, to allow a 'common word' to resonate in all of us. Our aperspectival consciousness rediscovers mythical and magical narratives and images, energetic, dynamic, in all indigenous and aboriginal cultures around the world and all so-called higher civilizations. Modern arts feed on them, new 'spiritualities' often quarry and exploit them, the sciences marvel at their levels of insights and sophistication, or steal their knowledge of medicinal powers in plants etc. An aperspectival consciousness implies a dialogue that includes the sciences and the arts – most of which is beyond the scope of this anthology.

The reader will discover that Gebser's intimations foreshadow those of Rabbi Zalman Schachter- Shalome half a century later and much else besides. Gebser calls this new consciousness: 'integral'. So does his contemporary Sri Aurobindo. Recently Shin Gwydiion Fontalba introduced the term: 'integral learning'. From all this I have learned to move from my notion of 'homo cardinalis', from the way I tried to characterize the new consciousness (which should govern the structure of University Education), to a notion of 'homo integralis': looking back over the more than sixty years since I wrote 'Studium Generale' report in 1960, (see My Story) I realize that my world-view has seldom prevented me from becoming wider, deeper and richer through interacting with people, especially students, from different world-views, through reading, through meetings, hints, whatever…and I learned (through this study) that 'resonance' is a key to integration at an aperspectival level. My view can still be focused on one point, but it can no longer be hemmed in by blinkers, the visible world has become round, surrounding me. Like the experience I had as a fruit picker in a huge tree full of plums: up the ladder and half immersed in leaves and plums myself, I gradually started to pick fruits that were fully out of sight, on the other side, but my hands knew, where to find them…There is a visual 'resonance'. What Cézanne, Picasso, Mondrian and Paul Klee and numerous others have done to make each of us see the world differently, And in education this doesn't mean, however, that educators should do the integrating for their students.

This need for open space and unhurried time is, at this chapter's end, reinforced by a philosopher of science and a neurobiologist, who both became urgent, radical renewers beyond their field, when faced and shocked by the current state of humanity in their self-created world: the experience of this confrontation will be one of many that are chronicled in the chapter that follows next.

Texts

The author (G.E. Lessing) has therefore seated himself on a hill, from which he believes to oversee somewhat more of the road than is prescribed by his present day. But he doesn't call any hasty traveler, eager to reach his destination for the night, away from his path. He doesn't desire, that the vista, that fills me with delight, should also delight the eye of anyone else. And thus, I thought, one could let him stand still and be astonished where he stands and wonders. Would that he offer only a hint – out of the immeasurable space, neither fully veiled nor fully revealed by a soft evening red – to something that has escaped me so often.

What I mean is this.

Why don't we – in all positive religions – prefer nothing more than face up to the one and only course along which the human intellect everywhere ought to be able to develop and evolve even further; rather than just smile and get angry by the thought of such? This our scorn, this our unwillingness, there is nothing in the best of worlds that would deserve this: and only the Religions should deserve this? God would play his hand in everything, only not in our mistakes?

Gotthold Ephraim Lessing
The Education of the Human Race
1780
[Foreword translated by Henk Bak]

Creative power of religions

The general public knows and lives the creative truths of a religion or culture always at the level of the general public, i.e. it knows and lives - in a distant periphery thereof – often only a dangerously hollowed-out interpretation of the same. It is clear that its 'truths' that are the first that are being compromised and jettisoned. And it is equally clear, that what has been - for centuries – the creative power of a culture always represents infinitely more than what a periphery can lose in times of crisis.

There is, however, still something else. Buddhism, Shintoism, Confucianism have – for centuries long – been able to nourish the human being in Japan, not only a spiritually uneducated, spiritually less hygienic general public, but more significantly, a spiritually creative minority and this in the first place, and this with the best qualities of its humanity. Everything that

Japan has brought forth during its history as cultural, i.e. spiritual, moral, intellectual and artistic formative power, the whole of this doubtless uncommon achievement, has been brought forth by these great religious movements, through the creative forces which they, in an elite, were capable to initiate and to awaken and – for centuries long – to keep nourishing. This in itself is already reason, why it should not be much of a foregone conclusion, that these life-sources would suddenly have dried up forever, or be incapable of still appealing to the best in the human being.

But there is more. The eastern religions, Buddhism, Hinduism, are essentially redemptive religions, not primarily sacrificial and devotional religions or primitive magical rites. They point a way which guides the human being here and now – and for the here and now towards inner freedom, an inner redeemed life. And they redeem in actual fact the human being very deeply and very beautifully. When India says that it possesses a "divine revelation, and a revelation just as intimately interwoven with its history and its being as was the revelation for Jewish people in Israel" 1) and adds to this: "the authoritative interpreters of this revelation have never found it failing in the fruits of grace and of redemption." Then, however much one want to play down this word, one finds herein not only confirmation of Koester's statement…regarding "God's all-embracing testimony active in these religions", but also ground for seeing in the experience of an inner redemption the explanation of the fact that the religions of the east have remained capable for centuries of nourishing a spiritual minority in the best of its humanity and to elevate ever and again to such undeniably sublime heights of moral and spiritual life, and to bring forth religious cultures of such great devotion, beauty – and profound divinity. All this which without doubt may be called the upper reaches of human existence and 'natural religions', is not possible if the religiously lived truth is not in one way or other a deep and truthful response to the human being's essential questions regarding human existence and if it not in one way or other stands guard for 'imperishable light-traces' of an imperishable divine truth. It is very well possible, that these religions are temporarily - at a turning point in history – at a loss for a response to the questions and problems thrown up by new revolutionary life-consciousness - (Christianity knew and knows this powerlessness as well, with all the disastrous consequences thereof) – it is not in the least to be taken for granted that they, after having given such most high proof of abundant creativity and vitality, should lack the capacity to renew themselves in their own right.

[Then follow as examples: in India, Ramamohan Ray, Ramakrishna, Vivekananda, Gandhi, Rabindranath Tagore,

*Aurobindo and in Japan the City of Kyoto and the philosopher
Nishida Kitaro (1870-1945) and the monastery Myoshinji]*

Henri Bruning
Vormkracht en Onmacht der Religie Missionair Christendom
1961, pp. 92-93

*I want to overhear passionate arguments about what we are and what we are
doing and what we ought to do.*
*I want to feel that art is an utterance made in good faith by one human being
to another.*
*I want to believe that there are geniuses scheming to astonish the rest of us,
just for the pleasure of it.*
I miss civilization, and I want it back.

Marilynne Robinson
The Death of Adam: Essays on Modern Thought
2005, p. 4

*God help us with ideas, those thoughts which inform the way we
live and the things we do. Let us not seize upon ideas, neither shall
we hunt them nor steal them away. Rather let us wait faithfully for
them to approach, slowly and gently like creatures from the wild. Let
them enter willingly into our hearts and come and go freely within the
sanctuary of our contemplation, informing our souls as they arrive
and being enlivened by the inspiration of our hearts as they leave.*

*These shall be our truest thoughts. Our willing and effective ideas. Let us
treasure their humble originality. Let us follow them gently back into the
world with faith that they shall lead us to lives of harmony and integrity.*

Amen

Michael Leunig
The Prayer Tree
1994

*Wherever there is life there is movement and growth. Wherever life
manifests itself we have to be prepared for surprises, unexpected changes,
and constant renewal. Nothing alive is the same from moment to moment.
To live is to face the unknown over and over again. Life requires trust.
We never know exactly how we will feel, think, and behave next week,
next year, or in a decade. Essential to living is trust in an unknown
future that requires a surrender to the mystery of the unpredictable.*

*At such time of ours, in which everything has become unhinged and there
is little to hold on to, uncertainty has become so frightening that we are*

tempted to prefer the certainty of death over the uncertainty of life. ...

Henri Nouwen
Peacework: Prayer, Resistance, Community
2014, p. 65

Ever present origin as ever present wellspring of renewal.

Origin is ever present. It is not a beginning, since all beginning is linked with time. And the present is not just the "now", today, the moment nor a unit of time. It is ever-originating, an achievement of full integration and continuous renewal. Anyone able to "concretize", i.e. to realize and effect the reality of origin and the present in their entirety, supersedes "beginning" and "end" and the mere here and now.

The crisis we are experiencing today is not just a European crisis, not a crisis of morals, economics, ideologies, politics or religion. It is not only prevalent in Europe and America but in Russia and the far East as well. It is a crisis of the world and mankind such as occurred previously only through pivotal junctures – junctures of decisive finality for life on earth and for the humanity subjected to them. The crisis of our time and our world is in a process - at the moment autonomously – of complete transformation, and appears heading to an event which, in our view, can only be described as a "global catastrophe." This event, understood in any but anthropocentric terms, will necessarily come about as a new constellation of planetary extent.

We must soberly face the fact that only a few decades separate us from that event. This span of time is determined by an increase in technological feasibility inversely proportional to man's sense of responsibility – that is unless a new factor were to emerge which could effectively overcome this menacing correlation.

Jean Gebser, Noel Barstad and Algis Mickunas (Translators)
The Ever-Present Origin / Part One: The Foundations of the A perspectival World
(1949) 1989, p. xxviii

The second part of my 'Ever-present Origin' is the attempt to answer the question: What is to come? At first glance it may be seen that this is only a question about the future, but in fact it is primarily one about our present situation. The events of tomorrow are always latently present today...

[ ]

Thus it is not a question of analysis or diagnosis, nor even of prognosis, but rather a matter of discerning in the manifestations of our age in what respects they differ from those of earlier epochs. I have called such new or novel manifestations 'aperspectival' because one of their characteristics is that they are neither unperspectival or perspectival; rather they are free of that form of thinking which, since the Renaissance, has characteristically been aimed at some goal or telos and bound to space...

[ ]

...This examination has extended over nearly twenty years and has included the forms, statements and expressions of the natural sciences, the humanities, and the arts. Only by demonstrating, which I believe to have done, that in all of these areas there is a common (and for the most part hidden) concern, would our discerning have a binding character. Thus the attempt had to be made to examine not only contemporary physics and biology, but also present-day jurisprudence and sociology, even interdisciplinary and dual sciences such as quantum biology, psychosomatic medicine, and parapsychology, and of course the principal arts —architecture, music, the pictorial arts, and literature... p. 277

Jean Gebser, Noel Barstad and Algis Mickunas (Translators)
The Ever-Present Origin / Part One: The Foundations of the Aperspectival World
(1949) 1989, p. 277

The Challenge of the New Millennium

Besides the challenge of past history we also face the challenge of the present millennium. This era is empirical, experiential, humanistic, multi-optional, fluid, mystical; it is existential, integrative, ecumenical, aware of nonverbal dimensions, with a view of God that is radically immanent, while at the same time utterly transcendental, non-anthropomorphic, and apopathic. Instead of being particularistic in regard to salvation and the conditions that make for it; it is universalistic and non-institutional; heuristic and empirical. This view takes most seriously "by their fruits ye shall know them," and the fruits are manifest in the realm of better human living and interaction. It demands to see the fruits in better and more harmonious relationships, and to see a consciousness that is higher, more integrated with the physical, multidimensional, centered, and ecologically aware. The new humanism wedded to trans-personal psychology has challenged all of us by presenting a viable and deeply religious option to the Bible religions.

Here, too, we make some acts of faith. I believe that there is something in Judaism that is in some sense closer to the divine intent than even the best that modern psychology can produce. At the same time I maintain that Judaism without holistic modern psychology will be farther from the divine intent than psychology alone. We three can meet the challenge of psychology most significantly in the field of spiritual direction, Tarika, Musar, and Kabbalah. About these things we must talk with one another from real live experience, not only from books.[ ]

Whenever a religion refuses to renew itself, it finds itself without adherents. How do we steer the course between removing all the surface tensions between religions, thus losing what is special in each, and the building of concrete walls between us? Perhaps we need to explore this again and, after exploring, reformulate our teachings on the differences of our religions. Let us each look at the teachings concerning the status of the adherents of our sister faiths.

The Emerging Cosmology
Rabbi Zalman Schachter-Shalomi
[Excerpt from an Unpublished Manuscript]

Balancing educating the mind with educating the Heart

The problems we face at this time don't seem to yield to the solutions our traditions and lineages have provided. Each of them had, built-in a high degree of surface tension and saw itself as sharply separate from others. Often universalistic statements were made which in subtle and not so subtle ways where what people call inclusivistic: that is to say "If you come under our umbrella, as a lesser adjunct, or a minor satellite, we will legitimate you." Still the attitude was basically triumphalistic; when the Mashiach – Christ – Madhi – avatar – Matreia – comes, we will be proven right, and you will end up to be on a lesser plane than we.

Then came Auschwitz – Hiroshima-Nagasaki – the moonwalk – the internet; and now we can no longer afford any reality-map that does not base itself on an organismic view of life on this planet. Our traditional theologians, in order to defend themselves against existential terror and high anxiety the spiritual vacuum in which they have to preach - have by and large been co-opted by those haves, who have the deep pockets to hold on to the status quo - or by the have-nots who want to return to implausible security of the old time religion.

More and more have deep thinking eco-theologians come to the conclusion that each religion is like a vital organ of the planet and that we for the planet's sake need, each of us, to aim to stay alive and devout in the most healthy way we can manage. Hence for all my universalism, I still need to be the best and healthiest Jew I can be and urge my co-religionists to become the best and healthiest Jews they can be in order to contribute to the healing of the planet. While I have gained much help from our tradition which provided me with the sacred tools and the means to higher consciousness, many of them seem not to be immediately applicable to our current situation.

However, there is clearly a revelation coming down to us from helpers above our ken, as well as a chthonic[2] push up from below, from our mother the Earth. This leads me not so much to offer answers as to raise questions. Therefore my contribution will be to raise questions and they are all intertwined.

As each generation comes it needs answers for the problems which the old answers have created. Example, nuclear fuel, pesticides and herbicides - soon we will also have to deal with questions which genetic engineering is creating in bio-engineered plants and who knows how soon? Even with human genetic stock. The urge we experience to grow in awareness is often blocked and opposed by forces that want to cut us off from that urge and addict us to mind deadening distractions. Yet, at meetings like this one, we want to amplify that urge that has the push of our earth's need of healing as well as the pull of the vision of organismic health that wants to birth itself in us. Here we want to wake up ourselves and wake others up to even more awakedness.

We have become habituated to find the easiest and the most immediate answers so that we do not have to stay in the anxiety of holding on to the question. The answers, easily available, don't work to stave off the impending disaster of our accelerating global dying. So what are some of the questions?

First: What ideas of Cosmology do we have in order to approach the healing of the planet. Apparently, the reality-map we have at this time is not correct. Our sense of the direction to which the possible harmonious life-matrix points, demands, that we change that map. Creativity does not reside in the way we are imprisoned to repeat precedent. It is in daring – to be outrageous, to play with the least probable possibilities, the ones more weird and spiritual where we may find answers. These possibility-forms dance before the mind's eye, and from that vision will emerge an unexpected form with its creative proposal and therefore new way to understand and map reality. We need to learn this process of questing in order to discover— and this is urgent— to co-create, with the integral planetary mind – the cosmology we have to have in order to approach the healing of the planet.

Secondly: What is the basic health ethos arising from that new cosmology? The cosmology of the industrial revolution gave us an ethos to productivity at any cost. The cosmology of corporate capitalism and globalization pushes an ethos to consumption at any cost. The cosmology we seek to find should produce, first and foremost, an ethos that honors harmonious biological health in the individual and in the matrix of the most harmonious biological health of the environment. In order to co-create this cosmology, we can no longer rely on a single mind. The complexity and with it the responsibility of what we have to mind in the world and in life is too great to bear for only one person. The only way to get it together is together. I plead for research that would discover what it takes to enable us to operate in webs of consciousness, in mind networks. At least for a small group of prepared minds to seek to merge dreams and behold visions. These people would serve as our psychonauts and contact minds on other regions. We are quite underdeveloped in this area. We have very low ideas how groups really work. While there is immense sophistication in the technological area of military systems and lethal Weapons of Mass Destruction, we are very low in understanding but our understanding of how we need to handle conflict resolution. We need to explore and develop much research needs to be done to help us achieve optimal social and political harmony and this cannot wait.

What do we need to do in order that there be that cultural revolution that is now urgently needed? I have often challenged educators to plan the curricula for handling information with ecological wisdom, for the formation of character, for education of the heart, for raising the emotional IQ, for teaching skills of cooperation that would produce the Adepts, saints, Zaddikim, rishis, bodhisattvas and shamans which we will need at this time.

Third Question : What are the upaya, the 'skill-full means', needed to lift our cultural trance, and to launch the awareness of the emerging Cosmology?

Current consensus mind leads us to ever-greater crises. We must do the miraculous work of altering millions of people's awareness. We must go deeper and deeper into regions where we cannot use muscle-effort, which is of no use, where only awareness can shift awareness which as one of my friends remarked is changing the tires while the car is – moving fast! We need so to update the inner resources of our spiritual traditions, the 'technologies' that once worked well but which were associated with flesh-rejecting monastic Asceticism. If our suggestions for spiritual study and practice exceed 20 minutes in the morning, and 20 minutes in the evening I will not do them and the old traditions demand more time than I can afford.

So we need to look at what still works among the old techniques and enhance their yield by learning to attune our consciousness to achieve the optimal transformational power. These actions take place in other than the mind of the shopping mall. When I think of the turbulent mind-space we inhabit at this time I get close to schizophrenia. I can't hear the sacred, choral-symphonic music of a sacred common dream. Just as some people once lamented the 'twilight of the gods,' so it seems that we now experience the 'twilight of the life-affirming archetypes!' How can we access them? How can we empower them? How can they empower us?

We need have come to realize that we are not on the top of the chain of being. What do we, as spiritual people, have as means to access the waiting helpers from higher planes? What do we need to do to address the matrix of the great life-process on the subtle plane to gain understanding of the deep life-process? Only then can we embark on designing the needed education of heart and spirit. Last: What adjustments in psychology, anthropology, biology, physics medicine, philosophy, political science, theology, spiritual technologies, economics, the arts, communications and most of all, the ethics, in order to heal the planet?

So the big questions remain. The current state of the disciplines of Transpersonal Psychology and Transpersonal Sociology is too primitive to handle our crisis. You who are here, my colleagues in the dais, as well as you in the audience I invite you to help find the answers to the questions we raised. We need to relearn the technology of blessings.

May the people who organized this event, the people who contributed with effort and finances, may we who spoke and you who listened be blessed with energy, vigour, resourcefulness, joy, health and well-being, harmony in your family and work-life, to actualize our renewed hope. May the words of my mouth, and the concerns in our hearts, be received and responded to by the One in whom we find refuge and redemption.

Amen.

> An address given at the Roundtable Dialogue for the visit of His Holiness the 14th Dalai Lama with other Nobel Laureates in Vancouver, B.C., entitled "Balancing Educating the Mind with Educating the Heart," held at the Chan Centre for the Performing Arts, on Tuesday, April 20, 2004.

(This is the text as it appeared on Rabbi Zalma's website after the event. It was later edited by Netanel Miles-Yépez)

The nineteen sided light pyramid

All roads must get narrower when reaching higher. Only together, yet multi-coloured, can the great problems be solved and the important tasks fulfilled.

Shin Gwydiion Fonalba.
Imbolc (Celtic) Festival Vevey Switzerland
Feb. 2012

How could this have happened?

When we studied together at a madrassa, Rashid Moosagie had a very low opinion of my politics. I was disenchanted by the academic, abstract nature of our curriculum at the Deoband seminary, some 100 miles from New Delhi, where I was enrolled in 1978; I desperately wanted the wisdom of my faith to help shape the world, and I had begun to lose myself in the writings of political Islam.

Rashid had just arrived to apprentice under some scholars after completing his religious education elsewhere, and he thought my notion of "applied Islam" was nonsense. The ideas I loved offered heady rhetoric but little substance, he argued. And eventually I came to agree with him that the madrassa approach, focused on tradition and piety, along with an infusion of new knowledge, was the best way to revitalize Islam. By that time, Rashid had become a successful imam in his native South Africa.

I was very confused to learn that, this year, Rashid immigrated to Syria and joined the Islamic State. He left Port Elizabeth with his wife, adult sons and daughter and parted with the circle of clerics in a city where he had served for more than 30 years. His brother Allie told a reporter that he is trying to persuade Rashid to return. In a letter he sent home and audio recordings I obtained from someone close to him who asked not to be named, Rashid claims it is theologically mandatory for a Muslim to migrate to a land where God's law is applied. "I am very happy here," he said. "Here I found what I missed all my life."

[ ]

How could this have happened? Islamic orthodoxy, which controls mosques and institutions worldwide, is out of step with the world in which the majority of Muslims live. In few places is orthodox Islam independent of the state; it is often a political tool used by authoritarian regimes, which explains why the Muslim intelligentsia does not respect it. Its hallmark is archaism in theology and ethics, and its reach covers most of the global community of faith. Once a robust intellectual tradition, today Islamic orthodoxy is in serious need of a makeover. Mainstream theologians who cater to the majority of lay Muslims, both Sunni and Shiite, are unable to address such critical moral and theological challenges as evolution, gender and sexuality, or the role and meaning of sharia in a modern nation. That's because theological education is steeped in ancient texts with little attention to reinterpretation.

[ ]

My old friend's new approach blends Salafism and millenarianism, a lethal combination. Salafism rejects any interpretation of scriptural sources. In this sense, Salafism is to sharia as formaldehyde is to a dead body. It prevents decomposition but also creates the illusion that the body is alive. But a sharia that truly lives would help Muslims adapt to a changing world.

[ ]

The Islamic State outlook does not threaten only groups like the Yazidis, Jews, Christians and Shiites. It poses an even greater threat to Islam. As long as mainstream Muslim authorities keep Islamic learning in formaldehyde, they make it easier for many more like Rashid to head for the violent apocalyptic theaters of the Islamic State in Iraq and Syria.

I don't doubt Rashid's sincere intention to live a pious life any more than I did when we studied together. But he was able to embrace the Islamic State as its lodestar only because Islamic orthodoxy has not offered a humane alternative.

Ebrahim Moosa
***Confronting the Problem with Islamic Orthodoxy**, Sydney Morning Herald*
October 4, 2015

Our magnificent position in the international balance of states: regression or renewal?

We are going through a strange period: light and darkness are intermingled, day and night move abreast; those drifting to death en masse are on the one side, and those reviving on another as if woken by the Trumpet of Archangel Israfil. Breezes of spring are wafting on one side, storms of total destruction rage on the other...

[ ]

We sometimes feel joy by ascribing the fortunate happenings to the extra blessing and special bounties of God Almighty, and sometimes we feel bitter in the face of various troubles and writhe in disappointment, as we see the crude behaviour of people whom we thought to be more mature than that, as we think about the coarseness and bigotry of the souls fixated on denial and unbelief, the faithlessness of friends, the peculiar attitudes of shoes who stand close but seem distant, and the continuous inconsistency of those who waver. How could a people whose past is so sound and whose spiritual roots are so splendid become such a society of contradictions with these warped thoughts and in this condition!

Unfortunately we were in a daze that was incompatible with our character and were unable to see what was happening. Every day we were debasing ourselves more and more and going through successive disappointments which affected the hue and pattern of our collective spirit.

[ ]

There came a time when all of those misfortunes totally upset our stance. Fissures began to appear in the spirit of togetherness and unity. Individuals in society were scattered like the beads of a broken string. The people were manipulated and society was polarized...what made it worse was the fact that the great self-sacrificing spirits with bleeding hearts through whom we hoped for a solution were muzzled.

[ ]

We have no right to complain about the present picture for sure. On the other hand, it is unthinkable for believers who care about their society to overlook what is happening. Unfortunately, with a distorted understanding which has its roots in the very distant past, we corrupted religious life just as we corrupted ourselves. And we sacrificed the spirit of unity to our whims. Instead of leaving matters of logic to our reason, and then turning reason in the pull of our heart and spirit towards sublime notions, thereby adorning our hearts with knowledge of God, we just turned our backs on our faculties such as insight (basira), will (irada), consciousness, feeling, cognition, and spiritual intellect (latifa al-Rabbaniya) and thus darkened both the corporeal and spiritual worlds... We just cannot manage to organize ourselves, focus on a single objective, in doing so turn to God wholeheartedly.

[ ]

Our collective nature and character seem to have become so deformed in recent years that now we are embarrassed to be ourselves; we turn our backs on the values that we held for several thousand years, and we deny – though not all of us – our own spiritual roots and historical dynamics. Instead of proclaiming our unfading magnificent historical heritage everywhere and letting everybody see its depths, we just listen to the disturbing growls of certain powers, and suffer from a certain sickness.

Since the day we lost our magnificent position in the international balance of states, the world has been run by unruly ones; the face of humanity has been entrusted to the unscrupulous. Everywhere, looters have been looking out for new targets to ransack. The blessings of the earth are in the hands of the ungrateful. The idea of right and considerations of fairness and justice are reduced to cries for help occasionally uttered by the wronged. The feeling of mercy and compassion has simply disappeared from hearts. Feelings of faith, loyalty, and trust have become blunted: and it seems that honor, dignity and self-respect are forgotten.

For centuries we have been oblivious to our most vital values and have turned our faces completely away from the centuries-long cultural heritage. Furthermore we have corrupted the minds of the young with foreign perspectives which do not suit us at all, but which we gathered from different corners of the world and attempted to use to replace our cultural and spiritual values. Now these young people, most of whom have become aimless, are condemning their own values, insulting the national spirit and thought, trying to destroy every part of the ancient inheritance and heading toward "nothings" in different lanes divided into so many factions. Despite of all this, the number of those who correctly see and interpret what is going on is not small. However, most of these just keep biting their tongue as if they were muzzled and they remain in silent contemplation.

[ ]

For years, no matter how sound its past was, society has been left squirming with its heart and mind detatched from each other; it can neither come up with a reasonable interpretation of the universe and what takes place in it, nor make a sound evaluation of social development. It just gapes around and is carried here and there on different winds. To tell the truth, this lack of direction seems likely to continue until the moment we come to ourselves and once again interpret the whole of existence, events, and ourselves correctly, and once more express ourselves through a new analysis synthesis. I wish we had been able to change this inverted course of fate!...

[ ]

...For years we have lived an unfeeling life. But considering the position of our people, we should have some stories from the heart to tell the entire world! In the world of the future, there should have been some colours from our looms of thought as well...

[ ]

It is still not too late; we have a world of opportunities before us. The number of those devoted to God is not small. I think all that is left to do is to seize the reigns in a firm grasp and set off with love and zeal, rely on God, knock on His door, open up in tears and say, "We have come". ...

M. Fethulah Gülen
Speech and Power of Expression / Chapter: A Blessed Region's Years of Alienation / On Language, Esthetics, and Belief
2010, pp. 77-82

Call for reinterpretation of the Qur'an

Although there are no historical connections between women in different parts of the Muslim world that make up this "movement", many – from Egypt, Jordan, Morocco, Sudan, Turkmenistan, Kazakhstan and Uzbekistan – have found in their faith not only a guide, but a powerful source of contestation. Many groups (which also include men) are calling for a reinterpretation of the Qur'an in hope of expanding what has been a rigid orthodoxical space for women. Their goal is gender justice. This "gender jihad" is a struggle, not against men, but for Islamic gender parity. This struggle binds women to the archetypal figures of the Qur'an – both male and female: In the face of hardship, they seek refuge in Him alone.

Hibba Abugideiri
George Washington University

Call for pluralism

In their cultural-religious progress, many Muslims today strive for pluralism, both inside and outside ummah. They seek to open up a broader spectrum of interpretations and practices considered Islamic, and epistemologically follow a pluralistic approach to the pursuit of knowledge and truth. While receptivity to dissent counteracts rigidity and dogmatism, familiarity with competing interpretations and different points of view, in fact, leads to flexibility and intellectual maturity. Perhaps the most exciting of the new emerging initiatives among Muslims is that progressives everywhere are seeking one another out, reading each other's work, cooperating with one another's organisations.

Dzavid Haveric
Islam and Pluralism within the West. A Collection of Essays
2014, p. 88

Raising Children with Qur'anic training

As a matter of fact, in a period when power is used as means of oppression and the truth is being violated, it is extremely important to remain on the straight path in terms of feelings and thoughts and to preserve the honor of being human. Therefore I believe that nurturing a generation with Qur'anic principles in education and training, enabling them to develop a Qur'anic moral value system, educating them to be loyal followers of God, and raising their physical, mental and spiritual capabilities to a level of unwavering resistance against formidable corruptive forces are among the most crucial steps in preserving our spiritual existence. One sees that the establishment of an ideal society, both in the world of conscience and senses, and in the real world is made possible only with the Qur'an.

[ ]

Understanding the Qur'an and its revival depends on deepening one's grasp of its core messages... The real issue in the context of our relation with the Qur'an is to feel it with all the dimensions of our self, approaching it with our hearts, our minds, our consciousness, and our comprehension. We feel and hear God's address and message through such an approach and in such a state of mind, and we can then experience a sudden revival. We can reach different depths in every word and in every sentence of a verse and reach the horizon where we witness maps of our spirits alongside maps of the heavens.

In my view, a new generation can only be formed in an atmosphere that is the same as the one described above; in the meantime a process of the formation of a "righteous circle" will begin. The Qur'an pours its secrets into our hearts, thus as much as we ascend from knowledge (science) to faith and from faith to wisdom with this richness, we also attain inner profundity as a result of the differentiation in the levels of becoming His addressee. We then attain such profoundness that we are able to comprehend the immensity of God's words in a distinct way. Primarily, the action-oriented and practical-axis based discipleship of the Qur'an is the only means to unravelling the message of the Qur'an... The core of the problem regarding the relationship with the Qur'an is about activating the whole human system that goes beyond knowledge. It is essential to execute whatever is learned from the Qur'an, according to the conditions, and atmosphere that one finds oneself in, by turning the acquired knowledge into a driving force. If this can be achieved, then human beings will find their place on the right track, one that is in accordance with the purpose of their creation and they will be able to avoid a disreputable extinction.

Upholding Sensitivity in Nurturing

Explaining a truth and installing a thought are one thing, while sustaining them is completely another. There have been numerous examples of ideals carefully executed and institutionalized. Although nothing is lacking in their foundations and in their day-to-day operations, neither has there been any progress, as no real attention has been paid to their development. Moreover some of these ideals and institutions are doomed to failure and have thus collapsed right at the time of their birth, due to bad management.

As a matter of fact, the construction of something is very important. However, ensuring the further development and continuation of whatever has been built is more important. The first Muslims were exceptionally careful to transmit all of the dynamics that keep a society alive in the community. They were also very cautious about the preservation of these dynamics and therefore they did not allow the emergence of logical, mental or emotional vacuums. They made no mistake about putting into practice what they believed. Here of course I am not referring to individual mistakes. I am referring to the fundamentals of a healthy society and those necessary for its survival. At a later period, some people, who had no grasp of the core of the matter and who approached Islamic issues from a single aspect only, radically destroyed what had been accomplished, and we have been unable to develop the historical legacy we inherited. In fact we have impoverished this heritage.

M.Fethullah Gülen

From Seed to Cedar: Nurturing the Spiritual Needs in Children
2014, pp. 108-109

Bahá'í New Culture

Though the Bahá'í Faith has very little in the way of public rites and rituals, a broader consideration of the usage of this term and the practices of the Bahá'í community into which a new convert needs to be acculturated invites further comment. Since about 1996, the whole Bahá'í community has been in the process of being reoriented toward a new culture or ethos. This new culture has not yet fully come into existence and so may more accurately be described as an ideal. But enough of it is in place in enough parts of the world to be able to characterize it. It does not contradict what is described above in that it does not replace or suppress local culture but rather can overlay this and indeed encourage it to flourish.

Among the features of this new culture is its orientation toward serving the wider community. Thus, Bahá'í institutions are introducing a systematic program of peer-mentored study circles that will give every Baha'i the skills to be able to institute such services as children's classes, junior youth groups, devotional meetings, and study circles. The range and complexity of these service activities is gradually being extended, and it is anticipated that they will become increasingly focused on the social and spiritual needs of the wider local community.

Another aspect of this new culture is that it is a culture of learning, where local groups of Bahá'ís come together at reflection meetings to consult about the needs of their community and the resources they have and then to draw up plans for local action. The experiences of other areas and guidance coming from the national or international level of the Bahá'í community are fed into this consultation process. Once the plans are made and executed, the whole community meets again to reflect on the successes and failures of the plan, studying what lessons are to be learned, and consulting about new plans of action.

There are several other features of the new culture that Bahá'ís are trying to create. One is the fact that there are no individuals in hierarchies of power in this culture. Authority and direction come from the elected institutions at local, national, and international level. However, it is the institutions that are authoritative, rather than the individuals in these institutions. The decisions made by these institutions are the result of a consultative decision-making process. Furthermore, except for extreme circumstances when an individual's behavior is threatening to cause divisions in the community or is bringing the religion into disrepute, power resides largely with the individual Bahá'ís. The institutions have the authority to lay plans of action before the Bahá'í community but they do not have the power to coerce Bahá'ís to carry out these plans. Initiative and the power to carry plans forward rest with individuals.

Another aspect of the new culture that Bahá'ís are trying to create is its openness. The Bahá'í culture aspires to be open to all of the positive aspects of every local culture. It also tries to be inclusive in the sense of welcoming anyone who wishes to cooperate with the Bahá'ís in advancing the social principles and carrying out local plans of action formulated by the community, without necessarily becoming full members of the Bahá'í community. The cluster meetings at which many of these plans are formulated are open to all. Furthermore, the Bahá'í community is willing to cooperate with any other organization that is advancing such plans, provided their course of action does not involve partisan political action (which Bahá'ís do not take part in because of its divisive nature).

Baha'i, Rituals and Worship, Religion
https://www.patheos.com/library/bahai/ritual-worship-devotion-symbolism/rites-and-ceremonies

Resurrection: source of renewal

There are Christians whose lives seem like Lent without Easter. I realise of course that joy is not expressed the same way at all times in life, especially at moments of great difficulty. Joy adapts and changes, but it always endures, even as a flicker of light born of our personal certainty that, when everything is said and done, we are infinitely loved. p.13

[ ]

Let us believe the Gospel when it tells that the kingdom of God is already present in this world and is growing, here and there, in different ways: like the small seed which grows into a great tree (cf. Mt. 13:31-32), like the measure of leaven that makes the dough rise (cf. Mt. 13:33) and like the good seed that grows amid the weeds (cf. Mt. 24-30). The kingdom is there, it returns, it struggles and can always pleasantly surprise us.

Christ's resurrection everywhere calls forth seeds of that new world even if they are cut back, they grow again, for the resurrection is already secretly

woven into the fabric of this history, for Jesus did not rise in vain.

Pope Francis
Evangelii Gaudium
2013, pp. 196,197

Secularization to gain access to sources of renewal

In giving up on so much, we have allowed religion to claim as its exclusive dominion areas of experience which should rightly belong to all mankind – and which we should feel unembarrassed about reappropriating for the secular realm. Early Christianity was itself highly adept at appropriating the good ideas of others, aggressively subsuming countless pagan practices which modern atheists and rearticulation. now tend to avoid in the mistaken belief that they are indelibly Christian. The new faith took over celebrations of midwinter and repackaged them as Christmas. It absorbed the Epicurian ideal of living together in a philosophical community and turned it into what we know now as monasticism. And in the ruined cities of the old Roman Empire, it blithely inserted itself into the empty shells of temples once devoted to pagan heroes and themes.

The challenge facing atheists is how to reverse the process of religious colonization: how to separate ideas and rituals from the religious institutions which have laid claim to them, but don't truly own them. For instance, much of what is best about Christmas is entirely unrelated to the story of the birth of Christ. It revolves around themes of community, festivity and renewal which pre-date the context in which they were cast over the centuries by Christianity. Our soul-related needs are ready to be freed of the particular tint given to them by religions – even if it is paradoxically, the study of religions which often holds the key to their rediscovery.

What follows is an attempt to read the faiths, primarily Christianity and to a lesser extent Judaism and Buddhism, in the hope of gleaning insights which might be of use within secular life, in particular in relation to the challenges of community and of mental and bodily suffering. The underlying thesis is not that secularism is wrong, but that we too often secularized badly – inasmuch as, in the course of ridding ourselves of unfeasible ideas, we have unnecessarily surrendered some of the most useful and attractive parts of the faiths. pp. 15-17

[ ]

Meditative walk: we become disinterested surveyors of our own existence

Later in the morning, we go outside for another spiritual exercise called a walking meditation, pioneered by the Vietnamese Zen monk Thich Nhat Hanh. We are instructed to empty our minds and wander the landscape without asking anything more of it than to observe it, freed for the moment of those ego dominated habits of ours which strip nature of its beauty and give us a misleading and troubling sense of our own importance in the cosmos. Under tutelage, we proceed at a camel's pace, our consciousness untroubled by any of our ego's customary ambitions or chidings – in a state as much prized by Buddhism as it is reviled by capitalism, and known in Sanskrit as apranihita, or aimlessness – and thereby become newly attuned to a thousand details of our surroundings. There is a shaft of sunlight filtering through the trees, in which miniscule particles particles of dust are dancing. There is the sound of running water from a nearly stream. A spider is making its way across a branch above us. Buddhist poetry is dominated by records of similar encounters with just such tiny facets of the world, which reach our senses only after our egos have loosened their grip on our faculties

> *Coming along the mountain path*
> *I find something endearing*
> *about violets.*

reads a poem by the Zen poet Basho. Working our way through the underground, we become disinterested surveyors of our own existence, and hence ever so slightly more patient and compassionate observers of the planet, its people and its small purple flowers.

The specifics of the exercises taught at Buddhist and other retreats are perhaps not as significant as the general point they raise about our need to impose more greater discipline on our inner life.

If the predominant share of our distress is caused by the state of our psyches, it seems perverse that the modern leisure industry should seek always to bring comfort to our bodies without attempting simultaneously to console and tame what the Buddhists so presciently term our 'monkey minds'. We require effective centres for the restoration of our whole beings; new kinds of retreats devoted to educating, through an array of secularized spiritual exercises, our corporeal as well as psychological selves. pp.256-258

Alain de Botton
Religion for Atheists: A Non-Believer's Guide to the Uses of

The centre needs to hold. Renewal needs to come from the field

Firstly I would like to state – as point of departure – that it is true, that the Church i.e. the clergy – is conservative. The work of moving forward comes principally, if not exclusively – either from laypeople or from the general world-historical situation. Certainly does the Church (clergy) recognize in time everything, that has shown itself as true and necessary, it happens always with a delay. This is how practically every time there is a stretch or zone of no-mans-land between the 'not yet recognized' on the side of the clergy and the recognized on the side of educated lay people. It takes an amount of time and the not-recognized is being recognized (e.g. the millions of years of earth evolution. It is how it is).

Now we ask ourselves, however, how this would be, if the church did not do this – if, in other words, she would be progressive? Then, two things would happen: firstly the collective strength, attentiveness and work of the clergy would not be dedicated to the redemptive truths, but to progress in their peripheral areas, so that the danger would indeed occur, that the redemptive truths – which after all have eternity value – can end up in the background, even being overshadowed by progress. Secondly the free life of progress would be made impossible for laypeople, because all new developments would be straight away added to the body of Church doctrine – and therewith irreparably crystallized.

We laypeople can endeavour to do research on our own terms – voice opinions of doctrine and then – after years – modify them or even withdraw. The Church cannot do that. She cannot take part yet another time in a 'copernican-pro-polemaean' controversy.

Progress is therefore the task of the layperson. You write, rightly so, I think, it is the duty of the layperson. Yes, it is our duty – and thousands and thousands of us take part in the further development of the sciences, the arts and social conditions.

Now there remains, however, one area, that is in need of progress: – the super-sensible, as you write, The super-sensible in the way it is found in Jungian depth-psychology, in parapsychology (hypnosis, suggestion, telepathy, clairvoyance), para physiology (Justinus Kerner, Prof van Rijnberk etc.) and is taught in certain metaphysical philosophies (e.g. Pythagorean, Leibniz,

Fechner), mystic teachings (yoga, Vedanta, kabbala, gnosis, Christian nature mysticism) and occult teachings (alchemy, astrology, magic, hermetic teachings, theosophy and finally also anthroposophy) is definitely not identical in meaning with the 'supernatural' of theology, nor with the 'supernatural' of natural science. That they all to a certain extent across a given - and as real experienced – border is obvious and is also expressly admitted by themselves. This 'super' as border to the super-sensible is not only admitted, but also often and from different points of view. warned against. So we find e.g. in the treatise Chagiga 14 b of the Talmud [ ] the following story: "Four scholars tried to enter into heavenly paradise, (i.e. the mysteries of divine creation). One, Ben Asai, lost thereby his life; the second, Ben Zouma, lost his mind; the third, Elisa ben Abuja, lost thereby – which is worse - the faith and only the fourth, Rabbi Ben Akiba entered happily and came back in good health."

This story, written down 18 centuries ago, contains two things: on the one hand encouragement, but on the other hand warning that the super-sensible is not without reason 'supersensible' and that crossing the border involves danger for life, for spiritual sanity and moral health – because the three scholars lost in turn life, mind and faith.

Elizabeth Heckmann and Michael Frensch
Valentin Tomberg: Leben, Werk, Wirkung Band 1.2, 1944-1973.
2005, pp. 273-4

Forgiveness as condition for renewal

If we turn to humanity's path of development in recent times, and especially to the history of the twentieth' century – perhaps the most painful and most tragic of the whole of mankind's earthly existence – we may come to realize the extent to which it is preoccupied with the problems of 'guilt'. In our century it has again and again been discussed in all its many aspects with the 'guilt' of one person towards another and ending with the 'guilt' of one nation with regard to another.

[ ]

In the great majority of the discussions .... there has generally been an almost total failure to take into account the counter-pole of the negative conception of 'guilt', namely the positive conception of forgiveness. This circumstance has been particularly associated with the fact that the problem of 'guilt' or 'innocence' is primarily a legal affair while that of 'forgiveness' is an ethical or moral question. Contemporary humanity is, in the present epoch of materialism and one-sided intellectualism, orientated to a considerable greater extent toward abstract legalistic concerns – both in social affairs and in individual conduct – than toward moral or spiritual impulses. In this sense the 'commandments' or 'laws' that are given to an individual or a social group form without play a far greater part in our society than do a person's own moral intuitions which, springing from the innermost part of his being, have their source in that stage of individual development which Rudolf Steiner, in his book The Philosophy of Freedom, *refers to as 'ethical individualism'.*

[ ]

It is this central need of modern man to reach also the moral impulses of human evolution through spiritual knowledge… pp. 3-5

[ ]

Thus in these following two German words, which both mean forgiveness, we find that the genius of language has given us an impression of both these principal characteristics of true forgiveness: verzeihen, the overcoming of the lower ego by the higher (self-overcoming), and vergeben, the total outpouring (self-giving) of the higher ego to the world! p. 76

[ ]

Plato (in the Menon) once called all true knowledge recollection (anamnesis). And if we consider the process of forgiveness from an occult point of view, this ancient truth can acquire for us an entirely new significance.

It is, of course, the case that in pre-earthly existence, a human being sets himself the most diverse goals and tasks with respect to his impending incarnation. Which of these does he recall in the first instance in the process of forgiveness? He initially recalls those which then come to manifestation in the act of forgiveness itself. Thus he recalls the need in earthly life for a continual self-overcoming and also… (an) outpouring of self into the world of love… p. 79

Sergei O. Prokofieff
The Occult Significance of Forgiveness
2004

Our not yet discovered capacities and their potential for renewal.

Human beings, even if we postulate a process of evolution, also possess a uniqueness which cannot be fully explained by the evolution of other open systems. Each of us has his or her own personal identity and is capable of entering into dialogue with others and with God himself. Our capacity to reason, to develop arguments, to be inventive, to interpret reality and to create art, along with other not yet discovered capacities, are signs of a uniqueness which transcends the spheres of physics and biology. The sheer novelty involved in the emergence of a personal being within a material universe presupposes a direct action of God and particular call to life and to relationship on part of a "Thou" who addresses himself to another "thou". The biblical accounts of creation invite us to see each human being as a subject, who can never be reduced to the status of an object.

Pope Francis
Laudato Si: On Care for our Common Home
2015, pp. 69-70

Even our known faculties need re-discovering: experience grounded in the body and developed through all the senses.

Needed are open and supervised places, where the visitor walking, sitting, lying, standing can converse with the elements fire, water, air, and with light and its colour-generating wrestling with darkness. Above the entrance of the temple of Delphi it stood carved in stone:

'Man, become what you are'
'Man, know yourself'
'Man, be'

What is needed is a new Delphi. Needed is the self-building of a Delphi. Whereby the experience becomes alive, then that building is the building.

[ ]

What the public needs are opportunities to converse meaningfully with the phenomena, through which the laws of polarity, symmetry, periodicity, magnetism are accessible for immediate bodily responses. Needed is such Delphi-like immediate equipment, to serve as study resources for the building of kindergartens, care centres, schools, buildings for healing, factories, offices, universities, and – not least – of housing in a form that works in accordance with life. Only the human being who lives out of the experience of the lawfulness of his or her own body is capable – on the basis of capacities thus gained – of instilling a lawfulness in the processes of world and earth that is demanded by this time in history.

It is an illusion to want to bring the world gone astray back into order with an attitude through which accidents of industrial technology get fixed. To this end the human being needs the awakening of the consciousness that is born into the needs of his/her body, that relates as effectively to the world and the earth as the organs and organic system of his/her physical nature between themselves.

[ ]

…What does make sense is the attitude of the man who knowing that tomorrow the world perishes, yet still plants a tree right now; brings his house in order; pays his debts. The attitude of such a man will – in as far as it is alive in an individual or in a community of individuals – take care to make arrangements in which all the needs subordinated to the bodily integrity of man are looked after. 'Looked after' in the double meaning of the phrase – of recognizing and safe keeping.

Hugo Kükelhaus, Rudolf zur Lippe
Entfaltung der Sinne: Ein Erfahrungsfeld zur Bewegung und Besinnung
2008, pp. 47-48

Ahimsa – nonviolence, restraint, stillness: the only means to realize Truth

My uniform experience has convinced me that there is no other God than Truth. And if every page of these chapters does not proclaim to the reader that the only means for the realization of Truth is Ahimsa, I shall deem all of my labour in writing these chapters to have been in vain. And even though my efforts in this behalf may prove fruitless, let the readers know that the vehicle, not the great principle is at fault. After all, however sincere my strivings after Ahimsa may have been, they have still been imperfect and inadequate. The little fleeting glimpses, therefore, that I have been able to have of Truth can hardly convey the idea of the indescribable lustre of Truth, a million times more intense than that of the sun we daily see with our eyes. In fact what I have caught is only the faintest glimmer of that mighty effulgence. But this much I can say with assurance, as a result of all my experiments, that a perfect vision of Truth can only follow a complete realization of Ahimsa.

To see the universal and all-pervading Spirit of Truth face to face one must be able to love the meanest of creation as oneself. And a man who aspires after that cannot afford to keep out of any field of life. That is why my devotion to Truth has drawn me into the field of politics; and I can say without the slightest hesitation, and yet in all humility, that those who say that religion has nothing to do with politics do not know what religion is.

Identification with everything that lives is impossible without self-purification; without self-purification the observance of the law of Ahimsa must remain an empty dream; God can never be realized by one who is not pure of heart. Self-purification therefore must mean purification in all walks of life. And purification being highly infectious, purification of oneself necessarily leads to the purification of one's surroundings.

Mohandas Karamchand Gandhi, Mahadev Desai (Translator)
An Autobiography: The Story of my Experiments with Truth
1983, pp. 452-453

Atheism as purification

There are two atheisms of which one is a purification of the notion of God.

Perhaps every evil thing has a second aspect, a purification in the course of progress toward the good, and a third which is the higher good.

[ ]

Religion, in so far as it is a source of consolation, is a hindrance to true faith: in this sense atheism is a purification. I have to be atheistic with the part of myself which is not made for God. Among those men in whom the supernatural part has not been awakened, the atheists are right and the believers wrong.

Simone Weil
Gravity and Grace
1997, pp. 167-8

Dialogue between secular and religious world-views: a source of renewal

Juergen Habermas Interviewed by Eduardo Mendieta

EM: Over the last couple of years you have been working on the question of religion from a series of perspectives: philosophical, political, sociological, moral, and cognitive. In your Yale lectures from the fall of 2008, you approached the challenge of the vitality and renewal of religion in world society in terms of the need to rethink the link between social theory and secularization theory. In those lectures, you suggest that we need to uncouple modernization theory from secularization theory. Does this mean that you are taking distance from the dominant trends in social theory in the West, which began with Pareto, continued through Durkheim, and reached their apogee in Weber, and thus also from its explicit and avowed Eurocentrism?

JH: We should not throw out the baby with the bathwater. The debate over the sociological thesis of secularization has led to a revision above all in respect to prognostic statements. On the one hand, the system of religion has become more differentiated and has limited itself to pastoral care, that is, it has largely lost other functions. On the other hand, there is no global connection between societal modernization and religion's increasing loss of significance, a connection that would be so close that we could count on the disappearance of religion. In the still undecided dispute as to whether the religious USA or the largely secularized Western Europe is the exception to a general developmental trend, José Casanova for example has developed interesting new hypotheses. In any case, globally we have to count on the continuing vitality of world religions.

In view of the consequences of which you speak, I consider the program of the group around Shmuel Eisenstadt and its comparative research on civilizations promising and informative. In the emerging world society, and concerning the social infrastructure, there are, as it were, by now only modern societies, but these appear in the form of multiple modernities because the great world religions have had a great culture-forming power over the centuries, and they have not yet entirely lost this power. As in the West, these "strong" traditions paved the way in East Asia, in the Middle East, and even in Africa for the development of cultural structures that confront each other today -- for example, in the dispute over the right interpretation of human rights. Our Western self-understanding of modernity emerged from the confrontation with our own traditions. The same dialectic between tradition and modernity repeats itself today in other parts of the world. There, too, one reaches back to one's own traditions to confront the challenges of societal modernization, rather than to succumb to them. Against this background, intercultural discourses about the foundations of a more just international order can no longer be conducted one-sidedly, from the perspective of "first-borns". These discourses must become habitual [sich einspielen] under the symmetrical conditions of mutual perspective-taking if the global players are to finally bring their social-Darwinist power games under control. The West is one participant among others, and all participants must be willing to be enlightened by others about their respective blind spots. If we were to learn one lesson from the financial crisis, it is that it is high time for the multicultural world society to develop a political constitution. p.1

[ ]

EM: In your manuscript "The Sacred Roots of the Axial Age Traditions", you offer us a sweeping and synoptic overview of anthropological and social theory in order to explore the relationship between myth and ritual. You set out to demonstrate that symbolic interaction has its anthropological roots in ritual practices. While you acknowledge the difficulty of acquiring archeological evidence for the priority of ritual to mythological narratives, you do seem to argue that the propositional dimensions of linguistically mediated interaction go back to the evolution of ritual, which, at the very least, we know antedates their symbolic representation in the form of cave paintings. Are you suggesting that before humans became Homo sapiens, we were Homo ritualis?

JH: You are referring to a chapter of a work in progress. In it, I resume an old theme in light of new investigations: the origins of language, that is to say, the use of symbols that have the same meaning for members of a collective. In the broad temporal periods of the evolution of Homo sapiens, our ancestors must have had this use at their disposal at, at the latest, the point at which groups organized their living together by means of symbolically generalized kinship relations -- that is, when they lived together in families. All parents, uncles, and children are assigned the same status as parents, uncles, and children. Since grammatical languages have a complex structure that -- pace Chomsky -- cannot have emerged overnight, today one rather (or, better: again) supposes a prior level of gestural communication that is not yet propositionally differentiated. And, apparently, the ritual practices we know from cultural anthropology belong to this level, even if they distinguish themselves from everyday communication between sender and recipient by means of their strangely circular and self-referential structure. Thus, there is some evidence for the view that, in terms of developmental history, ritual is older than mythical narratives, which require a grammatical language. Be that as it may, this time I am interested in the complex of ritual and myth, not for social-theoretical reasons (as in The Theory of Communicative Action), but because ritual survives in the communal cult practices of world religions. When we ask ourselves today what distinguishes "religion," in this narrower sense of the still formative "strong" traditions, from other worldviews, then these practices are the answer.

Religions do not survive without the cultic activities of a congregation. That is their "unique distinguishing feature" ["Alleinstellungsmerkmal"]. In modernity, they are the only configuration of spirit [Gestalt des Geistes] that still has access to the world of experience of ritual in the strict sense. Philosophy can only recognize religion as a different and yet contemporary configuration of spirit if it takes this archaic element seriously, without devaluing it a fortiori. After all, ritual has been a source of societal solidarity for which the enlightened morality of equal respect for all does not provide a real, motivational equivalent -- nor do Aristotelian virtue ethics and the ethics of the good. This of course in no way precludes the possibility that this source, protected in the meantime by religious communities, and often used toward politically questionable ends, will run dry one day. p. 5

Juergen Habermas
A Postsecular World Society? On the Philosophical Significance of Postsecular Consciousness and the Multicultural World Society
2010

Working with images, stories, aesthetic education necessary for renewal

Quantitative educational reform means industrializing, standardizing of education for all with a "curriculum" as vehicle. Qualitative reform in contrast allows and facilitates authentic ways of access to the world and to oneself, for everyone in the relations with history and one's life story, and therewith in the interesting – even though partially problematic – distinctions of cultures, groups. For this all must be gradually brought closer to the aesthetic depth dimension of life's development, which all humans carry within themselves.

With this timely/untimely 'votum' do artists, philosophers, educators not stand alone in this. It are especially the great physicists, who began thinking already in this direction for over half a century. The significant German nuclear researcher Ernst Schroedinger has realized and stated, that the necessary one-sidedness of the natural scientific image of the world makes the correspondent necessity of an image thinking immediately evident as a matter of course. He says something like: "The model lacks colour, tone, tangibility. In the same way and on the same grounds the world of the natural sciences lacks everything that has significance for the consciously contemplating, perceiving and feeling human being". "From a purely natural scientific standpoint" the essential can not be seen at all. "Life is a worth in itself". Through this the scientific world image becomes false. The great Anglo-Saxon biologist, ethnologist, psychologist Gregory Bateson expresses this at present: "Purposive rationality unaided by myth, religion and the like becomes pathogenic and destructive of life." When we include with the images of art and myth also those of dreams, we have a close family relationship with the ground concept of Surrealism, the basic question, the answer to which might well be different today, but hardly the question itself: how do we create a new connection between the rational and the non-rational dimensions of human consciousness? How do we gain for the dimensions of reality again a recognition for the social organization of life and work, which through the industrial image of a mechanistic world and through the behaviouristic image of the functional human being have been suppressed?

Meanwhile this question is no longer a question for artists and literati, who certainly did connect already with the language of a revolution in poetry and in political ideas. The problematic nature of a consciousness divided between expert rationality and lay experience is since 1980 by the Club of Rome recognized as the actual problem of humanity's survival, under the heading 'The Human Gap'. What is essential in being human is neglected as a matter of principle. This does not only fail to individually provide for a healthy and balanced, fulfilled life, but also fails humanity in a way that is decisive for life. I speak of the Learning Report to the Club of Rome, that therefore demands an innovative and integrative learning for all human beings, and indeed in their social living communities.

The voice of Africa provided us with an early answer through the design of a totally different world culture or cultures. Leopold Senghor placed the artistic-existential demand opposite the intellectual artistic questions as posed by surrealism – to rather shift our attention again to the sous-reality, to the despised depth-dimension of nature's openness to human experience and her living differentiated forms of consciousness. Not only out of African tradition does the mediating concept 'Rhythm' ring through. But – as Frobenius admitted already – the modern societies can themselves also be encouraged by the Africans. Encouraged to overcome the secondary primitivity of the industrialized attitudes of what is natural in the human being. Africa has, in contrast to us, to an exemplary high level, developed a representative and imaginary ability - of perception and expression in images - through the richly differentiated phases in history when humanity still lived close to nature. Following on from Senghor, Wole Soyinka has developed the design of sous-realism more radically, but also critically opposed to him. In 1986 the Nobel prize for Literature was awarded to him. I feared that there are still too few people to whom it is clear, that through this award in the deepest sense also the political significance of these dimensions of human-historical consciousness for the whole world has been highlighted. Such and similar ways of thinking are gaining anyhow to a considerable extent increasing attention. In North America itself and in Europe the questionable adventure-romanticism of the old style Indians books is in the younger generation making place for an interest in images of a brotherly/sisterly experienced nature, that often open to us hardly familiar relations to creation, often strengthen the buried memories. Ever so often do the imaginary world experiences as we find them in the creation mythos of Nez perce or in the much quoted speech of chief Seattle support an argument when it comes to an important decision. I am convinced that we can also gain models for our thinking out of the traditions, that are different from the one-sided causally identified logic. Here I will name by way of example only the early Indian Veda's, because their conception of the world as forming and shaping itself ever new, could meet so beneficially the modern thinking in guaranties, divorced from all movement and all presence.

However, it is exactly these old traditions with their creative images of the world, whether images of language in thinking or images of art in everyday buildings and temples, that have been driven into resistance or scattered.

In all countries the television screen captures an overpowering influence in guesthouses and homes as well as the monitors do in the workplace and the places of learning. Even there, where traditional culture should be fostered via films, it is being distorted through the fact that their medium is missing, the shared communicative experience, evocative communication, vicariously enacting what is to be shown by mimesis.

Being instantly available everywhere for reception and reproduction does not only replace living recreation, it displaces it. The transistors have in the last decade driven out the story tellers from Indian daily life, regardless of their broadcasting pop-music or mythological stories.

Secondly, the break down of the understanding of what an image actually is: Its unique origin, its connections with the history of an imaginary representation and the experience in the course of an artist's life, become uneconomic. To look at the image with questions of the culture out of which it arises and for the way it gives form to the life it wants to serve, appears ridiculous in the face of the senseless way graphic reports are taken for granted beyond all and everything; in the face of the apparent immediacy to which images of horror or joy do appeal.

The world of images and imaginative education belongs to another economy. They are not governed by abbreviation but by concern, concern with constant renewal, enrichment, where every instant of life gives a sense and premonition of its fullness. Real images are always transparent and therewith symbolic, as they reflect the strength of the experience as well as the way it is given form and shape, from which they come; likewise reflecting the untraceable movements of life, which are being experienced and enable life to give form. Images are economic in their way. They allow in dialogue to mediate and introduce a third, through which people experience that they don't have to fight over rules and interpretations. We can let ourselves rather be guided by images on the way to making sense of the world, to come closer to that of which images speak: an organization of human existence intelligently fostering different ways of human life and different movements in the life of nature.

[ ]

I see the task of art educators essentially more offensive. The achievements in the domination over humans and nature as well as the adaptation to the domination – that are the main directions which still keep being meant with "achievement" – cannot be driven further. All dimensions of lived and experienced life have shrunk in the "one-dimensional man" (Herbert Marcuse).

This point is identical with the vanishing-point of the central-perspectival representation of the world in the "correct rendering" through modern civilization. This accepts as valid only a reconstruction out of the eye-point of a vision. Past this presently arrived-at point, it only goes further in the artificial dimensions of digitalization.

This is what happens and art teaching should not pass it over. It should neither practise nor reject this industrialized world. We have to do something more important: neither fixate children on the vanishing point out there, nor to guide them to a flight inwards, but to work with them on seeing, on listening, on sensing the world from within. Education must become the art of knowingly and consciously helping the children to express and develop that which they - without science and historical consciousness - know better than we teachers. The point is not to pull the children towards - what we already think to know to be - the goal of the docile human being. Rather to support them, to encourage them in connecting with the ground within themselves, enabling them to go where-to their own life's intelligence, doubled by our elucidation, leads them. To this point it is right that we shouldn't expect the changes to come from the politicians or else whatever institutions. And that we better get on the way ourselves. The strategies and calculations of the institutions have after all penetrated our thinking and experience for a long time, so that we have to drive them out in ourselves, for the children, in them and with them as part of life's history.

Then we can perhaps historically also reverse the domination of machines: because the substantial machines make their appearance always then, when people collectively have accepted surrendering themselves to thinking and behaving in the way machines actually work. This is not least shown when examples of refusal in the face of the logic of 'development as progress' are often met with ridicule and insult. The reversal would mean, that we humans each for oneself in ourselves and many together seek to imagine the advantages and disadvantages of the machine, of the industrialization of life, to totally and independently determine their relative value and to act accordingly.

This will take much longer and will probably lead into fully unknown territory than the politicians like to think. It is therefore of primary significance, when we here, by a representative of the Federal Government – a very understanding one – are still being admonished not to undermine the unity of art and technology, when in reality this unity does not exist at all, can't exist and to keep "images and reality apart", where only through our image-thinking unity could become real again.

Out of inwardness, from an in itself developed – conscious - inner space and out of an inner world-space, from the world around for the world around, are we able to understand the beings and things that – out of their inwardness - come to meet us This doesn't mean 'I'-like and not merely structurally. With this the fragments of the one image of the world grow – as in dialogue – together. False measures let themselves only to a certain extent be corrected by better ones. There it happens as in a medical school that only knows poison and counter-poison. To detoxify ourselves and the world, to learn from children, what else there is: only this helps us to get away from the "problem of problems", which only ever generates new symptoms in the human-created hunger, the human- created population explosion, in the human-created armament race as well as the human-created mass-loneliness.

Through the children we can learn, in particular, that our contribution must not always be programmatic and met with official blessing.

Let's learn from them the still certainty that we otherwise deprive them of, and the cleverness of their intelligence. Teachers must learn not to drag the children along, but to carry them.

INSEA Weltkongreß
Das Bild der Welt in der Welt der Bilder
1987
[Translated by Henk Bak]

...to bring order and coherence to a confusing part of everyone's life

I started The School of Life from a sense that schools forget to teach you so much of the stuff we need to get by in this world. Where is instruction in relationships, in the management of career, in the raising of children, in the pursuit of friendship, in the wise approach to anxiety and death. All this sort of stuff I craved to learn about when I was a student and down to this day. I wanted to make the school a one-stop shop for information about the area of life I call emotional intelligence. We have been going for several years now and we have done a lot. It's the thing I'm proudest to have done in my life. We're trying to bring order and coherence to a confusing part of everyone's life.

Alain de Botton – Writer and Founder of The School of Life
The School of Life was founded in London in 2008 and is now open in Paris, Amsterdam, London, Melbourne, Antwerp, Belgrade, and Istanbul.
School of Life Melbourne Website
2019

True sources of religious and spiritual cultures as inexhaustible sources of renewal.

All the great utterances of man have to be judged not by the letter but by the spirit – the spirit which unfolds itself with the growth of life in history. We get to know the real meaning of Christianity by observing its living aspect at the present moment – however different that may be, even in important respects, from the Christianity of earlier periods.

For western scholars the great religious scriptures of India seem to possess merely a retrospective and archaeological interest; but to us they are of living importance, and we cannot help thinking that they lose their significance when exhibited in labelled cases – mummified specimens of human thought and aspiration, preserved for all time in the wrappings of erudition.

The meaning of the living words that come out of the experience of great hearts can never be exhausted by any one system of logical interpretation.

They have to be endlessly explained by the commentaries of individual lives, and they gain an added mystery in each new revelation. To me the verses of the Upanishads and the teachings of Buddha have ever been things of the spirit and therefore endowed with boundless vital growth; and I have used them, both in my own life and in my preaching, as being instinct with individual meaning for me as for others, and awaiting for their confirmation, my own special testimony, which must have its value because of its individuality. p. viii

[ ]

When the first Aryan invaders appeared in India it was a vast land of forests, and the new-comers rapidly took advantage of them.

[ ]

Thus in India it was in the forests that our civilisation had its birth, and it took a distinct character from this origin and environment. It was surrounded by the vast life of nature, was fed and clothed by her, and had the closest and most constant intercourse with her varying aspects.

[ ]

Having been in constant contact with the living growth of nature, his mind was free from the desire to extend his dominion by erecting boundary walls around his acquisitions. His aim was not to acquire but to realise, to enlarge his consciousness by growing with and growing into his surroundings. He felt that truth is all-comprehensive, that there is no such thing as absolute isolation in existence, and the only way of attaining truth is through the interpenetration of our being into all objects. To realise this great harmony between man's spirit and the spirit of the world was the endeavour of the forest-dwelling sages of ancient India. pp. 3-4

[ ]

The Infinite in India was not a thin nonentity, void of all content. The Rishis of India asserted emphatically, "To know him in this life is to be true; not to know him in this life is the desolation of death." How to know him then? "By realising him in each and all." Not only in nature but in the family, in society, and in the state, the more we realise the World-conscious in all, the better for us. Failing to realise it, we turn our faces to destruction.

[ ]

It was not a mere play of the imagination, but it was the liberation of consciousness from all the mystifications and exaggerations of the self. These ancient seers felt in the serene depth of their mind that the same energy which vibrates and passes into the endless forms of the world manifests itself in our inner being as consciousness; and there is no break in unity. For these seers there was no gap in their luminous vision of perfection. They never acknowledged even death itself as creating a chasm in the field of reality.

[ ]

Everything has sprung from immortal life and is vibrating with life, for life is immense.

This is the noble heritage from our forefathers waiting to be claimed by us as our own, this ideal of the supreme freedom of consciousness. It is not merely intellectual or emotional, it has an ethical basis, and it must be translated into action. In the Upanishad it is said, The supreme being is all-pervading, therefore he is the innate good in all. To be truly united in knowledge, love and service with all beings, and thus to realise one's self in the all-pervading God is the essence of goodness, and this is the keynote of the teachings of the Upanishads: Life is immense. pp. 20-22

Rabindranath Tagore
Sadhana: The Realisation of Life
1914

Perfectibility as potential and responsibility for renewal – Pomponazzi's perspective.

Taking over an Aristotelian classification, Pomponazzi distinguished between three forms of intellect: the theoretical, the practical, the productive. All men, he says, possess these three forms of intellect in some degree. They possess some knowledge, however rudimentary, of fundamental theoretical truths – such as that nothing can be both be and not be at the same time. They are 'productive', they can create and build. They are 'practical' in Aristotle's sense of the word, capable, that is, of making moral and political decisions. But only the 'practical' form of intellect, according to Pomponazzi, is proper and peculiar to man, and this is the only form of intellect which all men must attempt to develop in its full perfection.

It is neither possible nor desirable for all men to perfect themselves as metaphysicians or as builders. But it is both possible and desirable, according to Pomponazzi, for them to perfect themselves morally. 'As to the practical intellect', he writes, 'which is proper to man, every man should possess it perfectly... For the whole would be most perfectly preserved if all men were righteous and good, but not if all were philosophers or smiths or builders'.

Pomponazzi's reference to 'the whole' is particularly significant. By 'the whole' he meant 'mankind' or 'the human race'. There was nothing new is thinking of mankind in this way as a single whole; the Greeks had not done so, but Augustine had. What was novel in Pomponazzi's approach is that he takes as his point of departure the perfecting of 'the whole' – of mankind – rather than the perfecting of the individual. In so doing, he anticipated the characteristic approach of modern perfectibilism, at least since the eighteenth century. The individual is to be perfected only as part of the perfection of mankind. And if mankind as a whole is to be perfected then – unless within a Buddhist-type theory of reincarnation – the ideal of perfection has to be set at a level which men can, in their present life, hope to achieve. And this is the case, Pomponazzi is suggesting, if perfection is identified with moral or 'practical' perfection.

If it be objected that the perfection of the practical intellect will not of itself bring men perfect peace, Pomponazzi's answer is that men are not to expect perfect peace. Were, indeed, a human being to arrive at a state in which, like the Stoic sage, he was entirely free of anxiety, he would cease to be human. Nor should men repine at the fact they will know all that they might wish to know, and will never be secure in an eternal happiness. A mortal being ought not to desire eternal happiness, 'since the immortal is not fitting for a mortal. '. He should abandon his desire to be like God, whether in knowledge, in security or in happiness. It is characteristic of the temperate man to be content with what suits him and what he can have.'

John Passmore
The Perfectibility of Man
1970, pp. 151,152

The universe is after fullness, not perfection.

Which do you prefer, a tombstone artistically formed and decorated or soberly inscribed with Roman capitals?"

I don't want a tomb, I want life!

We are after unity

The universe is not about perfectionism.
If you are perfect you are dead.
The point is, that every stage is an opening for the next.
The universe is about fullness, not perfection.
Go for the highest divine love: the spirit, creator of
the good, beautiful, true spiritual world.

Shin Gwydion Fontalba
at Seminar at Frederikswark, Denmark 20 June 2000
[Seminar notes by Henk Bak]

The one who says 'I', source of renewal beyond doctrine or theory.

Dear Friends, we find ourselves these days in a certain way placed here in the epicenter of the Movement, in that vibrating centre namely, from which waves are moving outward.

We have in the course of our work considered how the Movement could positively unfold itself. In regard to this we have remarked, that by staying with our old habits and attitudes, together with all the implications playing into them, we are not going to generate anything new. And we must say, too, that nothing new would ever be possible at all, if the human being would merely consist of these old practices, habits and structures.

The human being however carries within himself completely new powers.

We have spoken about the dreams of the time when we were young, about the visions in the years of one's youth. About the noble and charming wish in children to grow up into a healthy human being, entering into a rich and meaningful adult world. We have spoken about the ideals, about the plans. We know: that - hidden and imprisoned beneath the surface – many of these such wishes, visions, ideals and dreams are definitely carried by all of you and many other human beings in every country. As long as these remain - psychologically spoken - repressed, because society could not have any use for these ideals or because the parents and the environment were not able to understand the visions and dreams, as long as these gifts, these powers and capacities that have retained their youthfulness remain out of bounds, so long does humanity, the people, society lack the youthful power to build something new. A newly initiated, sensitive awakening and cultivation of these gifts that children and young people are bringing to humanity here on earth, can lead to new steps in development that are quite astounding.

This however is not the only 'youngest' in every human being that wants to be respected and honoured: the child in you, the young human being within you. It is also – transcending this – the impulse- bringing power of life itself wanting to be respected, enhanced and cultivated. Even that is not the only element of youth that lives in you When we study this we can find in many religious streams and what has been carried in an outstanding form in early Christianity: that you carry something as well, that is not of this world. It is not of this world mechanism, not of this secondary world that human beings have artificially created for themselves.

It has been said of 'Isha", 'Jeshua', who has been called the Christ, that he is not of this world. And this is something which could be understood in a confessional sense or in a religious sense or one could understand it in a philosophical sense. What if, however, it is a spiritual scientific, an unequivocal statement? If it is science? If it is not the case of a master having placed himself above others, but of one demonstrating by the example of his own life something that applies equally to others, human beings, the disciples themselves? And the latter resonates clearly and consistently when in many further statements it is not only often said 'I have come down from above – you come from below' as against many others:

> *"I am not of this world and you, however, are also not of this world!*
> *Love the light and abide in it!"*

If all this, dear friends, now once more thought through after 2000 years, is in accordance, not necessarily with a religious interpretation, but with a scientific aspect founded on deep, initiation knowledge. If this is science*. If he then has passed on to human beings something, that we need to know, what then have we accomplished with this knowledge in the last 2000 years?

"Don't you know that you are gods?" (John 10:34)

Shin Gwydion Fontalba
Public Address on the launch of a Free and Worldwide Movement
for Human Dignity
Oberstdorf, Germany, October 2009 begins of 2nd part, reflecting
on context

---

* 'science', the English translation of the German 'Wissenschaft', refers to any form of methodical knowledge, not just physical science.

Natality – Remembrance – Narrative: central to Hannah Arendt's Understanding

From conditions it is impossible to extract any strategy for manipulation. Although the substance of history is free human action, that freedom is never freedom to impose one's own will on reality. Lenin's Bolsheviks designing and "making" the new society were bound to fail. But Arendt did not understand this frailty and ambiguity of human action against a "law of history" which overrules human agency. If communism became Stalinism, this was not because the invisible hand of the market always rules, or that history dictates that Socialism comes after capitalism. It is because the worldly nature of human action is to be always for and with others, which means that consequences of action are never determinable, no matter how efficiently an action is planned or how force accompanies it. A Women's Studies program may result not in new dignity for women professors but in marginality for women's scholarship. The establishment of a Jewish homeland can lead not to a non-discriminatory society, but to a racially exclusive enclave.

The source of this indeterminacy, for Arendt, is not the philosopher's mortality – the necessary deterioration, decay, imperfection of all mortal things – but "natality" – the coming into the world of "strangers", capable of doing new things, capable of acts of foundation and beginning again. Natality, like giving birth, is not omnipotence. One person cannot, by act of will and with sovereign power, construct a new reality, any more than a child born into the world will fit his parents' preconceived images of who that child should be. Action, like a child, is born into a world of human relationships in which it must find its own place. Nothing can dictate what that place must be.

It is with these concepts – natality, remembrance, narrative – anomalous in philosophy – that Arendt understood both the particular meaning of the holocaust and the larger failure of modernity and Western culture that it signalled. Thought is historical for Arendt not only in the sense that the subject matter of her concerns is drawn from her own particular situation – German, Jew, woman, emigrant: in this case thought might still proceed rationally to produce objective truth. Her thought, itself, is historical, situated "nowhere", in a suspension of time between past and future, at a precarious intersection through which weave through "trains" of remembrance and anticipation. The very motive force of thought, its dynamic, comes from temporal positioning in the present and a resulting struggle with the future against the past and with the past against the future. If a woman does not lose her nerve and escape into idealism, cynicism, or despair, if she does not succumb to the temptation to stop thinking, she can, when she thinks, manage to walk a diagonal between past and future, forward and then back again, precariously and painfully.

Andrea Nye
Philosophia: The thought of Rosa Luxemburg, Simone Weil and Hannah Arendt
1994, pp.150-151

The expecting mother: embodiment of hope for the new in becoming...

---side by side with the ego revelation of the prophets, there had always been another current of revelation present. It was the current of the heart-revelation present. This was the current of the heart-revelation of the mothers and grandmothers of the expected Messiah. For the Messiah was not only prophetically promised, but also knowingly loved and lovingly known in the silent depths of the heart. The love knowledge was not unclear; it was a wordless, silence cognition, but that doesn't mean that it was dim or uncertain. For though a great clearness and certainty may exist in the discernment of the heart, there may nevertheless be no organ to express it in words. Such a wordless, dumb knowledge dwelt for many centuries side by side with the cognition proclaimed in words by the prophets. In fact, side by side with the written book of the Old Testament, we must think of another, unwritten book of the wordless revelation of the heart of Sophia. A radiant comprehension of this invisible book dwelt in the heart of Mary, whereas an intellectual comprehension of the written book was in the consciousness of Joseph, who, on that account, is represented in traditional art as an "old man" ....

Valentin Tomberg
Anthroposphische Studies of the Old Testament (1933)/ 2nd edition
1985, p.176

Reincarnation in the East

He (the Buddha) by Himself thoroughly understands, as he sees, as it were, face to face, this universe – the world below with all the spirits, and the world above, of Mára and of Brahmã and all creatures, Samanas and Brahmanas, Shining Ones and men, and He makes His knowledge known to others.

Tevija Sutta, in: Annie Besant
The Universal Text Book of Religion and Morals. Volume 1 & 2

1910, p.74

*One's own self conquered is better than all other people ; not
even the Shining One, Gandharva, not Māra with Brahman
could change into defeat the victory of a man who has
vanquished himself, and always lives under constraint.*

Dammapada, ii. 30, in: Annie Besant
***The Universal Text Book of Religion and Morals. Volume 1
& 2***
1910, p.74

*He who is calm, having left behind good and evil, free from
defilement, having understood this and the other world, and
conquered birth and death, such a one is called a Samana.*

Sabhiyasutta, 11, in: Annie Besant
***The Universal Text Book of Religion and Morals. Volume 1
& 2***
1910, p.107

*The man who knows his former dwellings, who sees both heaven and
hell, and has reached the destruction of births, him I call a Brahmāna.*

Vāsettasutta, 54, in: Annie Besant
***The Universal Text Book of Religion and Morals. Volume 1
& 2***
1910, p.107

Reincarnation in the West: the process by which humanity is being educated through the ages

80*
*For in this selfishness of the human heart to will to practice the understanding
too, only, on that which concerns our corporal needs, would be to blunt
rather than to sharpen it. It absolutely will be exercised on spiritual objects,
if it is to attain its perfect illumination, and bring out that purity of
heart, which makes us capable of loving virtue for its own sake alone.*

81
*Or, is the human species never to arrive at this highest
step of illumination and purity?—Never?*

82
*Never?—Let me not think this blasphemy, All Merciful!
Education has its goal, in the Race, no less than in the Individual.
That which is educated is educated for something.*

---
* This text comprises 100 propositions in total. These were numbered by the author. It is an unusual text for the time in that it argued 'systematically' for reincarnation.

83

The flattering prospects which are open to the people, the Honor and Well-being which are painted to him, what are they more than the means of educating him to become a man, who, when these prospects of Honor and Well-being have vanished, shall be able to do his Duty?

84

This is the aim of human education, and should not the Divine education extend as far? Is that which is successful in the way of Art with the individual, not to be successful in the way of Nature with the whole? Blasphemy! Blasphemy!!

85

No! It will come! it will assuredly come! the time of the perfecting, when man, the more convinced his understanding feels itself of an ever better Future, will nevertheless not be necessitated to borrow motives of action from his Future; for he will do the Right because it is right, not because arbitrary rewards are annexed thereto, which formerly were intended simply to fix and strengthen his unsteady gaze in recognizing the inner, better, rewards of well-doing.

86

It will assuredly come! the time of a new eternal Gospel, which is promised us in the Primer of the New Testament itself.

87

Perhaps even some enthusiasts of the thirteenth and fourteenth centuries had caught a glimpse of a beam of this new eternal Gospel, and only erred in that they predicted its outburst at so near to their own time.

88

Perhaps their "Three Ages of the World" were not so empty a speculation after all, and assuredly they had no contemptible views when they taught that the New Covenant must become as much antiquated as the old has been. There remained by them the similarity of the economy of the same God. Ever, to let them speak my words, ever the self-same plan of the Education of the Race.

89

Only they were premature. Only they believed that they could make their contemporaries, who had scarcely outgrown their childhood, without enlightenment, without preparation, men worthy of their Third Age.

90
And it was just this which made them enthusiasts. The enthusiast often casts true glances into the future, but for this future he cannot wait. He wishes this future accelerated, and accelerated through him. That for which nature takes thousands of years is to mature itself in the moment of his existence. For what possession has he in it if that which he recognises as the Best does not become the best in his lifetime? Does he come back? Does he expect to come back? Marvellous only that this enthusiastic expectation does not become more the fashion among enthusiasts.

91
Go thine inscrutable way, Eternal Providence! Only let me not despair in Thee, because of this inscrutableness. Let me not despair in Thee, even if Thy steps appear to me to be going back. It is not true that the shortest line is always straight.

92
Thou hast on Thine Eternal Way so much to carry on together, so much to do! So many a side step to take! And what if it were as good as proved that the vast flow wheel which brings mankind nearer to this perfection is only put in motion by smaller, swifter wheels, each of which contributes its own individual unit thereto?

93
It is so! The very same Way by which the Race reaches its perfection, must every individual man—one sooner—another later—have travelled over. Have travelled over in one and the same life? Can he have been, in one and the selfsame life, a sensual Jew and a spiritual Christian? Can he in the self-same life have overtaken both?

94
Surely not that! But why should not every individual man have existed more than once upon this World?

95
Is this hypothesis so laughable merely because it is the oldest? Because the human understanding, before the sophistries of the Schools had dissipated and debilitated it, lighted upon it at once?

96
Why may not even I have already performed those steps of my perfecting

which bring to man only temporal punishments and rewards?

97
And once more, why not another time all those steps, to perform which the views of Eternal Rewards so powerfully assist us?

98
Why should I not come back as often as I am capable of acquiring fresh knowledge, fresh expertness? Do I bring away so much from once, that there is nothing to repay the trouble of coming back?

99
Is this a reason against it? Or, because I forget that I have been here already? Happy is it for me that I do forget. The recollection of my former condition would permit me to make only a bad use of the present. And that which even I must forget now, is that necessarily forgotten forever?

100
Or is it a reason against the hypothesis that so much time would have been lost to me? Lost—And how much then should I miss? —Is not a whole Eternity mine?

Gotthold Ephraim Lessing
The Education of the Human Race
1780

Birth and rebirth as integral part of a process of involution and evolution.

If there were no need of self-finding but only an eternal enjoyment of this play of Sat-Chit-Ananda (Being-Consciousness – Bliss)...then evolution and rebirth need not have come into operation. But there has been an involution of this unity into the dividing Mind, a plunge into self-oblivion by which the ever-present sense of complete oneness is lost. And the play of separative difference, phenomenal, because the real unity in difference remains unabridged behind – comes to the forefront as a dominant reality. This play of difference has found its utmost term of the sense of division by the precipitation of the dividing Mind into the form of body in which it becomes conscious of itself as a separate ego. A dense and solid basis that has been laid for this play of division in a world of separative forms of Matter by an involution of the active self-conscience of Sachchidananda is not a phenomenal Nescience. It is this foundation in

Nescience that makes the division secure because it imperatively opposes a return to the consciousness of unity; but still, though effectively obstructive, it is phenomenal and terminable because within it, above it, supporting it is the all-conscient Spirit and the apparent Nescience turns out to be only a concentration, an exclusive action of consciousness tranced into self-forgetfulness by an abysmal plunge into the absorption of the formative and creative material process... That assumption of body we call birth, and in it only can take place here the development of self and the play of relation between the individual and the universal and all other individuals; in it only can there be the growth by a progressive development of our conscious being towards a supreme recovery of unity with God and with all in God: all the sum of what we call Life in the physical world is a progress of the soul and proceeds by birth into the body and has that as its fulcrum, its condition of action and its condition of evolutionary persistence.

Birth then is a necessity of the manifestation of the Purusha (spirit) on the physical plane; but this birth, whether the human or any other, cannot be in this world-order an isolated accident or a sudden excursion of a soul into the physicality without any preparing past or any fulfilling hereafter. In a world of involution and evolution, not of physical form only, but of conscious being through life and mind to spirit, such an isolated assumption of life in the human body could not be the rule of the soul's existence; it would be a quite meaningless and inconsequential arrangement, a freak for which the nature and system of things here have no place, a contrary violence which would break the rhythm of the Spirit's self-mainfestation. ... For here life upon earth, life in the physical universe is not and cannot be a casual perch for the wanderings of the soul from world to world; it is a great and slow development needing, as we know, incalculable spaces of Time for its evolution... This ascent can only take place by rebirth within the ascending order; an individual visit coming across it and progressing on some other line elsewhere could not fit into a system of this evolutionary existence.

Sri Aurobindo, Robert Mc Dermott (Editor)
The Essential Aurobindo / The Philosophy of Rebirth
1987, pp.106-108

The notion of reincarnation elucidated 1:

...reincarnation is in no way a theory which one has to believe or not believe. ...Just as one does not make propaganda for or against the fact that we sleep at night and wake up anew each morning – for that is a matter of experience – so it is the fact that we die and are born anew a matter of

experience. i.e. either one has certainty about it or else one does not. But those who are certain should know that ignorance of reincarnation often has very profound and even sublime reasons associated with the vocation of the person in question... The priest, doctor and judge have to concentrate themselves in such a way on the tasks of the present that they must not be distracted by memories of former lives. Letter IV The Emperor Pages 92-93

[ ]

In order to resolve the contradiction between hereditary which only reproduces, and general evolution, which demonstrates creativity, it is necessary to have recourse to a further dimension, i.e. to add the vertical dimension to that of the horizontal continuity in time – the latter being that of hereditary, which connects successive generations. It has to be admitted that acquired characteristics are accumulated somewhere else other than the mechanism peculiar to heredity, and that "heredity" and "acquired characteristics" (which latter do not disappear but are simply relegated "somewhere else") there is an active tension which manifests itself in education and self-education as well as in the arising of intellectual and moral geniuses as fruit of a mediocre line of forefathers. This tension between the mechanism of heredity and characteristics acquired through experience – and accumulated "somewhere else" - leads in the long run to the prevalence of the latter, and a kind of "eruption" of acquired characteristics takes place in the hereditary mechanism. The fruits of past experience, so to say, "reincarnate".

[ ]

It is true that Jung designated the realm where past experiences are buried as the "collective consciousness". Why collective? Why not individual consciousness? Is it simply because experiences of the past, which arise from the depth of consciousness, have much in common? ... that they resemble one another?

But it are human beings in whom experiences of the past arise. It is therefore quite natural that they have much in common – in fact, as much in common as human beings have in common. For this reason alone, is it necessary to postulate the collectivity of subconscious (or superconscious) memory, that spans millennia? Is it not more simple and natural to conclude that the one who remembers an experience is also the one who experienced it?

Anonymous (Valentin Tomberg)
Meditations on the Tarot: A Journey into Christian Hermeti-

cism / Letter X The Wheel of Fortune
1991, p. 254

The notion of reincarnation elucidated 2:

(Goethe) was not referring to heredity when he said: "I bear in myself seeds of sickness since three thousand years," or when in a poem dedicated to Frau Von Stein he wrote: "once you were my sister or my wife". What was meant was the experience of destiny in repeated lives on earth. The belief in reincarnation is not confined to the world of Buddhism and Hinduism; it extends far beyond their frontiers. But how does the age-old and widespread conviction that there are repeated lives on earth relate to the ideal of resurrection?

[ ]

First we must point out and emphasize that reincarnation, or the repetition of lives on earth is not an ideal: it does not even qualify as a way of salvation. It is valid merely as a fact which by some is regarded as regrettable; by others, in contrast, it is judged to be necessary. Therefore, although we can place the ideal of resurrection over and against the ideal of Nirvana (the release from the wheel of rebirths), we cannot compare faith in reincarnation with the ideal of resurrection.

[ ]

It is simply the extent of the opportunity for experience, which makes a difference. For, just as an eighty-year old person has had more opportunity to acquire experience and to work upon himself than a twenty-year old, so has an individual who has lived ten times on earth had comparatively more opportunities than a person allotted only one short life.

[ ]

...reincarnation does not only mean repeated opportunities to gather experience and to overcome the trials of earthly lives, but it signifies also the repetition of earthly constraints of suffering, sickness and death.

[ ]

Resurrection on the other hand, is also a reappearance in the body, but without the constraints of suffering, sickness, and death, [ ] It is the

*great hope of final victory over constraint, sickness and death, i.e. it is
the meaning and goal of repeated earthy lives. It is solely the hope for
resurrection which makes it worthwhile to live many times on earth.*

Valentin Tomberg
***Covenant of the Heart: Meditations of a Christian Hermeticist
on the Mysteries of Tradition.***
1992, pp. 59-63

Krishna explains the difference between reincarnation as an individual's path of development and repeated divine incarnations as God's way of bringing humanity back on the right path.

*4. Arjuna said: The Sun-God was one of the first born of beings (ancestor
of the solar dynasty) and Thou art only now born into the world; how
am I to comprehend that Thou declaredst to him in the beginning*

*5. The Blessed Lord said: Many are the lives that are past and thine also,
O Arjuna, all of them I know, but thou knowest not, O scourge of the foe.*

*6. Though I am the unborn, though I am unperishable in my self-
existence, though I am the Lord of all existences, yet I stand in
my own nature and come into birth by my self —Maya.*

*7. Whensoever there is the fading of Dharma and the uprise
of unrighteousness then I loose myself forth into birth.*

*8. For the deliverance of the good, for the destruction of the evil-
doers, for the enthroning of the Right, I am born from age to age.*

Sri Aurobindo
***Bhagavad Gita and its Message: with Text, Translation and
Sri Aurobindo's Commentary***
1995, pp. 70-1

A lonely voice?

*I am of the opinion that it would signify an important step
forwards, if one would divulge the teaching of reincarnation.
In this way many riddles which now veil the spirit and
intellect of people in the mist, would be solved.*

Archbishop Louis Puecher Passavalli (1820-1897) in: Karel Douven
***Het Christendom op Weg naar the 21e Eeuw [Christianity on
its Way to the 21st Century]***

1988, p.190
[Translated by Henk Bak]

Science's first contribution to renewal: take a step back

Science is one Ideology among many and should be separated from the State just as Religion is now separated from the State.

I started by stipulating that a free society is a society in which all traditions have equal rights and equal access to the centres of power.

This led to the objection that equal right can be guaranteed only if the basic structure of society is 'objective', not influenced by undue pressure from any one from the traditions. Hence rationalism will be more important than other traditions.

Now if rationalist and the accompanying views are not yet in existence or have not power then they cannot influence society as planned. Yet life is not chaos under such circumstances. There are wars, there is power-play, there are open debates between cultures. The tradition of objectivity may therefore be introduced in a variety of ways. Assume it is introduced by an open debate – then should we change the form of the debate at this point? Intellectuals say, because of the 'objectivity' of their procedure – a pitiful lack of perspective as we have seen. There is no reason to stick to reason even if it was reached by open debate. There is even less reason to stick to it if it was enforced by force. This removes the objection.

[ ]

To find out (differences in results) we must let all traditions freely side by side as is at any rate required by the basic stipulation of a free society. It is quite possible that an open debate about this development will find that some traditions have less to offer than others. This does not mean that they will be abolished – they will survive and keep their rights as long as there are people interested in them – it only means that for the time being their (material, intellectual, emotional products play a relatively small role. But what pleases once doesn't please always; and what aids traditions in one period does not aid them in others. The open debate and with it the examination of the favoured traditions will therefore continue: society is never identified with one particular tradition, and state and tradition are always kept apart.

The separation of state and science (rationalism) which is an essential part of the general separation of state and traditions cannot be introduced by a single political act and it should not be introduced in this way: many people have not yet reached the maturity necessary for living in a free society (this applies especially to scientists and other rationalists). People in a free society must decide about very basic issues, they must know to assemble the necessary information, they must understand the purpose of traditions different from their own and the roles they play in the lives of their members. The maturity I am speaking about is not an intellectual virtue, it is a sensitivity that can only be acquired by frequent contacts with different points of view. It can't be taught in schools and it is vain the expect that 'social studies' will create the wisdom we need. But it can be acquired by participating in citizens' initiatives. This is why the slow erosion of the authority of science and other pushy institutions that is produced by these initiatives is to be preferred to more radical measures: citizens' initiatives are the best an only school for free citizens we now have.

Paul Feyerabend
Science in a Free Society
1987, pp. 106-7

Two mutually enhancing ways of thinking: potential for a shared road towards renewal...

The most often asked question about the Wandjina is why there is no mouth. Mowaljarlai explained that the void is unspeakable, because it is beyond our understanding. Years later, as I tried to come to terms with computer technology, I learned that it all operates on patters of 0 and 1. It was amazing to me, that the ancient Wandjina and twentieth-century technology used the same two symbols to create patterns for communication with the world.

The utter consistency of the basic premise of Ngarinyin philosophy throughout every facet of cultural and social life defies explanation. After more than two decades of listening, challenging, and learning, I continue to discover the contemporary relevance of their stories and way of seeing. In 1989 Mowarjarlai and I decided to name the Ngarinyin worldview "Pattern Thinking" because the whole of their cosmology is inextricable interconnected according to and as a reflection of the immutable Law of Relationships. By comparison the Western way of seeing is reductionist, linear, singular and fragmented while its law is made by men with power and is very changeable. We named this system "Triangle" because power concentrates in an ascending cone toward the top where One rules. Pattern thinking reflects the Law of Relationship, so not only are there no bosses but relationships are an integrated pattern between the masculine and the feminine. Triangle thinking, the systems of relationships for all patriarchal civilizations, reflects the power of the masculine One and its authority to own, control and hold dominion over all else. Pattern Thinking and Triangle Thinking seem, at first glance, mutually exclusive. The fact is, however that as we approach the third millennium , both are unsustainable in their own right, and both have much to learn and incorporate from each other. Pattern Thinking in its original form is unsustainable because of the very Law of which it is a reflection. Because Ngarinyin Law is a reflection of the laws of nature it cannot be changed by humans. It is embodied in the stories, songs, dances. and paintings about ancestral spirits whose presence in Creation is constant and literal. This mythic view of the world can only adapt at the pace of change in the natural world. The law is therefore immutable. In its application as a literal doctrine by the Ngarinyin has resulted in their inability to abstract, analyse, synthesize, and project and the arts and skills of control and dominion that characterize Triangle Thinking. On the other hand, Triangle Thinking, in its current expression is unsustainable because it fails to reflect, incorporate, or respond to the reality of natural law with its primary law of relationship. Consequently, Triangle Thinking is fundamentally out of balance, limited as it is to a masculine, "right-handed" interpretation of the world. Without a fully recognized and incorporated feminine, Triangle Thinking is inherently non regenerative and therefore decadent.

Hanna Rachel Bell
Men's Business-Women's Business: The Spiritual Role of gender in the World's Oldest Culture
1998, pp. 126-127

Brain Plasticity: Science's own step forward to renewal

How can we – better than until now - help each other to become conscious of our dignity as human beings?

That all parents succeed in this with their children remains a pious wish. In any case, as long as there are parents, who have not yet themselves become conscious of their own worth. Who often not even have a concept yet of what their dignity entails.

[ ]

The process of developing a self-image, that has interiorised one's own becoming integrated into a human community and serves the child as an inner compass in order to so shape its relations with others that their dignity is not violated, needs time. That doesn't let itself be taught. It can only be developed through each child's favourable individual experiences with other people. The accompanying and gradually more reflective and self-forming process doesn't let itself speed up. It can only succeed in an unhurried/sheltered environment that offers the child the necessary leisure for it. The ancient Greek seem to have understood this already, for they introduced the word 'sgolè' for it, which then by the Romans was taken over as 'scola', in German 'Müsse' (English 'leisure').

In most today's schools nothing is to be seen of the 'leisure' that is required for self-determination and self-finding. Where do the young when growing up still find opportunity there, to try out and playfully try out their inborn talents and gifts and to pursue their natural pleasure in independent discovering and creating something together?

Instead they are being informed, instructed, controlled, tested and assessed, exactly so as if they were objects malleable after the ideas of the adults.

No wonder, that for them the appetite for learning drains away...

[ ]

Perhaps you begin by now to get a sense of what had shocked me when watching both documentaries. (Showing well educated men responsible for environmental destruction etc. See: (Ch 4) It became clear to me as by a stroke of lightning, that our educational system is absolutely not equipped to assist the younger generation in strengthening their sense for what constitutes their dignity, let alone to develop their own concept or even an awareness of their dignity...

Gerald Hüther
Würde: was uns stark macht-als Einzelne und als Gesellschaft [Dignity: What makes us strong - as Individual and as Society]
2018, pp. 147-150

4. Experience

...my main concern is that a conversation take place about what it means to be a human being.

Brecht Molenaar in: Trouw 14 July 2018

Introduction

After three chapters dealing with viewpoints, clarification, concepts, teaching, language, joining in with the current dialogue and sharing the call for renewal of both the dialogue itself and the world-views of its participants – before plunging into the 'deep end', i.e.: the practice of transformation, the breaking of old forms and the birth of young, new possibilities responding to new needs, situations, insights as well as generating these out of a new consciousness – this chapter on experience is central to both the 'theory' and the 'practice'.

It is also the ground on which spiritual leaders and scholars meet, or where they could and should meet with their people, their communities and with humanity at large. Nothing in their teachings and directions would be valid if not grounded in experience: experience understood as direct cognition through individual perception – from thoughtful perception to perceptive thought: sensing and making sense in the widest and deepest meaning of the word. Not just through the obvious or not so obvious five senses, not just sensing based in living physiology, known or unknown, human, animal, plant, but also through those faculties of imagination, (inspiration*), intuition, memory, moral and common sense advocated by John Ralston Saul in his On Equilibrium and the more hidden organs of the soul, which in the East are called chakras, wheels, or 'lotus flowers' - and 'roses' in the West.

Experience, or rather experiencing, occurs not only in thinking but also in the whole spectrum of feeling and emotion, motivation and will. A range so wide, deep and enduring, that – to represent it adequately in an anthology like this – would explode the framework of its chapters.

In this selection it is assumed that some form of experience underlies most, if not all, the texts in these anthologies. I have chosen them guided by a sense of relevance and authenticity, ultimately a very individual journey, but one that I hope others may make sense of, also. The selection in this chapter, focused on experience itself, features the experiences of old and young, women

---
* 'inspiration' added by author

and men, with humanist, atheist, spiritual, religious orientations - with all varieties and shades in between.

Benedictine brother David and the Buddhist monk Thich Nhat Hanh open the selection with texts which make clear, that at the heart of religion is experience, inner, personal experience. The subtitle of Brother David's talk: 'towards a worldwide real ecumene of religions' (1985), nearly a quarter century after Henri Bruning introduced this concept in 1961, gives me a sense of recognition for Bruning's vision.

The full range of experience is rather to be found in music, poetry, dance, theatre, novels and the visual and plastic arts. For the purpose of this book, I selected texts that are testimony to the experiences of a lifetime as well as those of fresh, new life beginnings. For the latter I am especially indebted to 'God Within. our Spiritual Future as told by Today's new Adults' Skypaths Publishing, whose other thematic books have been also very useful. 'God, Faith & Identity from the Ashes. Reflections of Children and Grandchildren of Holocaust Survivors', is intensely and movingly relevant to considerations of 'experience'.

It is not only the emphasis on 'think-for-yourself' that can make education a much-needed instrument against indoctrination of any kind, but also an insistence on experience, on aesthetics in the original sense of the word: Greek 'aisthesis', which means 'sensing, feeling, perceiving'. Herbert Read had responded to the spectacle of the most cultured nations slaughtering each other in a barbaric war for the second time, by writing in 1943 his seminal 'Education Through Art'. He felt that the only hope would lie with a new generation, educated not just intellectually, but through sensing and feeling, i.e. through art. The international movement inspired by his book became a welcome instrument for continuing communication and exchange between art teachers from countries on both sides of the 'iron curtain' between East and West in the cold war. Read had referred back to J. Friedrich Schiller, known for his 'Ode to Joy' in Beethoven's ninth symphony. Schiller wrote his 'Letters on the Aesthetic Education of Man' 1792 in response to the terror of the French Revolution. High minded ideas had been abruptly put into practice, without considering the passions and savagery that this would unleash, without any intermediate stage of experimentation in a safe space, one removed from the pressing realities of public life: a time to play. Schiller estimated it would take one hundred years before people would be sufficiently mature to implement democracy. Schiller himself had evoked the experience of the several revolutions and struggles at the birth pains of the modern European nations, from Switzerland in 'Wilhelm Tell', over England in Mary Stuart, the Netherlands in 'Don Carlos' to Germany in 'Wallenstein' and others.

In the 20th century Steiner's new approach to education, with its strong emphasis on both independent thinking and perception, intelligence of feeling (Robert Witkin) and work, was a response to the Great War, in the spirit of Schiller, like Read's response later.

Experience, including aesthetic experience became the driving force in those 1960's movements like Provo in the Netherlands and Flower Power in California. 'Homo Ludens', (Human being – playing being), Johan Huizinga's notion that play is the primal source of all cultural expressions, including religious ones, became an inspiration in the '60's. Insisting on playfulness in public life, experimentation with new forms, re-introducing nature into the cities, creating car-free malls and other open spaces. 'Imagination au Pouvoir' ('Let Imagination reign') became the catchcry of the French uprising in that time (1968).

The new generation felt a craving for experience outside the constrictions of the predominant culture. The secrets of the early cultures were explored and often exploited. And, within the current culture, spirituality acquired a psychological dimension often to the point where 'spirit' became absorbed in 'soul' or 'mind'. Christianity and Judaism became enriched by Jungian and humanist psychology and different modes of therapy, which allowed experience to play a crucial role in what often had become empty words and practice. The availability of the most diverse cultural experiences, which is still rapidly growing, poses a challenge for the individual to become the conscious and responsible judge beyond the experiences themselves: the one who integrates specific experiences and lets other ones go. The spirit one is, within and beyond the soul one has., i.e.: Soul as the inner space in which the Spirit makes sense of experience, learns and gains wisdom.

In this context I find it significant that Pope Francis in his encyclical letter 'Laudato si' does not only call for activating all faculties/capacities of our consciousness that we can muster, the known and the not yet known (!), but also for a heightened appreciation and activation of the aesthetic qualities of life. People's dignity is significantly diminished by surrounding them with monotony and ugliness, visual and audial pollution, and forcing them to live in smell, smog and squalor. "We only wake up to environmental degradation when it happens faster than the degradation of our senses." (Klaus Michael Meyer Abbich, Kritik der Sinne –Erinnerung der Sinne (Critique of the senses – Memory of the senses) Poesis 5/1989. University Oldenburg Germany p. 20.

Meanwhile another new generation is consciously rejecting the ways in which institutional religions are failing to recognize their new and open sense for the sacred and the spiritual in all aspects of their lives and in all forms that are available to it. A generation of 'new adults', grown up with unlimited access to all expressions of the spirit worldwide, able to choose from many sources, to meet in various circles, outgrowing the spiritual/religious structures in which they were brought up, are finding new and better suited ones or endeavouring on their own. All guided by experience, not by doctrine or established practice. A recent publication of 'Prayers of a Secular World' Melbourne 2014/15 with an insightful introduction by David Tacey, author of 'Edge of the Sacred', offers 96 poems. Gathering some of those contemporary experiences I feel myself turning into a kind of dinosaur, an extinct species, a museum piece, when I keep referring to old and ancient texts that this generation might never read and to which they may have no living experiential connection.

And then I notice, that for this generation the search goes on, not so much a soul-searching as in the 60's, but a search for meaning in nature, the world and the cosmos. Deep ecology (Arne Naess 1912-2009), ecosophy, an awareness that one can't heal oneself without healing the earth. (Robert Sardello: Facing the World with Soul. The Reimagination of Modern Life Harper Perennial 1992). The search seems now to be for what in this vast field of cultural and spiritual experience throughout this age-long trajectory of time shows up as fresh and meaningful. Ancient texts and old traditions re-appear in a new light, a 21st century light, when layers of accumulated certainties have shifted or disappeared under the pressure of our new realities: the breakthrough of a new, self-directed consciousness emerging from experience and new thinking, uncensored by spiritual or secular authority.

As Rabbi Zalman noticed earlier: Latin has been replaced by national languages and people turn to Sanskrit. Gregorian chant has been abandoned in the church and Hildegard's music from the 10th century reaches the top charts in the world. Rabbi Zalman referred to Huston C. Smith (1919-2016) as the most influential pioneer towards religious renewal and interreligious awareness in America beyond established institutions. In 2016 I attended a lecture on meditation in Judaism at the Leo Baeck Centre for progressive Judaism by Jerome Winston, who had been inspired by Huston Smith when – as student – he attended Huston Smith lectures at MIT in the USA. Later that year I learned that my friend Lisaruth had attended Huston Smith's lectures at Syracuse University and had participated in a yearlong overseas journey to experience a diversity of religions in the world. I asked her to write about her experience, which I with her permission included in this selection, which again confirms how – through one person – the spirit of renewal may affect people's lives in ways in which they recognise their own spiritual path....

In this section, Lauren Winner tells of having moved from Judaism to Christianity, but then wanted the Talmud back. Sumi Loudon finds many of her generation turning to Buddhist meditation for its highly developed and systematic approach. This sounds like an artist lecturing in the 1980' to our students recalling how his generation resented being taught techniques in the 70's and now, 10 years later, was quickly catching up on learning them.

The challenge for institutional religion and humanism, it seems to me, is to create new forms or find new meaning in the old ones. Which is what is happening. And this anthology wants to serve to articulate this challenge and to uncover some vague contours of what seems to appear on the horizon as new patterns, dynamic interrelated processes rather than fixated forms of a new orthodoxy.

At least two areas of interest, steeped in experience, have been basically left out in this selection: 'Mysticism' and 'Perennial Philosophy'. Happold's (1893-1971) 'Mysticism. Study and Anthology', Penguin Books 1935, has been an inspiration for this book and is a rich source in itself. And 'Meditations on the Tarot' by Anonymous (Valentin Tomberg), described by Father Bede Griffith as 'the most comprehensive Philosophia Perennis he had ever read', remains a source for inter-religious and humanist understanding in its own right. Whilst Happold's 'Mysticism' offers texts which record mystical experience, the 'Meditations' are a reflection of the authors experience and thinking, living with this perennial wisdom throughout the ages during his lifetime. A third source that I feel is comprehensive and based on his own experience is that by his holiness the Dalai Lama (2004) with his reference to his meetings, conversations, sharing of ceremonies and pilgrimages with all the world's main religions, saints and scholars, but also with the local Muslim watch repairer in his youth, who admonished him use his time well, to begin with. In the 1980's the Dalai Lama had been presented with a list of different religions' expression of the Golden Rule. This list seems identical with what I received from a friend as a Christmas message in the 90's, which became a focus for my meditative walks, with the question: how can religions and spiritual movements restore the public function that this rule must have had at the beginning of their development and of which this rule is a crystallization? It is this question that animates the final three chapters of this book.

After having laid out, drafted and 'filled in' as it were the pages of this book, I find myself revisiting especially chapters 3 and 6 on the basis of what I have been learning whilst composing it. These two chapters have therefore become the most personal, subjective, biased or partisan parts of the whole project. Paradoxically it is for the sake of objectivity that I tentatively but deliberately include here my own - considered – understanding, according to which renewal of world-views may be, or may become, a unique source of renewal for their own institutionalized expressions (Chapter 3) and of today's society that appears to have lost its capacity for evolution. (Chapter 6). And on both 'fronts', indeed 'confronting' challenges, I found a key in Martin Buber's 'I and Thou' –and in his aphorism: "Alles wirkliche Leben is Begegnung". "All real life is encounter". Both the 'Be-' in the German 'Begegnung' and the 'en-' in the English 'Encounter' suggest that more is involved than a simple 'ending up at the same point', having come from different directions. Rather an 'implied mutuality', a 'face-to-face'. The German 'Be-' suggests some 'embrace', the English 'en-' suggests a shared space, even if ever so briefly: i.e. a potential relationship.

Recent encounters may serve as examples:

In the experience of an independent thinker, philosopher of science Paul Feyerabend, a neurobiologist, Gerald Hüther, who both were mentioned in Chapter 3, of John Dupuche, a Catholic Priest and Theologian, pioneering the dialogue between religious world-views, especially between Shaivism and Christianity, as well as in the experience of a musician as song-writer, it might become clear how an individual experience may not only change the direction of one's own life, but also the direction of the world one is involved in. And where those experiences and 'revelations' are very recent, one might do well to pay attention, take note and consider if and where those experiences may need to have an impact, too.

The same counts, too, for a recent and compelling experience of the sacred nature of the encounter between spiritual or pastoral carer and her client that can be found in an interview with Brecht Molenaar, where she pleads for a religious dimension in her profession as a humanist counsellor, and by which I conclude the collection of texts for this chapter: the last not only for its recent publication, but also for the way it reflects many of the elements touched upon in this chapter, and – most importantly – reflects back to the time straight after World War II, with its urgent need to ensure that people be rooted in themselves in such a way, that they would not be swept up again by totalitarian ideologies, a need that has become again just as urgent, if not more so, in recent years...

Interlude

Even though 'face-to-face' firstly points to a direct and literal form of encounter, it lends itself also to a rich reservoir of metaphors...let's face it...at face value...the face of the earth...facing extinction...Chapter 1 offers a rich selection of examples. It also contains a number of texts that emphasize the vital role of language in any form of dialogue.

There is a wealth of beautiful nature films, especially of the earth's wildest areas. With stunning overviews and intimate close-ups, they give concrete meaning to Buber's 'All real life is encounter'. The manifestation of life in all its volume and diversity is overwhelmingly beyond imagination. Yet – in close up – in every pocket of these massive eco-systems all life hangs together through encounters: caring, scaring, courting, nest-building, foraging to feed the young, hunting to still the hunger. No cubic inch seems to be devoid of encounters. Unselfconscious they may be, but not without an innate or acquired intelligence, alertness and sharpness of perception. And – indeed – faces everywhere: varieties of ears, eyes, noses, mouths etc. and even plants, shrubs and trees have 'feelers', sensing, excreting, encircling, winding, trapping...taking an active and foundational part in the overall manifestation of life. Life wants to live and be lived to the full, and one of its 'mechanisms' may be driven by individual or collective survival instincts, its overall, overflowing energy, formative wealth and playfulness suggest even a certain indifference regarding perpetuity and survival, certainly at the level of individuals, less so at the level of species. But even there the inventiveness displayed in those survival 'techniques' seem to demonstrate a masterly command of the technical dimension of their 'reactions' or 'solutions' in favour of what the Dutch phenomenologist F.J.J. Buytendijk (1887-1974) used to call a 'demonstrative wealth'.

This is – of course – not 'science'. On the contrary it is what happens when sciences, arts, technologies are prepared to come face-to-face with one another with their expert skills, experience and knowledge, with myself as onlooker and as 'layman' who over a lifetime has gathered some experience in appreciating 'experts'. If religious experience and expertise seem absent in this summary of all-encompassing encounter, it is because whatever in any world-view is considered highest, sublime, most profound or divine, sacred, stream of consciousness, personal or impersonal, creating or emanating etc. etc., may be the fruit of facing this very 'real life' that by its very nature is 'encounter'.

This all-encompassing pulse and breath of life doesn't stop at a macroscopic scale, it continues down the scale into microbiological life and up the scale towards earth life and humanity as a whole: there is encounter at every level and beyond, if one counts encounters in soul and spirit, embodied and beyond as well.

Before embarking on the second half of this project, dealing with the golden rule past and present, and closing with a chapter on prayers, rites and rituals, I feel the need to remind myself and my readers, that this project started and is continuously nourished by meditative walks over a wide clearing in bushland, at Evera, out under the sky between clusters of trees and shrubs. Sacred sites, not replacing places of worship and reflection in towns and cities, but complementing them: opportunities to concentrate on world-views' essential meanings and messages and on their interconnectedness, common ground and common sky, nature, winds, clouds, bird calls and songs…a dialogical space between heaven and earth. It is not just the walk and not just the conversation, but the space in which they happen, not to be measured in acres or hectares, but to be experienced and enjoyed as an invitation to open up and play together.

I would like to complement Rabbi Zalman's notion of 'dialogical mentality' with a concept of 'dialogical space'. On the one hand a space that only takes on form when we walk it, on the other hand metaphorically a space where people have walked before, not only literally in the last twelve years or so at Evera, but also in time and space, worldwide and in particular regions and times, around the Indian Ocean, the Pacific, the Mediterranean and the Middle East, and in recent times the Parliament of World's Religions and interfaith groups. A space also found in libraries and archives and in special places like the Cathedral of Toledo, where the building itself tells of Islamic and Christian interaction and where the University has become a centre for inter-religious dialogue and study.

This space-awareness is also significant in another sense: texts, customs, doctrines don't 'live' in isolation, without context they are or become lifeless, incapable of relationships and growth.

Texts

Peace is an exceedingly high good, for which we should expect we would have to pay an exceedingly high price... In my opinion the only force in human life that generates the energy enough that can get that we are willing to pay that price is religion.

[ ]

What makes religion religious?

[ ]

When you look at the heart of religion, which every religious tradition calls its heart, what every religious tradition calls as its starting point... What is it?

It is the profound limitless sense of belonging. There is no religion in the world that would not subscribe to that...This deep sense of belonging. It is not something out there, it is in here – personal. You experience it personally. And in the moment in which you have personally - I appeal to your personal experience - have experienced that deep sense of belonging, you experience peace...Religion is peace... (It is) that religion that makes religions religious.

Brother David Steindl-Rast
Let Religions be Religious / Towards a Worldwide real Ecumene of all Religions
[Transcribed and slightly edited excerpts from a lecture, recorded on audio tape, at an international interfaith conference in Amsterdam, 1985]

Authentic experience makes a religion a true tradition. Religious experience is, above all, human experience. If religions are authentic, they contain the same elements of stability, joy, peace, understanding, and love. The similarities and the differences are there. They differ only in terms of emphasis. Glucose and acid are in all fruits, but their degrees differ. We cannot say that one is a real fruit and the other is not.

[ ]

The absence of true experience brings forth intolerance and a lack of understanding. Organized religions, therefore, must create conditions that are favourable for true practice and true experience to flower. Authentic ecumenical practices help different schools within a tradition learn from one another and restore the best aspect of the tradition that may have been eroded. [ ] And it is possible to go even further. Different religious traditions can engage in dialogue with one another in a true spirit of ecumenism...

Thich Nhat Hanh
Living Buddha, Living Christ
1995, pp. 195-196

The feeling of being absolutely dependent: so breath is - so is religion

Life is breath, and there are two kinds of breathing: the breathing of air, which maintains the bodily penetration with oxygen, ozone and the life element (prana, as it is designated in Sanskrit), all of which are necessary for life, and the inner breathing of the soul, which "breathes in" God through prayer and meditation, as the body takes in air. The one kind of breathing is that of health, the other is that of religion. And just as the human being needs the air to breathe for his physical life, so he also has need of breathing in God — through religious prayer and meditation — for his soul-life. The primal religion of humanity (religio naturalis) is grounded and rooted in the breath of life, spoken of in the Bible (Genesis 2:7). The breath of life never ceases and will never cease; it lasts eternally. The German theologian and philosopher Friedrich Schleiermacher, held that religion results from the feeling man has that he is absolutely dependent. This feeling of dependency is actually the feeling of being breathed out from God. It is the primal human experience — and the most universal one — of the reality of God, and is the main "proof" of God for the human soul.

Valentin Tomberg Covenant of the Heart
Meditations of a Christian Hermeticist on the Mysteries of Tradition
1992

Imagined experience: empathy with one's fellow's fate

Of two men who have no experience of God, he who denies him is perhaps nearer to him than the other.

The false God who is like the true one in everything, except that we cannot touch him, prevents us from ever coming to the true one. We have to believe in a God who is like the true God in everything, except that he does not exist, since we have not reached the point where God exists.

The errors of our time come from Christianity without the supernatural. Secularization is the cause — and primarily humanism.

Religion, in so far as it is a source of consolation, is a hindrance to true faith: in this sense atheism is a purification. I have to be atheistic with the part of myself which is not made for God. Among those men in whom the supernatural part has not been awakened, the atheists are right and the believers wrong.

A man whose whole family had died under torture, and who had himself been tortured for a long time in a concentration camp. Or a sixteenth-century Indian, the sole survivor after the extermination of his people. Such men if they had previously believed in the mercy of god would either believe in it no longer, or else they would conceive of it quite differently than before. I have not been through such things. I know however, that they exist so what is the difference? I must move toward an abiding conception of the divine mercy, a conception which does not change whatever event destiny may send upon me, and which can be communicated to no matter what human being.

Simone Weil
Gravity and Grace
1997, pp. 167-8

What is special in the aesthetic experience

How does one come to being conscious? Surely only in a complex process of connecting remembering and presentiment, darkly sure experience, discerning perception and active thinking – this means: in the interweaving of all reactions to a situation, in which an individual I explores and moves. "Coming to one's senses", "making sense" in these and other everyday life expressions, give an inkling, that consciousness has something to do with wakeful senses. Yet we are equally strongly guided by what arises from an inaccessible unconscious as from the conscious; we know since long, that we cannot too much rely on our rationality, that much lies hidden behind it, continuously influencing us in our thinking and actions.

[ ]

Emotionally becoming aware is not yet experience. Living through some event, feeling and perceiving as an immediate way of becoming aware are pre-conditions for experience, but not experience itself. This arises in processes of working-through, in which moments of bodily-sensory, psychological and spiritual dynamically interconnect and at the same time are gathered in a consciousness that becomes aware of itself. Such working-through requires repetition of certain events and active perceptions, it requires remembering what has happened before [and anticipating what might happen next (?), translator] and as such is a process of lived time. Without the time of working-through, only in the pleasure and feeling of the moment, experience does not succeed – it can easily be missed.

What is special about the aesthetic experience is its comprehensive character, engaging all capacities of feeling/ sensing and all capacities of perceiving/thinking.

Gert Selle
Gebrauch der Sinne: eine kunstpädagogische Praxis [Engaging the Senses]
1988, pp. 28-9

In praise of the poetic dimension of science

If everything is judged by how 'useful' it is – useful for staying alive, that is – we are left facing a futile circularity. There must be some added value. At least a part of life should be devoted to living that life, not just working to stop it ending. This is how we rightly justify spending taxpayers' money on the arts.

[ ]

Isn't it a noble and enlightened way of spending our brief time in the sun, to work at understanding the universe and how we have come to wake up in it? This is how I answer when I am asked – as I am surprisingly often – why I bother to get up in the mornings. To put it the other way round, isn't it sad to go to your grave without ever wondering why you were born? Who, with such a thought, would not spring from bed eager to resume discovering the world and rejoicing to be part of it?

Richard Dawkins
Unweaving the Rainbow.
1998, pp. 5-6

A Child's Experience – a Seed for Life

Even the most perfect and complicated structures in the organic world may be traced back to a single cell, a seed. Similarly, the result of growth in the realm of spiritual life can also be followed back to a certain "seed" experience or "seed" thought. And the author of this fragment is no exception here. It is thanks to a kind of "seed" that he owes his growth to the heights, breadths and depths of the many-branched tree of knowledge of God. From this seed, growth has taken place throughout the several decades of his life, enabling him to feel and think his way into all forms of mankind's religious life from different countries and different times in history. In this it was neither a matter of an analytical study of research into the comparison of religions nor a case of building up a syncretistic philosophical system. Rather, the author's endeavour was purely and simply to inwardly sense and experience whatever is to contribute to a deepening, to an elevation, and to an expansion of the fundamental "seed" thought and "seed" experience, which became conceived and arose in the author as follows.

One day, sixty-eight years ago, when the author was four years old, he was playing with some building blocks whilst sitting on a colored carpet on the floor. The window was wide open, through which a cloudless sky could be seen. Close by, the child's mother was sitting in a chair watching the child playing. Suddenly the child looked up and, gazing at the blue heavens, asked his mother, without any prompting the question: "Where is God? Is he in heaven? Does he float there? Or is he sitting here? Where?"

The child's mother sat up straight and gave the following answer, which remained valid and meaningful to the child for decades: "God is everywhere: where the air is invisible and penetrates everything. Just as we live and breathe in the air, and it is thanks to the air that we live and breathe, so our souls live and breathe God and it is thanks to him that we live."

This answer was so clear and convincing that, like the breath of fresh air, it blew away all conceptual problems and left behind certainty concerning God's invisible presence everywhere. This "seed" thought later grew into the heights and depths and breadths, representing the primal seed from which grew a many-branched tree of insight and faith during the subsequent decades of the author's life.

Valentin Tomberg
Covenant of the Heart: Meditations of a Christian Hermeticist on the Mysteries of Tradition.
1992, p. 240

My Faith, My Sustaining Guide

The Qur'an does not speak only to men. It speaks, quite explicitly to women. I knew this at a young age, not because I read the Qur'an, but because I talked to God all the time. I knew with certainty that He responded. May be this spiritual consciousness was a result of my Sufi ancestry; my grandfather and father were Sufis of the popular Tijaniyyah order in Sudan. Sufism has historically welcomed women's spiritual connection to God. Or maybe it was because it never occurred to me that my gender could impede a relationship with God. These conversations taught me that intellect was connected to faith. As an adult, I found it unreasonable that God would prefer men to women in anything, but especially in terms of worshipping Him.

Hibba Abugideiri
George Washington University

A Student's Experience

What is most memorable to the course my life took during my time as a student of Huston Smith at Syracuse University was the entrance into my awareness of guiding thoughts; thoughts starkly different from any other mental thought content. They came as a sudden knowing setting me on a particular course of exploring, knowing and doing a task that I was uniquely fitted for.

If I reflect, this phenomenon had been there years before as a child and an adolescent, but as a young woman new to the higher learning of university and uncertain of what direction my studies would or should take, its presence, beginning in the lecture hall of Huston Smith's course on Chinese religion, had a remarkable formative power.

Sitting near the front of a large lecture hall listening to that slow deliberate cadence of Professor's Smith speech I heard his announcement that he would take a group of graduate and undergraduate students on a yearlong course around the world to study comparative religion and philosophy. In that split second after registering the words, I knew that I would do all I could to be one of those students. With the idea came the strength to realize it. I was accepted on for the year of the International Honors Program, primarily on the basis, Huston Smith explained, of my strong determination to go!

Huston Smith did more for my true education than any professor could sitting within the walls of a university. He dared to bring 30 students and 3 faculty and their families (himself, his wife and one of his daughters included) on a year-long trip beginning in Bath England, ending in Hawaii with one month or longer stops in Morocco, Iran, Israel for a shorter visit, India, Sri Lanka, and Japan to meet and study with teachers and practitioners of Islam, Buddhism, Hinduism, and other faiths. It was a wild year long journey of freedom and purpose and how its content lived in me shaped me as a seeker, student, and later, professional.

In India we arrived just as millions of pilgrims, holy men and women, sadhus, maharajas and others were converging at the place of confluence of three holy rivers; the Ganges, Yamuna and Saraswati. My introduction to India became truly the most cacophonous convergence of sensory impressions that I had ever witnessed before or since. We slept in a tent on the sandy banks, that had become camping spots to the multitude of participants for this month long celebration of cleansing and renewal in the holy confluence of rivers under the most propitious star arrangements. I remember waking up one night with a scream as though my western mind could only process all of this by ejecting a cry of overwhelm.

During these days we would emerge from our tents and be engulfed by the crowds making their way to the water. In the chaos and press of so many, all one could do was keep awake to it all and let oneself be moved by the crowd. It was during one of the auspicious bathing days when the crowds parted to make a 15 foot wide pathway for a procession of holy participants to be the first ones to bathe at the confluence. I cannot remember how it was that I could see what unfolded. I do remember seeing people perched on electricity poles or poles for megaphones hanging on to see the maharajas sitting under parasols and carried on or riding on horses as they proceeded to the bathing place. By some perch I was able to witness several groups of sadhus as they ambled down the wide sandy lane. First, the much photographed naked sadhus gesticulating with their ash covered arms and faces, then, to my astonishment a group of women sadhus clad in dust colored cloth, several with matted hair and to my memory also skin tinged with ash. I was astonished to watch how they moved and interacted with each other. As a portion of the group moved forward those behind would also move forward, but as they reached the line they would not stop in time, but as though in a somnolence of sorts nudge into the group ahead.

It was as I watched this scene unfold that there came to me an idea, an idea full of insight and will not born of my usual mental thinking. The thought was simply this; This extreme asceticism is not how I want to worship God. I knew then that I wanted to worship on a way that included the beauty and dignity of the human body as a full expression of our humaneness. I didn't know it at the time, but here was a pointer which would lead me to explore movement and dance as a way on a spiritual/religious path. At its core/heart is the idea that the body is an image, a microcosm of the divine and that movement and dance can convey unique keys to living and to our part in the, so to speak, cosmic whole including the divine, the spark and source of life itself. I must say here that the point of this thought which I apprehended while witnessing the sannyasins (Hindu *mendicants) move towards the Sangam (confluence) was not a critique of asceticism, but a pointer to the direction which my life would take. The important word here is my, my life. This connection to dance as a path had no connection at the time with any conscious interests or plans. It would be years from that moment before I found myself studying dance and then finding the opportunity to learn with Shin Shiva Swayambhu (known as Shin Gideon Fontalba in the West) the deepest connections of body, soul, spirit, creation and Creator through Cosmic Dance.*

During our International Honors Program travels another experience became a template for how I would engage in my inner questing for knowledge and direct experience of truth. We were staying in Bodhgaya and had the opportunity to participate in a 10 day course with a renowned teacher, Goenka, in the practice of Vipassana (Buddhist) meditation. During this experience of sitting watching the breath, scanning the body, and putting all our focus on the arising and passing of mind/body phenomena this doing of a spiritual practice opened the insight that, as it is through our consciousness that we have experience of the world, we might be able to train our consciousness to make room for awareness of life itself before the mental, emotional conditions which are present as normal daily content. That we might aim to experience first-hand the primal ground of existence as inner experience and so begin to know directly who we are as conscious beings and to intimate our part in the greater whole. So began my study of religion as a momentum to turn inwards; momentum to witness and to seek being, the essential being of my living consciousness and the greater Being from which this arises. This seeking would find its home, years later, in the teachings of Shin Shiva Swayambhu and Sarvajnana-Vidjnana Yoga; teachings which continue to offer insights and paths to transformation and experience and understanding of ourselves as conscious creative beings in this cosmic whole.

I was nineteen years old when I began travels with Huston Smith. It was not until many years later that the ideas that came from these experiences began to move and shape my life.

Through these travels I learned what education might be. The year was about meetings; encounters with sadhus, monks, with my inner world and in these meetings ideas came as pointers for my life. This is what I now consider true education and learning.

Lisaruth

Postscript

Since this trip I have learned through my teacher about asceticism and the deeper meaning of the naked sadhus and their ash covered bodies which I saw all those years ago at the Kumbh Mela. What I now understand is represented in their gesture and striving fills me with deep respect.

Lisaruth

An awareness of being carried

On the 9/11 2001 attack on the twin towers, the question was not: 'Can I be American and Muslim?' But 'How could someone do this in my name'
"It only made me want to delve more into this very beautiful mysticism that I'd already begun to connect with and I wanted to have more of my life".

On her subsequent years with bouts of paralysis and blindness:

But through that time of illness, what came forward was not only the strengthening of our partnership, but also this awareness of being carried by Allah. Even as my body was breaking down around me, this spiritual intensity, awareness, and growth was coming to the forefront and carrying me through this time ...

a really permanent and deeply rooted joy, a very beautiful and healing part of my life. When you go through something like paralysis or blindness and come out on the other side of it, there's not one day that goes by that you're not reminded of that time. You remember when you could not walk, couldn't see. Allah feels very near to me because of what was taken away and what was given back.

Ayesha in:
Lana Dalberg
Birthing God: Women's Experiences of the Divine
2013, pp. 199-201

Chernobyl 1

News of Chernobyl (26 April 1986) was broken to me in an evening class with Art School students, practicing artists, craftspeople: pottery, jewellery, glass, metalsmithing, teaching aesthetics, anthropology and history of the arts/crafts. My response was on the one hand a sense of overwhelm, the enormity of the catastrophe too overwhelming to take in. On the other hand, I sensed that the kind of work these students were doing and the kind of consciousness-raising on my part might be the most healthy and meaningful response to this news at this time. And so I said. Thus we did continue with what was at hand. I have now forgotten what. The question, however, 'where were you, when Chernobyl news broke?' kept haunting me long after.

Later I discovered that Gert Selle (Gebrauch der Sinne/ Engaging the Senses Rowohts Reinbek near Hamburg 1988, pp. 236-7) had discussed with his class, art students working with him in the studio, whether they would cancel the class and join the mass demonstration in the city that afternoon. The class decided, that turning their work into something meaningful in response to Chernobyl would ultimately be more effective than a mass demonstration. The point of his 'art education in action' was, that 'experience encompasses more than a mental working through.

This in turn reminds me of a conversation in the Amsterdam Steiner School between form 10 students and their class guardian, who had refused to go with them in school time to a demonstration against Franco. His explanation:

"For me the best way to fight fascism is to teach in this school."
As their history teacher I had joined the students, because I wanted to share their experience and the demonstration had been an utterly uninspiring event, with a poor turn out and tired slogans.

Henk Bak

Chernobyl 2

The next afternoon the planned excursion in the forest has to be postponed; nobody wants to go out. Shortly before we had still been lying on the earth full of curiosity and trust; now each contact with nature appears to be threatening. What to do? The question confronts everyone. Practically there are three responses possible: to act out of one's own helplessness in an extended collective protest (visit to an institute of physics); the inactive resignation in diffuse anxiety; or a reaction by means of exercise in the working through of this new experience of the sinister. Whatever we do, basically it must remain helpless and incommensurate, expressive of perplexity and powerlessness. Some vote for information (and come later back into the workplace, frustrated by having merely to listen). Others decide on a personal positioning in the framework of the exercise.

Existentially being involved now stands so clearly at the foreground, that for the remaining group an individual working through in an artistic activity shows up as more or less the obvious thing to do. So the picture full of tension arises, that we are contemplating new possibilities of expression, whilst outside a silent march is in progress. A tension develops between the two possible responses, which all are sensing. Half a year later it is still spoken about; but all are of the opinion that it had been right to stay there and in a practical sense to search for a special expression of the Chernobyl experience and to say something personal, not only to be silent symbolically and to march.

For the rest of the afternoon we worked on the alienation of the already familiar materials or of objects earlier found on the forest-floor and were still left. Materials that were reserved for totally different purposes are sacrificed, the disruption does something more to it. One works in silence; only at the end an exchange takes place in conversation.

So fields and objects emerge, which then lie visibly on the floor of the old refectory. Nobody thinks of commenting on them. They lie there for passers-by as admonition and as document of an attempt to react on the event that involves all in a way that is different from the usual, but not quite merely private; that cannot change anything, but opens a possibility for reflection as well as a working through of this shattering event.

Gert Selle
Gebrauch der Sinne: Eine Kunstpedagogische Praxis [On Using the Senses: Art Education in Action]
1988, pp. 247-48
[Translated by Henk Bak]

Experience in the Shadow of the Holocaust

It is my mother, Chris Lerman, who speaks about her personal relationship to God. In 2006, she guided her grandchildren through Auschwitz-Birkenau, describing her arrival at age eighteen. "Here is where they stripped me naked and tattooed my arm; here is where they shaved my head; here the wooden platform where I slept. You could see the chimney belching flames from this window." ... "One night, a woman risked her life to visit our barracks. She carried two wax stubs hidden in her rags. 'Tonight is Kol Nidrei,' she told us. 'Let's light the candles and pray.'"

Jeanette Lerman-Neubauer in: Menachem Rosensaft
God, Faith & Identity from the Ashes: Reflections of Children and Grandchildren of Holocaust Survivors

> 2015, p. 196

> *My relationship with God and the Jewish faith remained a complicated one throughout my life. A defining moment I will never forget was my first trip as a scholar to Auschwitz, where I saw prayer shawls on display. I felt an immense sense of anger at God and at the Jewish men who naively believed that they were going to live and pray in a place where God could not be present. Yet, when I lead groups to the sites of life and death in Poland, in each site I direct the group to recite the Jewish prayers in honor of the dead, Kaddish and El-Maleh Rachamim. Anger and prayer live side by side in my heart.*
>
> Tali Nates in: Menachem Rosensaft
> **God, Faith & Identity from the Ashes: Reflections of Children and Grandchildren of Holocaust Survivors**
> 2015, p. 251

> *It was time to tell him about our family. As I mulled lover how I would introduce him to the ghosts, I recalled something a friend had told me. He is a black man who grew up in the white Midwest, and he had heard terrible truths from his family as he was growing up, too. We were both traumatized by what we had learned in our families, and we didn't want to induce trauma in our own kids. "So maybe," he said, "we need to stop telling them we are the victims and tell them instead that we are the victors. We are here, today, because those people who came before us made it out alive."*

> *…When I finally told him about his great-grandparents, his eyes were shining with admiration as he asked me, "They must have been very strong to survive, right?" I hugged him hard. Focus on the survivors now, I thought. The ghosts can wait.*
>
> Natalie Friedman in: Menachem Rosensaft
> **God, Faith & Identity from the Ashes: Reflections of Children and Grandchildren of Holocaust Survivors**
> 2015, p. 163

Navigating Judaism with a Female Compass

> *One Simchas Torah when I was young, my childlike quest for inclusion found me marching in the circlke along with the boys, carrying a mini-Torah and singing gleefully. I innocently disregarded the gender roles assigned by Judaism because I wanted to celebrate the completion of the yearly Torah reading in the same way my male classmates did. The rabbi, however, was not entertained by my shirking of tradition and pulled me outside his circle. He reminded me that I was a girl and that girls don't march with the Torah on Simchas Torah, which also meant that they didn't on any other occasions, either.*

At the time, I might not have realized the injustice or the sexism, for I don't remember crying. I imagine I took comfort in the existence of such traditions, and followed the rabbi's instructions like a good little girl. I greatly respected my rabbi, with his warm, large hands and kind eyes, and I wanted those eyes to look down on me favourably.

[ ]

As I came of age I began to wonder if that was all there was to the prayer experience and to synagogues in general. Though I was eager to participate, it seemed that my sex and the very traditions I followed withheld me from the service. I was introduced to the brick wall just as my adult spiritual journey was beginning.

As a young adult, in the Boston suburb of Brookline, I now live close to temples, kosher restaurants and other Jews, and this has infused me, seemingly instantaneously, into a community. I have tried a few of the popular social events, formed new friendships, and made possible romantic connections.

[ ]

I have no doubt that when and if I marry a Jewish man, I will become both more religiously and more spiritually Jewish. I am just unsettled by the reality that even in this new century, one Jewish woman's desire to gain access, no matter how strong, can be unsuccessful, simply because she is outside a community's boundaries and single.

[ ]

Following men's examples it's no wonder, that I eventually found myself lost. Men are fundamentally incapable of guiding an experience that falls completely outside their own patriarchal traditions. And how could I have expected them to? It was women whom I needed as guides – women who were, on the whole, lost themselves. Like me, they had been thrown into the thick of Judaism with no female compass.

Jodi Werner
God Within: Our Spiritual Future – as Told by Today's New Adults
2001, pp. 105-8

Psalm Eight…God as a presence…I am never not instructed …

One Easter I went with my grandfather to a small Presbyterian church in Northern Idaho, where I heard a sermon on the discrepancies in the gospel accounts of the resurrection. I was a young child with neither the habit nor the expectation of understanding, as the word is normally used, most of what went on around me. Yet I remember that sermon and I believe, in some degree I took its meaning.

As an older child in another church and town, on no special occasion, I heard the Eighth Psalm read, and kept for myself a few words from it, because they heartened certain intuitions in me – "When I consider the heavens, the work of thy fingers, the moon and the stars…what is man, that thou art mindful of him? And the son of man, that thou visitest him? For thou has made him a little lower than the angels…" I quote the King James Version because those were the words I heard and remembered. The thought never entered my mind that the language could be taken to exclude me, perhaps because my experience of it was the religious one, of words in some exceptional sense addressed precisely to me.

[ ]

I doubt I concealed my restlessness, or much of it, and I doubt my grandfather knew the hour was anything but tedium for me. He would not have known, because no one knew, that I was becoming a pious child, seriously eager to hear whatever I might be told. What that meant precisely, and why it was true, I can only speculate. But it seems to me I felt God as a presence before I had a name for him, and long before I knew words like "faith" or "belief". I was aware to the point of alarm of a vast energy of intention, all around me, barely strained, and I thought everyone must be aware. I found the majestic terrains of my childhood, to which my ancestors had brought their ornate Victorian appreciation at daunting cost in life and limb, very disturbing, and I was coaxed to admire, and I would not, admiration seeming so poor a thing in the circumstances. Only in church did I hear experience like mine acknowledged, in all those strange narratives, read and expounded and for all that as opaque as figures of angels painted on gold.

[ ]

By the standards of my generation, all my life I have gone to church with a kind of persistence, as I do to this day…I go to church for my own gratification, which is intense, though it had never occurred to me before to describe it to myself.

The essence of it, certainly, is the Bible, toward which I do not feel in any degree proprietary, with which after long and sometimes assiduous attention I am not familiar. I believe the entire hypertrophic bookishness of my life arose directly out of my exposure, amongst modest protestant solemnities of music and flowers, to the language of scripture. Therefore I know many other books very well and I flatter myself that I understand them – even books by people like Augustine and Calvin. But I do not understand the Bible. I study theology as one would watch a solar eclipse in the shadow. In church, the devout old custom persists of merely repeating verses, one or another luminous fragment, a hymn before and a hymn afterward. By grace of my abiding ignorance, it is always new to me. I am never not instructed. pp. 227-8

Marilynne Robinson
The Death of Adam: Essays on Modern Thought
2005, pp. 227-8

I cannot just take a quick look, and think myself informed

The committee retreat's theme, this year is "together with the healing spirit". So my contemplation began with: "In what way am I together with the healing spirit?" and "how do I keep the healing spirit in connection with me – in what I think, and what I say?" I realise that by studying Anthroposophy, by being a Christian, that that is what I have chosen to do in this life – to function in my daily life, as much as I can, by being Conscious to live together with the healing spirit – or I could even say, the Holy Spirit, the spirit of love; this, for me, means that whatever my interaction with you, or you, or you, whatever the interaction is, (I pray) may be governed by love. Love heals everything; and love is blind, of course! So aren't I lucky. But "blind", not oblivious – because blind in fact requires me to be not at all oblivious, but in other ways more attentive, more seeking and perceptive; and it takes a conscious effort. (And there is nothing to stop anyone with physical sight from also practising those manifold ways of careful perception).

I quietly let my inner resonance resonate with your presence so that I may sense your gifts – and they are what defines who you are – your gifts, your talents. Hopefully you will feel a loving acceptance from me. I think the flowering of the plant is drawn by the warmth of the sun.

I remember that when my mother met a visitor, it was firstly with quiet slow contemplation – and it seemed to me that she was letting the visiting person's particular qualities show themselves. And then she would greet. I think of her as being merciful and just. You might think that being 'just' implies judging – but it doesn't, because if one wants to be 'just', one realises that I can never know the full details of your circumstances, so I had better be merciful. That is what being 'just' means to me.

Now remember that we are still with the theme of "being together with the healing spirit", and that when we say that "love is blind" that doesn't mean love is not sentient, not aware! To me it means that love is merciful. Love is a sense, as well as a feeling – with loving openness I can sense your talents, and the defects that you are challenged to learn from. Emphasising that the deficits in your character are the difficulties that we have been incarnated with, to use as lessons for our further flowering, it is possible that I have chosen to live this life as a blind person so I cannot just take a quick look, and think myself informed. If you want to know some things as a blind person, it takes time – you have to explore, you have to try many ways to access whatever it is - be it a terrain or a person, or a biology experiment. The few maps of areas I know are within me, they are very much 'within' me; I feel the movements of the directions. And that is a paradigm for knowing a person too. Perhaps I have said enough, except that I must repeat that this is how I can function because I keep together with the healing spirit. It is the light by which I see. Perhaps the Healing Spirit has gathered for me all that I have learned from past incarnations – and it resounds that within me now. And that's a good starting point.

Rebecca Maxwell
Together with the Healing Spirit A Cogitation
A contribution to a Christian Community Retreat Melbourne
2019
[Made available by the author]

Wisdom of Confucius – a Spring of warm, living water

When entrusted the manuscript of my book to the Zhongua Book Company in China at the end of 2006, I was content but also a little troubled. I started my Master's degree in pre-Qin Dynasty literature at the age of twenty-one, and I had grown up immersed in books from the Zhongua Book Company, but I would never have dared to dream that one day this elite publishing house might bring out a book of mine, no more than I would have presumed to entertain the hope that I would ever dare to stand up and talk about the Analects of Confucius on television.

I have always respected this book rather than fearing it, and my feelings towards it have always been plain, simple and warm.

Once, in a small town in North China, famous for its hot springs, I saw something called the 'Ask Sickness Spring', it is said that anybody who takes a comfortable soak in its water will at one at once understand the source of their illness: people with arthritis will get a tingling feeling in their joints, those with gastro-intestinal problems will experience a hot sensation in their gut, while people with skin complaints will feel a pleasant flush all over their skin as if a layer of skin is being washed away, like the sloughed-off skin of a cicada.

For me, the wisdom of Confucius is just such a spring of warm, living water.

With my limited knowledge, even if I truly wanted to write an in-depth analysis of Confucius, I would never, ever dare to do such a thing. It would be like sending me off to make a chemical analysis of that hot spring, when I am totally unequipped to do so. The only possible role for me is that of someone who has been immersed in the spring myself, testing with my own body and blood, like the thousands and thousands of people who over the last two hundred years and more have steeped themselves in this hot spring, and experienced its gifts.

The good will see goodness in it, and the wise see wisdom. Perhaps the value of this classical text is not in rituals and reverence that inspire awe and fear, but in the inclusiveness and fluidity, he wisdom in which so many people have immersed themselves down the ages, so that every life and every individual, through perceiving it differently, and following different paths, can arrive at last at the same final goal. In China we say 'The truth has never been far away from ordinary people' and here that is certainly the case.

Yu Dan
Confucius from the Heart: Ancient Wisdom for Today's World
2019, pp. 2-3

Human Being: Cosmic Eye

Crossing a bare common, in snow puddles, at twilight, under a clouded sky, without having in my thoughts any occurrence of special good fortune, I have enjoyed a perfect exhilaration. Almost I fear to think how glad I am...Standing on the bare ground, - my head bathed by the blithe air, and uplifted into infinite space, - all mean egotism vanishes. I become a transparent eye-ball. I am nothing. I see all. The currents of the

> *Universal Being circulate through me, I am part and particle of God. The name of nearest friend sounds then foreign and accidental. To be brothers, to be acquaintances, - master or servant, is then a trifle and a disturbance. I am the lover of uncontained and immortal beauty...*
>
> Ralph Waldo Emerson's Nature (1844), pp. 12-13
as cited in Gay Wilson Allen's Waldo Emerson
1982, p. 277

Conscious experience makes old scripture yield 'new revelation'.

> *It is true that, so far as such statements of Script are mysteries, they are relatively to us but words, and cannot be developed. But as a mystery implies in part what is incomprehensible or at least unknown, so does it in part imply what is not so; it implies a partial manifestation, or a representation by economy. Because then it is in a measure understood, it can so far be developed, though each result in the process will partake in the dimness and confusion of the original impression.*

[ ]

> *This moreover should be considered, - that great questions exist in the subject matter of which the Scripture treats, which Scripture does not solve; questions so real, so practical, that they must be answered, and, unless we suppose a new revelation, answered by means of the revelation which we have, that is, by development.*
>
> John Henry Newman
Essay on the Development of Christian Doctrine
1845, p. 44

Paths appear to me in the woods.... I always know where true North is

> *I had many spiritual experiences as a child. I had a working mother, and after school I practically lived on the banks of the Willamette, which is a very large river in Oregon. My mother used to tell a story about me running into the house shouting, 'Mommy, the wind talked to me!'*

> *I've always been very connected with the animistic forms of holiness. Mother earth taught me so much. Just by listening, by sitting quietly for hours on the banks of the river, or in a redwood forest, or the desert, you learn. Things come to you: ideas that can be manifested and brought to life in reality...*

The Spirit talks to me when I get to that tranquility level...

...your mind goes inward. Mine does anyway, so it feels like a direct connection. That's the only way I can explain it. Rocks talk to me. Paths appear to me in the woods. I've never lost my way, have never been lost in my life. I always know where true North is.

Kirstin in: Lana Dalberg
Birthing God: Women's Experiences of the Divine
2013, pp. 229-30

From Christianity to Spirituality and Community

Spirituality: I started doing yoga when I was nineteen. And then I started to hear about the Hindu's viewpoint, and I started doing meditation, and I didn't think about it as religion either. I just thought we were breathing and feeling. After Hinduism, I went into Taoism and Chinese medicine, and again I thought the philosophy made so much more sense than anything I'd studied, but it was just a collection of thoughts or philosophies.

That's where we make our mistakes: making all the rules. Spirituality is not written down, it's felt. In order to have a true spirit of the Divine, you need to have an open mind and an open heart. You don't need any isms or structures. It's structure-less and if you put any structures on it, it really doesn't exist anymore because it's structure-less. It's like the Tao that can be named is not the true Tao. The minute you put a name on it, it's no longer divine.

Community: The earth. Everything enhances my relationship to the Divine. When I hike, I see the trees swaying in the wind. When I walk in the street, I talk to them, they kind of talk back. Making love to my husband connects me to the Divine.... He is my favourite community.

Allison in: Lana Dalberg
Birthing God: Women's Experiences of the Divine
2001, pp. 207-8

How experience, deeply felt and thought through, may change one's profession 1.

From 1958 I was a professor of Philosophy at the University in California in Berkeley. My function was to carry out the educational policies of the State of California which means I had to teach people what a small group of white intellectuals had decided was knowledge. I hardly ever thought about this function and I would not have taken it very seriously had I been informed. I told the students what I had learned. I arranged the material in a way that seemed plausible and interesting to me — and that was all I did. Of course, I had also some ideas of my own — but those ideas moved in a very narrow domain (although some of my friends said even then that I was going batty).

In the year 1964ff. Mexicans, Blacks, Indians entered the University as a result of new educational policies. There they sat, partly curious, partly disdainful, partly simply confused hoping to get an 'education'. What an opportunity for a prophet in search of a following! What an opportunity, rationalists told me, to contribute to the spreading of reason and the improvement of mankind! What a marvelous opportunity for a new wave of enlightenment! I felt very differently. For it dawned on me that the intricate arguments and wonderful stories I had so far told to my more or less sophisticated audience might just be dreams, reflections of the conceit of a small group of people who had succeeded in enslaving everyone else with their ideas. Who was I to tell these people what and how to think? I did not know their problems though I knew they had many. I was not familiar with their interests, their feelings, their fears though I knew that they were eager to learn. Were the arid sophistications which philosophers had managed to accumulate over the ages and which liberals had surrounded with schmaltzy phrases to make them palatable the right thing to offer to people who had been robbed of their land, their culture, their dignity and who were now supposed to absorb patiently and then repeat the anaemic ideas of the mouthpieces their oh so human captors? They wanted to know, they wanted to learn, they wanted to understand the strange world around them-did they not deserve better nourishment? Their ancestors had developed cultures of their own, colourful languages, harmonious views of the relation of man and man and man and nature whose remnants are a living criticism of the separation, analysis, self-centeredness inherent in Western thought. These cultures have important achievements in what is today called sociology, psychology, medicine, they express ideals of lie and possibilities of human existence. Yet they were never examined with the respect they deserved except by a small number of outsiders, they were ridiculed and replaced as a matter of course, first but the religion of brotherly love and then by the religion of science or else they were defused by a variety of 'interpretations'. Now there was much talk of liberation, of racial equality — but what did it mean? Did it mean the equality of these traditions and the tradition of the white man? They did not. Equality meant that the members of different races and cultures now had the wonderful chance to participate in the white man's mania's, they had the chance to participate in his science, his technology, his medicine, his policies. These were the thoughts that went through my head as I looked at my *audience and they made me recoil in revulsion from the task I was supposed to perform. For this task – this now became clear to me – was that of a very refined, very sophisticated slave driver. And a slavedriver I did not want to be.*

Experiences such as these convinced me that intellectual procedures which approach a problem through concepts and abstract from everything else are the wrong track and I became interested in the reasons for the tremendous power this error has now over minds. I started examining the rise of intellectualism in ancient Greece and the causes that brought it about. I wanted to know what it is that makes people who have a rich and complex culture fall for dry abstractions and mutilate their traditions, their thought, their language so that they can accommodate the abstractions. I wanted to know how intellectuals manage to get away with murder – for it is murder, murder of minds and cultures that is committed year in ear out in schools, universities, educational missions in foreign countries. The trend must be reversed, I thought, we must learn from those we have enslaved for they have much to offer and at any rate, they have the right to live as they see fit even if they are not as pushy about their rights and their views as their Western Conquerors have always been. In 1964-5 when those ideas first occurred to me I tried to find an intellectual solution to my misgivings that is, I took it for granted that it was up to me and the likes of me to devise educational policies for other people. I envisaged a new kind of education that would live from a rich reservoir of different points of views permitting the choice of traditions most advantageous to the individual. The teacher's task would consist of facilitating the choice, not in replacing it with some 'truth' of his own. Such a reservoir, I thought, would have much in common with a theatre of ideas as imagined by Piscator and Brecht and it would lead to the development of a great variety of means of representation. ... Why should knowledge be shown in the garment of prose and reasoning?...

I now realize that these considerations are just another example of intellectualistic conceit and folly. It is conceited to assume that one has solutions for people whose lives one does not share and whose problems on does not know...So what remains?

Two things remain. I could start participating in some tradition and try to reform it from inside...I have not much enthusiasm for such work especially as I think that fields such as the philosophy of science, or elementary particle physics, or ordinary language philosophy, or Kantianism should not be reformed but should be allowed to die a natural death (they are too expensive and the money spent on them is needed more urgently elsewhere).Another possibility is to start a career as entertainer. This is very attractive to me. bringing a faint smile to the faces of people who have been hurt, disappointed, depressed, who are paralysed by some 'truth' or by the fear of death seems to me an achievement infinitely more important than the most sublime intellectual discovery...

Paul Feyerabend
Science in a free Society
2017, pp. 118-21

How experience deeply felt and thought - through may change one's profession 2.

Like so many others I was since long already sufficiently informed as to how effectively smart traders on the stock-market, real estate agents and investment bankers utilize without restraint their opportunities to enrich themselves at the expense of others. And since years already I knew of course also that the managers of the large food-companies leave no opportunity unused to maximize their profits...But it had not really touched me. I have bought more environmentally friendly food, occasionally even got upset about it, for the rest I lived my life as usual. Until I watched, a couple of years back, two documentaries by the Austrian filmmaker Erwin Wagenhofer. 'Lets make money' and 'We feed the world'...It was horrifying, through such hard-hitting images once more to be confronted with all this. But what did really terrify me was something that till then I had never thought of: those responsible for these conditions, those also, who had developed all these cunning financial transactions and who had built up these corporations that dominate the world-market, were formally well educated people. They had attended the best schools and had completed them with the best exam-results. They had studied at the most renowned Universities and had been rewarded with the highest distinctions for their academic achievements. Following from there they had arrived at their leading positions and that they made themselves in those positions not only unaccountable but also acted highly motivated out of their own conviction, was precisely what both films had showed my eyes with such directness.

I found it unbelievable how these leading powers enrich themselves at the expense of others and with such indifference in the face of the consequences of their profit-focused actions.

What shocked me most deeply, however, and what caused me a few sleepless nights, was the realization that they had enjoyed the very education that we

*class as optimal. That this education obviously had in no way generated
in them a concept - let alone a consciousness - of their own dignity, could
hardly have been brought more clearly to expression... The films have opened
my eyes for what in our educational institutes up to this day is missing.*

*When a human being in the course of growing up doesn't by chance
meet a teacher who assists him or her in developing a concept and a
consciousness of his/her own dignity, then an inborn sense for this has
been suppressed. In the case of many, possibly in particular the most
successful graduates, so deeply, that it never resurfaces during their
lifetime. That has shocked me. That was important for me, that affected
something in me. Which also includes the decision to write this book.*

*But how can we — better than until now - help each other
to become conscious of our dignity as human beings?*

*That all parents succeed in this with their children remains a
pious wish. In any case, as long as there are parents, who have not
yet themselves become conscious of their own worth. Who often
not even have a concept yet of what their dignity entails.*

[ ]

*The process of developing a self-image, that has interiorised one's own
becoming integrated into a human community and serves the child as
an inner compass in order to so shape its relations with others that their
dignity is not violated, needs time. That doesn't let itself be taught. It can
only be developed through each child's favourable individual experiences
with other people. The accompanying and gradually more reflective and
self-forming process doesn't let itself speed up. It can only succeed in
an unhurried/sheltered environment that offers the child the necessary
leisure for it. The ancient Greek seem to have understood this already,
for they introduced the word 'sgolè' for it, which then by the Romans
was taken over as 'scola', in German 'Müsse' (English 'leisure').*

*In most today's schools nothing is to be seen of the 'leisure' that is
required for self-determination and self-finding. Where do the young
when growing up still find opportunity there, to try out and playfully
try out their inborn talents and gifts and to pursue their natural*

pleasure in independent discovering and creating something together?

Instead they are being informed, instructed, controlled, tested and assessed, exactly so as if they were objects malleable after the ideas of the adults.

No wonder, that for them the appetite for learning drains away...

[ ]

Perhaps you begin by now to get a sense of what had shocked me when watching both documentaries. It became clear to me as by a stroke of lightning, that our educational system is absolutely not equipped to assist the younger generation in strengthening their sense for what constitutes their dignity, let alone to develop their own concept or even an awareness of their dignity...

Gerald Hüther, Uli Hauser
Würde: Was uns stark macht – als Einzelneund als Gesellschaft / [Dignity: That which does make us Strong as Individuals and as Society]
2018, pp. 147-154

Experience: the memory of a songwriter

Be there for the source, respect the source...

...Neil Young

Please allow me to digress a little. We are, first and foremost, songwriters. It is a craft in which the mind of the crafter entertains myriad tantalising thoughts and suffers long periods of agonising self- doubt and disappointment. This is a private craft, often selfish and divorced from the usual conceits and vanities rather entertains myriad tantalising thoughts and suffers long periods of agonising self-doubt and disappointment. This is a private craft, often selfish and never entirely divorced from the usual conceits and vanities that invade all artists' emotional lives. We live in our minds, and it is sometimes a battle between being lost for good reason, and just being lost.

So how does songwriting actually work in reality? It is the kind of process you will never workshop at a songwriting seminar. There was an astonishing moment in an interview with Neill Young on Charlie Rose's PBS chat-show, when Young was prompted by Rose to explain Living With War, his impassioned 2008 album and associated with anti-George W Bush campaign, complete with documentary videos.

Replying Young gave a highly charged description of his songwriting process and the inspiration for the record. It involved a hotel foyer, a coffee, a glance at a USA Today front-page headline, and a large colour photograph depicting an airborne operating theatre aboard a military transport plane en route from Iraq. There was blood everywhere and dying soldiers evenly spaced on operating tables. Rather than it being a story about suffering and futility, however, the editorial substance seemed to have been more about the remarkable advances being made in military medicine.

Young described an immediate departure to his room, tears flowing, and the intense composition of the song 'Families', which is on the album, accompanied by an abject personal horror at what the Iraq war was doing to the American family. The song portrays a kind of remote consciousness of a doomed young soldier, with a hand out to his family, and also to the artist who will convey his pain.

[ ]

This is nothing new in the context of lyrical composition and how inspiration strikes. It is about the need, the power of the senses. The need to express is all. If you go back over 200 years to the beginning of the nineteenth century, you find William Wordsworth penning the famous preface to his and Coleridge's Lyrical ballads, in which he explains their philosophy that poetry is indeed 'the spontaneous overflow of powerful feelings'. In Nature, he writes there exists a spirit, , indefinable and beyond organised religion. Wordsworth's 'Ode: Intimations of Immortality' characterises the power of the mind and the imagination as a 'light' and a 'mirror', illuminating and reflecting this spiritual essence. A little later, John Keats wrote that true poetry was by necessity 'of the senses'.

Dave McArtney
Gutter Black: A Memoir
2014, pp. 106-7

Still – Simple – Content

In a set of 5 precepts, to purify body, life and soul the Buddhist way, those three concepts: stillness, simplicity and contentment fascinated me most. I learned them from Pam, our Buddhist friend in the peace-meditation.

Perhaps a good way to enter the Christmas season and whatever is left of its meaning in today's society.

Stillness is more than absence of noise, sound, movement or any other sensory experience: a presence so powerful that many are afraid and drive it away. Whatever meaning is left, the message of peace or celebration of family and friendship, is easily replaced with emptiness.

Simplicity is more than cutting out the clutter. An approach to life that comes from within: to 'be' rather than 'have', a Christmas 'created' rather than 'bought' or happening 'on automatic'. And contentment?

Stillness: Christmas 1944, The Hague, Holland, 'hunger-winter' in the war. My brother (11) and I (13) were walking from church to home along a wide avenue.

We were approaching the crossing with another avenue, just as wide. A vast open space, totally empty, nobody there except a lonely soldier approaching the crossing from the left. On the crossing we met.

Simplicity: the soldier opened his mantle and offered us a loaf of bread. We both refused.

Contentment? Without a word the soldier understood and covered the bread with his mantle and continued his walk.

At home our dad was relieved that we had followed his instructions. But my oldest brother (18) disagreed: we had deprived this man, far from his family, the opportunity to do something good…We had acted 'on automatic', the soldier with intent. The longer I live, the more I agree with my brother, even though empathizing with our parents who had a hard task bringing a family of 7 safely through the war…

Final peace meditation for the year: 18 December – first in the new year: 8 January

Happy Christmas, Henk

Trentham Trumpet
[Newsletter, December, p. 8]
2017

Tantric experience – where millennia old traditions find their common source

The expressions of the Word are necessarily inadequate since the divine glory weakens as it radiates. If we remain at the level of words, and if we confuse religions and theologies, double belonging is impossible. We have always to go beyond the words, however necessary they may be, in order to arrive at their source. That being said, the experience of unity between religions must also be expressed. We would eventually need to perform an act which manifests externally and publicly that which is mutually felt in the depths of the spirit.

The sharing is enriching. Consider the following analogy: a single eye sees only the vertical and horizontal dimensions, but our two eyes which do not see in exactly the same way – allow us to see the third dimension: depth. Similarly, the two ears which do not hear in exactly the same fashion, allow the listener to determine from which direction a sound is coming. In an analogical way, the irreconcilable differences between religions are of inestimable value since they make us go beyond the merely mental to discover the Word which is at the origin. If there were no compatibility between religious traditions, we would finally have no complete access to the divine source which surpasses all knowledge.

The act of sharing is in fact a proto-evangelisation, since during the meeting we hear a sort of 'buzz' which is the Word in its first stage of manifestation. It is the resonance of the Word which manifests at the level of intuition before becoming explicit in words. The Word reverberates in us and enables us to hear the reverberation which occurs in others. The participants of the interreligious meeting recognize, one in the other and each in their own selves, the supreme Word from which all rites and teachings arise. It is the same Word which is manifest in the prophets of every age, in the Old Testament and in all the testaments, in the glory of the world. (Rom 1:20) and in the emotions of the human heart, in the ceremonies and the holy places of all religions. To refuse the expressions of the Word in other traditions would mean turning away from the Word itself; it would be apostasy.

John Dupuche
***Towards a Christian Tantra: The Interplay of Christianity
and Kashmir Shaivism***
2009, pp. 94-95A

The experience of a religious humanistic spiritual carer – an interview

She worked for 20 years as humanist spiritual carer in a hospital in Rotterdam, and what Brecht Molenaar was sad to see happening in the course of the years was this: humanism lost its religious dimension and the spiritual care lost sight for the world-view on which it is founded... 'My main concern is that a conversation take place about what it means to be a human being.

[ ]

Did you call yourself there explicitly humanistic?

> *Mostly I said that I wasn't religious, but that I didn't have anything against the faith. For many patients it actually didn't matter much – humanism, humourism, they found it best, as long as they were able to have an open conversation with me. And those who belonged decidedly to a church and had genuine problems with the faith, did of course have their own spiritual carers.*

> *Nowadays I teach the subject 'religious humanism and being present' in a liberal training course, and when I was asked there, I have entered more deeply into this, and I saw: yes, that is precisely what I am: a religious humanist.*

What is that?

> *For me it boils down to me saying: you turn up in the world, but how this has happened is a mystery. Even given a big bang it still remains utterly miraculous, that I am here now, that we all are, and I don't know how it goes further. And the beauty is that Jaap van Praag, the pioneer of the Humanistisch Verbond (Humanist Fellowship), thought along these lines, too. Van Praag, chairman from 1946 to 1969, was Jewish, but secular, and he considered himself a religious humanist, too. May I read to you the closing words of his course for spiritual counsellors from 1953? 'So the counsellor commits himself humbly to his task, entering in the reality that has found form in another human being, thoughtfully aware of the word: take your shoes from your feet, for you stand on sacred ground'. A biblical text. Van Praag draws the concept 'sacred' into the humanist discourse. This speaks strongly to me. In the first declaration of the Humanist Fellowship's principles, there was mention of 'the reverence for the human being as a special part of the cosmos as a whole'.*

What does this mean?

> *I sense awe, astonishment, not-knowing and I see this as reli-*

> *gious terms. One didn't assume a personal God, but He was also not – as a matter of course - denied, and in that time there were also many liberal protestants member of the Humanist Fellowship. But in the course of the years that element has disappeared, whilst for me it was very significant: it informed my attitude to the human beings who tell me about their lives. What mattered for me: if I am with them in such a way that they feel being seen and being heard, and being confirmed in their dignity, then I make humanism true as well.*

Did in such conversations the approaching death play a role?

> *Not that often, actually. But also when the dying was coming closer, it went much more about life than about death. Happened also because of me, perhaps. People who for example feared hell would most probably rather speak to a pastor. With many modern people, being seen and acknowledged is, certainly in the tragedy and in the task ahead, all the consolation that would in earlier times have been offered by explicit salvation ideologies.*

> *Interviewer: Makes me think of what Henk van Os recently told, how he after the passing of his oldest son had been consoled by a painting of Rembrandt: Jeremias grieving over Jerusalem. Therein didn't lie any solution for the suffering, but certainly an unnameable solidarity.*

> *Yes, that is it! precisely.*

Yet, after twenty years, you left this work.

> *What I experienced was, to be honest, modernity-over-the-top. The illusion that everything can be manufactured, the emphasis – precisely also with the Humanist Fellowship – on self-determination and autonomy, such as you also come across in the thinking about 'completed life'. And then, that billboard, partly on behalf of the Fellowship, 'There is probably no God, dare to think for yourself and enjoy life!' The Humanist Fellowship had to profile itself on the 'meaning-of-life' market and chose more and more for atheism or perhaps even for being antireligious: 'become a member, otherwise you are at the mercy of the gods.' I could not identify with that.*

Was that your reason to stop?

> *In addition the professional association for spiritual carers began more and more to move towards health and well-being as product. The focus shifted towards the working and effectiveness of our conduct. The spiritual carer applies methods more and more based on the social sciences, and these assist the patient in managing his problems with finding meaning. The faith or the view of life of the carer doesn't play a role in this. Since 2015 they are no longer mentioned in the definition of what spiritual care is. It fits in with the trend of secularization, even if there is here in fact more a case of breaking people's connection with tradition, because many people are still concerned with faith, only not any more in the church. My fear is that one is going to say: faith and world-view is all private, with as consequence that nobody still dares to take in a normative stand-point. In the care this means, that morality is being totally erased from peoples thinking, with the effect that one often thoughtlessly goes with the flow of neo-liberal thinking, with its emphasis on own strength, everything can be manufactured, and so on. And this whilst offering empathy, which is what care actually is, is a through and through a moral preoccupation.*

It sounds on the other hand pretty good: confirming human beings in their strength, facilitate self-management, promote positive health.

> *It is very good as well, but every time you use the word 'strength' you must also mention the word 'vulnerability', because this threatens in this way of thinking to become a non-value. Whilst all that is valuable carries vulnerability within. Everything that is important for you, you can lose. To deal with that together represents a value in itself. That whole strength story is at a certain moment no longer realistic. It by-passes what life is, and then you can also give no good care. And in that reality I felt myself insufficiently supported by the Humanist Fellowship.*

[ ]

The development with the Humanistic Fellowship seems to run parallel with that within the Christian sector, where in the last decades the identity was also a point of discussion.

> *... yes indeed: the fellowship has now also to deal with the fact that people don't become member of such organizations: they go once to a festival, they participate in a project, but that's it. For me that doesn't matter so much, my concern is that a conversation take place about what it means to be a human being and to live together. And that we have a language for this – regardless of whether we come from a humanistic or a Christian tradition – so that we don't stand defenceless in the face of the neo-liberal thinking, that - before all - places the ego on the throne.*

Van Praag saw the battle against nihilism as the most important task. After the second World War, during which masses had let themselves be swept up by a 'demonic' ideology, humanism should offer an alternative. But what is nihilism?

> *I think that Van Praag would say: not being able to independently maintain a view on life. To let yourself be carried away by whatever. It thereby doesn't imply that everyone has to be able to formulate one's own thought-through a world-view, but yes, that you have a lived morality, established on experiences of being a human being. If on the contrary, you put all your cards on your own freedom, then you move in the direction of the nihilism against which humanism precisely then wanted to offer a counterweight.*

Stevo Akkerman in: An Appeal for the Sacredness within Humanism / Interview with Brecht Molenaar, in Trouw, 14 July 2018, Dutch daily newspaper [Translated by Henk Bak]

5. The Golden Rule

The heart of the person before you is a mirror,
See there your own form.

Shinto

Introduction

Before embarking on the second half of this project, dealing with the Golden Rule past and present, in chapters 5 and 6, and closing with chapter 7 on prayers, rites and ceremonies, I feel the need to remind myself and my readers, that this project started and is continuously nourished by meditative walks over a wide clearing in bushland, out under the sky between clusters of trees and shrubs. Between sacred sites, which don't replace places of worship and reflection in towns and cities, but complement them, there are opportunities to concentrate on multiple world-views, one by one and in relation to one another, their essential meanings and messages and on their common ground and common sky, nature, winds, clouds, bird calls and songs and our own involvement in them, a dialogical space between heaven and earth. It is not just the walk and not just the conversation, but the space in which they happen, not to be measured in acres or hectares, but to be experienced and enjoyed as an invitation to open up and play together.

When in 1994 I modelled my questions for the religious conversation at the Caulfield campus of Monash University. Melbourne, on Buddha's eightfold path, I understood "Right mindfulness" to include "Right memory" as it has been sometimes translated. I suggested that "right" memory implied on the one hand an uncompromised or not distorted understanding of a religion's original impulse and on the other: a sense of a next step in its evolution, which would be a truthful, uncompromised continuation of the impulse into the future. In the eight sessions in each of the three years it was this same question, each time formulated in tune with the year's theme, to which none of the participants, Muslim, Buddhist, Jew or Christian had an answer. In the first round it was agreed that much depended on the culture in which a religion had been developed or introduced. It was assumed that the integration in any such culture would compromise at least something of the original impulse.

Thus "culture" became the theme of the second round of 8 sessions. And when, in the second session, the theme was narrowed down to aesthetic expression, as in architecture, the question became more complicated: how to find a form for an impulse that hardly had a tradition: a building that reflects the togetherness of all world's religions under one roof? This in response to the intention of Community Services and the Caulfield campus manager of Monash University, to build a purpose built multi-faith building for the increasing number of students and staff from different religious backgrounds in need of a suitable place to meet and worship. The current location for Buddhists and Muslims in the 1990's was too small and seriously inadequate.

This challenge is not totally new. The Pharao Echn Amon changed his name to Echn Aton, to reflect the fact that he didn't rule over Egyptians alone, but over many other peoples with their own gods and forms of worship. He chose the image of the sun disc as the over-lighting divine presence for all. The Romans, ruling over many different spiritual cultures created the "Pantheon" as a temple for all the gods. And at Monash itself, its main campus - in Clayton - has a spacious, purpose designed building for all religions, which was built with private money.

There are other buildings of this nature: the Bahá'i Temple and Shrine in Haifa, Israel and many others; the House of One, a complex being built in the centre of Berlin, comprising a Mosque, a Synagogue and a Church as well as a common meeting hall. And Shin's Gangavareshlinga temple in Garhwal, on the east bank of the Ganges in Northern India, as part of an International Centre for Peace reflects an Indian/Garhwalli Hindu style and Shaivic context. It contains a dedicated space, open for all religions to present their own symbols and to conduct their own rites. At the time of writing this project is nearing completion.

Present day public life runs its course on thought-patterns and systems, that breach at every turn of the road the law that once had given shape to public life in many, if not all, spiritual cultural traditions. This law was condensed and crystallized in what since the 16th century became known as the "Golden Rule". It was Rabbi Hillel's answer to the Gentile who demanded to be taught within the time he could stand on one leg. And it was, and is, the more complete answer, that the unnamed Jewish lawyer gave to his own question when asking Jeshua: "What is the Law". When Jeshua agreed with his answer and told him to act accordingly, the lawyer asked further: "Who is my neighbour?" Which allowed Jeshua to bring the formula to life with the story of the "Good Samaritan", a narrative that on the one hand anchors its truth firmly in time and space – the road from Jericho, the oldest known city in the world – to Jerusalem, a most sacred centre for three of the main world religions. And, on the other hand – as a story – has taken root in the heart of all of humanity, whether religious or not.

After having dealt with dialogue, doctrine, renewal and experience, it is the renewal of this particular, fundamental human calling, that forms the theme of this chapter and the next. Two elements in the Golden Rule are especially addressed:

1. The "horizontal" and the "vertical" dimensions of the rule: World-views, secular and religious, find themselves on common ground in the horizontal dimension, i.e. where social issues are poverty, slavery, disease, exploitation, torture etc. The vertical dimension, a relation to the Highest, God, the most sacred, the "Good", is gradually coming back, often via concerns with the plight of the earth, mother earth, Goddess, nature, the environment as something alive and sacred.

2. Human dignity as the foundation of all human rights, and – as Simone Weil pointed out, five years prior to the Universal Declaration of Human Rights in 1948 – of all human obligations, the most fundamental and universal obligation: respect.

In this chapter formulations of the Golden Rule are taken from the most diverse cultural contexts, showing how different aspects of this rule have been emphasized according to the time and place in which these cultures evolved and how - over time - a new consciousness lead to different ways of expressing this rule, notably and impressively by Immanuel Kant and in a clear, concise but comprehensive articulation by Simone Weil (1943).

The diversity of expressions of the Golden Rule in the various contexts out of which this diversity arose draws attention to the fact that the Golden Rule used to function as an organizing principle for the whole of the society in which this Rule arose.

In this Anthology one finds especially the Judaic and Islamic formulations that are extensively represented and by implication the Christian continuation of the Jewish tradition, gradually enriched by the cultures in which Christianity took roots. The same had been true for the Judaic form, which was rooted in an older Mesopotamian and then Egyptian culture; and later – in the diaspora, the dispersion of the Jewish faith outside Palestine – in the Greek and Roman worlds, including Eastern Europe and Spain etc. Islam also took root in a great diversity of cultures which all interpreted the Sharia, according to their own cultures as well. Of the Hindu culture, it is in Bali that a comprehensive societal tradition still exists. Originally governing village life, it now also functions in cities, and Kerobokan's governor Siswanto has introduced a Banjar structure in the prison in his care (Sydney Morning Herald 23 January 2010). I include the text of a relevant blog in this selection. An Australian woman who had married a Balinese man comments on the internet, that for her the Banjar system was restrictive and limiting. In present day consciousness there might be a need for more space in which the individual may be expected to find their own way to realize their responsibilities towards the economic, cultural/ religious and communal responsibilities, perhaps within a 'functionally differentiated' Banjar, as will be the main theme of chapter 6.

The chapter has been developed into four sections:

a. short formulations of the Golden Rule, clearly crystallizations of what in different cultures used to live as rules and practice.

b. more elaborate texts of traditional arrangements or laws that were in place and often still are.

c. texts on a virtue-based ethics. The more our societies become legalistic, i.e. on the letter of the law only, the more there is a need for those who make law, enforce them and obey them, to be honest, just and caring themselves…

d. an elaboration of the understanding of the words '…as yourself', an implied 'love yourself' as integral part of the Golden Rule, which appears to be passed over in the current interfaith dialogue, whilst in society at large it has been compromised, undervalued and undermined.

The Golden Rule itself is based on virtue: love God, love the Good, love your neighbour, your fellow human being, yourself. And to be able to practice the Golden Rule, one needs to be trained in many virtues, to be courageous as well as to be patient. Restraint is just as important as being valiant, generous and frugal etc. Virtues hang together organically, Margaret Somerville sees them as a constellation. And as we will see in the next chapter, living in three domains, cultural/spiritual, political/legal and economical/ecological is to live in three forms of lawfulness, each requiring three different constellations of virtues. The virtues may be the same, but their relevance and practice may vary with context.

From this point, the format of the selection of texts has changed: rather than introducing them in detail in the introduction that comes before the texts, I have inserted 'orientations' in front of a number of texts that deal with a particular theme. This might become especially useful in Chapter 6, where a detailed introduction to the whole would be too far removed from what is actually presented during the lengthy walk or wandering through the texts themselves.

Texts

A: The Golden Rule - Crystallization

Christianity:	*All things whatsoever ye would that men should do to you, do ye even so to them: for this is the Law and the Prophets.* Matthew; 7.12.
Judaism:	*What is hateful to you, do not to your fellowmen. That is the entire Law; all the rest is commentary.* Talmud, Shabbat, 31 a.
Brahamanism:	*This is the sum of duty: do naught unto others which would cause you pain if done to you.* Mahabharata, 5, 1517.
Buddhism:	*Hurt not others in ways that you yourself would find hurtful.* Udana Varga, 5.18
Confucianism:	*Surely it is the maxim of loving kindness: Do not unto others that you would not have them do unto you.* Analects, 15, 23.
Taoism:	*Regard your neighbour's gain as your own gain, and your neighbour's loss as your own loss.* T'ai Sheng Kan Ying P'ien.
Zoroastrianism:	*That nature alone is good which refrains from doing unto another whatsoever is not good for itself.* Dadistan-I-dinik, 94,5.
Islam:	*Not one of you is a believer until he desires for his brother what which he desires for himself.* Sunnah

The Golden Rule in the words of Hillel the Elder (ca 110BC -10 CE)

The comparative response to the challenge of a Gentile who asked that the Torah be explained to him while he stood on one foot, illustrates the character difference between Shammai and Hillel. Shammai dismissed the man. Hillel chided the man for his behaviour, but in a constructive way:

"What is hateful to you, do not do to your fellow: this is the whole Torah: the rest is explanation; go and learn"

(Shab.31a)
Hillel recognized brotherly love as the fundamental principle of
Jewish moral law
(Lev. Xix.18)

Aboriginal perspectives

Nobody living outside the sharing system
Kids – wives – husbands
All inside... everything all inside...
Bird...every animal, dog
no one outside the line
they always be inside the Wunan
they all inside this Wunan.

Nyawarra in: Dulman Mamaa's
Gwion Gwion – Secret Pathways of the Ngarinyin Aboriginal
People of Australia
2000, p.182

They (Wodoi and Djingun) started the sharing system, with the first two branches of a network of 'lines', or pathways that some call 'songlines'. Eventually this sharing system embraced all of Australia. The Old Man told the story to the point where Emu comes from the East and steals sacramental food that the ancestral beings are sharing, one after another, to show their commitment to the new Law. Emu, like all materialists, is greedy and won't wait, stealing all the sacramental food for personal gain.

John Allen in: Steve Biddulph (editor)'s
Stories of Manhood / Remembering Mowaljarlai
2000, p. 174

'Jagali' Carved Pearl Shell, symbol of the Wunan Sharing System

Story of Wodoi and Jungun stealing the sacred and magic tokens of justice, to make them available to all people.

Ngarinyin People, Kimberley

*Ancient Egypt: Do for one who may do for you,
that you may cause him thus to do.*

> The Tale of the Eloquent Peasant, 1970-1640 BC, quoted by Simone Weil in The Need of Roots
> 2003

*Thousands of years ago, the Egyptians believed, that no
soul could justify itself after death unless it could say:
'I have never let anyone suffer from hunger.'*

> Simone Weil
> **The Need of Roots**
> 2003

*Shinto: The heart of the person before you is a
mirror. See there your own form.*

*Yoruba, Nigeria: Someone going to take a pointed stick to pinch a
baby bird should first try it on oneself to feel how it hurts.*

Jainism: Know that violence is the root cause of all miseries in the world.

Violence, in fact, is the knot of bondage. (no source)

*Therefore, neither does he (a sage) cause violence
to others nor does he make others do so.*

Hindu: the Bhagavad Gita

*"A man should not hate any living creature. Let him be friendly
and compassionate to all. He must free himself from the delusion
of I and mine. He must accept pleasure and pain with equal
tranquility. He must be forgiving, ever contented, self-controlled,
united constantly. His resolve must be unshakable."*

*"He neither molests his fellow-men, nor allows himself
to become disturbed by the world. He is no longer
swayed by joy and envy, anxiety and fear."*

*"His attitude is the same toward friend and foe. He is indifferent
to honour and insult, heat and cold, pleasure and pain. He values
praise and blame equally. He can control his speech. He is content
with whatever he gets. His home is everywhere and nowhere."*

Swami Prabhavananda and Christopher Isherwood (Translator)
Bhagavad Gita: The Song of God
1947

Hinduism, Bali: We Balinese have an essential concept of balance. It's the Tri Hita Karana; a concept of harmonious balance. The balance between god and humanity; humanity with itself and humanity with the environment. This places us all in a universe of common understanding.

It is not only nuclear bombs which have fallout. It is our job to minimize this fallout for our people and our guests from around the world, Who did this? It's not such an important question for us to discuss. Why this happened – may be this is more worthy of thought. What can we do to create beauty from this tragedy and come to an understanding where nobody feels the need to make such a statement again? This is important. This is the basis from which we can embrace everyone as a brother; everyone as a sister.

It is a period of uncertainty. It is a period of change. It is also an opportunity for us to move together into a better future. A future where we embrace all of humanity in the knowledge that we all look and smell the same when we are burnt. Victims of this tragedy are from all over the world.

[ ]

We want to send a message to the world – Embrace this misunderstanding between our brothers and lets seek a peaceful answer to the problem which brings us to such tragedy.

We embrace all the beliefs, hopes and dreams of all the people in the world with love.

[ ]

Tat Wam Asi – You are me and I am you.

Asana Viebeke L. from a message on behalf of the Samigita ("Think Tank")
for the Banjars of the Kuta, Legian and Semyak areas (village councils), Bali, 25 October
in response to the bomb-attack in Kuta, 12 October 2002 killing 202 people from 21 nations

Judaism

You shall love HASHEM, your God, with all your heart, with all your soul, and with all your resources.

Deuteronomy 6:5

You shall not take revenge and you shall not bear a grudge against the members of your people; you shall love your fellow as yourself. - I am HASHEM.

Leviticus 19:18

*One expresses love of God by performing His commandments lovingly. With all your soul, i.e. even if your devotion to God requires that you forfeit your life (Rashi)
And with all your resources, i.e. even if love of God causes you to lose all your money.*

Deuteronomy 6:5

Comment: R'Akiva said: that this is the fundamental rule of the Torah (Rashi; Sifra)

Leviticus 19:18

Comment: Hillel paraphrased: "What is hateful to you, do not do to others"

Shabbos 31a

Comment: We must wish upon others the same degree of success and prosperity we wish upon ourselves and we must treat others with the utmost respect and consideration. (Ramban)

Nosson Scherman (Editor)
The Artscroll English Tanach: Stone Edition / The Jewish Bible
2011

Ancient Greece and Rome

Do not do to others that which would anger you if others did it to you.

Socrates 5th Century BCE

Do not expect strangers to do for you what you can do for yourself.

Quintus Ennius (239-169 BCE)

Treat your inferiors as you would be treated by your superiors.

Seneca (1st Century CE)

There is nothing more painful than the insult to human dignity,
Nothing more humiliating than servitude.

Human dignity and freedom are our birthright.
Let us then defend them or die with dignity.

Marcus Tullius Cicero (106-43 BCE)

Christianity

There was a lawyer who, to disconcert him, stood up, and said to him, 'Master, what must I do to inherit eternal life?'

He said to him, what is written in the Law? What do you read there?

He replied: 'You must love the Lord, your God, with all your heart, with all your soul, with all your strength, and with all your mind, and your neighbour as yourself '

'You have answered right, said Jesus 'do this and life is yours'.

Luke 10:25-28

The lawyer's source:

"Listen, Israel: Yaweh our God is the one Yaweh. You shall love Yaweh your God with all your heart, with all your soul, with all your strength."

Deuteronomy 6:5

You must not exact vengeance, nor must you bear a grudge against the children of your people. You must love your neighbour as yourself. I am Yaweh.

Leviticus 19:18

Sikh Religion

Service of one's fellows is a sign of divine worship.

Bai Gurdas
The Times World Religions
2002, p. 195

Bahá'I Faith

*O son of man! If thine eyes be turned towards mercy, forsake
the things that profit thee and cleave unto that which will profit
mankind. And if thine eyes be turned towards justice, choose
thou for thy neighbour that which thou choosest for thyself.*

Bahá'u'lláh
The Third Leaf of the Most Exalted Paradise, Tablets

Sufi View

*The basis of Sufism is consideration of the hearts and feelings of others.
If you haven't the will to gladden someone's heart, then at least beware
lest you hurt someone's heart, for on our own path, no sin exists but this.*

Dr Javad Nurbakhsh, Master of the Nimatullahi Sufi order

20th Century Humanism

*It's a little embarrassing that, after forty five years of research and study,
the best advice I can give to people is to be a little kinder to each other.*

Aldous Huxley in: Buzzy Jackson's
The Inspirational Atheist
2014, p. 104

Human Dignity as Idea

On the last day of creating the world, God created the human being: so that
he may know the laws of the universe, love its beauty and admire its grandeur.

He did not tie him to any fixed place nor to a set pattern of behaviour
or any inevitable necessities, but He gave him mobility and free will.

"I have placed you in the middle of the world" - the Creator says to Adam
– "so that you are better placed to look around and see all that is in it".

I created you as a being that is not just only heavenly, mortal or
immortal, so that you may be your own free maker and conqueror. You
can degenerate to animal or you can raise yourself to divine being.

What animals bring out of their mothers' body is what they shall have.
The higher spirits are, from the very beginning or soon after, what they will

remain in eternity. Only you have been given the ability to evolve, to grow out of free will. You have the germ of all kinds of life within you.".

From: Pico della Mirandola (1463-1494)'s De Dignitate Hominis
[Translated by Henk Bak from Valentin Tomberg's German transcript]

On Dignity: which all human beings possess in one form or other, and in some, though by no means in exact, proportion to their higher faculties, and which is so essential a part of the happiness of those in whom it is strong, that nothing which conflicts with it could be, otherwise than momentarily, an object of desire to them.

John Stuart Mill
Utilitarianism
1861

Responsibility: a person's dignity

The existential choice of goodness is the gesture of taking responsibility. Responsibility, in general, is one of the fundamental moral concepts; every kind of responsibility is at bottom a moral one. Taking responsibility is also a matter of a person's dignity, one respects another person's dignity if one treats him or her as a responsible being.

Agnes Heller.
The Elementary Ethics of Everyday Life.
Rethinking Imagination Conference Papers Melbourne 1991

Human Rights in History

Historical landmarks of human rights date from deep into the past, from Hammurabi's Code in ancient Babylon (in what is now Iraq) to the Enlightenment philosophies of the West. Between those times, Buddhist and Hindu teachings brought forth precepts of ecological responsibility; Confucius proposed a form of universal education; the Greeks practised democracy and first raised the idea of natural laws pertaining to human rights, and early Islam established limitations on the authority of rulers, and advocated an independent judiciary to protect and respect human dignity. Historically, however, religious and political movements that invoke the common good have tended to exclude certain groups: women, homosexuals, lower classes, enslaved people, or those born with disabilities, and many continue to do so to this day. Groups that populate the movement, in contrast, largely understand human rights from the viewpoint of the oppressed, not from that of the elite.

Along with gross violations of human rights are other endless indignities that billions endure: loss of water for agriculture, theft of local resources by government and corporations, incursions of mining companies that pollute, political corruption and hijacking of governance, lack of health care and education, big dams that have displaced millions of poor people, loss of land, trade policies that bankrupt small farmers and more...

Paul Hawken
Blessed Unrest
2007, p. 13

B: Golden Rule as an underlying, organizing principle of social life.

Orientation

Beginnings of a 'golden rule' in public life are to be found in traditions going back to the dawn of time: e.g. the oral and imaginary tradition of the Ngarinyin people of NW Australia is perhaps one of the longest unbroken, yet marginalized, traditions on Earth. Rock formations and narrative mutually support each other in transmitting the teaching from generation to generation, perhaps over more than 20,000 years. Here as elsewhere cave - and rock - paintings are kept alive, a primeval skill that enabled a delegation of the Ngarinyin people to show UNESCO experts, how European cave paintings might have been done...

Prometheus, the half-god in Greek mythology stole fire from heaven to give humanity a new lease of life and was punished for it. Two friends, Jungun and Wodoi, stole the law from a priestly, blind magician and made his secret public and got the magician's blessing, their friendship a symbol for the friendship between peoples, expressed in a pattern of inter-marriage arrangements.

The narrative nature of this unique document warrants an extensive quotation. When Banggai says: 'That symbol we look at here', he points to the configuration of standing stones around a large flat stone roughly the shape of a giant table top, to which Nyawarra adds: 'like a parliament'. And when Banggai uses the words 'title' and 'land rights', he places a millennia old, unbroken, lawful tradition as a rock rooted deeply underneath the shallow, legalistic quicksand of today's Australian context. 'Wunan' means 'Law. Banggai is David Mowaljarlai's other name.

The first people who put their foot tracks
their foot prints still in the stone
hardened up from long long time…darrawani
Wibalma…then he came out…he said
"I'm happy and let's do it…
Let this Wunan lay down forever!"

And they put it that way…
"We didn't have law
we want to make law now…new law
we can share and really marry one another"

Banggal

[ ]

Jungun and Wodoi right then
been make the big party see
like a parliament
or something that they do like that
and when they had that party over there
…put in this Wunan
they wasn't there…these two wasn't there
that Wodoi and Jungun you know?
It's only all the Wunan people
The other mob that make the Wunan

Nyawarra

[ ]

Jungun said to Wodoi…
"And you can be my brother-in-law…
you can be my father-in-law.
You marry my daughter or my sister"
and Wodoi said…
"Okay! You marry my daughter
and my sister" to the Jungun
and Jungun said "Okay!"

Jungun take'em Wodoi
and Wodoi take 'em Jungun wives

Nyawarra
pp. 137-138

[ ]

*And the Gwion put it that way
Wunan…from that time
Wunan…we still hold it today*

*And here we are…
that symbol we look at there
we don't talk about it…
without looking at the symbol!*

*Because it's controlling us…
that Wunan symbol
you know…that table …angga
you know that Jallala?*

*If we died that thing angga
would still be there
Wunan would still be there
and the land itself still be there yet*

*The Wunan is there now
that's where the sacred places are
for us to look after 'em
you know every man and woman
got their responsibility*

*Kamali jallala…lawmaker stones
that's why all these jallala here*

*that's where the conversation was
agreements and all the title…
everything…land right and all that*

*But the Wunan system
we all have been created from there
nobody is forgotten…nobody outside
…that the land
but we not outside…we inside
we inside here
and once and for all we got that song*

angga...table first a bed of stringy bark tree
golani muna...big plum dish
turned into stone

Humans turned into birds
and then into stone

Where we own land...
where our symbols are...it started from here
we all in different areas
the nature that we look after
that's why it was formed here

[ ]

Whenever this Wunan was created
then everybody had his own symbols
own blocks for land
representing different symbols
like ah...my hibiscus...jirad
is my dambun name Brrejirad
So every man had his own place and symbols
and symbol is the one...is different tribes
Only those ones who got symbols
can tell his own story
because he is the manager
he the servant of that place
because he look after the whole area

Banggai

That's why we say this land is like a pattern
see those marks there they are like that
no place not clear...they all covered in the land
Wunbanburan...old time...fixed

Nyawarra

Dulman Mamaa
Gwion Gwion: Secret and Sacred Pathways of the Ngarinyin
Aboriginal People of Australia
2000, pp. 140-142;168-169

Aboriginal words for Law

Wik-Mungkan: aak = ground, place, tradition, law
Wik-Mungkan: thayan = law, strong words
Wik- Mungkan: wik = language
Meryan Mir: gelak = law, rule
Ngiyampa: ngiya = word, talk, law
Ngiyampa: ngiyampa = word-world, language
Datiwuy: ruum (rom) = law, custom, culture
Dja Dja Wurrung: tallingingorak = word
Dja Dja Wurrung: talle; wurrung = speech

Aboriginal Words
The Macquarie Library Pty Ltd NSW 1994
John Tully
DjaDja Wurrung Language of Central Victoria
1997

On Banjar Bali: Village level government

Every area in Bali is run by a local banjar with the male heads of each family representing each family. This traditional town council meets twice a month at the banjar pavilion in a central location, close to the pura desa, or village temple.

•What is the banjar
The banjar are adjudicators of adat, traditional law and determine dates for religious events, collect money for ceremonies, allocate temple maintenance, oversee land sales and on occasion hand out summary punishment to troublemakers.

•How the banjar fits in with Balinese village structure
Bali is divided into kabupaten (districts), kecamatan (municipalities) and kelurahan / desa (villages). Traditionally a banjar will control a desa, more accurately the inhabited land. The sawah (rice-fields) are governed by the subak, another integral part of Bali's social system. The subak will determine when a farmer can flood his fields and its primary role is the control of water, since Bali's economy and culture depend on the production of rice. Both the banjar and the subak each with their temples and organizations.

Balinese villages have an organizational structure. If you look into the family compounds you will see red tiles roofs, various family bale structures and other familiar buildings. You will also see the same family temples (sanggah/merajan). A large tree will indicate the banjar pavilion, with 2 slit logs hanging from the branches, as well as religious shrines. This is where the banjar meets to discuss important village issues and is a community meeting place. Banjar means 'neighborhood' and people feel this place is where they can come and feel at one with the community.

•*Banjar society*
Membership to the banjar is mandatory for each Balinese married man. The banjar has its own system of lending locals money for equipment. At the banjar pavilion everyone takes a turn at cooking, cleaning and performing menial duties. The leader of the banjar is elected and approved by the gods via a medium.

The basic social unit of the banjar is the pekurenan (couple). Only Balinese married couples are full banjar members and subjected to the banjar rights and obligations. Foreigners or other Indonesians cannot join the banjar as it is tied up with Balinese culture and the Agama Hindu religion. All banjar meetings are conducted in Basa Bali (Balinese language). The decisions are taken by the sangkep (assembly) of the banjar's male members, the krama banjar, which often occurs every 35 days.

[ ]

•*Banjar decision making*
The decisions are taken on the basis of unanimous agreement, unlike the western ideal of 'winner takes all' (majority rule), The banjar has been, since 1979, recognized by the Indonesian government and is the lowest administrative structure of the national administration. Fitting in directly under the authority of the perbekel / lurah (supra - village head) and beyond the traditional bendesa adat (village head).

There are also two types of kelian banjar, the kelian dinas, who is in charge of the administrative aspects of the banjar life, and the kelian adat, who looks after the customary aspects in collaboration with the bendesa adat. They usually work together, unless the two roles are fulfilled by one person.

•*Sharing the joy & pain*
The banjar has an association called the 'banjar suka duka' which means 'the association for the sharing of joy and pain'. This relates to the function played by the group in the organizing specific social services or work called ayahan. Every banjar member has responsibilities

in helping keep the temple clean, preparing for ceremonies, providing funds and offerings. These responsibilities are some of the most important of all found in the network of village associations and Balinese can get ejected from the banjar if they do not participate.

Banjar Balinese Community,
Baliaround.com
2013

Judaic law: Sabbath

Thus the heaven and the earth were finished, and all their array. By the seventh day God completed His work that He had done, and He abstained on the seventh day from all His work that he had done. God blessed the seventh day and sanctified it because on it he abstained all His work that God created to make.

Genesis 2:1-3

Remember the Sabbath day to sanctify it. Six days shall you work and accomplish all your work, but the seventh day is Sabbath to HASHEM, your God, you shall not do any work – you, your son, your daughter, your slave, your maidservant, your animal, and your convert within your gates – for in six days HASHEM made the heavens and the earth, the sea and all that is in them, and He rested on the seventh day. Therefore HASHEM blessed the Sabbath day and sanctified it.

Exodus 20:8-11

It happened on the sixth day that they gathered a double portion of food, two omers for each; and all the princes of the assembly came and told Moses. He said to them: "This is what HASEM had spoken; tomorrow is a rest day, a holy Sabbath to HASHEM. Bake what you wish to bake and cook what you wish to cook; and whatever is left over, put away for yourselves as a safekeeping until the morning. They put it away until morning, as Moses had commanded; in did not stink and there was no infestation in it.

Moses said: "Eat it today; for today is a Sabbath for HASHEM; today you shall not find it in the field. Six days shall you gather it, but the seventh day is Sabbath, on it there will be none" It happened on the seventh day that some of the people went out to gather, and they did not find.

Exodus 16:22-27

On six days, work may be done, but the seventh day shall be holy for you, a day of complete rest for HASHEM; whoever does work on it shall be put to death. You shall not kindle fire in any of your dwellings on the Sabbath day.

Exodus 35:2-3

HASHEM spoke to Moses on Mount Sinai, saying: Speak to the children of Israel and say to them: When you come into the land that I give you, the land shall observe a Sabbath rest for HASHEM.. For six years you may sow your field and for six years you may prune your vineyard; and you may gather its crop. But the seventh year shall be a complete rest for the land, a Sabbath for HASHEM; your field you shall not sow and your vineyard you shall not prune. The aftergrowth of your harvest you shall not reap and the grapes you had set aside for yourself you shall not pick; it shall be a year of rest for the land. The Sabbath produce of your land shall be yours to eat, for you, for your slave, and for your maidservant, and for your laborer and for your resident who dwell with you. And for your animal and for the beast that is in your land shall all its crop be to eat.

You shall count for yourself seven cycles of sabbatical years, seven years seven times, the seven cycles of sabbatical years shall be for you forty-nine years. You shall sound a broken shofar, in the seventh month, on the tenth of the month, on the Day of Atonement you shall sound the shofar throughout your land. You shall sanctify the fiftieth year and proclaim freedom throughout the land for all its inhabitants; it shall be the Jubilee Year for you, you shall return each man to his ancestral heritage and you shall return each man to his family.

Leviticus 25:1-10

[ ]

If your brother becomes impoverished and his means falter in your proximity, you shall strengthen him — proselyte or resident — so that he can live with you. Do not take from him interest and increase; and you shall fear your God — and let you brother live with you. Do not give him your money for interest, and do not give him your food for increase. I am HASHEM, your God, Who took you out of the land of Egypt, to give you the land of Canaan, to be God unto you.

Leviticus 25:35-36

At the end of the seventh year you shall institute a remission. This is the matter of remission: Every creditor shall remit his authority over what he has lent his fellow; he shall not press his fellow or his brother, for He has proclaimed a remission for HASHEM. You may press the gentile; but over what you have with your brother, you shall remit your authority. However, may there be no destitute among you, rather, HASHEM will surely bless you in the land that HASHEM, your God will give you as an inheritance, to possess it, only if you will hearken to the voice of HASHEM, you God, to observe, to preform this entire commandment that I command you today.

[ ]

If there shall be a destitute person among you, any of your brethren in any of your cities, in your Land that HASHEM gives you, you shall not harden your heart or close your hand against your destitute brother. Rather, you shall open your hand to him, you shall lend him his requirement, whatever is lacking to him. Beware lest there be a lawless thought in your heart saying, "The seventh year approaches, the remission year,' and you will look malevolently upon your destitute brother and refuse to give him – then he will appeal against you to HASHEM, and it will be sin upon you. You shall surely give him, and let your heart not feel bad when you give him, for in return for this matter, HASHEM, your God, will bless you in all your deeds and in your every undertaking. For destitute people will not cease to exist within the Land; therefore I command you saying, "You shall surely open your hand to your brother, to your poor, and to your destitute in your Land."

Deuteronomy 15: 1-5; 7-11

Moses wrote this Torah and gave it to the Kohanim, the sons of Levi, the bearers of the Ark of the covenant of HASHEM, and to all the elders of Israel.

Moses commanded them, saying, "At the end of seven years, at the time of the Sabattical year, during the Succos festival, when all Israel comes to appear before HASHEM, your God, in the place that He will choose, you shall read this Torah before all Israel, in their ears. Gather together the people – the men, the women, and the small children, and your stranger who is in your cities – so that they will hear and so that they will learn, and shall fear HASHEM, your God, and be careful to perform all the words of the Torah."

Deuteronomy 31:9-12

The Dao

The Way is constantly nameless.
Though in its natural state it appears to be unimportant,

No one in heaven or earth dares to make it his subject.
Were marquises and kings able to maintain it,
The ten thousand things would submit to them on their own.

Heaven and earth come together and send forth sweet dew,
No one causes this to be so, of itself it falls equally on them.

When we start to "regulate" or "put into order" there will be names.
But when names have indeed come into being, we must also know that it is time to stop.
Knowing [when] to stop is the way to avoid harm.

The Way's presence in the world,
Is like the relationship of small valley streams to rivers and seas.

Li Kang (ca 196-264)
Robert G. Henricks
Lao Tzu: Te-Tao Ching: A New Translation based on the recently discovered Ma-wang Tui Texts
2000, p. 53
Guodian documents. C. 300 BC
Confucius

His student Zigong once asked him what conditions were
necessary for a country to be at peace, with a stable government.
Confucius's reply was very simple. There were only three: enough
arms, enough food and the trust of the common people.

[ ]

This student was always full of awkward questions. He said
that three conditions were too many. Tell me, if you have to
do with one of these which one would you remove first?

Confucius said: 'Give up arms.' ...
...If you had to get rid of another one...

Confucius in all seriousness told him: 'Give up food.'...

He continued: 'Death has always been with us since the beginning of time,
but when there is no trust, the common people will have nothing to stand on.'

To do without food will certainly lead to death, but from ancient times
to this day has anyone ever cheated death? So death is not the worst
thing that can happen. The most terrible thing of all is the collapse and

breakdown that follow when a country's citizens give up on their nation.

Yu Dan
Confucius from the Heart: Ancient Wisdom for Today's World
2010, pp. 17-18

When a tree stands above all the rest of the forest,
The wind is sure to break it, and when a mound stands out from
the shore, the fast flowing water is sure to overwhelm it.

Islam: Teachings from the Qur'an on economic life:

1. Means of production and transport as part of God's Creation.

1

It is he Who brought down from the heaven water,
With which We bring forth vegetation of all kinds,
From which We bring forth greenery,
From which We bring forth close packed grain,
And from the palm tree, from its wreaths, clusters of dates, near to hand,
And gardens of vine, olive and pomegranate,
Resembling and not resembling one another.
Behold their fruits when ripe and ready to pluck!
In these are signs for a people who believe.

2

He it is Who created gardens, trellised and untrellised, and palms
and plants of diverse fruits, and olives and pomegranates, like and
unlike. Eat of its fruit when ripe, and deliver up its due the day it is
harvested. Do not be immoderate; He loves not the immoderate.

3

God it is, Who created the heavens and the earth,
Who made water descend from the sky,
from which He brought forth nourishment, a bounty upon you;
Who made ships to serve you,
Running in the sea, by His command,
And made rivers to serve you;
Who made the sun and moon to serve you, alternating,
And made night and day to serve you;
Who granted you all you asked Him.
Were you to count the bounties of God, you could not take stock of them.

4

It is He Who made the sea to serve you so that you may eat from it soft flesh and extract from it jewellery for you to wear.
Therein you can see ships ploughing through the waves,
that you may seek of His bounty — perchance you will give thanks.
He cast upon the earth towering mountains,
lest it should shake you violently, and rivers and highways — perhaps you will be guided aright — and signposts; with the star they will be guided.

5

It is God Who made your homes to be places of rest, Who made for you of cattle- skins tents you find light to carry when you travel and where you put up, and from their wool, furs, and hair furnishings and enjoyment, for a while.
It is God Who made for you, amongst what He created, the shades, and made the mountains for your places wherein to hide, and made for you shirts to protect you from the heat, and other shirts to protect you in battle. Thus does he complete His bounty upon you; perhaps you will submit to Him.

6

It is a mercy from Him that he created for you the night and the day, in which you may find rest or seek His bounty: perhaps you will give thanks.

7

It is God Who created cattle for you upon which you ride, and from which you eat. From them you derive other benefits, or else fulfil some desire of your hearts.
Upon them, and upon ships too, you are carried.
He shows you His wonders: which of Gods wonders do you deny.

2. Fair and right measurement in dealings, caring and sharing
Sun and moon move in measured order;
Shrubs and trees bow down;
The sky He raised, and established the balance,
So that you do not infringe the balance,
But measure in fairness, and not short change the balance.
The earth he laid out for the living,
Wherein there are fruits and palms in clusters,

Grains upon stalks and sweet-scented flowers.

The All-Merciful 54:9-12, p. 441

It is He Who made the earth a bed for you, the sky a canopy; Who causes water to descent from the sky with which He brings forth fruits as sustenance for you. Do not, therefore, set up any equals to God when you know better.

The Cow 2:22, p. 5

Virtue does not demand of you to turn your faces eastwards or westwards. Virtue rather is:

He who believes in God, the Last Day, the angels, the Book and the prophets;
Who dispenses money, though dear, to kinsmen, orphans, the needy, the traveller, beggars and for ransom;
Who performs the prayer and pays the alms,
Who fulfil their contracts when they contract;
Who are steadfast in hardship, calamity and danger;
These are the true believers.
These are truly pious.

The Cow 2:177, p. 23-24

Those who consume usury shall not rise from the dead except like those whom Satan causes to babble from madness. This is because they allege that commerce is the same as usury. But God has made commerce licit and usury illicit. So he to whom a word of counsel from his Lord has reached, and desists, may keep his previous profit, and his affair is up to God. But he who relapses, these are the inhabitants of the fire, in which they dwell eternally. God annuls usury and augments free gifts. God loves not every impious lawbreaker.

The Cow 2:276, p. 39

O believers, fear God and abandon what remains of usury if you are true believers. If you do not, be forewarned of conflict with God and his messenger. If you repent, you will keep the capital of your wealth, neither wronging nor wronged. If a person is in difficulties, let there be respite until a time of ease. And if you give freely, it would be better for you, if only you knew. Fear a Day in which you shall return to God, when each soul shall be paid back that which it has earned. And they shall not be wronged.

The Cow 2:281

Do not come near the property of orphans, except in the fairest manner, until

*the orphan attains manhood. Be faithful to your compacts, for a compact shall
be a thing questioned about. Be fair in measures when you measure out, and
weigh with a balance that is true: that would be better and more rewarding.*

The Journey by Night 1:34, p. 224

3. Notes on the selected texts:

*In the first sequence of verses, taken from the Qur'an, on the
theme of economy in terms of 'livelihood' and 'bounty', the
emphasis is on Gods role in creating not only 'natural' things,
but also artefacts like gardens, clothing, roads and ships.*

It places the human being right in the middle of economy as Gods 'household'.

The texts are taken from the new Penguin edition of the Qur'an,
translated and introduced by Tarif Khalidi. Penguin Classics (2008)
London, New York, Camberwell Vic. Australia, 2009 etc.

1. Cattle 6:99
2. Cattle 6:141
3. Abraham 14:32-34
4. The Bees 16:14-16
5. The Bees 16:79-82
6. The Narrative 28:73
7. Forgiver 40: 81

*In the second selection of texts above, the emphasis is
on fair and right measurement as a reflection of the way
God created the world with measured order.*

*Together both sets of texts bring out the two aspects contained in the word:'
economy':
from the Greek 'oikos' or 'ecos' = house, home, dwelling place, estate, the
earth as 'home'
and 'nomos' from 'nemein' = giving, allocating, sharing in good measure.*

*The prohibition of usury has found its modern expression in Mahammed
Yunus's founding and developing the micro-credit movement through
the Grameen Bank in Bangladesh, initially reducing the interest on
loans for women from 1000 percent per year to ca. 17 percent...*

The parable of the good Samaritan

There was a lawyer who, to disconcert him, stood up and said to him, 'Master, what must I do to inherit eternal life?' He said to him. 'What is written in the Law? What do you read there?' He replied, 'You must love the Lord your God with all your heart, with all your soul, with all your strength, and with all your mind, and your neighbour as yourself'. 'You have answered right,' said Jesus 'do this and life is yours.'

But the man was anxious to justify himself and said to Jesus, 'And who is my neighbour?' Jesus replied, 'A man was once on his way down from Jerusalem to Jericho and fell into the hands of brigands: they took all he had. Beat him and then made off, leaving him half dead. Now a priest happened to be traveling down the same road, but when he saw the man, he passed by on the other side. In the same way a Levite who came to the place, saw him and passed by on the other side. But a Samaritan traveller, who came upon him was moved and with compassion when he saw him. He went up and bandaged his wounds, pouring oil and wine of them. He then lifted him on to his own mount, carried him to the inn and looked after him. Next day, he took out two denarii and handed them to the innkeeper. "Look after him,", he said "and on my way back I will make good any extra expense you have." Which of these three, do you think, proved himself a neighbour to the man who fell into the brigand's hands?' 'The one who took pity on him' he replied. Jesus said to him, 'Go, and do the same yourself'.

Luke 10:25-37
Jerusalem Bible
Popular Edition
1974

C: Virtues as pre-condition of rules and the source of new capacities to live by them

Orientation

The above selection of texts represents a range of examples of virtue based and law-based precepts. Where the rule requires love, it requires a virtue; where rules order to do such and such and/or refrain from something, they require compliance; when compliance requires the practice of a virtue, compliance itself becomes obedience. One cannot obey a rule, only the giver of a rule or law. A just ruler requires justice in those who obey him or her. The Golden Rule is a crystallization of whatever virtues and laws were shaping the cultures and societies in which they were expressed. Even though human goodness weaves as a common thread through the different collections of those expressions, the expressions themselves seem to reflect something of the culture in which they are found. The Japanese Shinto's 'seven gods of happiness' don't rule but they reward virtues and the root of all virtues is sincerity. In Buddhism the Golden Rule is formulated as a precept or rather a prohibition.

In Hinduism the set of 33 virtues of Bhairava reflects the moon-cycle and when considered in sets of three shows a certain organic process culminating in the 'highest freedom'. Because the threesomes form a certain unity, the last set can be adjusted to the different numbers of days in a month.

In the Jewish tradition Rabbi Hillel's summary of the Law was based on brotherly love, whilst the lawman in St Luke's Gospel quotes the Jewish Bible as commanding love, i.e. as a virtue, so in effect commanding to cultivate an inner quality, not to follow an outer law. This is an injunction that is re-enforced as the actual fulfilling of the law in Jeshua's 'Sermon on the Mount' as reported by St Mathew. "Perhaps this is why the behavioural likeness of the virtue enforced by external authorities (e.g. religious institutions or educational bodies) can feel like such a betrayal and entrapment" (Tineke Bak Friendships within friendships, see Texts).

When the philosophers of the 18th century endeavoured to formulate an ethics based on rational thinking, they removed the law-maker but kept thinking in laws and rules. The task was to find a moral principle general enough that all moral insights and decisions could be based or justified on that. A purely rule-based ethics replaced the earlier ethics based on rules and virtues interwoven. Both Kant and Coleridge maintained that morality ultimately rests with the individual. Kant searched for a rule for himself, which would be valid for everyone. The only one he could find was his famous maxim, which implies the rejection of a utilitarian ethics, a rejection which Coleridge, thirty years later, explicitly confirms. A 'scheme of ethics' lacks the foundation to be found in virtues.

With the spiritual revival since the end of the 19th century the virtues found a new insight and appreciation within the Theosophical and Anthroposophical movements and with women philosophers like Simone Weil, Hannah Arendt and Elizabeth Anscombe, but never became part of mainstream thinking. Yet, in a recent collection of essays on the ethics of warfare, virtues like courage, solidarity, integrity, not rules determine effective outcomes, when combatants are under fire. Islam traditionally teaches degrees of 'effective altruism', to the point of a 'type of self-annihilation', now horribly misinterpreted, misunderstood and misused as justification and incentive for suicide bombings and all their destructive consequences. Taken out of context even Fettullah Gülen's text could be vulnerable to manipulation...

For Simone Weil virtues are for the soul what food and shelter are for the body: she lists and describes them in opposite pairs, and warns to not understand those oppositions as mediating 'equilibriums' cancelling them out. For Hannah Arendt an ethics of 'following rules' prevents one from self-responsible thinking. Elizabeth Anscombe's pioneering essay of 1958 appeared in the context of a dominating English, analytical and rule-based moral philosophy. Her demand for a more concrete understanding of virtue itself etc., had been partly anticipated in Simone Weil's articulation of essential psychological needs and a similar demand has later been part of research into an interrelationship between virtues, a pattern or organism, as well as the practice of the virtues as a source of lasting moral strength. Margaret Somerville characterized such cluster of virtues as a 'constellation.' St Francis' "Greeting the Virtues" is imagined as a pattern with its inner 'logic'. And his concept of 'Obedience' can be read as the foundation for today's responsibility for the environment.

The 'Devotio Moderna,' mentioned as the context for Dirk van Herxen's little teaching, began as an order of laypeople, called 'brothers of the communal life', bound by promises, no by vows, initiated by Geert Groote (1340-1384), which after his death soon spread as a monastic order, a reform movement, engaged in education, schools, study and art. Its most well-known member was Thoms of Kempen, author the Imitation Christi, and its settlements spread all over Germany and Poland. The movement was part of a catholic reformation, predating and then running parallel to what is now known as the {protestant) Reformation. Desiderius Erasmus and Nicolaus Copernicus were directly influenced by it....

In the 20th century, out of an open ended Anthroposophical background philosopher and poet Martin Krüger and psychologist and healer Tineke Bak develop the awareness that the process of practising virtues results in developing lasting strengths.

In the 21 century the bio-ethicist Margaret Somerville dedicates in her Ethical Imagination a whole chapter on the development of the virtues as the urgent and necessary condition for any meaningful and effective ethical approach to the increasingly harrowing complexities humanity is facing in our time, due to what becomes technologically possible and financially exploitable. Her metaphor of 'constellations' of virtues resonates well with notions of 'pattern' and' organism' as means to acknowledge the interrelation between the different virtues. Her insights and those of Nassim Nicholas Taleb form a meaningful closure of this chapter. And in Somerville's understanding of hope and Taleb's understanding of the Golden Rule as a 'generator' rather than a 'summary' we are already anticipating the theme of chapter 6, that follows on from here.

Hinduism: Moon-cycle of virtues --- Names of Bhairava

Pristine purity ---Friendliness --- Positivity
Simplicity --- Harmony --- Sensitive consideration, perceptive tact
Good will ---Integrity --- Truthfulness
Contentment --- Moderation --- Nobility
Compassion --- Loyalty to the truth --- Serenity
Equanimity --- Inner firmness --- Perseverance
Decisiveness, determination --- Staying Power ---Reliability
Many-sidedness --- Capacity for wonder ---Awakened awareness (discernment)
Obedience, keeping one's vow --- Certainty --- Accuracy, precision
Magnanimity --- Benevolence, generosity --- Gentleness, tenderness
Highest freedom

Sanskrit names given by Shin Gwydion Fontalba
Translated by a team at Seminar in Bhairava Nagar/Shivaland,
Sirasu, India
November 2008

Mr Vidgi Sharma from Varanasi explained the Sanskrit words to us, one by one, with a story...I added 'perceptive tact' to the translation of 'Anakulata' as 'sensitive consideration', as it was the way an Aboriginal Artist, Robert Lee, a former student of mine, intending to work in a project with 5 Aboriginal communities, expressed his conclusion. He had a conversation with the architect Greg Burgess who had designed an Aboriginal Cultural Centre in collaboration with 5 aboriginal communities in Halls Gap, in the Grampians, after which he expressed for himself the need for "perceptive tact". I was supposed to make notes of that conversation, but these two words were the only ones I wrote down. In true Indian/Sanskrit fashion, this choice of words reflects my story...

Henk Bak

Greeting of the virtues (On the virtues that adorned the holy virgin and must adorn the holy soul.)

St Francis of Assisi

I greet you, Queen Wisdom. May the Lord bless you, together with your sister Donna Pure Simplicity.
Donna Poverty, may the Lord bless you, together with your sister Humility.
Donna Charity, may the Lord bless you, together with your sister Obedience.
Most sacred virtues, the Lord - from whom you come
and to whom you return – may bless you all.

No one in the whole world is guilty or suffers an untimely death, if he or she has one of you.
Who-ever has one and does not offend against the others has
them all;- and who-ever offends against one has none and offends
against all; - and each of them overcomes vices and evil.

Sacred Wisdom confounds Satan and all his malice.
Sacred, pure, Simplicity confounds all worldly wisdom and the wisdom of the flesh.
Sacred Poverty confounds all greed and avarice and worldly worries.
Sacred Humility confounds arrogance and all people and everything in and of this world.
Sacred Love confounds all diabolical and sensuous
temptations and all bodily fears.

Sacred Obedience confounds all bodily and sensuous urges and the spirit holds the disciplined body in obedience to oneself and to one's brother.
It causes the human being to respect all human beings on earth and not only people, but also all living creatures, tame and wild, in order that they are able to live out of whatever has been ordained for them by the Lord from above.

Salutatio Virtutum
Opuscula Sancti Patris Francisci Assisiensis
1949, pp. 20-21
[Translated by Henk Bak]

Devotio Moderna (14th-16th Centuries)

Patience, trust and contentment:
three important things.
Patience generates rest,

trust brings joy,
contentment leads to gratitude.
Whoever possesses these three
will live here on earth in happiness.

Dirk van Herxen (1381-1457)
Zorgzaam en toegewijd 600 jaar moderne devotie (Caring and dedicated 600 year devotio moderna)
1984, p.7
[Translated by Henk Bak]

Virtues in relation to others

We have already the broad division of Virtues and Vices, springing from the Emotion of Love and the emotion of Hate, the constructive and destructive elements in nature and in man. The subdivisions of those in relation to others are conveniently suggested by the phrase about the world which is filled with a man's "elders, equals, and youngers". *) The duties we owe to our superiors , our equals, and our inferiors, give us a natural division of Virtues and Vices, and all subclasses grow out of these. Out of the Emotion of Love to our superiors grow all the Virtues that are of the nature of Reverence. Those which grow out of the emotion of love to our equals are of the nature of Affection. Those which grow out of the emotion of love for to our inferiors, are of the nature of Benevolence. Similarly with the Virtues that grow out of the emotion of Hate: these show themselves to our superiors in forms of Fear; to our equals in forms of Anger, to our inferiors in forms of Scorn.

Annie Besant
The Universal Text Book of Religion and Morals. Volume 1 & 2
1910

Morality based on virtue versus ethics based on utility

Let it be granted, that in certain individuals from a happy evenness of nature, formed into a habit by the strength of education, the influence of example, and by favourable circumstances in general, the action diverging from self-love as their centre should be precisely the same as those produced from the Christian principle, which requires of us that we should place our self and our neighbour at an equal distance, and love both alike as modes in which we realize and exhibit the love of God:; wherein would the difference be then?

I answer boldly: even in that for which all actions have their whole worth and their main value – in the agents themselves.

So much indeed is this of the very substance of genuine morality, that wherever the latter has given way in the general opinion to a scheme of ethics founded on utility, its place is soon challenged by the spirit of honour. [   ] Honour implies a reverence for the invisible and supernatural in our nature, and so far it is virtue; but it is a virtue that neither understands itself or its true source, and therefore often unsubstantial, not seldom fantastic, and always more or less capricious.

S.T Coleridge
The Friend / Section 2 Essay 2
1866, p. 283-284

Respect to be expressed through the medium of earthly needs, of body and soul

The fact that the human being possesses an eternal destiny imposes only one obligation: respect. The obligation is only performed if the respect is effectively expressed in a real, not a fictitious, way; and this can only be done through the medium of Man's earthly needs.

On this point the human conscience has never varied. Thousands of years ago, the Egyptians believed, that no soul could justify itself after death unless it could say: 'I have never let any one suffer from hunger.'

[ ]

So it is the eternal obligation towards the human being not to let him suffer from hunger when one has the chance of coming to his assistance. This obligation being the most obvious of all, it can serve as a model on which to draw up a list of eternal duties towards each human being. In order to be absolutely correctly made out, this list ought to proceed from the example just given by way of analogy.

[ ]

The first thing to be investigated is what are for the life of the soul what the needs in the way of food, sleep and warmth are for the life of the body.

[ ]

They are much more difficult to recognize and to enumerate than are the needs of the body. But everyone recognizes that they exist. All the different forms of cruelty which a conqueror can exercise over a subject population, such as massacre, mutilation, organized famine, enslavement or large scale deportation, are generally considered measures of like description, even though a man's liberty or his native land are not physical necessities. pp. 6-12

List of soul needs analogous to food.

Order is the first of all; it even stands above all needs properly so-called. The be able to conceive it, we must know what the other needs are.

The first characteristic which distinguishes needs from desires, fancies or vices, and foods from glutinous repasts or poisons, is that needs are limited, in exactly the same way as are the foods corresponding to them.

[ ]

The second characteristic, closely connected with the first, is that needs are arranged in antithetical pairs and have to combine together to form a balance. Man requires food, but also an interval between his meals, he requires warmth and coolness, rest and exercise. Likewise in the case of the soul's needs.

What is called the golden mean actually consists in satisfying neither the one nor the other of two contrary needs. It is a caricature of the genuinely balanced state in which contrary needs are each fully satisfied in turn. P 12

[Here follow 27 pages with descriptions of six pairs of soul needs:

*Liberty and Obedience
Responsibility and Equality
Hierarchism and Honour
Punishment and Freedom of opinion
Security and Risk
Private property and Collective property*

The list begins with Order and ends with Truth:]

*Order stands above all other needs properly so-called
The need of truth is more sacred than any other need...*

[ ]

There is no possible chance of satisfying a people's need of truth, unless men can be found for this purpose who love truth. pp. 38-39

Simone Weil, Arthur Wills [Translator]
The Need of Roots
2003, pp. 6-12

On the virtue of Gratitude

Let us look at a humble virtue, that of gratitude. With this virtue alone, the world could be at peace. We need to recognize that everybody in the world is the benefactor of everybody else. Not only people: even cats and dogs are benefactors of mankind, even birds. If we remain aware of the debt of gratitude that we owe to these things, we will be unable to act in any way that hurts or oppresses them. With the power of the virtue of gratitude, we can help the world.

Buddhadasa Bhikkhu
Thailand 1906-1993

Re-introducing a virtue-based moral philosophy

It may be possible, if we are resolute, to discard the notion "morally ought," and simply return to the ordinary "ought," which, we ought to notice, is such an extremely frequent term of human language that it is difficult to imagine getting on without it. Now if we do return to it, can't it reasonably be asked whether one might ever need to commit injustice, or whether it won't be the best thing to do? Of course it can.

And the answer will be various.

One man – a philosopher – may say that since justice is a virtue, and injustice a vice, and virtues and vices are built up by performances of the action in which they are instanced, an act of injustice will tend to make a man bad; and essentially the flourishing of a man qua man consists in his being good (e.g. in virtues); but for any X to which such terms apply, X needs what makes it flourish, so a man needs, or ought to perform only virtuous actions; and even if, as it must be admitted may happen, he flourishes less, or not at all, in inessentials, by avoiding injustice — so he still needs to perform only good actions.

That is roughly how Plato and Aristotle talk: but it can be seen that philosophically there is a huge gap, at present unfillable as far as we are concerned, which needs to be filled by an account of human nature, human action, the type of characteristic a virtue is, and above all of human "flourishing." And it is the last concept that appears the most doubtful. For it is a bit much to swallow that a man in pain and hunger and poor and friendless is "flourishing," as Aristotle admitted.

Further, someone might say that one at least needed to stay alive to "flourish."

Another man, unimpressed by all that will say in a hard case "What we need in such-and-such, which we won't get without doing this (which is unjust) — so this is what we ought to do."

Another man, who does not follow the rather elaborate reasoning of the philosophers, simply says, "I know it is in any case a disgraceful thing to say that one had better commit this unjust action."

The man who believes in divine laws will say perhaps "It is forbidden, and however it looks, it cannot be to anyone's profit to commit injustice";

He, like the Greek philosophers can think in terms of "flourishing".

If he is a Stoic, he is apt to have a decidedly strained notion of what "flourishing" consists in;

If he is a Jew or Christian, he need not to have any very distinct notion: the way it will profit him to abstain from injustice is something that he leaves to God to determine, himself only saying "It can't do me any good to go against his law." (but he also hopes for a great reward in a new life later on, e.g. the coming of the Messiah; but in this he is relying on special promises.).

It is left to modern moral philosophy — the moral philosophy of all the well-known English ethicists since Sidgwick — to construct a system according to which the man who says "We need such-and-such, and will only get it this way" may be a virtuous character: that is to say, it is left open to debate whether such procedure as the judicial punishment of the innocent may not in some circumstances be the "right" one to adopt; and though the present Oxford moral philosophers would accord

*a man permission to "make it his principle" not to do such, they teach
a philosophy according to which the particular consequences of such an
action could "morally" be taken into account by a man who was debating
what to do; and if they such as to conflict with his "ends," it might be
a step in his moral education to frame a moral principle under which he
"managed" (to use Mr. Nowell-Smith's phrases) to bring the action:*

*Or it might be a new "decision of principle making" which was an
advance in the formation of his moral thinking (to adopt Mr Hare's
conception), to decide: in such-and-such circumstances one ought to procure
the judicial condemnation of the innocent. And this is my complaint.*

G.E.M Anscombe
Modern Moral Philosophy
Philosophy Vol. 33, No. 1, 24 January 1958, pp.15-16
[Lay-out edited by Henk Bak]

Virtue based ethics in warfare: Honour, not law

*The law of armed conflict (LOAC) 'obliges belligerent nations to keep
their armed forces disciplined under responsible command'. P20*

[ ]

*Given the importance of ethical warfare, the question remains of whether
today's combatants can agree on a single international code. Or instead,
are we destined to live in a world of ethical asymmetries? In the Western
world, we start from a universalist ethic based on human rights. In some
of the battlefields today, there is an opposing ethic. This ethic comes from
a view that defines the tribe, the nation, or the ethnic group...While
reciprocity was once the major sanction underlying the laws of war, it
has broken down with respect to non-state actors who are indifferent to
accepted legal restraints. Obligations without reciprocity risks the warfare
strategy breaking down. Particularly when one side feels bound to protect
the civilians of both sides, and the other side deliberately does not...*

*Should militaries yield to expedience if they want to defeat today's
adversaries? If militaries were to do so they would create a global political
environment where LOAC violations become rampant. So can ethics do
what reciprocity once did? 'Law is the judgement of the community at
large, but the impetus for ethical conduct among warriors must come from
among other warriors.' The challenge for commanders is to teach their
troops the 'ethos of the professional warrior'. It is not enough for soldiers*

to know the rules and follow them. Without deep reserves of character and moral strength, troops in today's high-stress battlefield situations may not be able to withstand the psychological toll and may give in to undisciplined impulses. 'Honor, not law, is the key to battlefield disciplines.'

Charles J Dunlop Jnr Why Ethics Matter in: Tom Frame and Albert Palazzo (Editors)
Ethics under Fire: Challenges for the Australian Army
2017, pp. 20; 29-31
Quotes: Lt Gabriel Bradley Honor, not Law in: Armed Forces 2012

Virtue based ethics in warfare: values beyond rules.

The Australian Army's values have a context of their own:

Courage: Every Australian soldier is expected to demonstrate physical and moral courage. To be courageous in the Army is to believe in the Army's mission, its goals and one's mates, and under the most demanding conditions.

Initiative: Every Australian soldier is expected to show initiative whenever required and to be committed to continuous learning and self-development. Initiative is fundamental to professional mastery and essential to the effective practice of mission command.

Respect: Respect is the glue that binds the other values together. It is the quality that will both temper and sharpen the hard edge that must be a part of military service in order to survive and prevail in war. Furthermore, the Australian nation must trust the standing army to respect the law of the land and be capable of restraint and prudence in using appropriate and sanctioned violence. Respect also extends to those whom the Army is entrusted to protect and support when deployed in Australia and overseas.

Teamwork: The Australian Army is a team of teams in which all soldiers are expected to be able to rely on their mates. Without a team a soldier is just another person. Robust, cohesive teams are the personnel building blocks of the Army's capability.

Chris Field The Practicalities of Ethical Accountability in: Tom Frame and Albert Palazzo (Editors)'s
Ethics under Fire: Challenges for the Australian Army / Chapter 17
2017, pp. 285,286

What is justice? Following orders or standing up for what is right?

I had the following conversation with prison inmates in 2004. This intervention demonstrates Dennett's "belief in belief". ...I like this dialogue, because it's brief and because it causes people to adopt the idea that they should "believe in the right stuff".

Researcher [Peter Boghossian]: What is justice?

Inmate 6: Standing up for what you believe in.

Researcher: What if you believe weird stuff? Like one of those lunatics who want to kill Americans? Or what if you're a pedophile?

(A twenty-second silence)

Inmate 6: I think if you can stand on your own feet and not care what anyone else thinks about you, and you are willing to fight for it and die for it or whatever, that makes you a man. Whether it's right or not.

Researcher: So being a man would mean to be resolute in your beliefs no matter what? What if you're in the military, like in Rwanda, and you're told to butcher all these people, and you have a skewed idea of loyalty. And you stand up for what you believe, for your country or tribe or whatever, and you just start butchering civilians? Hutus or Tutsis or whoever. Is that just? Does that make you a man?

Inmate 5: Yeah, good point. It happened in Nam [Vietnam].

Inmate 4: What are you saying? That justice isn't standing up for what you believe in?

Researcher: I'm not saying: I'm asking. What is justice? [Inmate 6] said it's standing up for what you believe in. But is it really standing up for what you believe in? Don't you have to believe the right stuff, then stand up for that? No

Inmate 6: Yeah, maybe. Maybe.

Peter Boghossian
A Manual for creating Atheists
2013, pp. 87,88

Virtue based ethics in activism: a new year's pledge for 2015

I pledge to live more by these 3 principles in 2015:

To show kindness and respect, strive for wisdom, and practice gratitude:

We will show kindness and respect towards ourselves and others whenever possible. And it's always possible, because everyone we meet is fighting a battle we know nothing about.

Strive for wisdom

We will seek to be wise in our decisions, listening deeply to ourselves and others, and balancing our heads, hearts and intuitions in a harmony that feels right.

Practice gratitude

We will regularly reflect on what we are grateful for, because it brings perspective, dissolves negativity, and grounds us in what's most important.

Our community has overwhelmingly voted for these 3 simple, powerful principles to support each other to follow... When 500.000 of us pledge, we'll invite world leaders to personally join us, and we'll all check in 3 times this coming year to see how we are doing.

AVAAZ Website
As of 18 August 2018: 505,490 signatures received

Manfred Krüger: Virtues and the capacities they generate

As one racticed it becomes clear that the virtues are related to the path of the Sun through the Zodiac, and should be meditated upon in this way. Each sign lends soul —strengths and —weaknesses. By racticed the appropriate virtue the various predominant —weaknesses can be overcome.

In the Mars sign —Aries, the human being is most eager to attack and least reverent or devotional. Should he ractice devotion, he will develop the capacity to sacrifice.

If the 'Bull' (Taurus) is irritated, he stands in great danger of losing his balance, his equilibrium in the realm of feeling. Should he strive after inner balance, this becomes for him the capacity to make progress.

*In the 'Twins'(Gemini) he mercurially swings from one thing to
another, and he lacks perseverance. In racticed perseverance, the
capacity arises to be true and loyal to something, or someone.*

*In the dream sign Cancer, the human being draws back on himself – he lacks
unselfishness. In racticed unselfishness he will be able to experience catharsis.*

*The 'Lion'(Leo) needs to learn compassion, then
he will be able to develop true freedom.*

*Virgo - intelligence sees the mistakes and failures of
others, and can be hurtful—courtesy should be racticed.
That will soon develop into tact of the heart.*

*In the 'Scales '(Libra) one is seldom satisfied, beauty is ephemeral. Should
he ractice contentment, however, he will be able to let its destruction pass
him by with equanimity and may well discover the beauty of autumn.*

*In Scorpio, the human being defends himself where perhaps there is no attack
at all. Above all he lacks patience, and in racticed this he will attain insight.*

*In Sagittarius, words slip more quickly over the tongue than thoughts can be
formed. Holding back the words gives him the strength to sense the truth.*

*In Capricorn ('mountain goat') courage is lacking. Should he be able to
muster courage nevertheless, the power to redeem will fill him. If – in his
position between Sagittarius and Aquarius - he has thoughtfully racticed,
passing on his own wisdom in Sagittarius, so he must securely protect what
others entrust to him in Aquarius. That will give him the power to meditate.*

*Pisces is the sign of death and resurrection. Here one needs
more than courage; one needs magnanimity, so that the new
can arise out of the old. Transformation is love.*

Manfred Krüger
Meditation: Erkenntnis als Kunst.[Insight as Art]
1988, p.40
[Translated by Tineke Bak, Evera 'Dewdrop' Newsletter. Vol 1 Issue
3, 2007 p.10]

Friendships Within Friendships

Virtues are qualities we instinctively recognize. Something in us knows

*them. We may not trust our own perception or the enduring nature of the
virtue in the other person, but we do recognize virtue when we encounter
it, especially when it is the real thing'. We do not have to invent it –
only discover it, find a language or a name for it, learn to deal with
those forces in an appropriate, creative fashion rather than leave it to
chance and circumstance to bring them to us, or us to them. Our being
instinctively responds to their presence around us, even if as children we
do not yet know how to generate these qualities consciously ourselves.*

*It is always like a homecoming to encounter the virtue in its true power. We
feel we can open safely, can relax, can be ourselves, are free, warm, and
accepted. Perhaps this is why the behavioural likeness of the virtue enforced by
external authorities (e.g. religious institutions or educational bodies) can feel
like such a betrayal and entrapment. When someone truly offers us devotion,
or compassion, is clear and patient with us – we KNOW we have been given
something essentially priceless, and something deep in our being responds to its
grace-full presence as if it were an echo of the paradise that once was home.*

*It is as if long ago we dwelt together with these great qualities
and within their care were truly at one, at peace, in effortless joy,
whole and complete. If we listen with great attentiveness to our
own response, we notice that we respond as if these qualities were
beings who surround us with their wings of power, their truly just,
loving guidance – like the safe protection of guardian angels.*

*It is as if we left their embrace to manifest on Earth, yet somewhere still
carry the memory of them buried deep within our heart-soul. It is as if we
are born – and expect the world to provide the same loving, just guidance.*

*Instead we find that life is imperfect here, is often chaotic, wild, unpredictable,
and soon we are so busy learning to cope with all the ways in which we
must adapt that we begin to forget this part of our primary knowing.
Eventually some of us even forget the hurt of discovering that this perfect
love is not there to catch us when we fall – and we find ourselves living
almost entirely within our adaptations, numb and blind to our loss.*

*But there is a part of us which never forgets. A part of us that steadfastly
remembers, and knows and recognizes these qualities of being, even in the
wilderness of life. And when we encounter them anew, we can notice that
in their presence the wilderness of life transforms its face and shows its
potential as a garden of Eden, a garden we can choose to re-create with*

*our choices. We can choose to remember these best of friends and we
can choose to cultivate the friendship consciously and deliberately – re-
creating old friendships with spirit in our human friendships on Earth.*

*These old friends will never let us down, but we have to choose to invite
them. They will never force themselves upon us in any way whatsoever.
Their bounty is free, and very potent, but this freedom is their protection from
misuse. Their bounty vanishes when that freedom of choice is compromised.
When we use them to enforce, to manipulate, to enslave them for our own
gain, our pride or status, our security, to look good, to get results, even to make
religious or spiritual ambitions happen – we find their bounty vanishes.*

*The virtues can be utterly trusted to shower their protection only in the
spacious light of free choice, free will, as an expression of love. In that light
their friendship flourishes and nourishes, guides and heals, and re-creates their
Garden within ours. The more we cultivate that ancient spiritual friendship,
the stronger these gifts can dwell and work in our life, our soul, and nurture
our becoming – and allow us to re-discover the Friend in the Other.*

*Which Virtues?
There are many, many virtues but we have been given twelve that
especially strengthen the power of the heart chakra to transform and
work. These twelve were indicated already by the Theosophists, and
confirmed by Rudolf Steiner and later, by Gideon Fontalba, and Shin.*

*How do we practice them?
To begin with, remember them – think about them, write about them in
journals or on café napkins, wonder about them, notice them, invite them, talk
about them, and try them out now and again, deliberately choose to interrupt
your reaction, and BE patient, clear, compassionate, etc., whatever is needed
in the moment. Most especially practice on yourself! Create the friendship
garden within yourself with yourself and rediscover your own being*

Tineke Bak
Dewdrop / Evera Newsletter Vol 1 Issue 1 Winter
2007 pp. 8-9

How virtues generate new capacities

*Devotion, when it truly lights up our heart, frees
up the soul to the power of self-sacrifice.*

Balance, when carefully and playfully racticed in daily

living, frees up the power to make progress.

Perseverance, when honestly pursued, gives rise to a deeper faithfulness, a capacity to be true to what we endeavour or commit ourselves to honour.

*Selflessness, when acted out becomes the power
of catharsis, of inner purification.*

*Compassion, when brought to a situation, awakens in the soul
a new power of freedom to act, to be, to feel, to perceive...*

*Courtesy or attentiveness, when woven into social interactions,
develops into a warmer power of intuitive heart-felt tact.*

*Contentment, faithfully sought again and again, gives rise to a
powerful state of inner composure, tranquility and serenity.*

Patience, when offered to life, builds an ever-deepening power of insight.

*Clarity, when striven for and acted out through control of the tongue,
unfolds a delicate yet powerful new sense and feeling for truth.*

*Courage brought again and again into life's challenges,
gives rise to the alchemical power to redeem.*

Discretion, racticed diligently, develops in the soul the power to meditate.

*Magnanimity and generosity of heart given freely
will unfold the power of love in the soul.*

Rudolf Steiner Start Now—A Book of Soul and Spiritual Exercises,
p. 143
in: Christopher Bamford's
Meditation: Erkenntnis als Kunst
2007, p. 40

Past Virtues for a Future World – Holding our Humanity in Trust

*In this last chapter, I want to explore the question of where we might
go from here in searching for ethics, whether as individuals, families,
communities, societies, or a global world. If we think back to the metaphor
I used at the beginning of this book of a constellation of stars, what
concepts, attributes, or capacities might we now want to find in that ethical
constellation? Some that come to my mind are respect for nature, a sense*

of the sacred, the intellectual joy of reason, hope, awe, wonder, mystery, courage, integrity, compassion, kindness, generosity, restraint, and, I would add, a sense of humour. These are not all of the same nature or of equal importance, but all have roles to play in helping us to find meaning in life – which means they all have roles to play in helping us to find ethics.

Complexity – Trust – Courage – Compassion – Generosity – Hope

Complexity.

I want to begin, however, by looking at a concept that is relevant to all of the virtues, that of complexity – especially in relation to uncertainty and meaning-making.

The Oxford English Dictionary defines complexity as "Involved nature or structure, intricacy. ... A whole comprehending in its compass a number of parts, esp. (in later use) of interconnected parts or involved particulars; a complex or complicated whole." I suggest that complexity and meaning-making have a symbiotic relation: complexity is necessary for meaning-making, and meaning-making is necessary to deal with complexity. I have come to that conclusion through long-time puzzling about what ethicist David Roy meant, when he said, "Suffering is where meaning crossed path with biology." This seemed to me an important statement, but the more I thought about it the less I understood it – that is, until I looked at it in the light of complexity. Suffering cannot be accommodated in our lives, or even partially understood, unless we see it as an immensely complex phenomenon. When we, as biological creatures, witness suffering or suffer ourselves, and we see this experience as complex, we have an opportunity to find meaning in life. It is not an opportunity the vast majority of us would seek – indeed, usually we do all we can to avoid it – but that does not take away from the great value many people find in suffering. Moreover, meanings are not always comforting and peaceful, and even when they are comforting they can be related to distressing ones. Roy relates how a patient describes the complex reality of finding meaning in suffering as experiencing the "sound of the soul singing, as it used to do before it lost its courage and the love." In short, finding true, complex meaning requires both courage and love.

There is a vast difference between simple and simplistic approaches to complex realities such a suffering and finding meaning. The former are valid and the latter are not. And when the simple is not sufficient, we need to tease out the elements that give rise to complexity if we are to deal with reality appropriately. My former law student Alicen Chen describes the complexity of a legal and ethical analysis of an issue this way: "an investigation that is textured, nuanced, layered and rich in traces of different cultures, disciplines, world-views, and understandings of both human nature and human as compared to nature."

To reach a complex understanding of an issue, we might need to consider notions of objective and subjective; the knowable and the unknowable; the individual and the collective; duties to act and obligations to exercise restraint. We can undertake an analysis within these tensions, in the spaces between and among them, for it is there that room exists for complex understanding. Note, however, that we choose what we see as opposing forces in these tensions, and our choices are not neutral. They result from our values. We also generate creative tension when we simultaneously seek a single or individual principle or good and a universal one, especially when these cannot be reconciled and we choose to live with that situation. This discussion leads us to the insight that we should try to establish "creative tension" when that is called for. pp. 199-203

Complexity requires being comfortable with ambiguities, ironies and contradictions – in short, being comfortable with uncertainty. p.203

Hope

…Because hope is linked to the future, it's linked to potentiality. For this reason, the ethics of potentiality and the idea that it can be ethically wrong to deliberately negate potential are relevant to the discussion of hope. We can describe hope as a sense of possibility – the sense that our best dreams, no matter how short-term they might be, are open to fulfilment. Helping others to find hope requires imagination and creativity on the part of individuals, institutions, and societies; our enemies in this enterprise are apathy, boredom, inactivity, and nihilism. I believe that acting in ways that cause such loss of passion should be viewed as an ethical "mortal sin".

I also believe it's a mistake to perceive hope as passive. Rather we can compare "making hope" with making war or making peace…p. 235

[ ]

Hope is a human good. It is real, but it is not a physical reality, not a scientific fact, and not necessarily based on reason (although it is not antithetical to reason). It simply belongs to a different order of realities. We can argue that it is inherently wrong to intentionally destroy hope – which is what torture does. p. 236

[ ]

Hope as a basis for a shared ethics raises the question: is searching for hope a religious pursuit or a secular one, or can it be both? Religion gives us one way to find hope. But many people are now also looking for new ways to find hope in our secular societies. I suggest that hope seems to be intrinsically connected with religion – in the broad sense of that word, where it implies bonding – because we appear to be turning some of these relatively newer ways of seeking hope into secular religions – for example scientism and atheism. Just as traditional religion is dangerous when it becomes moralism (which I define as morality practised impersonally, without sympathy or empathy, and to the exclusion of other relevant considerations), scientism and atheism are dangerous when they become secular moralism.

[ ]

While not abandoning religion for those who find hope through it, I believe we need to explore where and how we can find hope other than through religion. I have written elsewhere that hope is the oxygen of the human spirit: without it our human spirit dies; with it, we can survive appalling suffering and surmount incredible obstacles…pp. 237-238

Margaret Somerville
The Ethical Imagination. Journeys of the Human Spirit
2006

Compared with rules, virtues are 'antifragile'

Some things benefit from shocks; they thrive and grow when exposed to volatility, randomness, disorder, and stressors and love adventure, risk, and uncertainty. Yet, in spite of the ubiquity of the phenomenon, there is no word for the exact opposite of fragile. Let us call it antifragile.

Antifragility is beyond resilience or robustness. The resilient resists shocks and stays the same; the antifragile gets better. This property is behind everything that has changed with time: evolution, culture, ideas, revolutions, political systems, technological innovation, cultural and economic success, corporate survival, good recipes (say, chicken soup or steak tartare with a drop of cognac), the rise of cities, cultures, legal systems, equatorial forests, bacterial resistance…even our own existence as a species on this planet. And antifragility determines the boundary between what is living and organic (or complex), say the human body, and what is inert, say, a physical object like the stapler on your desk. pp. 3-4

As usual at the end of the journey, while I was looking at the entire manuscript on a restaurant table, someone from a Semitic culture asked me to explain my book standing on one leg. This time it was Saiy Pilpel, a probabilist with whom I've had a two-decade long calm conversation without a single episode of small talk.

With the previous book, one of his compatriots asked me the same question, but I had to think about it. This time I did not even have to make an effort.

It was so obvious that Shaiy summed it up himself in the same breath. He actually believed that all real ideas can be distilled down to a central issue that the great majority of people in a given field, by dint of specialization and empty-suitedness, completely miss. Everything in religious law comes down to the refinements, applications, and interpretations of the Golden Rule, "Don't do unto others what you don't want them to do to you." This we saw was the logic behind Hammurabi's rule. And the Golden Rule was a true distillation, not a Procrustean bed. A central argument is never a summary – it is more like a generator.

[ ]

The glass is dead; living things are long volatility. The best way to verify that you are alive is by checking if you like variations. Remember that food would not have a taste if were not for hunger; results are meaningless without effort, joy without sadness, conviction without uncertainty, and an ethical life isn't so when stripped of personal risks. pp. 421;423

Nassim Nicholas Taleb
Antifragile: Things that gain from Disorder
2014

D: '…as yourself': integral to the Golden Rule

Introduction

The reference to oneself in the succinct form of the Golden Rule has mostly been understood to imply a 'love yourself'. Most traditional forms include an: 'as you wish for yourself', 'desire for yourself'. Still, whilst 'unselfishness' seems to be valued as a virtue, it seems not clear whether 'self-love' is to be considered a virtue, too.

It seems logical, that without self-love one would not be able to how to love one's neighbour, real life, however, shows many examples of people who are good at loving their neighbours and fellow creatures, but not at all good at loving themselves.

Philosophers have often objected that what we love for ourselves doesn't need to be right for our neighbours at all: differences in age, in gender, in culture, in world-view may require different responses to their situation or need.

Only at the most elementary level of human needs, our responses to hunger, abject poverty, oppression and the like, our self-love might be a trustworthy guide. And then, again, at the highest level of human dignity, there where all human beings one by one are unique individuals: each of us is called to recognize the unique, individual other as unique and individual as one oneself is. In this sense the Universal Declaration of Human Rights of 1948 is founded on the same 'rock' as is the Golden Rule. In this sense also 'respect of self' is called for in the same breath as is 'respect for the other'.

In this train of thought we will have moved from a logical, perhaps even theological mode of thinking to a philosophical and finally an existential approach to the question: is loving yourself a virtue, a moral strength, an indispensable guide for life?

I suggest that this question is itself an 'existential' one. At least on three grounds:

Firstly, lack of self-love has become a pathology of our time. Not only in the sense that it has become a mental health issue world-wide, but also, because this pathology must be major factor in what drives human beings to violence, suicides, killings, rape. In a culture that treats human beings as disposable, superfluous commodities, not all of us have the moral resources that empower us to refrain from inflicting this violence on ourselves as well as on others.

Secondly, our consumer culture is degrading not only our environment but also ourselves, our dignity: it makes us directly or indirectly complicit in this environmental degradation. Our participation in this consumer culture, whether we want it or are aware of it or not, degrades every one of us.

Thirdly, with the degradation of the environment comes the degradation of our senses, a vicious circle: ugly, noisy, smelly, smoggy surroundings and junk food become standard and the lower the standard, the less we notice the degradation around us. The same is true of our moral sensitivity: coarse language, bad taste, offensive behaviour degrades the users as badly as it degrades the ones so abused.

We show up in a universe that exquisitely equips us for wondering, perceiving, experiencing the richness of its qualities and for recognizing its majesty and wisdom. The richer and more diverse our sense experiences, the greater scope for appreciating ourselves as 'cosmic marvels'. In the face of this cosmic generosity our self-love can guide us to use, enjoy and develop our senses unselfishly… Gratitude rather than gratification…

In the 'Study' part of this book, and in the Chapters 2 and 3 of the anthology, we have had ample occasion to distinguish stages of consciousness and constituent elements of the human being, most generally: physical and living body, sentience, soul and spirit. When we say 'I am' then we either say this out of the integrity of our whole being, or out of the dominance of one or other separate part, egotistic, egocentric, self-serving, sentimental, animalistic, materialistic…

Part of human development consists of leaving behind those false identifications that identify us with one part or other of ourselves rather than of with the One we truly are. Where this development is stunted or distorted, the false identifications take over.

The following texts emphasize the validity and meaning of self-love as part of our humanity, and contrast this with the other 'self-love', that separates us from our true selves, and therewith from the humanity we share with our neighbours as well.

Orientation

The ongoing climate emergency and the apparently transitory global health crisis have generated and are generating a groundswell of goodwill. The 'love your neighbour' seems to overshadow the '-as yourself 'part of the Golden Rule. The 'as yourself' understood as an implied 'love yourself' has always been problematic, increasingly so in a world of racial, ethnic, cultural and religious diversity, where what is meaningful, helpful and satisfying for oneself, might not be so for someone from a different religious, cultural and so on background. In less diversified or more homogeneous cultures it must be much easier to know how to respond to someone else's needs.

In most religious teachings as far as I know, there is a tendency to encourage or instil a preference for serving the other's needs over one's own.

This may be an inclination, naturally to be fostered in a family, tribal setting, community and society at large. I am reminded of the volunteers who recently risked their lives in the bushfires here in Australia, the technicians who risked their lives in cleaning up Chernobyl and Fukushima. Religious education and practise will have given depth, vigour and endurance to this altruism. But – hopefully – also an equilibrium, a sense of proportion. Any form of fanaticism, absolute self-denial, sacrificing one's own integrity, obstructing one's own eternal destiny turns altruism into pathology or crime. Only those who are healthy and strong in soul and spirit, fully themselves, are truly capable and authorized in sacrificing their earthly life for the higher good. Hence the extra horror of modern wars, where governments drive troops into battlefields regardless of the standard of their 'moral resources' and more often than not, for no higher good than their own power interests.

'Orientations' and 'texts' will alternate in the following part of this anthology.

Two examples of how altruism can be pushed to the limit and how it can be generous and relaxed.

Degrees of altruism

According to Gülen, there are degrees of ithar depending on the level of faith and quality of the representation of Islam:

To look after others while neglecting oneself, such as feeding others while remaining hungry. Observing the rights of all humans and being careful not to tread on any person's rights...I would call this "ithar bil aql" (altruism with the reasoning)

Despite everything, to use all bounties, including time, money, health, and personal abilities, only to earn Allah's pleasure, and then to keep these acts to oneself, or even forget the acts so as to remain humble...I would call it "ithar bil aql qalb" (ithar with the reasoning and heart)

The third degree is the highest level of devotion to the community. Gülen points to the sacrifice of Prophet Mohammed (pbuh) during the Ascension. The prophet had entered Janna and came close to the Divine presence, but returned to the world to save his umma from hell and to take his umma to paradise. This state is a type of annihilation of one's self. The last degree of ithar can be called ithar "bil aql wal qalb wa'r-ruh" (ithar with the reasoning, heart and soul). It can be called pure ithar as well.

Salih Yücel
A Life in Tears: Understanding Fettullah Gülen and his Call to Service
2018, pp. 173-4

One is loving-kind amongst God's servants who desires for God's creatures whatever he desires for himself; and whoever prefers them to himself is even higher than that. Like one of them who said, 'I would like to be a bridge over the fire (of hell) so that creatures might pass over me and not be harmed by it.' The perfection of that virtue occurs when not even anger hatred, and the harm he might receive can keep him from altruism and goodness.

Abü Hāmid Gazzālï, David B. Burrell and Nazih Daher
The Ninety-nine Beautiful Names of God
2011

Twenty century humanism

I have something that I call my Golden Rule… "Do to others twenty five percent better than you expect them to do unto you." … The twenty five percent is for error.

Linus Pauling in: Buzzy Jackson's
The Inspirational Atheist
2014, p. 103

Orientation

There may be two other considerations that favour the tendency to emphasise 'love thy neighbour' over 'love thyself'. One is the age honoured qualification: 'for the sake of God'. It had often puzzled me: how can one love someone if not for this person's own sake? Is it forbidden to find pleasure in another's wellbeing and happiness? To show one's pleasure with a smile? Two recently found sources helped unravel the puzzle for me. The formulations of the Golden Rule cited by Justin Parrott in his recent PhD dissertation (2018) interpret 'for God's sake' as 'without selfish intentions', which doesn't forbid me to enjoy my love for my neighbour, but also encourages me, to love him or her in case don't enjoy it. The second source is the Universal Textbook of Religions (1910) in which Annie Besant emphasized the relevance of a religious/spiritual understanding of the 'Universal Brotherhood of Man'.

A pre-syllogistic expression of the 'love your neighbour as yourself'

"We are one and the same person"

"We consider you siblings because we share the same struggle", said Pedro dos Santos Uriri, a Forest Guardians Commander wearing a peccary tooth necklace. He wept as he embraced his guests. "Why am I crying? It's because I feel we are one and the same person," the 55-year-old said to applause.

Forest Fight. Pereira's legacy kept alive in the Amazon
Guardian Weekly, UK, 26 August, 2022, pp. 22-23

Araboia indigenous people, activists, from Brazil's eastern region of the Amazon, having travelled 2500 km west to the Javari territory, close to the Peruvian border were welcomed by a Javari man in a Javari village. Their mission: to connect indigenous defenders from all around the Amazon, their territories against the onslaught of loggers, farmers and poachers. This pioneering project had been prepared by Pereira and Philip, the latter of who had recently been murdered whilst preparing this journey.

Universal brotherhood

It must be frankly admitted that, so far in human history, Brotherhood has been partial rather than universal, and the few precise texts that inculcate the universal are accepted for the most part as pious opinions rather than as living inspirations for the practical guidance of conduct. Hence arises the duty of every religion to emphasise the truth and cultivate the practice, to break down barriers and level separating walls.

This can never be done by insisting on acceptance of the religion as a condition for admittance to Brotherhood. It must be seen that Brotherhood is a fact in nature, rooted in the One Life whereof we are all partakers, ineffaceable by any crime, unescapable by any heights of attainment, including the vilest and the noblest, the lowest and the loftiest, the sinner and the saint, an indefeasible birthright beyond any confiscation. Wherever God is immanent, there Brotherhood exists.

Edited and introduced by Annie Besant
Universal Textbook of Religion and Morals
1910, pp. 174-5

Seated equally in all beings, the Supreme Lord of All, indestructible within the destructible: he who thus seeth, he seeth.

Bhagavad-Gītā. 13. 27 in: Annie Besant's
Universal Textbook of Religion and Morals
1910, p. 279

All men tremble at punishment, all men fear death; remember that you are like unto them, and do not kill, nor cause slaughter.

(Buddhist) Dhamapada. x. 129, in: Annie Besant's
Universal Textbook of Religion and Morals
1910, p. 182

The best of men is he from whom good accrueth to humanity. All God's creatures are His family; and he is most beloved of God, who trieth to do most good to God's creatures..

The Sayings of Muhammad p.8, in: Annie Besant's
Universal Textbook of Religion and Morals
1910, p. 189

The Master said, 'Tseng! There is a single thread stringing my Way together.' 'There is indeed,' replied Master Tseng. When the Master left, some disciples asked, 'what did he mean?' 'Be loyal to the principles of your heart, and treat others with the same loyalty, 'answered Master Tseng, 'that is the master's Way. There is nothing more.'

Adept Kung asked, 'Is there any other word that could guide a person throughout life?' The Master replied, 'How about 'shu' (empathy, altruism)? Never impose on others what you would not choose for yourself.'

Confucius and David Hinton Analects Counterpoint. 2014, in: Justin Parrott PhD
The Golden Rule in Islam: Ethics of Reciprocity in Islamic Traditions
2018, p. 7

Comment: Najm al-Tūfī (d1306) was a Hanbalī jurist known for his bold of the legal principle of public welfare (maslaha) often preferring ethical or utilitarian considerations over the literal letter of the law, an orientation that preceded and foreshadowed the intellectual activity of modernist reformers...(in the following text) he takes another bold stance on the centrality of religious love.

The objective of this tradition is to unite the hearts of people and rectify their circumstances, and it is a major principle in Islam that God Almighty has enjoined...In clarification of that, if every person loved for others what he loves for himself, he would treat him in the best manner, he would not harm them because he loves for himself to be treated well, and he himself would not be harmed. If he treats them well and does not harm those he loves, then love will emanate from that between people, and with the emanation of love between them will be the emanation of good and the removal of evil, and with that the rectification of daily life and habits and the improvement of people's circumstances.

...Al-Tufi sees the Golden Rule as an expression of religious love, to have transformation power in its ability to bring about positive change.

The commentators who proposed an idea of universal brotherhood ... almost always qualified their comments with the missionary imperative, that Islam should be shared with non-Muslims; a Muslim should desire for non-Muslims to embrace Islam...This does not necessarily preclude Muslims from wishing unbelievers to acquire permissible, worldly blessings as well. In this way, the utility of the golden rule as a conceptual vehicle for managing interfaith relations remains intact, an important development that would come to play a role in the modern period's focus on human rights and interfaith conflict.

Sulaymän ibn 'Abdal-Qawï Tüfi, Kitäb al-Ta'yin fï Sharh al- Arba'ïn
(Bayrüt: Mu'assasat al-Rayyän, 1998)
in: Justin Parrott PhD
The Golden Rule in Islam: Ethics of Reciprocity in Islamic Traditions
2018, p.33
[author's translation]

The Golden Rule anchored in humanity itself, Kant's maxim:

Act so, that you use your own personal humanity as well as the humanity in another person both as end, never merely as means.

Immanuel Kant (1724-1804; 1785)

Orientation

The reference to sisterhood/brotherhood clarifies the 'as yourself' in yet another way: I used to understand it as a 'measure', J. Parrott uses the word 'criterion', by which one can know how to love the other. If one does not love oneself, who can one love one's neighbour? Well, there are many people who don't love themselves, find themselves not good enough, inferior, not worthy...but are eminently capable of loving others. It makes me even reverse the formula and say to them: 'love yourself as your neighbour' i.e. recognize your love for your neighbour as your criterion/measure for your self-love, self-esteem, self-worth. And it is not forbidden to enjoy loving yourself, for goodness' sake! In this way the 'as yourself' points to the common root of both – what J. Parrott calls 'horizontal-elements' of the Golden Rule: sisters and brothers, partners in nature, born from nature, nature itself born out of itself, natura naturata, which makes animals plants rocks water air and fire our brothers and sisters, too.

As long as brotherhood was understood partially, confined to a tribe, a nation, a religion, the Golden Rule said often: 'love your brother'. Recently a shift was made to 'love your neighbour' as the more inclusive formula. A soon as a truly universal humanity emerges, the 'love your neighbour' might still be the most inclusive and preferable wording, at least in the English language...

> *As a man traversing the whole earth,*
> *Finds not anywhere an object more loveable than himself:*
> *Therefore, since the self is so universally loved by all,*
> *The man who loves himself so much,*
> *Should do no injury to others.*
>
> Dawsonne Melanchton Strong the Udâna, or the Solemn Utterances
of the Buddha 1902
in: Justin Parrott PhD
The Golden Rule in Islam: Ethics of Reciprocity in Islamic Traditions
2018, p. 7-8

Learning to love yourself needs guidance and education

> ...when God infused His own light into the soul, He adapted the light above all to this: that it might lead him to bliss, which consists in the possession of Him. To this we are led by four virtues: Prudence, Courage, Justice, and Temperance. Prudence first shows us bliss; those other three virtues, like three paths, lead to bliss. And so God tempers his own spark variously in various souls to this end, that under the direction of Prudence some

seek their author again through the offices of Courage, others through the offices of Justice, and others through the offices of Temperance. Certainly some, thanks to this gift, undergo danger and death with a brave heart, for the worship of God, for integrity, or for fatherland. Others arrange life so justly that they neither themselves do harm to anyone nor, insofar as possible, permit it to be done by others. Others master the appetites by vigil, fast, and work. These certainly proceed by three paths, but they all strive to arrive at the same end of bliss which Prudence shows them.

Accordingly those three virtues are also contained in the Prudence of God Himself. Enflamed with a desire for them, the souls of men seek to arrive at them, by exercising them, and then to cleave to them and possess them eternally.

The Courage of men which we call masculine because of its hardness and boldness. Temperance we call feminine because of a certain restrained and cooler habit of desire and its soft nature. Justice we call mixed. Feminine certainly in as much as because of its innocence it brings harm to no one. But masculine inasmuch as it does not permit harm to be done to others, and with very severe judgement levies punishment upon wicked men.

Marsilio Ficino, Sears Jayne (Translator)
Commentary on Plato's *Symposium* on Love (1469)
1985, pp. 77-78

The natural order as matrix of mature virtuous love

Finally, to speak briefly, Venus is twofold. One is certainly that intelligence, which we have located in the Angelic Mind. The other is the power of precreation attributed to the World Soul. Each Venus has as her companion a love like herself... These twin powers are two Venuses in us, accompanied by two loves. When the beauty of the human body first meets our eyes, our intellect, which is the first Venus in us, worships and esteems it as an image of the divine beauty, and through this is often aroused to that. But the power of procreation, the second Venus, desires to procreate a form like this. On both sides, there is a love there (with) a desire to contemplate beauty, here a desire to procreate it. Each love is virtuous and praiseworthy, for each follows a divine image.

What, therefore, does Pausanias censure in love? Indeed I shall tell you. If anyone, through being more desirous of procreation, neglects contemplation, or attends to procreation beyond measure with women, or against the order of nature with men, or prefers the form of the body to the beauty of the soul, he certainly abuses the dignity of love. This abuse of love Pausanias censures. He who properly uses love certainly praises the form of the body, but through that contemplates the higher beauty of the Soul, the Mind, and God, and admires and loves that more strongly. And he uses the office of procreation and intercourse only as much as the natural order and the civic laws laid down by the prudent prescribe. About these things Pausanias speaks at greater length.

Marsilio Ficino, Sears Jayne (Translator)
Commentary on Plato's Symposium on Love (1469)
1985, pp. 51-52

Self-love: the love emotion controlled by purified reason

In addition to the relation a man has with his surroundings, we must consider what a man should be as an individual in himself with certain qualities: these form the settled character of the man, and this general character will express itself in specialised virtues when it comes into contact with superiors, equals, and inferiors. This character should be the general expression of the love-emotion, controlled by the purified reason, and this character every man and woman, every boy and girl, must build up, if duty is righteously discharged, and life is to be made a blessing not a curse, both to themselves and others.

[ ]

Among these, first and foremost comes Truth, the foundation of all virtues, Truth in thought, in word, and in act. Well may all join in the sublime invocation:

*"O True of promise, True of Purpose.
Triply True, the Fount of Truth, and
Dwelling in the True, the Truth of
Truth, the Eye of Right and Truth,
Spirit of Truth, refuge we seek in Thee."*

"Thy law is the Truth", says the psalmist.

"By mercy and truth iniquity is purged", declares the wise King. "They who know Truth in truth, and untruth in untruth, arrive at Truth, and follow true desires," says the Buddha. "Lie not one to another", says the Apostle.

"No man is true," says the Prophet, "in the truest sense of the

word, but he who is true in word, in deed, and in thought. Truth is the eternal Brahman.... everything rests on Truth."

When Truth permeates the character it shows itself in all the relations in life as Truthfulness, Uprightness, Honesty, Integrity, Righteousness, Justice, Impartiality, giving rise to Trust, Confidence, and mutual Respect, and building a stable society.

[ ]

The next great virtue of the individual character is Self-Control, which leads to the nice Balance, Equilibrium, and Dignity which mark the well-evolved man. Self-control implies the recognition by the man that he is the Sprit, not the body, and that he rules the matter which he has appropriated for his own purposes.... Purity of mind, of speech, of body, are essential for true manliness and womanliness, and without self-control these are impossible. Control of the mind can be gained only by meditation, by persevering effort, by cultivating the habit of attention, by concentrating the thought on the task of the moment in daily life...

Annie Besant
Universal Textbook of Religion and Morals (Part II Ethics)
1910, pp. 46-49

A Buddhist view:

One's own self conquered is better than (conquest of) all other people; not even the Shining One, Gandharva, not Māra with Brahman could change into defeat the victory of a man who has vanquished himself, and always lives under constraint.

Dammapada, ii. 30 in Annie Besant's
Universal Textbook of Religion and Morals
1910, p.74

In the evolution from tribal to individual consciousness, mutual enhancement of loving partners' individual lives becomes more significant than preservation of the human species...

[Solovyov] opens with a biological survey which easily, and to my mind irresistibly, refutes the age-old assumption ... that the teleology of sexual attraction is the preservation of the species by multiplication. On the contrary, it is apparent from the whole tendency of biological evolution that nature's purpose or goal (or whatever continuity it is that the concept

of evolution presupposes) has been the development of more complex and, with that, of more highly individualized and thus more perfect organisms. From the fish to the higher mammals quantity of offspring steadily decreases as subtlety of organic structure increases; reproduction is in inverse proportion to specific quality. On the other hand, the factor of sexual attraction in bringing about reproduction is in direct proportion. On the next or sociological level he has little difficulty in showing that the same is true of the factor of romantic passion in sexual attraction. Both history and literature show that it contributes nothing towards the production of either more or better offspring, and may often, as in the case of Romeo and Juliet, actually frustrate any such production at all.

Why then has nature, or the evolutionary process, taken the trouble to bring about this obtrusively conspicuous ingredient in the make-up of homo sapiens?

Being, at the level of human individuality, is characterized above all by a relation between whole and part that is different from the everyday one that is familiar to us. We may catch a glimpse of it if we reflect, in some depth, on the true nature of a great work of art. ... It is a relation no longer limited by the manacles of space and time, so that interpenetration replaces aggregation; one where the part becomes more specifically and individually a part — and thus [to that extent] an end in itself — precisely as it comes more and more to contain and represent the Whole.

Sex-love is for most human beings their first, if not their only, concrete experience of the possibility of such an interpenetration with other parts, and thus potentially with the Whole.

Abstract by Owen Barfield of Solovyev's Meaning of Love (1890's)
2014, The Nature Institute, Article 22

Orientation

Apart from the time-honoured tendency to prefer the neighbour's above one's own and the emphasis on the impersonal, unselfish 'for God's sake', there is a relatively recent reason for avoiding too much attention to the 'as yourself' or 'self-love', namely contemporary consumer culture. It are corporations and their advertisers that 'teach' humanity how to 'love' oneself and – especially on Mothers' Day and on Christmas how to 'love' one's neighbour likewise: 'Love' as commodity, available on the market place. Even the fuzzy, feel-good phenomenon called "spiritual" or "spirituality" has become a lucrative commodity on the market.

Today's world market operates as a system which involves us all, mechanically/electronically, with little or no knowledge as to the effects of our participation on our fellow human beings or the environment where-ever else in the world. We clamour e.g. for renewable energy and have little or no knowledge at what environmental and social cost panels, turbines, batteries and the electronic hardware are being produced and so on.

Günther Anders, Austrian Philosopher, initiated a correspondence with the navigator who was instrumental in detonating the atom bomb above Hiroshima and who was locked in a high security military asylum, because of his public expression of his sense of guilt, regret and evil of what he had done. The correspondence had been conducted in English, but I have only the German original to work with. At the end of the correspondence Claude Eatherly was released from hospital. Here the beginning of the first letter in which Anders reflects on the consequences of a technologically fully integrated world:

Letter 1

Mr. Claude R. Eatherly
Formerly Major U.S. Air Force
Veterans Administration Hospital
Waco, Texas

Dear Mr. Eatherly, 3 June 1959

The writer of these lines is not known to you. You – on the other hand – are known to us, my friends and myself. How you cope or not cope with your tragedy, we follow with our hearts beating, regardless whether we live in New York, in Vienna or Tokyo. Not because we would be curious, or because your 'case' would interest us medically or psychologically. We are neither doctors nor psychologists. But because we are involving ourselves, full of anguish and concern involving ourselves to become clear about those moral problems, that obstruct the road for all of us these days. The technification of existence: the fact, that we unawares and indirectly, somehow like cogs in machines, can be slotted into actions, the effects of which we don't oversee and which – if we could oversee them – could not consent to – this fact has changed the moral situation for all of us.

Technology has brought with it, that we can become guiltless guilty in a way, that didn't exist in the technologically less advanced time of our fathers.

You understand what you have to do with this: Ultimately you surely belong to the first ones, who have found themselves actually caught in this new kind of guilt, in which today or tomorrow each one of us could find ourselves caught. To you has happened what tomorrow could happen to all of us. This is the reason why you play for us the important role as a key example, yes as a forerunner.

Rowohlt Hamburg
Off limits für das Gewissen: The correspondence between the Hiroshima-Pilot Claude Eatherly and Günter Anders
1961
[Translated by Henk Bak]

Orientation

On the day the news of Hiroshima reached him in London, Ronald Knox immediately wrote a letter to the editor with a plea not to throw a second bomb. On his way to the post-box he heard the paperboys shouting 'Nagasaki!' He, a clergyman, waited for someone in the church-hierarchy to take a stand. When this didn't happen, he wrote his God and the Atom and had it published before the year was ended.

Uniquely awake to the world-chattering consequences of the bombing of Hiroshima and of Nagasaki: Hiroshima and Nagasaki

If atomic power should manifest the same surprising capacities for making people comfortable, as it certainly has for making people uncomfortable, then we should be in danger of selling our souls to evil, and making up our minds to live contentedly in a world without freedom, without honour, without justice. If we do that, we shall be deserving, and probably earning, a far more grievous chastisement than in the worst days of the early forties.

Ronald Knox
God and the Atom / Chapter X Brother Atom
1945, p. 141

Orientation

Hannah Arendt, herself a refugee from Nazi Germany, attended and reported on the trial of Adolf Eichmann, responsible for the transport of thousands of Jews to the extermination camps. For her two main comments she was severely criticised: 1. She summed up her observations of Eichmann himself by saying how 'banal'– in his case – evil is: an ordinary man, totally dedicated to following orders, never thinking about the consequences of his deeds, abdicating his 'being himself'…2. She expressed her empathy with the members of the Jewish Council, who were forced to make choices that would destroy peoples' lives, whatever their choice. She said that they must have gone 'through dark times'. Which her critics heard as an accusation… What follows is an excerpt out of a recent publication urgently drawing attention Hannah Arendt's relevance for our time.

Who needs dictators if markets achieve the same.

The ultimate aim of totalitarianism is to make human beings as human beings superfluous. "What totalitarian ideologies aim at is not the transformation of the outside world or the revolutionising transmutation of society, but the transformation of human nature itself." The systematic attempt to eliminate any vestige of human spontaneity and individuality – to make human beings as human beings superfluous is what she called absolute or radical evil. The most disturbing sentence in The Origins of Totalitarianism is her warning: "Totalitarian solutions may well survive the fall of totalitarian regimes in the form of strong temptations which will come up whenever it seems impossible to alleviate political, social and economic misery in a manner worthy of man." These "strong temptations" have not been resisted in the massacres, genocides, rapes, tortures, and systematic lying by governments during the past seventy-five years.

R.J. Bernstein
The Urgent Relevance of Hannah Arendt, The Philosophers Magazine
2018

Orientation

Just as the hunger for material consumer goods, the 'spiritual supermarket' may also be a symptom of a real hunger for spiritual nourishment that doesn't only make one feel good, but also would sustain one on a chosen path of human development.

Much genuine inspiration can be found outside established spiritual traditions, in literature, music, the arts. No wonder that a philosopher of science like Feyerabend was attracted to the idea of becoming an entertainer. David Attenborough, Richard Dawkins in his role as interpreter of science to a wider public, and many others in different fields provide us with a wealth of more than just intellectual food, emotionally stimulating nourishment, and also with the hard-hitting information about how a world-economy fuelled by overconsumption is bringing the earth, nature and humanity to the brink of destruction.

Theatre, film, documentaries, music, dance, song, poetry, stories and so on, they all address us through our senses as well as to our intellect. Factual reports, systematic thoughts, however correct in themselves, don't draw us in as stories, songs or pictures do. Attention is a kind of actively 'holding in' and 'standing still' by what otherwise would not exist for us. Without attention we don't perceive: we may hear, but do not listen; see but do not look. Attention anticipates things, objects and people to show up around us. There seems to be a 'structural solidarity' between our senses and the cosmos (Minkowski). Our language seems to somehow 'complicit' with the world we speak of (Dufrenne). God's word and His work: a primal sensory, creative and reflective intelligence at the source of language (Qur'an). What we sense is meant to be 'proportionate' to our needs, sustaining and nourishing (Bonaventura). Today much is known about the nourishing and therapeutic qualities of the senses. Unfortunately oppressive regimes know too well: there is no crueller torture than sensory deprivation.

The world around us appears to correspond with our receptive openness.

> *When the similitude is seen as active and impressive, the impression will be well proportioned if the impressing agent feels a need in the receiver, that is, sustains and nourishes him, which is best observed in taste and touch.*
>
> Bonaventura
The Journey of the Mind to God
1259, II.5

Creation Reflects God's Goodness to Us

> *Creation is God's goodness, it is a reflection of His love and wisdom and it helps our spiritual journey towards God's Holy Trinity. Creation is where we experience our humanity and it's the world where God's artistry and fingerprints come to us through our senses and it is our senses we use to follow the footprints of Christ and to feel God's Holy Spirit around us.*
>
> *Sight – enables us to see beauty in everything from a clear blue sky, Autumn leaves to creeping creatures, insects and worms.*
> *Hearing – to listen to the sounds of creation's harmony, of birds singing, dogs barking, waves crashing and wind howling.*
> *Smell – to sense how God's words can have fragrance like flowers, aroma like*

*natural oils, the strength of a lion's roar and the sweat of a hard day's work.
Touch – to feel blessings, healing and compassion, to feel the warmth of the
sun and the coldness of snow, the solution of water to the harness of rock.
Taste – to experience God's sweet words expressed
in summer fruits and winter vegetables.*

*Our senses help our inner self experience, our outside self as part of, and
within, Creation – they are a bridge from the inner to the outer understanding
of our creature-ness as created by God and formed in love by His Holy Spirit.
Through creation we understand that God exists, that Divinity is pure spirit
and can be found in creatures, elements, plants, geography, geology and biology
as power, presence and essence and that creation is for us to enjoy and cherish.*

Part of Bonaventrura's 'Journey of the Soul' summarized in: Secular
Franciscans
The Soul's Journey into God
2023

Sensory experience resonates in our language

*Language cannot awaken in us the mechanism of comprehension unless
it has already realized a sort of organic complicity with the object.*

Mikel Dufrenne
Phenomenology of the Aesthetic Experience
1973, p. 188

Complicity between world and language at the heart of creation.

*And remember when God said to the angels: 'I shall appoint a deputy on
earth', and they answered 'Will you place therein one who sows discord
and sheds blood while we chant Your praises and proclaim Your holiness?*

God said: 'I know what you do not.'

*He taught Adam the names of all things. Then he displayed them to the
angels and said: 'Tell me the names of these things, if you are truthful.'*

*They said: 'Glory to You! We have no knowledge except what
You taught us. You! You are All-Knowing, All-Wise".*

*God said:' O Adam, reveal to them their names.' When Adam revealed their
names, God said:' Didn't I tell you that I know the unseen of the heavens
and the earth? That I know what you make public and what you hide?'*

Tarif Khalidi (Translator)
Qur'an / The Cow 2: 29-31
2009, pp. 6-7

Sense of touch in relation to all other senses

...Let's take the world in its immensity, in its inconsistency, in its unceasing flux; is it not a miracle that one can "touch" something, that one can make an unmediated contact with beings and with things?

The universe in its primitive nebulous, unfathomable state, where everything seems destined to disperse itself into fine dust, is now being enriched by the fact of touch, a particular quality. This is far from a simple sensory modality that penetrates into our life: it is the face of the world that changes. It is the element of cognition and of cohesion (and perhaps even coherence) that enters our life. The things 'stay put' now and we 'find our feet' and 'touch ground'.

...it is only through touching that something palpable arises, something that is consistent in the world, not before it nor beyond it. It is also this that in this particular case reveals to us the very sense of immediate contact which we then proceed to depreciate, sacrificing its proper quality for the idea of geometrical distance. Hence the paradox, for, as we have said, if there were no sense of touch, the face of the world with all its other sensory aspects would suddenly change. Deprived, underneath, of any point of support, of any cohesion, the world would evaporate, would turn into dust so to say.

The sense of touch therefore would appear as an essential quality, at least equivalent with the other ones, if not the most fundamental of them all. For touch seems to serve as a base for the other sensory qualities, and this not any more as the biology will have it, i.e. as inferior to the other senses arising from it. These overtake the sense of touch by their reach in space, but at the phenomenological level, i.e. because there is something really 'basic' in it, through its faculty of introducing consistency in the world and of 'consolidating' thus all other sensory qualities. Once more, could we fully perceive an object, standing still by it, attend to it, i.e. "touch it with our gaze" if touch had not revealed to us the profound significance of the 'tangible' in general? Fundamentally there is something 'tangible' in every perception because of what it characterizes in relation with other mental faculties. In thought, imagination, abstraction it is precisely the tangible that makes us "touch ground", that makes us – in as far the world is something consistent and perceptible – 'attend' to what underlies it all. Through this the 'tangible' furnishes us altogether with the certainty, that we should not bypass the direct and immediate 'grasp' of things.

Eugène Minkowski
Vers une Cosmologie: Fragments Philosophiques (Towards a Cosmology)
1936, pp. 179-181
[Translated by Henk Bak]

Ortientation

It was a filmmaker who inspired a neurobiologist, double doctor, professor at two universities, to give up his career and become a pioneer in educational reform, at the level of earliest childhood to begin with.

It is then and there that the foundations for a human being's self-trust, self-experience and self-worth are laid. Never in a human beings' life time is its appetite and capacity for learning stronger and the brain's capacity for absorbing and organizing what is being learned greater than in those early days, weeks and months… A diffused experience of waking and sleeping happens already before birth. It must make a difference whether after birth a child in its increasingly less diffused awareness feels itself safe in the constant moving in and out of sleep. Safe in a constant presence, attended to, cared for…An experience that gives direction to an innate instinctive self-centredness, a sense of self-worth, a first step in the direction of a healthy self-love. For a longer or shorter time, a child needs further guidance on this path. This raw natural self-centredness overshadows at first a just as raw natural altruism. Even though parents at first take the brunt of a baby's raw demands, earlier or later there will be a toy or a doll, which will be 'loved to bits' until the moment that the child starts to 'talk' to it, and if there are siblings or an animal around, educators can appeal to a child's natural altruism. It seems to me that love for oneself and love for one's neighbour right from the start have their natural roots in early childhood.

The Aboriginal experience

One last question remained to the topic of Dulugun: "In the olden days, David, did Aborigines commit suicide?"

No, never! Now they commit suicide, like in jails. They want to kill themselves because they are drunk. And there is no fire.

Fire is the spirit of life, love, family, all those

kind of things are tied up with that.

In the womb, we are in a little world. When we are born to the larger world, the first things we see are the sun, the family and the fire, these three important things.

We grow up with that spirit of caring and warmth of the sun, fire and love from our family. Those are the growth elements, the elements of Wandjina. Wandjina can't walk in jails.

When Aborigines are cut off from that, they want to kill themselves. They just die then and go to Dulugun. There is only that channel. And they are all coming back".

David Mowaljarlai and Jutta Malnic
Yorro Yorro: Aboriginal Creation and the Renewal of Nature
1993, p. 165

The first smile of a newborn child: an intimation of a first encounter

The child that with a smile reveals itself as human being, moving – being moved in the involuntary condition of its nature, in the manner that has been provided in its tissues, transcends therewith the – in the stream of time - unconscious compulsion, to take - as individual being - part in the timeless presence of a conscious 'being sheltered'. What wakes up in the child out of the slumber, like a bird in the morning, what wells up and radiates out of its inner depth, is like a remembering this origin and like a premonition of a destiny.

In the psychology of which the physiologists are the prophets, who when referring to observable facts don't know what hidden meaning is contained in their words, we speak of feelings and expressions, of inborn activity and imitation, of excitation of nerves and vegetative effects, of a "exitation modérée" and a "reaction facile", but all this becomes first transparent in the light of human existence.

By this light the mother, too, sees the first smile of her child, and understands like we ourselves, Frederik van Eeden, when he shares poetically his emotion:

> *When he did smile, the first in his life,*
> *He came floating, gliding out of far, still lands*
> *He sent to us the sign of love once more*

He himself laughed – and was lonely no more.
Even more profound, because succinctly containing the oneness of
living and knowing in the wakening spirit, does Virgil's song sound
throughout the ages:
Incipe, parve puer, risu cognoscere matrem.
Begin, little boy, to recognize mother through your smile.

F.J.J. Buytendijk
De eerste glimlach van het kind (The first smile of the child)
1947, pp. 116-117

Orientation

If someone, who has read the above, found it difficult to read it in a hurry, he or she finds him/herself in good company, I feel. In David Mowaljarlai's response thousands and thousands of years of experience and wisdom have been concentrated in a few short lines, holding out as rocks in the whirlpools of the rapidly changing streams of our time.

And his brief, articulate and poetic summing up of the many layered foundation of his tentative understanding of a child's first smile, just as tender as the smile itself, seems to betray the status of a man, who – physiologist, psychiatrist, phenomenologist, professor at three universities and teacher of a new generation of psychiatrists and a wider readership – radically and definitively helped break the spell that a rationalist, materialist and positivist world-view has held the human sciences in its ban for more than one century.

The kind of attention, the seemingly timeless presence surrounding and supporting any person's inner development, towards knowing oneself, accepting and appreciating oneself, being oneself and coming to one's senses, all of them…will at first and for a long time be the educational responsibility of the adult world, and gradually the responsibility of the person him- or herself. Teachers, educators, spiritual masters, gurus, rabbi's, priests, imams, counsellors and carers, friends, lovers and spouses, and sometimes total strangers, may offer guidance along the way. And on the path of self-development an inner dialogue or conversation will play a vital role: in his conversational letter Gideon Fontalba evokes the image of a bridge with on the other side an 'other' one sees every day, but never stops to speak to…

> What does the 'other', whom you meet on the bridge every day, want to say to you? He wants to say, 'Talk to me too sometimes!' It is his urgent request of you to speak together with him sometimes. It would make him happy if you were to be friendly with him, if you would converse with him

about worldly happenings and about his concerns. He would also gladly share what he daily observes about you, what he receives from you, and what it is about you which gives him happiness or grief. He would also like speak to you about his own cares an joys. And he wishes to help you!

[ ]

Who is the other one? You have already guessed! It is your twilight soul, your unconscious or dream-conscious being. It is that part of you which takes in all your experiences throughout daily life and who must bear and cope with all your repressed worries, fears, doubts and anger, as well as your suppressed or overly-indulged drives, impulses, desires and appetites. He is expressed in imaginative form as this 'other'.

[ ]

Many depressions arise out of not working through certain contents of the soul. Many oppressing experiences or bad habits that do not get any attention, and are not mastered in everyday life, express themselves eventually as depression or psychosomatic disturbances. Such illnesses of the soul have increased so much in our time that we should understand them as warnings. They are a sign that that much of our artificially-created world is out of line with the laws of the spirit and life. Our civilization and our life-orientation have become unhealthy. We know very well that the life of the individual human being is closely and finely interwoven with the larger community, the city, the nation, even with the whole of humanity and with the earth. Therefore, the harmonization of one's own being is as difficult as it necessary, because what is in the outer world works on the inner and vice versa. People who have become more harmonious in themselves can also have a harmonizing effect on their environment. That is why attention to one's own being, which wishes to purify and further develop itself, is at the same time a purifying impulse and higher developmental help for humanity and the earth.

Therefore, when we withdraw somewhat, at certain times during the day, in order to be all-one with ourselves and to take an interest in the other person in us, this is not then an act of egoism, but rather one of inner work, the consequences of which benefit all beings around us. By turning and talking with my friend in me, this other who patiently bears everything, I gain knowledge and experiences through the exchange with him which no other person in the world could give me. With this treasure I can then also help others in the world.

Gideon Fontalba
Talk with me Too Sometimes / Conversational Letters (1981-88)
2005, pp. 40-43
[Translated by Sally Duncan]

In my readings and in conversations with Christian participants in the meditative walks at Evera, I found quite a reluctance to affirm 'love of oneself' as a vital ingredient for a life lived well. In conversation with an Anglican Priest I encountered a refreshing and realistic exception: "After retirement, I was an interim minister for 6-9 months in neighbouring parishes. What could I achieve in a short time? One thing was to teach them my one basic sermon: God loves you, no buts. No, but you have to repent. No, but you have to love God back. God just loves you. During Advent I taught them to say it with me so they could repeat it aloud when they brought their children and grandchildren to church at Christmas. Some of them seemed to believe me and would say it if they met me in the shops. They began to smile when they saw me instead of the usual frown. On the first Sunday in Advent I gave them this task: Every day when you wake up, look in the mirror and say "God did a fine job when he made you." More than one person came to me after church and asked "Am I allowed to do that?" "Try it and see," I replied. I know one person who did it all Advent. I know because when she saw me at Christmas she flung her arms around me and declared "I love you!" I think she had begun to love herself."

At an interfaith workshop at Evera, Trentham, to mark the World Interfaith Harmony Week, entitled 'Reclaiming the Golden Rule for Public Life', on the 9th of February 2020, the first question was: 'From what or where does the Golden Rule need to be reclaimed?' Most answers pointed to corporate and political powers, corruption and greed. One answer, however, pointed to 'consciousness', our own. I suggested that we steer away from 'blaming' and 'bashing': the queue of 'culprits' would be endless. We rather concentrated therefore on a possible blind spot or area in our own consciousness and the apparently systemic condition that enables those culprits to operate freely, often even legally, as an evil force that holds humanity to ransom. The systemic tendency to underrate or to neglect the 'as yourself' as a constituent element of the Golden Rule seems to me such a 'blind spot'. Before we turn to its role in public life itself, we want to restore this missing element in the Golden Rule with an added emphasis…

Love God – Love the Good
Love your neighbour - and your fellow creatures – as yourself
Love yourself as yourself.

...a more comprehensive summation of the Law for this our time.

...way to maturity, a summation for this our time, to be read from below upwards:

LIGHT BEING

ONENESS OF BEING

9. *Self Responsibility*

CONFIRMATION OF BEING

8. *Self Realisation*

CERTAINTY OF BEING

7. *Self Knowledge*

LOVE OF BEING

6. *Self Confidence*

REVELATION OF BEING

5. *Self Expression*

GRACE OF BEING

4. *Self Perception*

WILL OF BEING

3. *Self Worth*

SOURCE-STRENGTH OF BEING

2. *Self Experience*

GROUND OF BEING

1. *Self trust*

FIRE BEING

Shin Gwydion Fontalba
[Translated by Henk Bak]*

---

*   FIRE BEING is indicated by red text, and LIGHT BEING by yellow text.

The meditative guide to a mature love of self 'From Fire Being to Light Being' has been included with the approval from its author, spiritual teacher Shin Gwydion Fontalba, who has been the inspiration of this book and has encouraged its publication.

Personally I have found this guide helpful and clarifying in more than one way: at 92 I find myself starting a walk on uneven terrain re-finding 'self-trust' as ground of being, re-finding 'self-experience of balance' as a 'source-strength of being' and so on. The nine steps don't only reflect the story of one's life, e.g. childhood (3 steps), youth (3 steps) and adolescence (3 steps), and then with adulthood finding one's feet again in this new stage of life. And so on. It may help reflect on one's own biography or on the role and relevance of parents and other educators, teachers and preachers.

6. The Golden Rule in the Public Sphere

The Ganges of rights originates in the Himalayan of responsibilities

Mahatma Gandhi

Introduction

The height of the Himalayas, the reach of the rivers it feeds and the width of the lands it dominates make it indeed an apt image of public life. The Law that has been summarised in the Golden Rule rules in domains much vaster, diverse and deeper, than what legislation is capable and authorized to regulate and codify through positive law, jurisprudence and enforcement.

Where all citizens are equal under the law, what governs the vast areas of public life where people are not equal?

This question may be a key to the central theme of this chapter: how to recognize, strengthen and renew the Golden Rule in public life. Unequal we are from the time, circumstances and conditions before conception and birth to the time we leave our body and die, no life story will be the same; nor will be our livelihood, our participation in the resources that nature and society has on offer…Equal before the law we are when and where – as humans – we recognize ourselves and our fellow humans as equal in our shared humanity; the law itself is meant to bring protection, justice, freedom and peace equally to all…

Private life enters public life from the beginning. Right from the start our private space extends with the public space we enter: privacy of intimate relationship, family, tribe, village – kitchen tables, boardrooms, committees – school rooms, consultations, artist studios, laboratories and religious services. Public life becomes public service as soon we leave our private space and encounter others in the 'outside world' with respect, courtesy, empathy and readiness to be at service…

These patterns of fluid transitions between life and service, private and public may have been so old as the world. What characterizes most if not all of pre-modern societies, is that they have been embedded in the natural world with its overall abundance and local conditions, with its seasons and continuity. And this natural world itself an expression and reflection of a spiritual world, which tended and tends to stratify those societies into hierarchies, in degrees from high to low. All the public services were embedded and integrated in these flat or steep hierarchies. And the vertical and horizontal 'dimensions' in the Golden Rule reflect their function in public as well as private life.

The last 300 years have seen a radical breakdown of the patterns that wove and held societies together. The rationalist enlightenment and the industrial revolution followed by the American and French Revolutions dethroned the spiritual and worldly hierarchies, without decentralizing political power. Public service became the outcome of a political struggle between 'brotherhood' and 'freedom'. In the face of object poverty and hunger as a consequence of ruthless exploitation and of the long term need to generate a larger and more sophisticated consumer public and workforce, governments extended their legislative reach into and alongside the areas of social and cultural development, that traditionally had been in the care of charities, religious and philanthropic foundations.

Colonization and then global centralization has expanded this new kind of public sphere worldwide, with the corporations, organizations, institutions and power structures to go with it. Legislative centralization at the root of modern democracy has expanded into global jurisdictions through treaties over wider territories or disciplines: from Regional Unions to United Nations, World Bank, UNESCO, international courts, World Health and Food Organizations. Political and non-political organizations like the World Economic Forum, the 'International Society for Education through Art' and the Parliament of the World's Religions concern themselves with the world from their different perspectives. Radio, printed and electronic media flood the worlds public space with truth and untruth, education and indoctrination, with spiritual and materialistic initiatives and everything in between.

The overall framework for this 'new kind' of public sphere are the market, the military and surveillance technology whilst its dominant view or world-image is 'mechanistic'. From the mechanism of 'checks and balances' in the political arena, to the 'mechanisms' that govern our health, our behaviour, our careers and our misfortunes, humanity is on the way to becoming a function of a world-mechanism and the electronic networks which in some public scenarios are already pictured as a 'no touch' world or a society which needs only one million technicians, programmers, operators to run it. The rest of humanity would be superfluous. The public sphere has in the meantime also expanded into the solar system and the floor of the world's oceans and is penetrating into the private sphere in sub-physical ways, where in earlier times spiritual masters, shamans and black magicians would have had access by non-physical powers.

This, of course, is a panoramic overview, which on closer look needs critical refinement, but may serve – for the sake of a dialogue on the Golden Rule in public life – as a sufficiently common reference. Out of this overview a closer look may vaguely reveal a new texture: that which in the past could be described as 'fluid' and 'interwoven', shows itself now as 'integrated', 'homogenized', a 'seamless grid', 'networks within networks' from which there seems no escape. The better the 'machinery' seems to work, the more dysfunctional humanity and the earth become within it: wars, famines, terrorism, climate crisis, epidemics, mental health crisis, refugees, racism, ideologies fundamentalisms, rampant consumerism. A closer look reveals also ominous cracks or fault-lines in this seemingly seamless global civilization: e. g. between so called developed and developing worlds; between autocratic and democratic regimes.

Zooming in – from this panoramic view via 'closer looks' – on ourselves as individuals, we see that modern public space is no longer lawfully shaped by the traditional Golden Rule, that addresses all of us as individuals. Even the Universal Declaration for Human Rights addresses governments, not individuals. And our obligations towards our fellow human beings, ourselves, the earth, and towards the for us highest, most sacred or divine presence in and beyond the universe, are in today's world for a significant part mediated through systems ruled by their own laws, that are often conflicting and draw us in opposite directions. Every time I buy something to feed myself and others responsibly I run the chance that I underpay someone somewhere in the world and so on.

A technologically/commercially integrated world makes us complicit in mistreating others, whether we know or intend it or not. 'What is hateful to you do not do to others' (Hillel 1st Century) – 'Human dignity is inviolable' (UN 1948): modern public space violates the latter, negates the former, and leaves the individual too often torn apart or paralysed as a mere 'function' in the system.

It needs a crisis to expose the dysfunctions of an integrated system, where if one thing goes wrong everything goes wrong. Each crisis means large scale suffering, not necessarily leading to the transformation needed for the creation of public space where individuals are enabled and encouraged to fully and generously live by the Golden Rule. In what follows one might find observations like: if Mosaic Law or Sharia Law had been in place, the global financial crisis would not have happened and there would have been no evictions…And another: "perhaps there is not enough democracy, love and scientific truth for social evolution to take place". If a health and economic crisis interlinked is already causing suffering on an unprecedented scale worldwide, an environmental catastrophe would be worse.

A transformation process must go through a vacuum, a breakdown, zero, a 'nothing' – no thing – out of which something new may emerge. Digestion and artistic creation are prime examples. The better our world-views go through a transformation process themselves, the better participation in a dialogue between them has a chance to open up new ways for the Golden Rule to function again in public life.

The first thing such dialogue needs is silence as a timeless space, open and still.

In the last chapter we considered a possible 'update' of the wording of the Golden Rule itself. In this chapter we consider how underneath the consolidated 'crust' of a homogenized society, the three ideals of the American and French revolutions have been growing and surfaced like trees and plants that grow through the cracks of a concrete slab. Especially the ideals 'freedom' and the (legal) 'equality', to a lesser extent those of the 'pursuit of happiness' and 'brotherhood' have been made to work in modern societies, but inequality in all aspects of life has grown and still growing everywhere as a cancerous weed, out of control, overgrowing and undermining any progress made in other areas.

Economy, politics and culture have long been identified as the three domains that constitute human society. The terms are modern, they have been conceptualized and organized as systems, but their functions go back to the beginning. What got lost in the process, is an understanding and appreciation of those functions themselves, which aspects of life they serve, under which conditions they serve best and what kind of dynamics is involved: rhythms, timeframes, form-tendencies, cyclic or hierarchical – economic different from cultural or political – and so on.

The Golden Rule addresses individuals. The Universal Declaration of Human Rights (1948) begins with declaring 'Human Dignity' the inviolable foundation of those rights and ends with addressing its signatories with the call to act on their obligations towards those rights. Obligations rest with individuals, not collectives or states. International law is 'humanity's law'. In an unprecedented move, in April 2020 the UN secretary general António Guterres, addressed – over the heads of UN delegates – more than 60 million individuals worldwide with an urgent appeal to make their governments keep the cease-fire for the duration of the Covid '19 crisis. This appeal was facilitated by Ricken Pavel and his team at Avaaz, the world's largest activist group, part of a movement of local, regional and national groups whose number runs into the millions. All committed to restore in their own environments and communities the dignity of caring for the earth, for one another, for oneself and for their culture and higher aspirations. Many members of the Parliament of the World's Religions take part in this movement as well.

World-views tend to be panoramic; perceptions of the world tend to be focused. Activists, perceptive, motivated and engaged individuals meet public servants at local levels and higher up. The more governments have invested in their public services, not only with proper funding and proper income, but also with training, equipment and trust in their areas of competence, the less there will be need for citizens' activism. Corporations and cultural institutions, schools, universities, hospitals and religious organizations are public services, too. The less public space is politicized, the more public service will be able to get on with being at service.

At this point the dialogue of world-views becomes a conversation on the field of action. We will meet economists, sociologists, educators, spiritual teachers, philosophers, activists, actors, psychologists, heads of state, financial experts, at least one novelist and one palaeontologist. In what they have to say their own world-views will ring through right unto the affairs of everyday life.

Out of the rich array of quotations I have chosen three texts which for me stand out as the most elementary pointers to the three directions into which the conversation may fruitfully unfold. In section A those elementary statements will be articulated after which in section B their understanding in potential and realization will be widely explored within and beyond their original scope. As in the former chapter, groups of texts will be preceded by an orientation. And when this work of this conversation is done, it will be time to stop, be still and silent, contemplate, meditate, pray and even sing…the theme of chapter 7.

I. Sense of direction:

...Union, the true upward union in the spirit, ends by establishing the elements it dominates in their own perfection. Union differentiates. In virtue of this fundamental principle, elementary personalities can, and can only affirm themselves by acceding to a psychic unity or higher soul. But this always on one condition: that the higher centre to which they come to join without mingling together has its own autonomous reality. Since there is no fusion or dissolution of the elementary personalities the centre in which they join must necessarily be distinct from them, that is to say have its own personality.

Pierre Teilhard de Chardin: Human Energy
Translated by J.M. Cohen
1969, p. 104

II. Principle of Compatibility between Essential Obligations.

The first of the soul's needs, the one which touches most nearly its eternal destiny, is order; that is to say, a texture of social relationships such that no one is compelled to violate imperative obligations in order to carry out other ones. It is only where this, in fact, occurs that external circumstances have any power to inflict spiritual violence on the soul. For he for whom the threat of death or suffering is the only thing standing in the way of the performance of an obligation, can overcome this disability, and will only suffer in his body. But he who finds that circumstances, in fact, render the various acts necessitated by a series of strict obligations incompatible with one another is, without being able to offer any resistance thereto, made to suffer in his love for the good. At the present time, a very considerable amount of confusion and incompatibility exists between obligations. Whoever acts in such a way as to increase this incompatibility is a trouble-maker. Whoever acts in such a way as to diminish it is an agent of order. Whoever, so as to simplify problems, denies the existence of certain obligations has, in his heart, made a compact with crime.

Simone Weil
The Need for Roots
Written in 1943 first English edition 1952. 2003 reprint, p. 10

III. Principle of Subsidiary Function

In any organisation, large or small, there must be a certain clarity and orderliness; if things fall into disorder, nothing can be accomplished. Yet, the orderliness, as such, is static and lifeless; so there must also be plenty of elbow-room and scope for breaking through the established order, to do the thing never done before, never anticipated by the guardians of orderliness, the new, unpredicted and unpredictable outcome of a man's creative idea.

Therefore any organisation has to strive continuously for the orderliness of order and the disorderliness of creative freedom...

[ ]

A famous formulation of this (first) principle (in an attempt towards a theory of large-scale organizations) reads as follows:

"It is an injustice and at the same time a grave evil and disturbance of right order to assign to a greater and higher association what lesser and subordinate organisations can do. For every social activity ought of its very nature to furnish help to the members of the body social and never destroy and absorb them.

[ ] Those in command should be sure that the more perfectly the graduated order is preserved among the various organisations, in observing the principle of subsidiarity function, the stronger will be the social authority and effectiveness and the happier and more prosperous the condition of the State."

(Pope Pius IX: Encyclical Quadragesimo Anno)

E.F. Schumacher Small is Beautiful: Economics as if People Mattered
1975 p. 244

Towards a new public embodiment of the Golden Rule

Three starting points:

Union, the true upward union in the spirit, ...differentiates.

Order: a texture of social relationships such that no one is compelled to violate imperative obligations in order to carry out other obligations that are equally imperative.

It is an injustice and at the same time a grave evil and disturbance of right order to assign to a greater and higher association what lesser and subordinate organisations can do.

Texts 6A

Orientation

The ancient examples of the second part of the last chapter demonstrate how they still have the potential to inform modern thinking, acting as a ferment or seed to generate new realities. Two approaches seem to stand out as recognizable starting points for public life to become an expressions of the golden rule.

1. Where public life has become increasingly complex, individual responsibilities are torn in different directions, which makes it imperative that the complexity is so arranged and managed, that individuals are not forced to sacrifice vital, essential responsibilities because they are in conflict with other responsibilities, just as vital: an arrangement away from the indifference of a homogenized society. Unity towards the spirit differentiates.

In both 'horizontal' and 'vertical' approaches it are ultimately the individuals, not the collectives, that are responsible for the relevant arrangements. In washing the feet of his disciples the master Jesus sets an example. And in this sense Martin Buber's insistence on the spirit, on relatedness, transcends a mere differentiation in functions: within each functional domain the spirit and relatedness must be actively present in all, and in each domain according to its nature.

2. By the time (1943) the French philosopher Simone Weil had formulated her understanding of 'order', Western society at large had already differentiated its complexity into three distinct domains: The state had emancipated itself from religion, and economy had recently emancipated itself from the state. Religion had generated a whole spectrum of disciplines, which became domains in their own right, which S.T. Coleridge in the 19thcentury summed up under the term "clerizy": arts, sciences, education, healing, sports…each with its own competences and commitments. What used to be referred to under the heading "church" or "religion", as in "separation of church/religion and state", would now need to be extended under the heading "culture":

'separation of state and culture'. What religion and those other areas have in common is a commitment for humanity to reach its full potential, individually and collectively, and to generate the conditions under which such full potential can be realized. In the German language the words for 'culture' and for 'humanities' have traditionally been: 'Geistesleben' (life of the Spirit) and 'Geisteswissenschaften' (sciences of the Spirit). Martin Buber's insistence on the working of the Spirit in all three domains serves to avoid any identification of Spirit and Culture alone. In other words, economic life needs to develop its own culture and so does political life.

The first condition would be the freedom to become and be 'the master of one's own destiny' (Allain de Botton). "Economy" on the other hand requires solidarity with one another and with nature, caring and sharing. And "State" needs rules and regulations under which all its citizens find protection, justice and peace. Those three sets of conditions need to be harmonized to make sure that the responsibilities towards each of those don't clash.

Simone Weil's understanding of 'order' in 1943 mirrored exactly its opposite which terrorized Europe in her time and which was later identified by Hannah Arendt as 'totalitarian logic', the devilish system under which human beings are crushed in what makes them essentially human. After Prof Bernstein's summary of Hannah Arend's, the thesis (1982) of the sociologist Niklas Luhman's vision reads as an antidote and safeguard against the totalitarian temptations that societies in the last 75 years have not been able to resist.

3. Only after those domains are recognized as functions on an equal footing, 'hierarchy' returns within each domain as a natural requirement and practical arrangement for those functions to 'function'. Age, experience, skill, talent, disabilities, needs, etc. place people 'naturally' in a 'vertical' order, with the responsibility of the ones in higher positions to enable those in lower positions to contribute, to the whole, according to their capacity. In his "Small is Beautiful" (1972) Schumacher finds this first principle in Pius XI 's summation of Leo XIII's 'subsidiarity principle', formulated in the negative: no higher placed individual should deprive a lower placed person from the opportunity to contribute according to her/his capacity (see above pp. 172,173). Here a text by Feyerabend warning against breaking down existing hierarchies prematurely.

In both 'horizontal' and 'vertical' approaches it is ultimately the individuals, not the collectives, that are responsible for the relevant arrangements. In this sense Martin Buber's insistence on the spirit, on relatedness, transcends a mere differentiation in functions: within each functional domain the spirit and relatedness must be actively present in all, and in each domain according to its nature.

Hierarchy becomes service

> *...Jesus got up from the table, removed his outer garment and, taking a towel, wrapped it round his waist; he then poured water into a basin and began to wash the disciples' feet and to wipe them with the towel he was wearing... When he had washed their feet and put his clothes on again he went back to the table. 'Do you understand', he said, 'what I have done to you? You call me Master and Lord, and rightly; so I am. If I then, the Lord and Master, have washed your feet, you should wash each other's feet. I have given you an example so that you may copy what I have done to you.'*
>
> *I tell you most solemnly,*
>
> *No servant is greater than his master,*
>
> *No messenger is greater than the man who sent him.*
>
> *Now you know this, happiness will be yours if you behave accordingly.*

John 13: 4-5, 12-17
Jerusalem Bible
Popular Edition
1974

In each domain it is in meeting the other that the individual spiritualizes society...

> *Man's communal life cannot dispense any more than he himself with the It-world – over which the presence of the You floats like the spirit over the face of the waters. Man's will to profit and will to power are natural and legitimate as long as they are tied to the will to human relations and carried by it. There is no evil drive until the drive detaches itself from our being: the drive that is wedded to and determined by our being is the plasma of communal life. The economy as the house of the will to profit and the state as the house of the will to power participate in life as long as they participate in the spirit.*

If they abjure the spirit, they abjure life. To be sure, life takes its time about settling the score, and for quite a while one may still think that one sees a form move where for a long time a mere mechanism has been whirring. Introducing some sort of immediacy at this point is surely futile.

[ ]

Neither work not possessions can be redeemed on their own but only by starting from the spirit. It is only from the presence of the spirit that significance and joy can flow into all work, and reverence and the strength to sacrifice into all possessions, not to the brim but quantum satis – and that all that is worked and possessed, though it remains attached to the It-world, can nevertheless be transfigured to the point where it confronts us and represents the You. There is no back-behind-it, there is, even at the moment of the most profound need – indeed only then – a previously unsuspected beyond-it.

Whether it is the state that regulates the economy or the economy that directs the state is unimportant as long as both are unchanged. Whether the institution of the state becomes freer and those of the economy more just, that is important, but not for the question concerning actual life that is being posed here: for they cannot become free and just on their own. What is decisive is whether the spirit – the You-saying, responding spirit – remains alive and actual; whether what remains of it in communal life continues to be subjected to the state or the economy or whether it becomes independently active; whether what abides of it in individual human life incorporates itself again in communal life.

But that can certainly not be accomplished by dividing communal life into independent realms that also include "the life of the spirit." That would merely mean that the regions immersed in the It-world would be abandoned forever to this despotism, while the spirit would lose all actuality. For the spirit in itself can never act independently upon life: that it can do only in the world – with its force which penetrates and transforms the It-world.

The spirit is truly "at home with itself" when it can confront the world that is opened up to it, give itself to the world, and redeem it and, through the world, also itself. But the spirituality that represents the spirit nowadays is so scattered, weakened, degenerate, and full of contradictions that it could not possibly do this until it had first returned to the essence of the spirit: being able to say You.

Martin Buber in: Walter Kaufmann's

I and Thou
1970 pp. 97-99

Obligations to be compatible for each individual.

Obligations are only binding on human beings. There are no obligations for collectives as such. But they exist for all human beings who constitute, serve, command or represent a collective, in that part of their existence which is related to the collective as in that part which is independent of it.

[ ]

The object of any obligation, in the realm of human affairs, is always the human being as such. There exists an obligation towards every human being for the sole reason that he or she is a human being, without any other condition requiring to be fulfilled, and even any recognition of such obligation on the part of the individual concerned.

[ ]

This obligation is an eternal one. It is coextensive with the eternal destiny of human beings. Only human beings have an eternal destiny. Human collectives have not got one. Nor are there, in regard to the latter, any direct obligations of an eternal nature. Duty towards the human being as such - that alone is eternal.

[ ]

This obligation has no foundation, but only a verification in the common consent accorded by the universal conscience. It finds expression in some of the oldest written texts which have come down to us. It is recognized by everybody without exception in every single case where it is not a result of interest and passion. And it is in this relation to it that we measure our progress.

[ ]

The fact that a human being possesses an eternal destiny imposes only one obligation: respect. The obligation is only performed if the respect is effectively expressed in a real, not a fictitious, way; and this can only be done through the medium of Man's earthly needs.

Simone Weil, Arthur Wills [Translator]
The Need of Roots

Totalitarian logic

In one of the most chilling chapters of (Hannah Arendt's) The Origins of Totalitarianism she explains the "logic" of totalitarian domination. The first stage is to kill the juridical person. This happens when people are stripped of their legal rights. This is what happened to Jews in Germany long before the final solution. The second stage is the murder of the moral person. This occurs when even martyrdom becomes impossible. Totalitarian terror achieved its most terrible triumph when decisions of conscience became impossible. "When a man is faced with the alternative of betraying and thus murdering his friends or sending his wife and children, for whom he is in every sense responsible, to their death: when even suicide would mean the immediate murder of his own family – how is he to decide? The alternative is no longer between good and evil, but between murder and murder. Who could solve the moral dilemma of the Greek mother who was allowed by the Nazis to choose which of her three children should be killed?" But this is not yet the worst. There is a third stage of this "logic" of total domination. After the killing of the juridical person and the murder of the moral person, the one thing that prevents human beings from becoming living corpses is their spontaneity and individual differentiation. "After the murder of the moral person and the annihilation of the juridical person, the destruction of individuality is almost always successful. . . . For to destroy individuality is to destroy spontaneity, man's power to begin something new out of his own resources, something that cannot be explained on the basis of reactions to environment and events" The ultimate aim of totalitarianism is to make human beings as human beings superfluous. "What totalitarian ideologies aim at is not the transformation of the outside world or the revolutionising transmutation of society, but the transformation of human nature itself." The systematic attempt to eliminate any vestige of human spontaneity and individuality – to make human beings as human beings superfluous is what she called absolute or radical evil. The most disturbing sentence in The Origins of Totalitarianism *is her warning: "Totalitarian solutions may well survive the fall of totalitarian regimes in the form of strong temptations which will come up whenever it seems impossible to alleviate political, social and economic misery in a manner worthy of man." These "strong temptations" have not been resisted in the massacres, genocides, rapes, tortures, and systematic lying by governments during the past seventy-five years.*

R.J. Bernstein
The Urgent Relevance of Hannah Arendt, Philosophers Mag-

azine
2018

Three domains functioning together without domination

We can no longer define society by giving primacy to one of its functional domains. It cannot be depicted as civil society, as capitalist/socialist society, or as a scientific –technocratic system. We must replace such interpretations by a definition of society that refers to social differentiation. Modern society, unlike all earlier societies, is a functionally differentiated system. Its analysis thus requires a detailed study of each of its functional subsystems. Society can no longer be grasped from a single dominant viewpoint. Instead, its dynamic is clarified through the fact that functional systems for politics, the economy, science, law, education, religion, family, etc. have become relatively autonomous and now mutually furnish environments for one another.

Niklas Luhmann
***The Differentiation of Society** / Preface*
1982, p. xi

Cognitive diversity – hierarchies function within traditions, not among them

The separation of state and science (rationalism) which is an essential part of the general separation of state and traditions cannot be introduced by a single political act and it should not be introduced in this way: many people have not yet reached the maturity necessary for living in a free society (this applies especially to scientists and other rationalists). People in a free society must decide about very basic issues, they must know to assemble the necessary information, they must understand the purpose of traditions different from their own and the roles they play in the lives of their members. The maturity I am speaking about is not an intellectual virtue, it is a sensitivity that can only be acquired by frequent contacts with different points of view. It can't be taught in schools and it is vain the expect that 'social studies' will create the wisdom we need. But it can be acquired by participating in citizens' initiatives. This is why the slow erosion of the authority of science and other pushy institutions that is produced by these initiatives is to be preferred to more radical measures: citizens' initiatives are the best and only school for free citizens we now have.

Paul Feyerabend
Science in a Free Society
1987, pp. 106-107

Orientation

Before presenting a variety of texts that elaborate on those three aspects of a framework for the golden rule for public life, directional: "towards the spirit"; horizontal: "functionality"; vertical: "subsidiarity", I insert a section on the 'threefold differentiation' through which our society wants to express its humanity: What in chapter 2 is presented as different approaches to 'being' as by its very nature 'threefold", not only divine being but also human being, comes to be mirrored in this chapter by an understanding of society in its present state as threefold as well. Hamlet's question 'to be or not to be' was not primarily concerned with life and death, but with being conscious, alive, responsible, truthful etc. as opposed to mere existence, merely part of a world of deceit, pretence, lies. A living human being is fully alive if it is fully conscious, self-willed with a rich inner life, through emotional involvement and sense experience. One wonders when and how humanity would be 'fully alive'. Etc.

> ...a year ago in Florence, a catholic priest told me that he was interested in learning more about Buddhism. I asked him to share with me his understanding of the Holy Spirit and he replied, "The Holy Spirit is the energy sent by God." This statement made me happy. It confirmed my feeling that the safest way to approach the Trinity is through the door of the Holy Spirit. pp. 13-14

[ ]

> When John the Baptist helped Jesus touch the Holy Spirit, the Heavens opened and the Holy Spirit descended like a dove and entered the person of Jesus. He went to the wilderness and practiced for forty days to strengthen the Spirit in Himself. When mindfulness is born in us, we need to continue to practice if we want to become solid. Really hearing a bird sing or seeing a blue sky, we touch the seed of the Holy Spirit within us. Children have little difficulty recognizing the presence of the Holy Spirit. Jesus said that in order to enter the kingdom of God, we must become like a child. When the energy of the Holy Spirit is in us, we are truly alive, capable of understanding the suffering of others and motivated by the desire to help to transform the situation. When the energy of the Holy Spirit is present, God

the Father and God the Son are there. That is why I told the priest that touching the Holy Spirit seems to be a safer way to approach the Trinity.

Discussing God is not the best use of our energy. If we touch the Holy Spirit, we touch God not as a concept but as a living reality...

Thich Nhat Hanh
Living Buddha, Living Christ
1995, pp. 20-21

Sometimes our orthodox friends call the Trinity their "social program." They begin with the Holy Spirit and the Son. The Father belongs to the realm of inexpressibility, but it is possible to touch the Son and the Holy Spirit. We have the capacity to recognize the presence of the Holy Spirit whenever and wherever it manifests. It, too, is the presence of mindfulness, understanding and love, the energy that animates Jesus and helps us to recognize the living Christ...

Thich Nhat Hanh
Living Buddha, Living Christ
1995, pp. 220-221

The perfect community of oneness, is both the pattern and the possibility for our living community

...If God on the inside is the community of Father, Son and Spirit, this overcomes what Colin Gunton has called the 'alienation' at the heart of much modern thought. We need not divide knowledge into 'objective' and 'subjective'. We are enabled to overcome the opposition raised between 'other' and 'self' in much modern thought. The distinction of the persons means there is already 'otherness' in the divine 'self'. God on the inside includes the possibility of God on the outside. God as triune allows for the coming into being of what is other to God. If God on the inside holds together knowledge and knowing, so may we. As Gunton writes,

The triune God is the one who, a creator and sustainer of a real world of which we are part, makes it possible for us to know our world.

So, in the doctrine of the Trinity, we have a basis for the pursuit of science with ecological sensitivity. It preserves us both from mere technology and also from naïve naturalism. We could trace out further such implications for the way we reason about living.

[ ]

Since God exists as Persons-in-relation, so too must we, in our common life. We are not made as autonomous individuals, to live privatized lives. We are made for community, for relationship. Certainly this community can be corrupted into totalitarian conformity. Yet its opposite is just as bad. God on the inside, the perfect community of oneness, is both the pattern and the possibility for our living community. This is what the gospel of Jesus offers us and demands of us. Sin has distorted human life, marring the divine image in which we are made. Yet the work of Jesus has restored our relation with God. The Spirit of Jesus brings us into this relation, gathering us into a renewed humanity in the process. So the gospel of the Triune God offers restoration, not only 'vertically' with God, but 'horizontally' with one another.

Charles Sherlock
God on the Inside: Trinitarian Spirituality
1991, pp. 203-204

Love doesn't rule – it instructs and educates.

The old Woman hastened away; and at that moment appeared the rising Sun, upon the rim of the dome. The old Man stepped between Virgin and the Youth, and cried with a loud voice: "There are three which have rule on Earth; Wisdom, Appearance and Strength." At the first word, the gold King rose; at the second, the silver one; and at the third, the brass King slowly rose, while the mixed King on a sudden very awkwardly plumped down.

[ ]

The Man with the Lamp now led the handsome Youth, who still kept gazing vacantly before him, down from the Altar, and straight to the brazen King. At the feet of this mighty Potentate lay a sword in a brazen sheath. The young man girt it round him. "The sword on left, the right free!" cried the brazen voice. They next proceeded to the silver King; he bent his sceptre to the Youth; the latter seized it with his left hand, and the King in a pleasing voice said: "Feed the sheep!" On turning to the golden King, he stooped with gestures of paternal blessing, and pressing his oaken garland on the young man's head, said: "Understand what is highest!"

During this progress, the old Man had carefully observed the Prince. After girding-on the sword, his breast swelled, his arms waved, and his feet trod firmer; when he took the sceptre in his hand, his strength appeared to soften, and by an unspeakable charm to become still more subduing; but as the oaken garland came to deck his hair, his features kindled, his eyes gleamed with inexpressible spirit, and the first word of his mouth was "Lily!"

"Dearest Lily!" cried he, hastening up the silver stairs to her, for she had viewed his progress from the pinnacle of the Altar; "Dearest Lily! what more precious can a man, equipped with all, desire for himself than innocence and the still affection which thy bosom brings me? O my friend!" continued he, turning to the old Man, and looking at the three statues; "glorious and secure is the kingdom of our fathers; but thou hast forgotten the fourth power, which rules the world, earlier, more universally, more certainly, the power of Love." With these words, he fell upon the lovely maiden's neck; she had cast away her veil, and her cheeks were tinged with the fairest, most imperishable red.

Here the old Man said with a smile: "Love does not rule; but it trains, and that is more."

Johann Wolfgang von Goethe, Thomas Carlyle [Translator]
The Green Snake and the Beautiful Lily
1832

Orientation

Differentiation in three domains implies a differentiation in lawfulness. If the golden rule is crystallization of existing law or seed for the unfolding of new law, then one might expect a transformation from 'law' as one single 'body' to 'law' as a differentiated 'body'. Each domain has its own 'lawfulness' and its own way of establishing this.

Primal examples of law in the Western tradition are the Ten Commandments, the Sermon on the Mount and most recently a not yet widely known Circle Verse of Transformation. In the first human beings are told 'from the outside' what to do and not to do; in the second they are told to fulfil the law 'from the inside', from the heart; in the new understanding human beings are learning to become 'co-creators' of law themselves.

As soon the law has to be lawfully differentiated, peoples' involvement in formulating the law for the different domains becomes indispensable…

The structure of Ten Commandments underlies all formulations of law in that they are short on positive precepts and long on negative ones. Honouring God or the Highest or Most Sacred and honouring one's parents, one's ancestors, tradition etc., and allow time for this, are sufficient to sum up one's responsibility towards the good, but the negative, bad or evil takes on ever new forms when new possibilities for it arise. Hence Valentin Tomberg – in his 'Covenant of the Heart' – sums up the six prohibitions under the first one: 'thou shall not kill'. Every further breach of the law is a form of killing. In his Encyclical Letter Gaudium Evangelii (2013) Pope Francis says the same.

The Sermon on the Mount addresses the human being as a self-responsible being, in whom 'being told' is no longer enough: one has to interiorize the law, so that one acts out of one's own 'being'. Martin Buber points to the way Jeshua says 'I' as something that every individual is called to realize through his or her own life. Rabbi Zalman speaks the language of the Sermon on the Mount, when he insists on the 'form' of the dialogue as being equally important as its content...

Behind Shari'ah stands the love of God for humanity. Any legalistic approach to the law is not shari'ah.

An ancient Celtic Tradition is resonating in Shin's 'Circle Verse of Transformation'. It makes the law transparent and available as a process for modern human beings, who are called upon to become co-creators of law, differentiated in the different domains. Even though 'love' only appears after 'justice', the cycle becomes mechanical and shallow, if love is not its prime mover from the start. It is, however, only after justice is done, that love surfaces as the law's true face. (In a court case e.g., love would come to expression in the punishment after a guilty verdict.) The cyclic nature of the transformation process enables one to begin each cycle at a higher level, closer to true lawfulness.

Lord Buddha's 'eightfold path' offers a similar opportunity for growth in true enlightenment, not only as a private practice, but also as a developing consciousness in public life. It is not without reason that the Sutra is named the "turning" of the wheel.

The Ten Commandments

> *I am the Lord your God*
> *1. You shall have no other gods before Me.*
> *2. You shall not take the name of the Lord your God in vain.*
> *3. Remember the Sabbath day to keep it holy.*
> *4. Honor your father and your mother.*
> *5. You shall not kill.*
> *6. You shall not commit adultery.*
> *7. You shall not steal.*

8. You shall not bear false witness against your neighbor.
9. You shall not covet your fellow's wife.
10. You shall not covet your fellow's possessions.

Exodus 20:1-14
(Abbreviated version)

From the Sermon on the Mount

Do not imagine that I have come to abolish the Law or the Prophets. I have come not to abolish but to complete them. I tell you solemnly, till heaven and earth disappear, not one dot, not one little stroke, shall disappear from the Law until its purpose is achieved. Therefore, the man who infringes even one of the least of these commandments and teaches others to do the same will be considered the least in the kingdom of heaven, but the man who keeps them and teaches them will be considered great in the kingdom of heaven.

For I tell you, if your virtue is not deeper than that of the scribes and Pharisees, you will never get into the kingdom of heaven.

You have learnt how it was said to our ancestors: You must not kill and if anyone kills he must answer for it before the court. But I say this to you: anyone who is angry with his brother will answer for it before the court; if a man calls his brother "Fool" he will answer before the Sanhedrin; and if a man calls him "Renegade" he will answer for it in hell fire. So then, if you are bringing your offering to the altar and there remember that your brother had something against you, leave your offering there before the altar, go and be reconciled with your brother first, and then come back and present your offering...

Matthew 5: 17-25

Circle Verse of Transformation

Law grants Protection
Protection grants Unfolding
Unfolding grants Strength
Strength grants Encounter
Encounter grants Appraisal
Appraisal grants Deliberation
Deliberation grants Hearing
Hearing grants Justice
Justice grants Love

Love grants Insight
Insight grants Truth
Truth grants Freedom
Freedom grants Peace
Peace grants the Good Law
This is the Seal of the New Reign.

Shin Gwydion Fontalba
[Translated by Helma and Henk Bak]
2008

Three stages in the evolution of law

I took the time to look at the three main guidelines for human behavior: The Ten Commandments given to Moses, the Sermon on the Mount spoken by Christ and the Circle Verse of Transformation given by Shin.

First the Ten Commandments: the language is direct and instructive. "I am the Lord, your God" and then follow the instructions how to honour God and one's fellow human being.

Language- and content-wise it are commands, not advice: just do. More like one speaks to the child from 4 to 12.

Christ explains in the famous Sermon on the Mount how you work with these instructions. If somebody slaps you on the cheek, you turn the other cheek. The basic rule became "Do not to others that which you do not want to be done to yourself". He calls this the fulfillment of the law.

Christ brought the awareness of the reality of the I AM, the spirit part of God, in each one of us.

These are the guidelines to show us how to lovingly live together, to help humanity through puberty from 12 to 18 and worthwhile to meditate on. This stage is not yet fully integrated.

But time moves on, so Shin now gives us the Circle Verse of Transformation also as fulfillment of the law.

These are concepts addressed to the insight of humanity, as adults, one could say.

The Circle Verse of Transformation gives the possibility to transcend the stage of instructions and invites us to creativity in problem solving.

The new time is what for the whole humanity is new.

The Circle Verse introduces a new way of working with the spiritual world and friends in our relationship with each other.

Helma Bak in a letter to friends
11 June 2013

Study of law: from knowledge to understanding good as well as evil

Juris prudentia est divinarum atque humanarum rerum notitia

atque justi atque injusti scientia.*

Justinianus
Corpus Juris

...Here (i.e. after 'notitia') do we stand at the point where the lawmaker knows the domain of facts and compares this with what is divine and ideal. When he then stretches the tension beyond the borders of the divine and human spheres, so that the divine superhuman stands in opposition to the diabolical sub-human, and through and out of this, insight (scientia) ripens – then we get the second part of Justinian's formula: 'justi atque injusti scientia'.

[ ]

Thus does the path lead from the notitia towards the scientia, from knowing the facts to understanding what adequate measures to take, as the thinking rises from the empirical domain up to the moral domain.

Valentin Tomberg
Degeneration und Regegeration der Rechtswissenschaft
1946, pp. 27-29
[Translated by Henk Bak]

---

* The body of legal knowledge and insight consists in an account of divine and humane realities and as well as an insight in what is just and injust. [Translated by Henk Bak]

The Golden Rule in International Law

The fact of peaceful dealings between mutually independent nations implies – as primal historical phenomenon of international law – for the human groups in question, some fundamental convictions, as if such must have been the 'logical thing to do'. For just as two human beings express, through the very fact of their dealings, the conviction, that each of them has the right to claim a similar treatment by the other – and on the other side has the obligation to treat the other similarly – thus the fact of peaceful dealings between two of more nations is grounded in the same conviction. Thus – in dealings under international law the assumption of equal rights, i.e. legal equality applies, except in the case of a formal agreement to the contrary. This assumption implies the ethical connotation of 'justice', when – in practice – it is being used as guiding principle.

Valentin Tomberg
Grundlagen des Volkerrechts als Menschheitsrecht [Foundations of International Law as Humanity's Law]
1947, p. 137
[Translated by Henk Bak]

Shari'ah: an expression of God's Love.

In his review of the English Edition of Prince Gazi's 'Love in the Holy Quran', the Reverend Dr. Munib A. Youman begins: "This book will open up to you that which stands theologically behind Shari'ah Law. And for those delving deeper than Shari'ah for the first time, you may well be astounded to find that, behind Shari'ah stands love. The love of God for humanity..."

Social development requires not only truth and democracy, but also love.

...the concept of functional supremacy is not concerned with comparing the intrinsic importance of specific functions. Instead, it refers to the position of a subsystem in the total context of social evolution – namely, the position of that subsystem which by virtue of its own complexity and dynamics guides social development and delineates for other subsystems their domains of possibilities.

It should not, however, be assumed that this subsystem defines the totality of the evolutionary constraints for a society. We could develop, as a contrast, the concept of evolutionary bottlenecks. We might ask whether there exists enough love or democracy or social-scientific truths for further social development.

Niklas Luhmann
The Differentiation of Society
1982, p. 225

...For the last century, without greatly noticing it, we have been undergoing a remarkable transformation in the range of intellect. To discover and know has always been a deep tendency of our nature. Can we not recognize it already in cave man? But it is only yesterday that this essential need to know has become explicit and changed into a vital autonomous function, taking precedence in our lives over our preoccupation with food and drink. Now, if I am not mistaken, this phenomenon of the individualization of our highest psychological functions is not only far from having reached its limits in the field of pure thought, but is also tending to develop in a neighbouring realm, which has remained practically undefined and unexplored: the 'terra incognita' of the affections and love.

Paradoxically, love (I understand love here in the strict sense of 'passion'), despite (or perhaps precisely because of) its ubiquity and violence, has hitherto been excluded from any rational systematization of the energy of man. Empirically, morality has succeeded more or less successfully in codifying its practice with a view to the maintenance and material propagation of the race. But has anyone seriously thought that beneath this turbulent power (which is nevertheless well known to be the inspirer of genius, the arts and all poetry) a formidable creative urge has remained in reserve, and that man will only be truly man from the day when he has not only checked, but transformed, utilized and liberated it? Today, for our century, avid to lose no energy and to control the most intimate psychological mechanism, light seems to be beginning to break. Love, like thought, is still in full growth in the noosphere. The excess of its growing energies over the daily diminishing needs of human propagation becomes every day more manifest. And love is therefore tending in a purely humanized form, to fill a much larger function than the simple urge to reproduction. Between man and woman a specific and mutual power of spiritual sensitization and fertilization is probably still slumbering. It demands to be released, so that it may flow irresistibly towards the true and the beautiful. Its awakening is certain. Expansion, I have said, of an ancient power. The expression is undoubtedly too weak. Beyond a certain degree of sublimation spiritualized love, by the boundless possibilities of intuition and communication it contains, penetrates the unknown; it will in our sight take its place, in the mysterious future, with the group of new faculties and consciousnesses that is awaiting us.

...Union, the true upward union in the spirit, ends by establishing the elements it dominates in their own perfection. Union differentiates.

> *In virtue of this fundamental principle, elementary personalities can, and can only affirm themselves by acceding to a psychic unity or higher soul. But this always on one condition: that the higher centre to which they come to join without mingling together has its own autonomous reality. Since there is no fusion or dissolution of the elementary personalities the centre in which they join must necessarily be distinct from them, that is to say have its own personality.*
>
> Pierre Teihard de Chardin, J.M. Cohen [Translator]
Human Energy
1969, pp. 128-130

Effectiveness of one's right depends on the effectiveness of the correspondent obligation.

> *The notion of obligation comes before that of rights, which is subordinate and relative to the former. A right is not effectual by itself, but only in relation to the obligation to which it corresponds, the effective exercise of a right springing not from the individual who possesses it, but from other men who consider themselves being under a certain obligation towards him. Recognition of an obligation makes it effectual. An obligation which goes unrecognised by anybody loses none of the full force of its existence. A right which goes unrecognised by anybody is not worth very much.*
>
> Simone Weil
In Need of Roots
2003, p. 2

Mahatma Gandhi, who was consulted about the UN Declaration of Human Rights, wrote per telegraph: (1948)

"*The Ganges of rights originates in the Himalayan of responsibilities*".

Hans Küng
Global Ethic and Human Responsibilities
2005

Validity of one's right is inherent in the dignity of being human

> *Of course it would be wrong to think that the legal validity of human rights depends on the actual realization of responsibilities. Human rights cannot*

be considered as a reward for good human behaviour. This would in fact mean that only those who had shown themselves worthy of rights by doing their duty towards society would enjoy rights. Such an absurd idea would clearly offend the unconditional dignity of the human person, which is itself a presupposition of both rights and responsibilities. No one has claimed and will claim that certain human responsibilities must be fulfilled first, by individuals or a community, before one can claim human rights. These are given with the human person, but this person is always at the same time one who has rights and responsibilities: All human rights are by definition directly bound up with the responsibility to observe them. Rights and responsibilities can certainly be distinguished neatly, but they cannot be separated from each other. Their relationship needs to be described in a differentiated way. They are not quantities which are to be added or subtracted externally, but two related dimensions of being human in the individual and the social sphere.

Hans Küng
Global Ethic and Human Responsibilities
Submitted to the High-level Expert Group Meeting on
"Human Rights and Human Responsibilities in the Age of Terrorism" 1-2, April 2005
Santa Clara University

Human Rights not only a legal matter: human dignity to be honoured in all three domains

A decision at Amnesty International's Council meeting in August 2001 to begin working on economic, social and cultural rights has led to the creation of the Human Dignity Campaign, which will be launched globally in 2008.

...It is unfinished business in the sense that economic, social and cultural rights are important rights enunciated nearly 60 years ago in the Universal declaration of Human Rights (UDHR) of 1948. The International Covenant on Economic, Social and Cultural Rights (ICESRCR) together with the UDHR and the International Covenant on Civil and Political Rights (ICCPR) form what has been termed an international bill of rights.

[ ]

(In response a criticism in The Economist):

"The right to adequate food, the highest attainable standard of health and education are as much human rights as are freedom of expression or the right

*to a fair trial." Amnesty International also said it widely recognized that
nobody could enjoy their economic, social and political rights unless their
economic, social and cultural rights were also respected, protected and fulfilled.*

Russell Solomon
in Amnesty International Publication, Australia 2007

First obligation towards needs of the soul: order

*Unfortunately, we possess no method for diminishing this
incompatibility (between obligations). We cannot even be sure that
the idea of an order in which all obligations would be compatible
with one another isn't itself a fiction. When duty descents to the level
of facts, so many independent relationships are brought into play
that incompatibility seems far more likely than compatibility.*

*Nevertheless, we have every day before us the example of a universe in which
an infinite number of independent mechanical actions concur so as to produce
an order that, in the midst of variations, remains fixed. Furthermore, we love
the beauty of the world, because we sense behind it the presence of something
akin to that wisdom we should like to possess to slake our thirst for good.*

Simone Weil
The Need for Roots
2003, pp. 3-13

Islam: Four texts on order, justice, and prayer

Sixty years of injustice against one night of chaos

*(Hussein) was not a warrior or a statesman. He was a revered
scholar, honoured since his brother's death as the one who more than
any man alive embodied the spirit of Muhammad, and he was
no longer a young man. Why not be content to live out his days
in the peace and quiet of Mecca or Medina? Why not leave the
business of politics and powers to those who could handle it?...*

*To Sunnies, Hussein's determination to travel to Iraq would be the proof
of his unsuitability to take the helm of a vast empire. They would call it
a quixotic and ill-fated quest, one that never should have been undertaken.
Hussein should have acknowledged reality, they say, and bow to history.*

In time they would cite the bitterly anti-Shia scholar Ibn Taymiya, whose writings are still central to mainstream Sunni thought. Sixty years with an unjust leader would be preferable to a single night with an ineffective one, Ibn Taymiya declared. His reasoning was, that without an effectively run state, the implementation of Islamic law was impossible. But he was also clearly stating that church and state, as it were, were no longer one and the same, as they had been in Muhammad's time.

Lesley Hazleton
After the Prophet. The Epic Story of the Shia-Sunni Split
2009, p.178

Sixty years under an unjust ruler are better than one night without a sultan.

To Ibn Taimiyah authority is preferable to anarchy. Although he asks Muslims not to obey orders contrary to the commandments of Allah and forbids them to cooperate with an unjust ruler, he does not advocate open rebellion or encourage overthrowing him. He quotes the saying: 'Sixty years of an unjust imam (ruler) are better than one night without a sultan.' Al-Ghazali and Ibn Jama'ah also take the view that any effort to depose even a tyrannous sultan is liable to create chaos and lawlessness. Following the Greek philosophers, St. Thomas Aquinas also adopts this view, on which William Archibald Dunning has commented: 'In respect to individual action in slaying tyrants, he observes that it is more often bad men than the good that undertake such an enterprise, and that, since bad men find the rule of kings no less burdensome than that of tyrants, the recognition of the right of private citizens to kill tyrants involves rather more chance of losing a king than of being relieved of a tyrant.'

Ibn Taymiyyah
On the Need for a State by 'Abdul'atheem Islaahi
In: Economic Concepts of Ibn Taimiyah / Courtesy Of: Islaam.com

One hour of justice outweighs sixty years of prayer

If the judge (Shanah-i 'adl) (ruler) does not regulate the affairs of the people, a clandestine rebel, abetted by tyranny, will destroy the lives of the nobility and plebeian alike. If the light from the candle of justice does not illuminate the sombre cell of the afflicted, the darkness of cruelty will blacken the entire country just as it does the hearts of tyrants.

Because rulers are but the reflections of the Creator, without the sun of their justice the expanse of the world is not illuminated...A just ruler is a refuge to the oppressed and a protector of fallen. In the Tradition (khabar) [it says] that "on a pair of scales, one hour of justice outweighs 60 years of worship". Indeed the benefit of praying is limited to the worshipper, (whereas) the benefit of justice reaches to the public in general, from high to low.

Muhammed Baqir Najm-I Sani
Advice on the Art of Governance 1612-1613
[Translated, Introduction & Notes by Sajda Sultana Alvi]
1989, p. 45

Institutionalise for the sake of order

For greater success, the institutionalisation of tamthil is necessary. For Gülen, every good and beautiful idea should be institutionalised. As Muslim individuals are responsible for being role models for their fellow human beings; similarly, institutions of all fields must be operated in the most productive and useful ways and should serve as role models for other institutions...

According to Gülen, for required tamthil, firstly, institutions must have a humanist vision and serve all human beings. Secondly, they should be a place where people are spiritually and morally elevated. Thirdly, they should be based on public support rather than that of the state. Finally, those who work for institutions must not use institutions for their worldly ambitions.

[ ]

In summary, all institutions (specifically non-profit ones) must provide services to the community regardless of their faith, ethnicity or social status. By operating in such a way, Hizmet's institutions look similar to the waafs of the Golden Age of Islam. The tamthil of institutions is more important than individual tamthil in Gülen's philosophy. To him, if institutions are not represented as required, their collapse is inevitable. If the successful members of a government or experienced executives of a state or institution demand the lion's share of benefits in consideration of their abilities and accomplishments, the government is paralysed: the state collapses, and the institution descends into chaos.

Salih Yücel
A Life in Tears: Understanding Fettullah Gülen and his Call to Service
2018, pp. 156-158

Declaration of Marrakesh

In the Name of God, the All-Merciful, the All-Compassionate

Executive Summary of the Marrakesh Declaration on the Rights of Religious Minorities in Predominantly Muslim Majority Communities 25th-27th January 2016*

> WHEREAS, conditions in various parts of the Muslim World have deteriorated dangerously due to the use of violence and armed struggle as a tool for settling conflicts and imposing one's point of view;
>
> [ ]
>
> WHEREAS, this year marks the 1,400th anniversary of the Charter of Medina, a constitutional contract between the Prophet Muhammad, God's peace and blessings be upon him, and the people of Medina, which guaranteed the religious liberty of all, regardless of faith;
>
> WHEREAS, hundreds of Muslim scholars and intellectuals from over 120 countries, along with representatives of Islamic and international organizations, as well as leaders from diverse religious groups and nationalities, gathered in Marrakesh on this date to re-arm the principles of the Charter of Medina at a major conference;
>
> [ ]
>
> AND NOTING the gravity of this situation aflicting Muslims as well as peoples of other faiths throughout the world, and after thorough deliberation and discussion, the convened Muslim scholars and intellectuals:
>
> DECLARE HEREBY our firm commitment to the principles articulated in the Charter of Medina, whose provisions contained a number of the principles of constitutional contractual citizenship, such as freedom of movement, property ownership, mutual solidarity and defence, as well as principles of justice and equality before the law; and that,
>
> The objectives of the Charter of Medina provide a suitable framework for national constitutions in countries with Muslim majorities, and the United Nations Charter and related documents, such as the Universal Declaration of Human Rights, are in harmony with the Charter of Medina, including consideration for public order.

* For full text of the Declaration of Marrakesh, see Henkbak.com

NOTING FURTHER that deep reflection upon the various crises afflicting humanity underscores the inevitable and urgent need for cooperation among all religious groups, we

AFFIRM HEREBY that such cooperation must be based on a "Common Word," requiring that such cooperation must go beyond mutual tolerance and respect, to providing full protection for the rights and liberties to all religious groups in a civilized manner that eschews coercion, bias, and arrogance.

BASED ON ALL OF THE ABOVE, we hereby:

Call upon Muslim scholars and intellectuals around the world to develop a jurisprudence of the concept of "citizenship" which is inclusive of diverse groups. Such jurisprudence shall be rooted in Islamic tradition and principles and mindful of global changes.

Urge Muslim educational institutions and authorities to conduct a courageous review of educational curricula that addresses honestly and effectively any material that instigates aggression and extremism, leads to war and chaos, and results in the destruction of our shared societies;

Call upon politicians and decision makers to take the political and legal steps necessary to establish a constitutional contractual relationship among its citizens, and to support all formulations and initiatives that aim to fortify relations and understanding among the various religious groups in the Muslim World;

Call upon the educated, artistic, and creative members of our societies, as well as organizations of civil society, to establish a broad movement for the just treatment of religious minorities in Muslim countries and to raise awareness as to their rights, and to work together to ensure the success of these efforts.

Call upon the various religious groups bound by the same national fabric to address their mutual state of selective amnesia that blocks memories of centuries of joint and shared living on the same land; we call upon them to rebuild the past by reviving this tradition of conviviality, and restoring our shared trust that has been eroded by extremists using acts of terror and aggression;

Call upon representatives of the various religions, sects and denominations to confront all forms of religious bigotry, vilification, and denigration of what people hold sacred, as well as all speech that promotes hatred and bigotry;

AND FINALLY,

AFFIRM that it is unconscionable to employ religion for the purpose of aggressing upon the rights of religious minorities in Muslim countries.

Marrakesh
January 2016, 27th

To 'present a viable alternative in scale': cohesion through (traditional forms of) centralization or through (new forms of) networking?

The as yet undelivered promise of this movement is a network of organizations that offer solutions to disentangle what appear to be insoluble dilemmas: poverty, global climate change, terrorism, ecological degradation, polarization of income, loss of culture, and many more. The world seems to be looking for the big solution, which is itself part of the problem, since the most effective solutions are both local and systemic. Although the groups in the movement are autonomous, the coming together of different organizations to address an array of issues can effectively become a systemic approach. Although the movement may appear inchoate or naively ambitious, its underlying structures and communication techniques can, at times, create a collective response that can challenge any institution in the world.

Paul Hawken
Blessed Unrest: How the Largest Social Movement in History
is Restoring Grace, Justice, and Beauty to the World
2007, pp. 20 -21

The unifying principle of the movement comes from within, in freedom:

In the midst of such giants a worldwide gathering of ordinary and extraordinary people are reconstituting the notion of what it means to be a human being. While they are organizing themselves into the largest movement in the history of the world, the movement only happens one person at a time. But how does one become an environmentalist or human rights campaigner? There are no missionaries. There are no postings offering lessons. Concerned individuals have to work it out for themselves and find colleagues who will mentor them. Movements are the expression of changed attitudes, and how each person comes to realize his responsibility to a greater whole is a unique experience.

Paul Hawken

Blessed Unrest: How the Largest Social Movement in History is Restoring Grace, Justice, and Beauty to the World
2007, pp. 23-24

MOTHER EARTH

Bestows her Love on all her children;
and according to divine laws
all beings have their nourishment,
their meaningful life and their task.
Human beings are learning to take care of,
and carry responsibility for, one another
and all fellow creatures.
Know that you are not alone upon the way!
The healing Spirit wanders through all
peoples. There are billions who carry this
in their hearts.
Come, go forward bravely and full of trust;
and you will find those friends who,
without self interest work together
to lovingly protect the Earth; and who raise up
their efforts and their consciousness to the
realm of perfect Love.
I – AM
*I YOU IT I WE**

Given by Shin Gwydion Fontalba in September 2001
© by Ganga Verlag, Walzenhausen, Switzerland

Indigenous Culture – the quiet hub of the new movement

Our fate will depend on how we understand and treat what is left of the planet's surpluses —its lands, oceans, species diversity, and people. The quiet hub of the new movement - its heart and soul — is indigenous culture. The acknowledgement of aboriginal cultures is not a romantic gesture or wistful plea, not does it value Neolithic cultures above modern ones, or native spiritual practices above other sacred traditions. Just as a wheel cannot turn without a stationary hub, the movement reaches back to the deep and still roots of our collective history, for its axle. Indigenous people have a different sense of time because they remember a different history, and that memory

---
* Read these as : "I AM I"
"I AM I" , "I AM YOU" etc.

brings an uncommon appreciation of their place in time. Simply stated, they possess patience. Things come and go; conquests, ideas, and leaders arise and fall away. For indigenous people, in the time that defines one's life, the relationship one has to the earth is the constant and true gauge that determines the integrity of one's culture., the meaning of one's existence, and the peacefulness of one's heart. In most indigenous cultures there are no separate social and environmental movements because the two were never disaggregated. Every single particle, thought, and being, even our dreaming, is the environment, and what we do to one another is reflected on earth just as surely as what we do to the earth is reflected in our diseases and discontents.

Paul Hawken
Blessed Unrest: How the Largest Social Movement in History is Restoring Grace, Justice, and Beauty to the World
2007, p. 22

6B Texts

Orientation

Central to an understanding, grasp and realization of functional differentiation is the faculty of imagination. J. Friedrich Schiller had already pointed to its essential role in his Letters on the Aesthetic Education of Man, in response to the Terror of the French Revolution; Rudolf Steiner had placed the development of imagination at the heart of his concept of education, after the 'Great War', and Herbert Read wrote his Education Through Art during the second world war, in response to the savagery and barbarism raging between highly civilized nations on earth. The 'Education through Art Movement' became an important, effective vehicle for mutual understanding between nations, otherwise separated from each other by the cold war. Here are some texts that point in a similar direction. Especially Owen Barfield's essay addressing the relation between parts and whole is directly pertinent to an understanding of society as a whole, functionally differentiated in three parts.

The visible and the Invisible

On the surface, beauty confers grandeur on order,
attractiveness on goodness, graciousness on truth and Eros on Being.
Thomas Aquinas and the medieval thinkers wisely recognized
That beauty was at the heart of reality;
it was where truth, unity, goodness and presence came together.

There is a profound equality at the heart of beauty;
A graciousness which recognizes and encourages the call of individuality
but invites it to serve the dream and creative vision of community.
Without beauty the Eros of growth and creativity
would dry up.
As Simone Weil says:
'Desire contains something of the absolute
and if it fails...
the absolute is transferred to the obstacle.'

John O'Donohue
Divine Beauty: The Invisible Embrace
2003

A modern social structure must be somewhere artistically right.

...Now the imagination or mens creatrix, the faculty to which we impute the provenance of art, has also frequently been spoken of as "organic", and indeed this quality is in some degree implied in the very use of an adjective as "creative". But if "organic" in this connection is to signify anything more than a lose analogy with the mysterious ways of "nature", we need to have a clearer idea of the general principle underlying "organic" processes. In short, we must know what "organic" means.

And it is here that Soloviev* comes to our aid, building up, through the concept of "organic solidarity", the image of a special relation between part and whole, which is neither serial nor spatial nor – as we shall see – hierarchical: the kind of relation, in fact, which the imagination, and only the imagination, detects between the parts and the whole of a living organism, and (which) both creates and detects organic solidarity between the parts and the whole of a work of art. For imagination is, precisely, that which experiences form.

Thus the body of a single animal – when regarded as a whole – manifests the principle of organic solidarity. But nature goes further than this. Though each body is in itself a whole, yet each animal, regarded as a unit of consciousness, is only a part. As such it is part of a race; and it experiences, the unity of the race in its full force at the moment of sexual impulse, when the inward unity or community with the "other", with the "all", receives its concrete embodiment in the relation to a single being

---

*   Soloviev, see: S.L Frank A Solovyov Anthology Greenwood Press Publishers, Westport Connecticut (1950) 1974 Vladimir Solovyov 1853-1900. Russian Philosopher. For Barfield's reference, see: Solovyov's Essay: The Meaning of Love 1892-1894 pp 150-179

of the other sex, which represents this complementary "all" in one.

But since the process of individualization is carried furthest of all in the human being, it follows that it is in human society that the all-one idea can be most fully realized. For man, too, that inward unity or community receives its concrete embodiment in the relation to a single person of the other sex; but the unity which he thus experiences, or ought to experience, is the unity not merely of the physical race, but of the social organism. The social organism "is produced by the same creative life-force of love, which gives birth also to physical organisms." The love between two human beings (and this strangely packed little book *) is primarily a disquisition on human love) is true to its own essence only if it functions as a sort of biological cell, with the potentiality of expanding to the entire social organism.

[ ]

Now the most distinctive feature of Soloviev's book is that it propounds an adequate concept of Christian love, without at the same time setting this over and against nature and the natural. On the contrary, by applying his concept of "organic solidarity", he reveals the same spiritual principle at work, on the one hand in nature and on the other in man and society. The aim and object of this principle is everywhere the same — the establishment of an "organic" relation between part and whole — and, when the "whole" in question is human society, the principle is usually called love. Such a conception of love, not exclusively as the fruit of "grace" supervening on "nature" from a contrasted source, but rather as a normal extension of the natural process itself, carries far-reaching implications; and it is my whole contention that these implications may be profitably considered and better understood in connection with a similar theory of imagination.

At the present junction of affairs the establishment of a true relation .... between part and whole in society is of great practical urgency...

[ ]

...a modern social structure must, if it is to be healthy and durable, be somewhere artistically right, this is exactly what we should expect...

Form in Art and Society in: Owen Barfield's
The Rediscovery of Meaning and Other Essays
1977, pp. 220,223-225

Aesthetic education an antidote against consumerism and environmental vandalism.

> ... *"the relationship between a good aesthetic education and the maintenance of a healthy environment cannot be overlooked" (1990 Message for the World Day of Peace) By learning to see and appreciate beauty , we learn to reject self-interested pragmatism. If someone has not learned to stop and admire something beautiful, we should not be surprised if he or she treats everything as an object to be used and abused without scruple. If we want to bring deep change, we need to realise that certain mindsets really do influence our behaviour. Our efforts at education will be inadequate and un-effectual unless we strive to promote a new way of thinking about human beings, life, society and our relationship with nature. Otherwise the paradigm of consumerism will continue to advance, with the help of the media and the highly effective workings of the market.*
>
> Pope Francis
Laudato Si: On Care for our Common Home
2015, p. 167

Cultural development depends in principle on asymmetrical relationships 1

Yet there are also many I-You relationships that by their very nature may never unfold into complete mutuality if they are to remain faithful to their nature.

Elsewhere I have characterized the relationship of a genuine educator to his pupil as being of this type. The teacher who wants to help his pupil to realize his best potentialities must intend him as this particular person, both in his potentiality and in his actuality. More precisely, he must know him not as a mere sum of qualities, aspirations, and inhibitions, he must apprehend him, and affirm him as a whole. But this he can only do if he encounters him as a partner in a bi-polar situation. And to give his influence unity and meaning, he must live through this situation in all its aspects not only from his own point of view but also from that of his partner. He must practice the kind of realization that I call embracing.* It is essential that he should awaken the I-You relationship in the pupil, too, who should intend and affirm his educator as this particular person; and yet the educational relationship could not endure if the pupil also practiced the art of embracing by living through the shared situation from the educator's point of view. Whether the I-You relationship comes to an end or assumes the altogether different character of a friendship, it becomes clear that the specifically educational relationship is incompatible with complete mutuality.

*Another, no less instructive example of the normative limits
of mutuality may be found in the relationship between
a genuine psychotherapist and his patient. ...*

[ ]

*The most striking example of the normative limits of mutuality could
probably be found in those charged with the spiritual well-being
of their congregation: here any attempt at embracing from the other
side would violate the consecrated authenticity of the mission.*

*Every I-You relationship in a situation defined by the attempt of one
partner to act on the other one so as to accomplish some goal depends
on a mutuality that is condemned never to become complete.*

*Umfassung

Martin Buber in: Walter Kaufmann's
I and Thou
1970, pp. 178-179

Cultural development depends in principle on asymmetrical relationships. 2

*... to acknowledge tacit thought as an indispensable element of all
knowing and as the ultimate mental power by which all explicit
knowledge is endowed with meaning, is to deny the possibility that
each succeeding generation, let alone each member of it, should
critically test all the teachings in which it is brought up... p. 60*

*....if indeed we recognize a great discovery, or else a great personality,
as most real, owing to the wider range of its yet unknown future
manifestations: then the idea of knowledge based on wholly identifiable
grounds collapses, and we must conclude that the transmission of
knowledge from one generation to the other must be predominantly tacit.*

*We have seen that tacit knowledge dwells in our awareness of particulars
while bearing on an entity which the particulars jointly constitute. In
order to share this indwelling, the pupil must presume that a teaching
which appears meaningless to start with has in fact a meaning which can
be discovered by hitting on the same kind of indwelling as the teacher is*

practicing. Such an effort is based on accepting the teacher's authority. p. 61

Michael Polanyi
The Tacit Dimension
1967

In a free society art is not a weapon...artists are not engineers of the soul.

John F. Kennedy
"Dedication"
Robert Frost's presidential inaugural poem
20 January 1961

We must not forget that art is not a form of propaganda; it is a form of truth

John F. Kennedy

A functionally differentiated society: a horizon rather than a program.

Imagine a society in which people have learnt to value the individual capacities and dignity of each single human being, to work with economic, social and legal, political bodies and resources, which are in tune with the natural foundations of life and make it possible for all human beings to live together in harmony and peace.

Gideon Fontalba
From a Letter 'Meditation of the Turning'
1992

Envisioning the "City of Dawn"

There should be somewhere on earth a place which no nation could claim as its own, where all human beings of goodwill who have a sincere aspiration could live as free citizens of the world and obey one single authority, that of the supreme truth, a place of peace, concord and harmony where all the fighting instincts of man would be used exclusively to conquer the causes of his sufferings and miseries, to surmount his weaknesses and ignorance, to triumph over his limitations and incapacities, a place where the needs of the spirit and the concern for progress take precedence over the satisfaction of desires and passions, the search for pleasure and material enjoyment. p. 46

[ ]

A new world will be born, if men are willing to make an effort for transformation, to seek for sincerity, it is possible. From animal to man, thousands of years were needed, today, with this mind, man can will and hasten a transformation towards a man who shall be God. p. 49

The Mother. August 1954, in: Robert N. Minor's
The Religious and the Secular: Auroville and Secular India
1999, p. 46

...sciences into which religion has breathed new life

With the natural environment unpolluted and in good order and harmony, its lovely towns and villages re-planned and re-designed, and its population equipped with such human values and virtues as belief, love, knowledge, mutual loyalty and high morals, this world would be a place fit for joyful , sincere-hearted people to dwell in a place where rivers of love and other sublime feelings flow, where works of the finest artistry appear side by side with those of the sciences into which religion has breathed new life, a place where families dwell whose members are attached to one another with love, respect and compassion. Those destined to live in this world will find it a Paradise-like place cleansed of all kinds of impurity and foulness, and purified of all kinds of misery and dissipation, where angelic souls fly around and all are for each other and each is for all.

Gülen Horizon of Hope, in: Salih Yücel's
A Life in Tears: Understanding Fettullah Gülen and his Call to Service
2018, pp. 45-46

The prospect (1945) of selling our soul to evil

If atomic power should manifest the same surprising capacities for making people comfortable, as it certainly has for making people uncomfortable,

then we should be in danger of selling our souls to evil, and making up our minds to live contentedly in a world without freedom, without honour, without justice.

If we do that, we shall be deserving, and probably earning, a far more grievous chastisement than in the worst days of the early forties.

Ronald Knox
God and the Atom / Chapter X Brother Atom
1945, p. 141

Come and dance with uncertainty

now come good people from the city and the town

from the field, from the forest and from working underground
do a quick two step and a one two three
and dance, yes dance, with uncertainty
look to the east and look to the west
north and south and right and left
there's no right answer to get you off the hook
there's no simple truth and there's no good book
we got a lot of
fundamentalism, feminism, pacifism, pragmatism
capitalism, corporatism, hedonism, humanism
romanticism, realism, anarchism, atheism
socialism, solipsism, cynicism, scepticism
christian, hindu, buddhist, muslim
bureaucracy, democracy, autocracy, theocracy
economy, ecology, biology, psychology
and each of them is right and each of them is wrong
and there is no holy, is no holy, is no holy, one
so move one way and then another
don't you move like a jerk,
but like you're dancing with your lover
there's a place for confusion
and there's fun at the fair
take a glide next step, like you're skating on air
skating, like you're skating on air
learn some elasticity
and dance, yes dance with uncertainty

Peter Fernon
Song and Dance as prelude of "This Jesus Story" as part of Words
in Winter celebration Trentham 27 August 2016
[Published in the Trentham Newsletter October 2016]

Orientation

Uncertainty permeates all of today's life experience. It makes us also sensitive to uncertainties that were part of life in times past. For present day readers, historical texts and scriptures may reveal uncertainties that earlier generations might not have noticed. Poet, actor and musician Peter Fernon places his exploration of how Jesus was experienced and perceived in the existentially uncertain world-view of today. The uncertainty of the people around Jesus, his disciples, his mother…even his own self-doubt, until Peter Fernon is confronted with the 'sermon of the mount' and the 'beatitudes': blessed are the meek, the poor of spirit, the down-trodden, the peace-makers. Paradoxically these outrageous claims sound true beyond any doubt, and so do the repeated contrasting pairs: 'you have been told...but I say to you!' Amidst all the uncertainties, it is here where the author finds his 'Torah', his law, his rock...It is this 'I saying' Martin Buber refers to in his "I and Thou". And it is the authenticity of this 'I saying' that is demanded by a world growing smaller by the day, for the human being to become larger: to the point that every human being lives up to the challenge of simultaneously participating in economic, political and cultural life: reconciling freedom and solidarity with equality, rather than being reduced to a 'function', a cogwheel in the machinery of ideological, political, economical systems and 'machinations'.

When I sketched my statement of intent in 1964, I had no idea what 'becoming larger' meant, apart from becoming 'big enough' to accommodate other peoples' different opinions etc. When the Dalai Lama uses the same words thirty years later, they get a new dimension by the re-introduction of the concept of 'family' at the most universal level. In family life it is quite natural that its members live this seeming opposition between economic, cultural and political demands: there are certain family rules that are to be obeyed by all, there are vital needs, food, clothing, shelter, that may change from age to age, physical condition etc. and children come with talents and disabilities which require the freedom and creativity to make the most of them...A natural differentiation which gets lost in the centralized structure of contemporary society...only to emerge at humanity's most universal level as aspiration towards the one human family.

The two interviews that both took place in June 2017, in locations as far apart as Switzerland and Manus Island and in situations as different as night and day, highlight the range over which this sense of humanity in the valley of deep despair as well as on the height of public office...Behrous Boochani is a poet and journalist, refugee from the Iranian part of Kurdistan, at the time of the interview imprisoned on Manus Island as part of Australian Government's 'deterrent' policy. Arnold Zable is a Melbourne author committed to the cause of refugees and other victims of public violence.

Even though the function and meaning of money would need to become part of the dialogue, especially now it has become a power of its own, with disastrous effects on real life issues, I have refrained from selecting texts on the matter, except two recent observations that under both Mosaic and Islamic Law, the recent global financial crisis would not have happened. I concentrate on economy rather than money partly to avoid an identification of money with economy, as most of the money operations have no connection at all with any substantial economic activity. Two things need to be kept in mind: the role of money changes in the transition between the three domains: what originates in economic activity, especially in horticulture and agriculture as the expression of surplus, functioning as 'purchase money', enters the legal domain when purchase is postponed and money is invested in productive projects: 'investment credit', to be distinguished from the 'consumption credit' which now has become rampant. Cultural projects and endeavours are in principle financed by 'gift money', in the form of grants, endowments, donations. The fruits of culture are priceless. Even though current thinking and language treats them as commodities that one sells and buys, money spent on cultural activities is money that makes them possible, not a price that matches their worth. This future thrust of money outside any financial markets permeates the whole of society. Etc. And there is the Son of Man saying: "give the emperor what is owed to the emperor and to God what is owed to God". No mention here, that money would ever be 'owed' to money.

The challenge of living in uncertainty was recently highlighted for me by two talks: the first was a talk by philosopher Peter Boghossian at an Atheists and Freethinkers Gathering in Kyneton (110 Km North of Melbourne) in 2015 where he opened his talk by distinguishing between being honest and being rude. Boghossian works with prisoners in Oregon, USA, to help them question their certainties, which lead them to keep re-offending. The questioning happens following a scale of 1 to 10, from the least certain to the most certain…and his method and his own honesty and humanity, give him a significant success rate. In his book: A Manuel for Creating Atheists (2013) he elaborates on the rich history of rationalism and a wealth of common sense. His book is highly instructive for anyone who wants to combat fundamentalism in whatever kind of world-view…

The second talk was at the 2018 Interfaith Conference in St Albans, Melbourne, the area disastrously affected by the machinations of the gambling industry. The keynote address, a faith-based response to gambling by Reverend Tim Costello, Baptist minister, identified four human certainties that gambling turns into illusions: a false hope, a false sense of community, a false sense of identity and a false sense of meaning. Costello made it clear, that it is no longer an issue of problem gamblers in need of help, but a nationwide structural and cultural catastrophe, the responsibility of those in corporate and political power, as well as educators and spiritual leaders of the country…Shariah law prohibits gambling, just as it forbids usury. Perhaps, again, if genuine Shariah would have been in force in Australia, this systemic humanitarian disaster might never have happened...

Niklas Luhmann adds to his outline of a society differentiated in domains the observation, that each domain functions in an environment that is undefined. Societal space is by itself not measurable, it is not a 'container', just as we know since Albert Einstein, that physical space is not a container...Without a societal space that by itself is undefined, the domains within that space have no room to develop and to relate with other domains, lacking the awareness that they are also environments to one another. Corporations should be aware that they function in a social environment with many other dimensions such as family, health, creativity, generation of meaning etc. Without such awareness a money flow that changes its function from 'purchase' to 'investment' to 'gift' would not be thinkable and one would still live in the illusion that one can 'buy' the gifts of human creative spirit, the majesty of nature or any inspiration or gift that comes from a divine or sacred source. Or that one can 'invest' in destruction. When money leaves the domain in which it has been generated it enters a societal space that by itself is undefined and hence uncertain...To live in a functionally differentiated society is to live in a space that is inherently uncertain, in which it is up to the human being individually and together to establish the trust that enables us to become the global family we may aspire to...

A world growing smaller asks for human beings growing larger

> *Science and technology, communication and mass-consumption make the earth more and more habitable for man. The world is growing smaller every day and peoples are brought together more and more.*

> *War has come to mean world war, and peace can only be imagined as world peace. And yet this intertwining of interests does not constitute real unity. For real unification involves collective striving towards the well-being of all, whilst the oneness of all people in every field has to be respected and appreciated.*

> *A world growing smaller asks for a man growing larger, a man who is able to live with people of a completely different opinion, who is "ready for discussion". The aim of the discussion is to free oneself and one's partner, opponent and enemy from fear, narrowness and hate. The aim of the discussion between peoples is not to solve final*

*problems, tensions and oppositions, but rather to make them more
clear, so that they become fruitful instead of poisoning everything.*

Ecumene of Cultures / General Introduction
1964
[Edited translation by Henk Bak from the Dutch draft statement of intent]

A global family

*The world is becoming smaller and smaller. Nations are far more
interdependent than before. Our generation has reached the threshold of
a new era of human history: the birth of a global family. Whether we
like it or not, all the members of our vast and varied human family have
to learn to live together somehow. We need to develop a greater sense of
universal responsibility, on both the individual and the collective level.*

Dalai Lama
The Dalai Lama's Little Book of Inner Peace
1996, p. 136

*Shouldn't we come to a different kind or concept of human dignity?
The dignity of the human being is sacrosanct.*

*Thus it is stated by the Declaration of Human Rights and this statement stands
as a rock in history. The will expressed in these words creates a strong
foundation stone for a healthy and noble unfolding of the individual in
the community and of the single nations in the community of nations: in
the family of mankind.*

*I may remind ourselves, that in the declaration of human rights,
in these fundamental laws, that are valid in the union of nations
of those who have accepted them, reference is made to the great
family. I think, this also ought to be remembered again.*

*Because, that even in the actual legal description 'Human Union', 'Human
Community', 'United Nations', 'Humanity' has been denoted as family, is an
indication that in that time, when this was formulated, the human beings were
intend to bring spiritual goodness and ahigh ideal down into earthly reality.*

*Yes. May the dignity of human beings be inviolable.
So be it really and in fact.
But human dignity also seeks to show itself in earthly life as active strength
and as a health bringing spirit. Human dignity wants to be lived, wants to*

prove itself, wants to bear flowers and fruits.
The dignity of the human being is not so easy to fathom.
It does not only want to be there as a declared law, through
which people agree to not harm each other. That point of view
would be insufficient, unsatisfactory, even unworthy.

[ ]

Shouldn't we come to conceive of a different kind of human dignity?
To the dignity of the true, spiritual being, which is specific to being human.
To the one becoming to the human being: the dignity of higher insight and
respectful willingness to serve the great universal life.
The human being will rise to a fuller dignity when he, in God's
will and – I might add to God's joy - decides with determination
and full strength to work for the earth, to work for nature and
all living beings in the great union of life on this planet.

Shin Gwydion Fontalba Public Address
at the launch of the 'Free and Worldwide Movement for Human
Dignity'
Oberstdorf Germany
October 2009

The new movement: Representative, not centralized; no ideology, yet common spirit?

If anything can offer us hope for the future it will be an assembly of humanity that is representative but not centralized, because no single ideology can ever heal the wounds of this world. [ ]

The movement, for its part, is the most complex condition of human organizations the world has ever seen. The incongruity of anarchists, billionaire funders, street clowns, scientists, youthful activists, indigenous and native people, diplomats, computer geeks, writers, strategists, peasants, and students, all working toward common goals is a testament to human impulses that are unstoppable and eternal. [ ] This is the promise of the movement, that the margins link up, that we discover through our actions and shared concerns that we are a global family. pp. 161 - 162

Paul Hawken
**Blessed Unrest: How the Largest Social Movement in History
is Restoring Grace, Justice, and Beauty to the World**
2007

"This republic breaks all the borders between human beings."

Zable: Perhaps it can be said that you created a republic of refugees or a republic of the stateless governed by a disciplined, peaceful act of civil disobedience. How would you describe this republic? And now that the literal fences of the centre have been torn down, do its outlines still exist?

Boochani: I think a republic is a political concept but yes, in some ways our resistance was a declaration of a republic and a political act. But in our hearts we wanted only to declare that we exist. And our language was our half-naked bodies and our peaceful resistance.

[ ]

But I think we should not reduce our protest to a political perspective only. Our resistance was a republic of love, peace and humanity, and it was a republic on behalf all stateless refugees in the world. We wanted to declare that we are human and that we have a right to live. That's why in my manifesto I wrote: This republic breaks all of the borders between human beings."

Our republic was built on dignity and genuine respect for difference. We were made up of many different individuals, ethnicities and beliefs, all resisting together.

Zable: You express this poetically in your manifesto, when you write that "our resistance is the spirit that haunts Australia". You have also said that "all the conversations are driven by one thing and one thing only, and that is freedom". During these dramatic weeks of resistance, it seemed that despite the great danger you faced - the threat of illness, exhaustion, food shortages and even death - you took charge of your own fate, your own destiny, and achieved a kind of desperate state of freedom. Is this how the men felt during that time?

Boochani: It's a great question, which creates a space for deeply understanding the resistance, and the true nature of the Manus prison. We were living under so many rules for years... We were living through a dehumanising system for years, and a system that humiliated us and ignored our human identity for years.

What did the resistance give us? We achieved a great feeling for the first time. The hierarchy completely disappeared for the first time and the rules disappeared for the first time. For the first time we were out of the system. The place was the same, we were even close to death, but we were free, we had control over our lives for the first time.

We created new rules for our community based on love, respect and peace. We created a society that was completely different from a system that was torturing us for years. We created a society based on concepts that were the opposite of the system that had robbed us of our humanity. We were close to death but we were living in freedom.

Behrouz Boochani and Arnold Zable
This Republic breaks all Borders
From a conversation that took place in June 2017 published in The Age
23 December 2017, pp. 20-21

...must one regulate at all? ... Perhaps new vessels are needed.

Q: Herr Thurnherr, you have as Chancellor of the Confederation, a unique insight into the working of government. One gets the impression that the Confederation Council mainly processes the issues of the individual departments and hardly touches on strategic questions. Is this impression deceptive?

The Confederation Council deals with ca 2600 items a year in ca 40 sessions. You yourself can calculate how much time it is able to spend per item. This works only, because the items are beforehand being prepared, pre-discussed and partly also pre-negotiated.at the level of administration and heads of departments. Amongst these issues there are in fact strategically important questions, which the Confederation Council must be able to discuss in further depth. For this year we have therefore set aside a whole raft of specific areas. For example agriculture, health or Europe. These time-frames are important because many topics become even more complex, intertwined and international.

[...after three more questions about the internal working of government, the topic shifts to the increasing pressure from the intertwining of institutionalized internal and international politics...]

Q: What is to be done about this? Should participation in the deliberations be restricted?

A: No. We should continue to take the time needed to think things through. As a rule laws become better through this, not worse. The question is more whether one is able to regulate differently. Does it always need a new law, or is a decree sufficient? Should one step up a goal-oriented and techno-neutral way of regulating and leave the way open towards this? That requires a certain trust in the administration and the Federation Council. There is a further-reaching theme: to recognize and decide early enough whether one must regulate at all. In this matter politics and administration should step up their cooperation with science and with economy.

Q: A kind of Think-Tank for early recognition of the need for regulation?

A: In earlier days the ETH (Engineering, Technology etc University, Zürich) was a kind of 'Competence Centre' for the Federation. Today one has clinically separated or outsourced everything. One must indeed not tinker with the independence. But the cooperation could again be strengthened. Our research institutions – such as universities and university level professional education institutes – become aware of certain developments earlier than the administration does. The same is true for the economy. In earlier days one assumed that the military system takes care of the necessary exchange. Today this is not so obviously the case. Perhaps, new vessels are needed.

Q: You have spoken of the added value of collective intelligence. How do you consider our government in this respect?

A: I am a fan of the system with seven federal councils. Value is added when one looks at a problem from seven different sides. In other countries decisions are often made much quicker, with also more mistakes.

Q: But does the collective intelligence in today's Federation Council also carry?

A: Now, that's not a fair way of putting the question. I mean yes. And it is reinforced by the fact – there are also scientific studies on this – that both genders are appropriately proportionally represented.

An Interview by Jan Fueckiger and Heidi Gmur published in Neue Züricher Zeitung, 13 June 2017, p. 15
[Translated by Henk Bak, 27 July 2017]

Under Islamic or Mosaic law, the global financial crisis might not have happened

1 Sharia: The conventional finance system has recently run out of control. Can the Islamic approach, where all financial transactions must be in accord with Sharia, be an alternative? Sabine Machhausen has for her PhD thesis assessed Islamic variations on conventional financial market instruments. Through this, investment funds and investors are able to gauge in how far the Islamic way of structuring finance products agrees with the basic principles of the religion.

The jurist says, she wants also to "contribute to the debate around the legal requirements of ethical investment". She presents parallels with other sustainable finance products and finds "the correlation with the general ethical or moral principles is so high, that religious differences fade into the background". Because what shows up as the basic principle of Islamic finance is simply the foundation for socially being in it together.

For example, legal equality in partnership of investment institution and investors, which are equally exposed to the chances and risks of the investment.

The Islamic economic law and its moral 'extra' could serve as an example when developing policies that guide the financial markets. "Because for Islamic Finance, the prohibition of interest or usury are not the only features of central significance. It forbids also excessive uncertain and purely speculative transactions as well as forms of gambling disguised as business".

With its mandated mechanisms orientated toward communal wellbeing, Islamic law challenges the conventional finance market to rethink its basic attitude which is exclusively profit orientated. And it is a reminder that the principles of Islamic economy are also to be found in western Christian ethics. They can help building a finance market architecture, that would diminish the risk of future crisis.

[ ]

On Islamic Financial Engineering to create a match against the current range of finance instruments the report notes that, although in Islamic Financial Engineering communal wellbeing and protection against unfair advantage through unequal economic strength play a role: a tension quickly arises.

[ ]

And it is no surprise, that Sabine also comes across black sheep, e.g. amongst the Islamic 'derivatives' on offer.

Report on German Study Prize results,
Dr. Sabine Machhausen, Islamic Finance: Sharia conform invest-

ment funds. A chance for more morality in the global economy or just a game of the conventional financial system under the guise of religion?
Dissertation Johannes Gutenberg University, Mainz 2011
Körber-Stiftung Forum for Impulse German Study Prize 2012

2 Deuteronomy and Leviticus: This is Deuteronomy 24:10-13: "When you make your neighbour a loan of any sort, you shall not go into his house to fetch his pledge. You shall stand outside, and the man to whom you make the loan shall bring the pledge out to you. And if he is a poor man, you shall not sleep in his pledge; when the sun goes down, you shall restore the pledge that he may sleep in his cloak and bless you; and it shall be righteousness to you before the Lord your God." The Geneva Bible has a note that makes the law gentler yet. It says, "As ye wouldst what to have appoint, that you have, but shalt receive what he may spare." No one can read the book of Moses with any care without understanding that law can be a means of grace. Certainly that law is of one spirit with the Son of man who says, "I was hungry and you fed me, I was naked and you clothed me". This kind of worldliness entails the conferring of material benefit over and above mere equity. It means a recognition of and respect for both the intimacy of God's compassion and the very tangible forms in which it finds expression. Cranky old Leviticus gave us – gave Christ not only "Thou shalt love thy neighbour as thyself" but also the rather forgotten "Thou shalt love the stranger as thyself", two verses that appear to be merged in the Parable of the Good Samaritan. Still, startlingly gentle laws like this fall under the general condemnation of Old Testament severity and Calvin's refinements with them.

The tendency to hold certain practices in ancient Israel up to idealized Western norms is pervasive in much that passes for scholarship, though a glance at the treatment of the great class of debtors now being evicted from their homes in America and elsewhere should make it clear, that from the point of view of graciousness or severity, an honest comparison is not always in our favour.

[ ]

The emperor Julian notes that no Jew is ever forced to beg. So this-worldly are God's interests that he cares whether some beleaguered soul can find comfort in his sleep. He cares even to the point of overriding what are called by us, though never by Moses or Jesus, the rights of property.

Marilynne Robinson

When I was a Child I Read Books / Chapter: Open Thy Hand
Wide: Moses and the Origin of American Liberalism
2012, pp. 72-73

Orientation

The following texts have been chosen for their authors' contributions towards clarifying the new relationships arising out of a functional differentiation of society. Firstly with a focus on state, secularism and religion or spirituality. Shin's understanding of the way Jeshua says 'I', resonates with Martin Buber's, in the sense that every human being has it in him/herself, to say 'I' out of the same depth of being, i.e. 'not of this world'. It is the individual who is responsible - as citizen of three "worlds" - for the functioning of all three in harmony. In all cases the role of the state is in principle limited to legislation etc., and by default extended to facilitate in areas where she must be neutral, but not indifferent. Separation of economic interests and the state is just as urgent as a separation between state and church, temple, mosque, synagogue, university, education, art, sport and health. An example of differentiation in action: After a 'guilty' verdict, which is the legal responsibility of the judiciary arm of the state, the establishment of appropriate punishment is a cultural/ educational responsibility carried out by the judge as the state's facilitator. [Rudolf Steiner's Towards Social Development, 1919; Freedom Charter, South Africa 1955; Simone Weil Punishment as Soul Need, in The Need for Roots (1943) 1949]. Niklas Luhmann's reflection on the consequences of the shift from hierarchical to functional differentiation of society has a special bearing on religious and non-religious world-views, because this shift places world-views on the same 'level' as say: science. It is the whole cultural domain that is at stake here, not just that of science. This means 1. that this domain can only function through mutual communication, conversation, and 2. that supremacy can only be earned for the cultural domain as a whole, if it wants to be functional for the whole of society. The State by itself cannot generate culture, but without a living culture the State degenerates and the Economy remains dysfunctional. There is a cultural aspect to economic and political life, just as there is an economic aspect to the state and cultural institutions. And aspects of governance are to be found in both cultural and economic life. Hence a variety of texts reflecting the variety of aspects to consider…

Dennis Kucinich: the state to be separated from religion, not from spirituality

While our fathers understood well the importance of the

separation of church and state, they never meant America to be separate from spiritual values. Spiritual values can improve our own health, our spirit, our nation, and the world.

Quoted in: Christian Science Monitor
January 2004

Our founding fathers never thought, that the state should be devoid of all spirituality

Dennis Kucinich
Interview with Barbara Graham
Tricycle; Buddhist Review Fall 2004

...the need for some universal action toward spiritual renewal...

If the salvation of the world depended upon people who were initiated personally, there would not be a foundation on which to build. The necessary foundation would not be available if there were no other methods and other ways. The relationship of teacher and pupil is really a very high thing. People can enter into this relationship truly, only when they are very close to perfection...You have heard this saying that two hundred conscious men can save the world, or this notion in one Judaic tradition of the thirty-nine Just Men who keep the world from disaster... if there is one man, who reached a high degree of perfection, and he wishes to help others, he can do it in two ways. One is in secret by what he does inwardly inside himself. The other is by spreading outwardly, but in order to spread, he needs people who are already receptive. That is why I said there would be not enough foundation if there were not some universal action, and therefore it is happening at this time that literally millions of people are being touched. Especially among young people; more particularly among those who were born after the end of the last war...

Intimations Talks with J.G. Bennet at Beshara
1975, p. 61

When mere legality, not justice, becomes the rule...

The political system of a highly differentiated society can no longer be understood as a means to an end and can no longer be regulated by rigid external guidance. In order to pursue its function it has become so differentiated from the rest of society, so autonomous and complex, that it can no longer base its stability on fixed foundations, practices or values. It can become stable only by creating possibilities for change... The system has to have command over possibilities for change, without thereby eliminating these possibilities by viewing what is new as definitive. Paradoxically, beyond a certain level of complexity, security can be achieved only by the detour of maintaining insecurity.

Some of the typical institutions in modern political systems focus on just this paradoxical problem. It seems that, in order to solve it, they make use of procedures that presuppose the reflexivity of power, transmitting it to decision making processes. The positivity of law, an orientation toward interests instead of truth, the pursuit of security through planning instead of tradition are some examples...

Law becomes positive when mere legality comes to be recognized as legitimate —i.e., when law is heeded precisely because it has been made according to definite rules by competent decisions. In this way, arbitrariness about a central question of social life becomes institutionalized...

Parallel to this normative determination of norms we find a similar degree of arbitrariness institutionalized in the evaluation of values. Underlying this development is the fact that values as well as the pragmatic reduction of horizons for action have lost their capacity of being true. Now values must themselves be evaluated according to their function in orienting action. In the political system truths are no longer at issue (although, naturally, firm everyday truths, such as that planes can fly or men must sleep, remain in use). Instead, it are interests that are at issue. Whoever still tries to advocate truths is making a mistake and is treated as doing so. pp. 158-159

Niklas Luhmann
Functional Differentiation of Society / Chapter 7 Politics as a Social System
1982

Consequences of a shift from hierarchical to functional differentiation of society.

In recent years ...new forms of self-reflection (at the level both of the economy and total society) have begun to emerge. In precise analogy to the liberal constitutionalist endeavours of early bourgeois society, they culminate in a self-limitation of the economy with an eye on its direct and indirect social consequences.

A brief allusion to the Club of Rome should suffice here. It is no longer simply assumed that the self-rationalization and self-optimization of the economic system yields adequate or desirable results. The economic system – and this means not only entrepreneurs but also, for example, consumers – must learn to view themselves as the environment of other social subsystems and also to be concerned about its impact on the total social environment. Hence there arises a demand for broad social criteria according to which we can evaluate and adjudicate narrow economic criteria. Whether such self-reflective achievements are possible within the structure of our economic system or whether they will require a re-politicalization of this system, (for example, new forms of nonmarket coordination between production and consumption) remains at present an open question. p. 342

...After our retrospective glance at the history of the previous self-thematizations of European society, it is tempting to seek the solution to our problems once again in the hypostatization of a part for the whole. The only change would be a shift in social primacy. Truth would take the place of power and money, and science would take the place of politics and the economy. We could prognosticate that the society of the future would be a societas scientifica. Science could pragmatically evade what were once unavoidable difficulties with the help of structures and processes which, although logically odd, are possible socially, compatible with other requirements of society, favourable to evolution, and institutionalized in a functionally adequate way in the scientific system.

If science ever assumes social primacy, the self-thematization of society will acquire a new centre of gravity and be beset with new problems. There would be a "change of command" in the key problems of which society identifies itself as being thus-and-so-and possibly-otherwise. In political society, the defining moment was the reconstruction of social contingency, through the alternative of justice and injustice and the attendant binary schematization of physical force as either for or against law and the state. In economic society, there was superimposed upon this the reconstruction of social contingency through scarcity in the monetary code and its binary schematization through property. This made possible a universal and unambiguous ascription of owning and not owning and, thus, exchange, and as a further result, a general separation between production and consumption. In both cases the main achievement of social evolution lay in the stress on a new binary scheme. It became futile to expect one half of either dichotomy to suppress its counterpart...Indeed, there is only one form of "cancellation" or Aufhebung possible. This would involve another schematism (for example, the true/false schema of logic) taking over the primacy. It would preserve the alternatives of illegal/legal behavior and of the ownership/non-ownership, but it would reform them and release them from their previous burdens. Problems stemming from the contingency of human behaviour (the elemental problem of society) would still plague the central binary schematization, in this case the assumption that there exists a perfectly clear-cut (mutually exclusive and jointly exhaustive) disjunction between truth and untruth

[ ]

The apparatus and knowledge of science are not necessarily the apparatus and knowledge of society. Scientific truths and falsehoods are not necessarily identical with the everyday truths and falsehoods of the rest of society...It is crucial to note that the risks accompanying the scientific production of truth cannot necessarily be borne. The chances exploited by science may well be hazards that are in no way socially useful. What is even more dangerous is the fact that science not only produces truths but also falsehoods. It discredits socially accepted truths regardless of whether they are still needed or not. Finally, the collaboration between science and the rest of society seems, at first, to take the form of defining priorities among subjects of research...pp. 357-359

Niklas Luhmann
The Differentiation of Society / Chapter 10 Self-thematization
1982

Next Step in Evolution?

Being compelled to make more of ourselves is the human lot. This book asks whether a significant portion of humanity has found a new series of adaptive traits and stories more alluring than the ideological fundamentalisms that have caused us so much suffering. [ ] How many new stories and groups will it take before the world recognizes its evolutionary potential, not just its baseness? [ ]

This movement is a new form of community and a new form of story. [ ] What are the characteristics of leadership required when power arises instead of descends? What would a democracy look like that was not ruled by a dominant minority? What would a world feel like that created solutions to our problems from the ground up? What if we are entering a transitional phase in human development where what works is invisible because our heads are turned to the past? What if some very basic values are being re-instilled worldwide and are fostering complex social webs of meaning that represent the future of governance? These are but a few of the questions collectively posed by a movement that has yet to recognize it is a movement.

Paul Hawken
Blessed Unrest: How the Largest Social Movement in History is Restoring Grace, Justice, and Beauty to the World
2007, p. 25

The State not to be indifferent to constitutive values.

A liberal and democratic state cannot remain indifferent to certain core principles, such as human dignity, basic human rights, and popular sovereignty. These are the constitutive values of liberal and democratic political systems; they provide these systems with their foundations and aims.

Although these values are not neutral, they are legitimate, because it is they that allow citizens espousing very different conceptions of the good to live together in peace.... They often arrive at them by very different paths, but they come together to defend them. The presence of what Rawls calls an "overlapping consensus" about the basic public values is the condition for the existence of pluralist societies. A Christian, for example, will be able to defend fundamental rights and freedoms by invoking the idea that the human being was created in God's image; a Kantian rationalist will say that it is necessary to recognize and protect the equal dignity of rational beings; a utilitarian will maintain that one must seek to maximize the happiness of sentient beings capable of both pleasure and pain; a Buddhist will invoke the core principle of ahimsa; nonviolence; and an indigenous person or deep ecologist, referring to a holistic conception of the world, will maintain that living beings and natural forces stand in a relation of complementarity and interdependence and that, consequently, each of them, including human beings, must be granted equal respect. All of them agree on the principle, even though they cannot reach an agreement about the reasons that warrant it.

[ ]

...In the realm of core beliefs and commitments, the state, to be truly everyone's state, must remain 'neutral'.

This implies that the state should adopt a position of neutrality not only toward religions but also toward the different philosophical conceptions that stand as the secular equivalents of religions. In fact, a political system that replaces religion with a comprehensive secular philosophy as the foundation of its actions makes all the faithful member into second class citizens. pp. 11-13

[ ]

Whereas political secularization finds its expression in positive law and public policies, social secularization is a sociological phenomenon embodied in people's conceptions of the world and modes of life. In accordance for the state's necessary neutrality toward conceptions of the good and the convictions of conscience, the state must seek to become politically secular but without promoting social secularization.

With that said, it is clear that such neutrality on the state's part will not impose an equal burden on all citizens. The liberal state, for example, defends the principle that individuals are to be considered autonomous moral agents, free to define their own conception of the good life. In the schools, therefore, the state will favour the development of students' critical autonomy. In exposing students to a plurality of worldviews and modes of life, the state is making the life of parents more difficult seeking to transmit a particular order of beliefs to their children and even more difficult for groups wishing to shield themselves for the influence of the larger society in order to perpetuate a style of life based more on respect for tradition than an individual autonomy and the exercise of critical judgement. The state's neutrality is, therefore, not complete. p. 16.

[ ]

In our view, secularism rests on two major principles, namely, equality of respect and freedom of conscience, and on two operative modes that make the realization of these principles possible: to wit, the separation of church and state and the neutrality of the state toward religion. The operative modes of secularism are not merely contingent means that can be disregarded, On the contrary, they are indispensable institutional arrangements. Nevertheless, they can be interpreted in different ways and can prove to be relatively permissive or rather restrictive with respect to religious practice.

At the level of principles, a democratic political system recognizes the equal moral value or dignity of all citizens and therefore seeks to grant them all the same respect. Realizing that aim requires the separation of church and state and the state's neutrality toward religious and secular movements of thought. On one hand since the state must be the state for all citizens, and since citizens adopt a plurality of conceptions of the good, the state must not identify itself with one particular religion or worldview. It is for that reason that the state must be "separate" from religion. It must be sovereign within the fields of its jurisdiction. The fusion between political power and a religious or secular conception of the world makes those who do not espouse the state's official doctrine into second-class citizens. p. 20

[ ]

It is important to understand that secularism is composed of a set of values and of means, or operative modes, which are so intimately linked that it is difficult to separate them. In our opinion, one of the sources of the impasse in debates both theoretical and practical on secularism is that the aims of secularism are not distinguished clearly enough from the operative modes. As a result, what belongs to means comes to assume a status equivalent to or even greater than that of the aims the secular state is seeking to achieve. p. 20.

[ ]

...Not all principles of secularism are of the same type. Equal respect and freedom of conscience are moral principles whose function is to regulate our behaviour (or, in the case at hand, the state's actions), whereas neutrality, separation and accommodation could be called "institutional principles" derived from the principles of equal respect and freedom of conscience. To use an analogy, the separation of the executive, legislative and judicial branches is not a moral principle. It is an indispensable institutional arrangement whose aim, as Locke and Montesquieu showed, is to safeguard the freedom of citizens and to avoid tyranny. The value of "institutional principles" is derived rather than intrinsic: they are essential means toward the realization of properly moral ends.

The complexity inherent in secularism can be better assessed by observing that it entails a set of ends and operative modes that can enter into conflict. In particular, tensions may arise between respect for moral equality and the protection of freedom of conscience and religion. pp. 23-24

Jocelyn Maclure and Charles Taylor, Jane Marie Todd [Translator]
Secularism and Freedom of Conscience
2011

What is complex needs not be complicated

The sophisticated arguments of those who say the issues of war and peace are too complex for us to understand seduce us into feelings of powerlessness and uselessness.

The truth, however, may be simple after all. May be the difficult grammar of warmaking, with words such as fusion, and fission, MAD, MARV, and MX, is nothing more than an elaborate screen hiding the face of the One who says: "You must love the Lord your God with all your heart, with all your soul, with all your strength, and with all your mind and your neighbour as yourself" (Luke 10;27). It is a simple but hard truth, requiring constant vigilance, resolution, and practice. This difficult truth, the truth of peace, has to be spoken and lived – directly, courageously, intelligently, gently, lovingly, and repeatedly.

Henri Nouwen
Peacework: Prayer, Resistance, Community / Introduction
2014, pp. 20-21

Search for a new form:

1. Oath of Citizenship

Under the sacred power who is the creator of this land and the guide of its people,

I, ... pledge loyalty to Australia, its nature and its laws, its Indigenous Custodians and the great diversity of people from all over the world who came to settle on its shores.

I honour their ideals and great achievements and I build on them.

I take part in our economy as a caring partner, in our democracy as a responsible citizen, and in our culture as a free individual.

I share responsibility for the vitality of our natural environment, for the integrity of our institutions and for the healthy development of both for the benefit of the earth, our children and future generations.

I support Australia as a nation in the community of nations and share its commitment to freedom, human dignity and life on this planet.

I trust that our loyalty to Australia and the world works both ways and leads to good neighbourship in the region and at home.

[The first sentence is from Les Murray's draft, 1992. The phrase '.... settle on its shores' echoes a favourite expression of the late Burnum Burnum]
Henk Bak
In: Functional Differentiation, From Welfare State to Well-Tempered Society

Discussion Paper for the Constitutional Debate. Trentham 1996

Promise before Parliament. A better alternative to the Lord's Prayer.

We come here today to do the business of governing. Members of this Parliament have pledged to improve the quality of this community and are entrusted with doing so.

As we gather, let us remember that though we have differences, we are linked by our common humanity.

We embrace many traditions and represent many demographics. We are Christians, Jews and Muslims, Hindus, Buddhists and Sikhs, humanists, atheists, rationalists and skeptics, the unaffiliated and the uncertain. We represent many races and nationalities, men and women, young and old, and all in between. We identify as libertarian, liberal, progressive, and conservative.

To be sure, we do not agree about everything and we often feel fiercely protective of what we believe. But there is one thing on which we can all agree and that is the goal of making our community the best it can be. We unite here today with that noble aim and common purpose.

Our meetings should be characterised with a healthy dose of humility and doubt, being receptive to the ideas of others and having the willingness to change our beliefs given good reason, argument and evidence.

Let us not have intellectual arrogance or emotional intransigence. Let us remember that our beliefs inform our actions and, translated into real-world impact, have the potential to help or harm others.

So, in the spirit of goodwill and common decency, may we always show respect to others, compassion for the needy, and integrity in our actions.

Dr Meredith Doig [President of the Rationalist Society of Australia]
Rationalist Society of Australia
February 2015

Humanity in need of balance...Ehrlich and Ornstein

Have you ever gone to the circus? Next time watch closely the person on the tightrope to keep her balance...You are, automatically,

> *feeling an intense connection and empathy with a stranger.*
>
> *The need to expand our connection and cooperation with strangers is essential right now. All of us, citizens of every nation, are now in the same family, are now in the same boat, walking the same tightrope, like it or not. The worst problems of the human predicament are common to all of us, from climate disruption, loss of biodiversity, and poisoning of the environment to pandemics, gross economic inequities, and the threat of nuclear war...*
>
> *Like it or not, we're all now balancing on that same global tightrope – and that means we have to change.*
>
> *We've got it in us to change. All human beings have a brain that evolved to give us an extraordinary ability to understand and to connect with others, but that primordial is much too limited for the complex world we have created in the twenty first century. p. 3*
>
> *[ ]*
>
> *One of our society's major problems is that there is, as Barack Obama said in his Martin Luther King speech in 2008, an "empathy deficit".*
>
> *[ ]*
>
> *One hopeful sign for promoting change is the new understanding of how the human brain operates; we're not, as it turns out, just simple "economic men", cold-blooded decision makers...the human brain/mind is highly influenced by the emotional tone of any situation, and emotions are essential to decision making. And it is the emphatic emotions that are falling short right now. p. 4*

Paul R. Ehrlich and Robert E. Ornstein
Humanity on a Tightrope
2010

A balancing act needs a lot of training...Tomberg

> *Look at a tightrope walker. He is evidently completely concentrated, because if he were not, he would fall to the ground. His life is at stake, and it is only perfect concentration that can save him. Yet, do you believe that his thought and his imagination are occupied with what he is doing? Do you think that he reflects and that he imagines, that he calculates and that he makes plans in regard to each step that he makes on the rope?*

If he were to do that, he would fall immediately. He has to eliminate all activity of the intellect and of the imagination in order to avoid a fall... It is the intelligence of his rhythmic system — the respiratory and circulatory system — which replaces that of his brain. In the last analysis, it is a matter of a miracle — from the view of the intellect and the imagination — analogous to that of St Dionysius, apostle of the Gauls and first bishop of Paris (who, according to legend, was beheaded before the statue of Mercury and walked two miles with his head in his hands from Montmartre to where he chose to repose.)

[ ]

Concentration without effort is the transposition of the directing centre of the brain to the rhythmic system — from the domain of the mind and imagination to that of morality and the will. pp. 9-10

Anonymous (Valentin Tomberg)
Meditations of the Tarot: A Journey into Christian Hermeticism
1991

Balance between good and bad

We have a concept in Bali, Ruwas Bhidena, a balance between good and bad. Without bad there can be no good. The bad is the 'sibling' of the Good. Embrace this concept and we can move forward into a better world.

There is Sekala/Nisikala — the underworld forever in darkness merging with our world in the light.

You love your husband and wife but sometimes you fight. Fear arises and shows its opposition to love. This is normal. This is a natural, essential part of life.

These are the concepts by which we, as Balinese, live our lives. Please we beg you, talk only of the good which can come of this. Talk how we can reconcile our 'apparent' differences. Talk of how we can bring empathy and love into everybody's lives.

Asana Viebeke L. from a message on behalf of the Samigita ("Think Tank")
for the Banjars of the Kuta, Legian and Semyak areas (village councils), Bali, 25 October in response to the bomb-attack in Kuta, 12 October 2002 killing 202 people from 21 nations

A tightrope walker: a visionary experience

...Bewildered by the sudden flooding of the bridge, he started to swim. He swam in a panic, forgetting what his guide had told him – that every moment he had to relearn what he already knew. And so the faster he swam, the slower he moved, till it appeared as if all his confused efforts only succeeded in making him go backwards. He resisted this paradox of motion with all his might and all his fear, and soon found himself near the beginning of the bridge again.

It was only then, that he remembered the mysterious quality of grace that his guide had hinted at. And he remembered only because he didn't want to have to go through it all over again, making all the mistakes of his confusion. So he swam more gently, more slowly, and he wasn't at all surprised that this made him travel faster through the water.

He was beginning to enjoy the serenity in this discovery when it occurred to him that he was swimming in the air, in an illusion, in a dream, and that at any moment he would fall through the water into the dreaded abyss below.

He had hardly completed this thought when he found himself in midair, with voices crying around him, with demons rushing past his face, whistling songs from his childhood. He noticed strange beings with green eyes, riding on yellow horses, drifting past his gaze. He was surprised to find people wandering past him in the air, dressed in blues and reds, with a distracted look in their eyes.

As if in a mist, he saw whole peoples rising from the depths of a great ocean, rising from the forgetful waters. Then, with a fixed and mystic gaze in their eyes, he saw them walking to an island of dreams. There they began building a great city of stone, and within it a mighty pyramid and universities and churches and libraries and palaces and all the new unseen wonders of the world. He saw them building a great new future in invisible space. They built quietly for a thousand years. They built a new world of beauty and wisdom and protection and joy to compensate for their five hundred years of suffering and oblivion beneath the ocean. They had dwelt as forgotten skeletons on the ocean bed, among the volcanic stones and the dead creatures that turned into diamonds, among the fishes of wonder that never come to the surface to bathe in its sunlight. He noticed that there is also light in the depths.

He saw all these things as he flailed in midspace. Then he realised that towards the end, the bridge had turned into air, and into dreams.

Ben Okri
Astonishing the Gods / Chapter Ten
1996, pp. 26-27

Modern day banjars

The banjar has anywhere from fifty and two hundred individual family compounds. The word banjar originally meant a row of houses, the clustering of compounds into a neighborhood, with a temple and a community. Nowadays, most of these banjars have split, and the banjar community is no more strictly territorial. Two banjars can occupy the same territory, and banjar members sometimes live far from the center of community. In densely populated areas such as Denpasar and Kuta, there are many banjars and they don't always get along, especially when residents choose to leave one banjar for another.

Effects of the banjar in modern times

The banjar have generally been a good thing for Bali and during the riots in 1999 banjar Kuta patrolled to keep rioting youths from destroying tourist infrastructure. The banjar is the main force that prevents the Balinese from becoming a disenfranchised population like some other cultures in the developing world. It insists locals are used for construction and hired as staff. During religious events the banjar will determine what streets are blocked off and this is enforced by the banjar traffic cops, the pecalang. It is the one social group in Bali that has the respect (in some cases fearful respect) of most people. A couple of years ago banjar Seminyak decided to close down all bars and nightclubs for a weekend to make a point. They stayed closed and the point was made.

Banjar Bali: Village level government
by Nick on April 12, 2007
[For the Ceremonial function of the Banjar see Chapter 7]

Four domains – four timeframes

WTO* policies engage and affect four chronologies or time frames, but WTO considers only one of them. The dominant time frame of our age is commerce. Businesses are responsive, welcome innovation in general, and have a bias for change. They need to grow more quickly than ever before, due to the integration of capital markets and globalization; they are punished, even bankrupted if they do not. With the efficiency of

* World Trade Organisation

worldwide capital mobility, companies and investments are rewarded or penalized instantly by a network of technocrats and money managers who move $2 trillion a day, seeking the highest return on capital.

The second time frame is culture. It moves more slowly, as cultural revolutions are resisted by deeper, established beliefs. The first institution to blossom under perestroika was the Russian orthodox Church. I walked into a church near Boris Pasternak's dacha in 1989 and heard priests and babushkas reciting the litany with perfect recall, as if seventy-two years of repression had never happened. Culture provides the slow template of change within which family, community and religion prosper. Culture stabilizes identity, and in a fast-changing world of displacement and rootlessness, becomes an ever more important anchor.

Between culture and business is a third time frame: governance, which moves faster than culture, slower than commerce. The fourth and slowest chronology is earth, nature and the web of life. As ephemeral as it may seem, it is the slowest clock, always present, responding to long, ancient evolutionary cycles that extend beyond any civilization's reckoning. Nature has the greatest inertia but the most resilience.

These chronologies often come into conflict. What makes life worthwhile and enables civilizations to endure are all the elements and qualities that have poor returns under commercial metrics: universities, temples, poetry, choirs, parks, literature, language, museums, terraced fields, long marriages, line dancing and art. Nearly everything humans hold valuable is slow to develop and slow to change. Healthy commerce requires the governance of politics, art, culture, civic society, and nature, to slow its pace, to make it heedful, to make it pay attention to people and place.

Paul Hawken
Blessed Unrest: How the Largest Social Movement in History is Restoring Grace, Justice, and Beauty to the World
2007, pp. 134-135

Orientation

Here are some texts that are directly focused on the nature of economic life as distinct from the current prevailing tendency to equate economy with business, in particular big business. What Niklas Luhmann has described earlier as 'functional domain' in general terms, becomes more concrete when one considers all of us as the constituency of this domain and takes the meaning of the word 'economy' as point of departure for a conversation on how to make this domain actually function for all. Paul Hawken contributes to this conversation by articulating the need to identify the different groups or categories which form this constituency entitled and responsible for the creation of a democratic, i.e. representative decision –making form of economic governance. Mao Tse-tung's understanding of the interplay between theory and practice is still static in comparison: interplay needs to be continuous, especially in economic life, where things are moving and changing by the day. Going to the people is no longer enough: the people need to be involved in the process of decision making. Theorists are 'people' too.

John Ruskin was brought to my attention through a proposal in the Guardian Weekly, to make his "Unto This Last" (1861) **COMPULSORY READING** for every politician.

This is a prophetic text in more than one sense: sharp in exposing the flaws in what is still the prevailing economic doctrine and realistic in its idealism by which it sets out the basic conditions for an economic life that is just and fruitful for all its constituents: unto this last…

I selected his image of the earth itself turning around its own axis as the ultimate source of all economic life, as a modern echo of the Finnish Sampo myth of the Kalevala: the 'sampo', a magic mill of cosmic proportions grinding salt, grain and money. The way the sampo is described in this Finnish Epic clearly points to the ribbon-like movements of the Aurora Borealis, which science now explains as the effect of interference of Sun energy with the earth's rotating magnetic field.

The text is very elaborate and concrete in what economy is not and what it could and should be. I have never read a text on economic life that is so through and through religious, christian, without being 'churchy', whilst through and through articulate in terms of the intellectual discourse of its time. And in it there is testimony out of the Judaic tradition to Martin Buber's saying: 'all real life is encounter', encounter between two men: one rich, one poor…

I have since learned that Mohandas Gandhi learned about Ruskin's book, in South Africa, studied it, took this text to heart, translated it and brought it into practice.

Ruskin's definition of economy of 1862 has been refreshed and extended by Pope Francis in his first Encyclical letter 'Gaudium Evangelii' of 2013.

In his chapter 'Towards a Theory of Large-scale Organisation' Schumacher begins with a quote from Pope Pius XI and ends with quoting Chairman Mao Tse Tung. The former has been quoted at length at the beginning of this Chapter 6. The latter will be quoted here below. Both formulations of this 'subsidiarity' principle will only be effective, if 1. it are ultimately the individuals themselves that are empowered to do what they do best. And 2. if there is constant feedback from the field of 'action' to field of 'theory'. At this time of writing, the worldwide Covid '19 crisis, putting unprecedented pressure on public services in the areas of health, economic welfare and education, workers in the field will have to 'think on their feet', and the workers who guide the action from above will need to adjust 'their theories' to facts. Public Services where people are trained to be competent and mutually trusting and trusted may in the end turn out to be the most effective.

The title of Ruskin's essay: 'Unto this last' comes from Jesus' parable of the workers in the orchard, which brings the nature of a fair wage (or salary, remuneration etc.) into sharp focus: a wage is not a price for work. Work is an integral part of a workers' life. Selling work is selling the worker, which is slavery. The notion of 'labour-market' denotes slavery under a different name. A wage is what makes work possible, i.e. makes the life of a worker possible with all that it entails, his or her responsibility for children, dependents etc...The parable is important enough to be presented here in full. Abolition of the notion and practice of 'labour-market', (worker as commodity), replaced by understanding wages and salaries etc. as a fair share in the revenue from the results of work, would be a first step in the direction of a functional economy.

Historic low for the human intellect

> So far as I know, there is not in history record of anything so disgraceful to the human intellect as the modern era, as the modern idea that the commercial text, "Buy in the cheapest market and sell in the dearest," represents, or under any circumstances could represent, an available principle of national economy. Buy in the cheapest market? Yes, but what made your market cheap? Charcoal may be cheap among your roof timbers after a fire, and bricks may be cheap in your streets after an earthquake; but fire and earthquakes may not therefore be national benefits. Sell in the dearest? – Yes, truly, but what made your market dear? You sold your bread well today: was it to a dying man who gave his last coin for it, and will never need bread more, or to a rich man, who tomorrow will buy your farm over your head; or to a soldier on his way to pillage the bank in which you have put your fortune?

None of these things you can know. One thing only you can know: namely whether this dealing of yours is a just and faithful one... sure thus to have done your part in bringing about...a state of things which will not issue in pillage or in death... pp. 23-24

John Ruskin
Unto This Last: Essays from the Cornhill Magazine
1860
[Reprinted as Unto This Last 1862]

Meeting face to face of rich and poor

Some centuries before the Christian era, a Jew merchant largely engaged in business on the Gold Coast...left amongst his ledgers some general maxims concerning wealth, which have been preserved...

[ ]

...the two most remarkable passages in their deep general significance are the following: -

"The rich and the poor have met. God is their maker."

"The rich and the poor have met. God is their light."

They "have met". More literally, have stood in each other's way (obviaverunt). That is to say, as long as the world lasts, the action and counteraction of wealth and poverty, the meeting face to face, of rich and poor, is just as appointed and necessary a law of that world as the flow of stream to sea, or the interchange of power among the electric clouds: - "God is their maker." But, also, this action may be either gentle and just, or convulsive and destructive: it may be by rage of devouring flood, or by lapse of serviceable wave: - in blackness of thunderstroke, or continual force of vital fire, soft, and shapeable into love-syllables from far away. And which of these shall be depends on both rich and poor knowing that God is their light, that in the mystery of human life, there is no other light than this by which they can see each other's faces, and live; - light, which is called in another of the books among which the merchant's maxims have been preserved, the "sun of justice,"... pp. 25, 27

Valor, from valere, to be well or strong; - strong, life (if a man), or valiant, strong for life (if a thing), or valuable. To be "valuable", therefore, is "to avail towards life." A truly valuable or availing thing is that which leads to life with its whole strength. In proportion as it does not lead to life, or as it is leads away from life, or as its strength is broken, it is less valuable; in proportion as it leads away from life, it is unvaluable or malignant.

The value of a thing, therefore, is independent of opinion, and of quantity. Think what you will of it, gain how much you may gain of it, the value of the whole thing itself is neither greater nor less. Forever it avails, or avails not; no estimate can raise, no disdain repress, the power which it holds from the Maker of things and of men.

The real science of political economy, which has yet to be distinguished from the bastard science, as medicine from witchcraft, and astrology from astronomy, is that which teaches nations to desire and labour for the things that lead to life; and which teaches them to scorn and destroy the things that lead to destruction.[ ] the great and only science of Political Economy teaches them....what is vanity, and what substance; and how the service of Death, the Lord of Waste, and of eternal emptiness, differs from the service of Wisdom, the Lady of Saving, and of eternal fullness; she who has said, "I will cause those that love me to inherit SUBSTANCE; and I will FILL their treasures." pp. 41-42

John Ruskin
Unto This Last: Essays from the Cornhill Magazine
1860
[Reprinted as Unto This Last 1862]

Interplay between theory and practice

The best formulation of the necessary interplay of theory and practice, that I know of, comes from Mao Tse-tung. Go to the practical people, he says, and learn from them: then synthesise their experiences into principles and theories; and then return to the practical people and call upon them to put these principles and methods into practice so as to solve their problems and achieve freedom and happiness.

E.F. Schumacher
Small is Beautiful: Economy as if People Mattered
1975, p. 253

An economy in search of representative form of governance?

Just as democracies require an informed and active citizenry to prevent abuse, markets require constant tending to prevent them from being diverted and exploited. A free market, so lovely in theory, is no more feasible in practice than a society without laws. Democracies can sustain freedom because their citizens and representatives continually adjust, maintain, and as necessary enforce standards, rules and laws. Markets are unequalled in providing feedback, fostering innovation, and allocating resources. Market competition is ultimately a matter of financial capital: those activities that most efficiently accrete and concentrate money gain market advantage; those that don't are marginalized. But there is no comparable competition to improve social or natural capital, because markets for such commodities simply don't exist. The only way those issues are dealt with is through legislation, regulation, citizen activity, and consumer pressure. Removing the laws and regulations that create market constraints leaves the body politic with very few means to promote economic democracy. The localized poor, primary forests, the stratosphere, and ecosystem viability, which are the source if life for every economy in the world, have no voice at all in market systems. The voice comes from citizen organizations, although when it does, it is often ignored or patronized.

Paul Hawken
Blessed Unrest: How the Largest Social Movement in History is Restoring Grace, Justice, and Beauty to the World
2007, p. 132

The earth: the mill and the house

The Earth: '...the eternal engine, whose beam is the earth's axle, whose beat is its year, and whose breath is its ocean, will still divide imperiously to their desert kingdoms, bound with unfurrowable rock, and swept by unarrested sand, their powers of frost and fire: but the zones and lands between, habitable, will be loveliest in habitation. The desire of the heart is also the light of the eyes...'

[ ]

'...all true economy is "Law of the house." Strive to make that law strict, simple, generous: waste nothing, and grudge nothing. Care in no wise to make more of money, but care to make much of it; remembering always the great, palpable, inevitable fact -- the rule and root of all economy -- that what one person has, another cannot have; and that every atom of substance, of whatever kind, used or consumed, is so much human life spent; which, if it issued in the saving present life, or gaining more, is well spent, but if not, is either so much life prevented, or so much slain...'

John Ruskin

Unto This Last
1862

The House: Our common home which is the whole world

Just as the commandment "Thou shalt not kill" sets a clear limit in order to safeguard the value of human life, today we also have to say "thou shalt not" to an economy of exclusion and inequality. Such an economy kills.

[ ]

Today everything comes under the laws of competition and the survival of the fittest, where the powerful feed upon the powerless.

[ ]

Human beings are themselves considered consumer goods to be used and then discarded. We have created a "disposable culture" which is now spreading.

[ ]

Exclusion ultimately has to do with what it means to be part of the society in which we live; those excluded are no longer society's underside or its fringes or its disfranchised – they are no longer even a part of it. The excluded are not "exploited" but the outcasts, the "leftovers".

[ ]

This opinion (the "trickle effect" theory), which has never been confirmed by the facts, expresses a crude and naive trust in the goodness of those wielding economic power and in the sacralized workings of the prevailing economic system. Meanwhile the excluded are still waiting.

Welfare projects, which meet certain urgent needs, should be considered merely temporary responses. As long as the problems of the poor are not radically resolved by rejecting the absolute autonomy of markets and financial speculation and by attacking the structural causes of inequality*), no solution will be found for the world's problems or, for that matter, to any problem. Inequality is the root of social ills.

*) This implies a commitment to "eliminate causes of global economic dysfunction" Benedict XVI 8 Jan 2007.

[ ]

We need to be convinced that charity "is the principle not only of micro-relationships (with friends, with family members or within small groups) but also of macro-relationships (social, economic and political ones). Benedict XVI 28 June 2009.

[ ]

It is vital that government leaders and financial leaders take heed and broaden their horizons, working to ensure that all citizens have dignified work, education and healthcare. Why not turn to God and ask him to inspire their plans? I am firmly convinced that openness to the transcendent can bring about a new political and economic mindset which would help to break down the wall of separation between the economy and the common good of society.

Economy as the very word indicates, should be the art of achieving a fitting management of our common home, which is the world as a whole.

Pope Francis
Gaudium Evangelii
2013, pp. 47-48,152-154

The Earth a Cosmic Mill

Then the winds arose in fury,
Blew the east wind, blew the west wind,
And the south wind yet more strongly,
And the north wind howled and blustered.
Thus they blew one day, a second,
And upon the third day likewise.
Fire was flashing from the windows,
From the door the sparks were flying
And the dust arose to heaven;
With the clouds the smoke was mingled.
Then again smith Ilmarinen.
On the evening of the third day,
Stooped him down, and gazed intently,
To the bottom of the furnace;
And he saw the Sampo forming,
With its brightly coloured cover.
Thereupon smith Ilmarinen,

He the great primeval craftsman,
Welded it and hammered at it,
Heaped his rapid blows upon it,
Forged with cunning art the Sampo:
On one side there was a corn-mill,
On another side a salt-mill
And upon the third a coin-mill.

Now was grinding the new Sampo,
And revolved the pictured cover,
Chestfuls did it grind till evening,
First for food it ground a chestful,
And another ground for barter,
And a third it ground for storage.

Now rejoiced the crone of Pohja,
And conveyed the bulky Sampo,
To the rocky hills of Pohja,
And within the Mount of Copper,
And behind nine locks secured it;
There it struck its roots around it,
Fathoms nine in depth that measured,
One in Mother Earth deep-rooted,
In the strand the next was planted,
In the nearest mount the third one.

Michael Branch, William Forsell Kirby (Translator)
Kalevala: The Land of the Heroes / Verses 393 - 431
1985

Aboriginal Economy is knowledge based

The Nhunggabarra – and most likely Australian Aboriginal societies – had developed something that the industrialised world is still struggling with: a truly sustainable society on earth. Isolated on the Australian island continent, they had developed and fine-tuned their model. It had withstood and proven its sustainability over ten-thousands of years of dramatic events until their economy was destroyed by a force coming from outside their system.

[   ]

A striking feature of the Nhuggabarra society is their knowledge based economy. Because food and a few personalised tools were the only tangible production that scientist and economists recognised and were able to measure, these scientists and economists long dismissed Aboriginal economy as producing very low value. What they missed was more than half the economy – that is, Aboriginal society's very high production of intangible value: education, knowledge, art, law, entertainment, medicine, spiritual ceremonies, peacekeeping and social welfare.

Karl-Erik Sveiby and Tex Skuthorpe
Treading Lightly: The Hidden Wisdom of the World's Oldest People
2006, pp. 169-172

The dignity of work and the educational effect of a societal arrangement

Unemployment is the most hideous of our social evils…It has not been sufficiently appreciated that this moral isolation is the heaviest burden and most corrosive poison associated with unemployment: not bodily hunger, but social futility…nothing will touch the real need except the man to do something which is needed by the community. For it is part of the principle of personality that we should live for one another…

The only real cure for unemployment is employment…beginning from the time when school education is complete and continuing, with no longer intervals than can be appreciated as holidays, till strength begins to fail. In other words we are challenged to find a social order which provides employment, steadily and generally, and our conscience should be restive till we succeed. Christian sympathy demands this.

…the second ground for the Church's concern in social questions (is) the educational influence of the social and economic system in which men live. …If the State is so ordered as to give great prominence to military leaders as Sparta was, as Prussia was, as Nazi Germany is, this must represent the fact that the effective body of citizens, which may be a compact minority, regards the military qualities as specially honourable or important; and the system expressing that estimate impresses it by perpetual suggestion upon every growing generation. So it is if wealth receives conspicuous honour…

…Our system is not deliberately planned but it produces effects just the

same. It offers a perpetual suggestion in the direction of a combative self-assertiveness. It is recognized on all hands that the economic is an educative influence, for good or ill, of immense potency...

...in the economic field, the reason why goods are produced is that men may satisfy their needs by consuming the goods. Production by its own natural law exists for consumption. If then a system comes into being in which production is regulated more by profit for the producer than by the needs of the consumer, that system is defying the natural law or natural order...

William Temple, Christianity and the Social Order, 1942, in: Canon
A.E. Baker's
William Temple and his Message
1946

There is no dignity in being treated as disposable...

We need to shift the way we define and perceive physical work. Replacing people has been defined as liberating people from work. Physical work has been defined as drudgery and as degrading.

[ ] Destroyers of work and employment always present destruction as liberation. Yet there is no liberation in being robbed of one's productive capacity. There is no dignity in being treated as disposable.

To make the energy transition beyond oil, we need to bring people back into the economy, bring human energy back into production, respect physical work, and give it dignity. Climate change is giving us adequate warning that substituting people with fossil fuel is ecologically unsustainable. Social and cultural breakdown should likewise be recognized as a warning about the social unsustainability of displacing people from work.

Vandana Shiva
Soil Not Oil: Climate Change, Peak Oil, and Food Insecurity
2009, pp. 186,188

Dignity of work: three functions, the Buddhist view

...the Buddhist sees the essence of civilisation not in a multiplication of wants but in the purification of human character. Character, at the same time, is formed primarily by a man's work. And work, properly conducted in conditions of human dignity and freedom, blesses those who do it and equally their products. p. 55

The Buddhist point of view takes the function of work to be at least threefold: to give a man a chance to utilise and develop his faculties; to enable him, to overcome the ego-centredness by joining with other people in a common task; and to bring the goods and services needed for a becoming existence. p. 55

E.F. Schumacher
***Small is Beautiful: Economics as if people mattered** / Chapter 4: Buddhist Economics*
1975

Parable of the vineyard labourers

Now the kingdom of heaven is like a landowner going out at daybreak to hire workers for his vineyard. He made an agreement with the workers for one denarius a day, and sent them to his vineyard. Going out at about the third hour he saw others standing idle in the market place and said to them, "You go to my vineyard too and I will give you a fair wage". So they went. At about the sixth hour and again about the ninth hour, he went out and did the same. Then about the eleventh hour he went out and found more men standing round, and he said to them, "Why have you been standing here idle all day?" "Because no one has hired us" they answered. He said to them, "You go into my vineyard too.". In the evening, the owner of the vineyard said to his bailiff, "Call the workers and pay them their wages, starting with the last arrivals and ending with the first". So those who were hired at about the eleventh hour came forward and received one denarius each. When the first came, they expected to get more, but they too received one denarius each. They took it but grumbled at the landowner. "The men who came last" they said "have done only one hour, and you have treated them the same as us, though we have done a heavy day's work in all the heat." He answered one of them and said, "My friend, I am not being unjust to you: did we not agree on one denarius? Take your earnings and go. I choose to pay the last-comer as much as I pay you. Have I no right to do what I like with my own? Why be envious because I am generous?" Thus the last one will be the first, and the first the last.

Matthew 20:1-16
Jerusalem Bible
Popular Edition
1974

Michael Moore: Call for a new economic order

What I am asking for is a new economic order.
I don't know how to construct that. I am not an economist.

*All I ask is that it has two organising principles.
Number one, that the economy is run democratically.
In other words, the people have a say in how it's run, not just the 1%
And number two, that it has an ethical and moral core to it.
That nothing is done without considering the ethical nature,
no business decision is made without first asking the question,
is this for the common good?*

Interview with Chris McGreal
Regarding his film: Capitalism: A Love Story
2010, pp. 32-33

Food Sovereignty

*Seed Sovereignty (Beej Swaraj), Food Sovereignty (Anna Swaraj),
Water Sovereignty (Jal Swaraj) and Land Sovereignty (Bhu Swaraj).
We need once more to feel at home on the earth and with each other.*

We need a new paradigm to respond to the fragmentation caused by various forms of fundamentalism. We need a new movement, which allows us to move from the dominant and pervasive culture of violence, destruction and death to a culture of non-violence, creative peace and life. That is why in India, Navdanya started the Earth democracy movement, which provides an alternative worldview in which humans are embedded in the Earth Family, we are connected to each other through love, compassion, not hatred and violence and ecological responsibility and economic justice replaces greed, consumerism and competition as objectives of human life.

Following Gandhji's inspiration from the Salt Satyagraha we declared the launch of 'Bija Satyagraha' against Seed Laws and Patent Laws that seek to make sharing and saving of seed a crime by making seed the "Property" of companies like Monsanto, forcing us to pay royalties for what is our collective heritage. The Bija Swaraj campaign, launched by Navdanya, demands that Indian laws do not legalise patents on seed and food, and TRIPs is reviewed to exclude patents on seed and food. Under Bija Swaraj, we pledge to protect sovereignty to save our seeds and grow our food freely without MNCs domination and control. We have received the precious gift of biodiversity and seeds from nature and our ancestors and we pledge to protect our rich biological heritage and fundamental freedom to save and exchange seeds.

At the Anna Panchayat (Public Tribunal on Hunger) in May 2001, Navdanya launched its campaign on food rights and food sovereignty

(AnnaSwaraj) for a genuinely decentralized democratic and sustainable food system. The entry of companies like Cargill into direct procurements, transportation and processing is leading to the closure of small local and larger agro-processing units that provide livelihoods to lots of people. We demand that food be accepted as a Fundamental Human Right and is produced and distributed in a democratic manner.

Pressured by the World Bank, W.T.O. and corporate interests, the Indian government has been trying to sign away water rights to giant MNCs like Coca Cola and Vivendi, ignoring concerns for people's needs, sustainability and democratic access to water. In the year 2000, Navdanya launched the Jal Swaraj Movement to protect our water from privatization and commodification and to promote traditional water harvesting systems and equitable access to water. RFSTE and Citizens Front for Water Democracy (a coalition of more than 100 groups) have successfully stopped the World Bank scheme of privatizing Delhi's water supply to Suez, effectively stealing Ganga water from farmers. We have also stopped Coca Cola's thievery of Kerala's ground water, creating profits by hoarding from and polluting the water that belonged to the commons. We are also collaborating with farmer groups from Bundelkhand and Uttarankhand to fight against the River Linking Projects like Ken-Betwa and Sharda-Yamuna, which are nothing but theft of our water and water heritage.

Bhu Swaraj is the foundation for economic and food security. Nevertheless, India's economic growth has violently dispossessed millions from their land and fundamental rights, as massive land grabs are perpetuated by the state and corporations. We oppose this corporate-hijack because land is a sacred trust for human sustenance and cannot be used as a commodity with no concern for the lives of people. Strongly believing that land must belong to those who till it and nurse it and for whom it is a source of sustenance, we immediately call for measures to ensure land sovereignty.

Vandana Shiva, Navdanya Organic
Food Sovereignty

Dao: the wisdom of restraint

It is best to have small communities with few people.
And although they have goods and equipment in abundance
few of them are even used.
They have great love of life,
and are content to be right where they are.

And although they have boats and carriages,
there is no place they particularly want to go.
And although they have access to weapons and machineries of war,
they have no desire to show them off.

Let people return to simplicity,
Then they will find joy in their food
Beauty in their simple clothes
peace in their living
Fulfilment in their traditions.

And although they live within sight of neighbouring states
And their roosters and dogs are heard by one another
The people are content to grow old and die
Without having gone to see their neighbour states.

Lao Tzu. Tao Te Ching/Chapter 80
Rev John Mabry
God as Nature Sees God: A Christian Reading of the Tao Te Ching
1994, p. 104

Two of the many texts on usury in the Holy Qur'an

Those who spend their wealth, night and day, in secret
or in public, shall have their reward with their Lord. No
fear shall fall upon them, nor shall they grieve.

Those who consume usury shall not rise from the dead except like
one whom Satan causes to babble from madness. This is because
they allege that commerce is the same as usury. But God has made
commerce licit and usury illicit. So he to whom a word of counsel from
his Lord has reached, and desists, may keep his previous profit, and
his affair is up to God. But he who relapses, these are the inhabitants
of the Fire, in which they dwell eternally. God annuls usury and
augments free gifts. God loves not every impious lawbreaker.

Tarif Khalidi
The Qur'an / The Cow 2:276
2008

O believers, fear God and abandon what remains of usury if you are
true believers. If you do not, be forewarned of conflict with God and his
messenger. If you repent, you will keep the capital of your wealth, neither
wronging nor wronged. If a person is in difficulties, let there be respite until

a time of ease. And if you give freely, it would be better for you, if only you knew. Fear a Day in which you shall return to God, when each soul shall be paid back that which it has earned. And they shall not be wronged.

Tarif Khalidi
The Qur'an / The Cow 2:281
2008

Investment credit: From 1000% (usury) to 17% (interest).

The prohibition of usury has found its modern expression in Mahammed Yunus's founding and developing the micro-credit movement through the Grameen Bank in Bangladesh, initially reducing the interest on loans for women from 1000 percent per year to ca. 17 percent...

Henk Bak

Enduring structures: time to process

...Complex systems need time to process information and come up with apt responses. As a consequence, they must include at least some structures or parts not directly embroiled in determining specific reactions. If external events required everything to be changed at once, all complex systems would be eliminated. System differentiation, in fact, is a structural technique for solving the temporal problems of complex (i.e. time consuming) systems situated in complex environments.

Niklas Luhmann
The Differentiation of Society
1982

Future oriented economy: real consumption versus illusory consumerism

...economic life does not seem to depend on specific determinable needs. Instead, it has to do with the possibility of deferring a decision about the satisfaction of needs while providing a guarantee that they will be satisfied and so utilizing the time thus acquired. From this point of view, the fundamental problem of the economy lies in the dimension of time. All life flows through the inescapable present. By opening up and pacifying a future perspective of this present, the economy is able to clear a space for action in the meantime and thus for rationality as well: we can specify needs and the means for satisfying them only to the extent that we can defer some of these needs and guarantee their satisfaction in the future.

[ ]

Our thesis that the problem to be focused upon lies in the temporal dimension can be checked if we look at the economy in its relation to the immediate satisfaction of needs (consumption). The real possibilities for consumption are held within anthropologically fixed limits and thus they remain very small... Today, through an illusory premium put on consumption, ...[economic development] creates the respect for money that is needed for a comprehensive mastery of the future. Here we can see that it is the temporal dimension that "leads the way". The conspicuous consumption described by Veblen forms only one aspect of this situation. Here too belongs above all the continual enshrouding of consumer goods with arbitrarily high values, as well as nonmonetary scales for heightening consumption – such as rarity, novelty etc. pp. 195-196

Niklas Luhmann
The Differentiation of Society
1982

In Praise of an Accomplished Woman

A perfect woman – who can find her?
She is far beyond the price of pearls.
The members of her household have confidence in her,
from her they will derive no little profit.
Advantage and not hurt she brings them
all the days of her life.
She is always busy with wool and with flax,
she does her work with eager hands.
She is like a merchant vessel
bringing her food from faraway.

She gets up while it is still dark
giving her household their food,
giving orders to the workers.
She sets her mind on a field, then she buys it;
with what her hands have earned she plants a vineyard.
She puts her back into her work
and shows how strong her arms can be.
She finds her labour well worth while,

her lamp does not go out at night.
She sets her hands to the distaff,
her fingers grasp the spindle.

She holds out her hand to the poor,
she opens her arms to the needy.
Snow may come, she has no fears for her household,
with all her servants warmly clothed.
She makes her own quilts,
she is dressed in fine linen and purple.
Members of her household are respected at the city gates,
taking their seats among the elders of the land.
She weaves linen sheets and sells them,
she supplies the merchant with sashes.

She is clothed in strength and dignity,
she can laugh at the days to come.
When she opens her mouth she does so wisely;
on her tongue is kindly instruction.
She keeps good watch on the conduct of her household,
no bread of idleness for her.
The members of her household stand up and proclaim her blessed,
her partners, too, sing her praises:
"Many households have achieved admirable things,
but you surpass them all!"
Charm is deceitful, and beauty empty;
a wise economy is the one to praise.
Give her a share in what her hands have worked for,
and let her works tell her praises at the city gates.

> This poetic picture of woman, here taken as embodiment of a healthy economy, has been, with only a few alterations, taken from The Book of Proverbs in the translation of the Jerusalem Bible.
> ***An Alphabetic Poem on the perfect Wife. Proverbs 31: 10-28***
> 1974, pp. 852-853

This picture could have been taken from everywhere in the ancient world around the Mediterranean, including the Greek world, where the word economy sums up its essence in the combination of

1. 'oikos' = house, dwelling place, now written as 'ecos', in ecology, the earth as the natural home for humanity; and,

2. 'nomos', from the verb 'nemein' = measuring, allocating rightly (cfr: astronomy = measuring, locating the stars, the heavens rightly).

So, together: house-hold on a farm, an estate, a merchant house in town, a family home, everywhere in traditional communities, even now, one can find them. Especially nowadays Grandmothers looking after families with parents away to work or war or who died of aids...

Comment in the Jewish Bible, the Tanach:

The concluding verses of Proverbs are the famous paean to the righteous woman, which is chanted in Jewish homes at the beginning of the first Sabbath meal. The Hebrew word Chayil as used in Scripture implies more than just valor; it includes the possession of whatever attributes are needed to carry out the task at hand. The hymn contains a Hebrew alphabethical acrostic as a further allusion her all-encompassing virtues. This passage has been interpreted as a metaphor for the Shechinnah (Divine Presence) the Sabbath, the Torah, and the soul.

N. Scherman
The Artscroll English Tanach: Stone Edition: The Jewish Bible
2011, p. 1053

Orientation

'How fortunate, that there are insights and documented facts to show the way, not only out of the sciences of spirit and culture (humanities), but also out of natural scientific perspectives.'

The discovery, in neuro-science, of the plasticity of the brain, less than half a century ago and subsequent development of neuro-biology, brings an extra dimension to all of the above and suggests how functional differentiation of society would reflect the very procedure, the brain itself would follow when faced with unmanageable complexity.

Avoiding incoherence is the brain's strategy to respond to a complexity that has become unmanageable. If state and society are considered and managed as one domain. And if this one domain has grown in complexity to a point, where its management is becoming incoherent, the intelligent strategy would be to differentiate the one domain into domains that by dint of a certain internal, 'natural' coherence might be less complex to manage. To govern a domain one needs experience and competence. Those responsible for governing society as one domain, are increasingly confronted by issues outside their experience and competence, which is to make laws and to enforce them. Abandoning the fiction that society and state are one, and recognizing society's other domains in their own right, would avoid incoherence for those responsible, ultimately for all of us. We would elect in each domain those who have shown experience and competence within the domain in question. This is not the place to work this out in detail, but as our world-views have a bearing on society as a whole, the issue of an intelligent and coherent response to an increasingly dysfunctional world must be an urgent theme for our dialogue…

Unprecedented increase in complexity calls for an inner compass

The highly technified, digital and globalized world arose as a provisional result of these themselves re-enforcing developments. And in this highly complex, inseparable entangled and in all areas mutually dependent world, a problem has now arisen, that in the whole history of humanity has never occurred. The old hierarchical ordering structure turns out to be in principle not suited to secure the stability of this highly developed society of today, let alone to steer its future development. It has lost its power to provide orientation and to establish order through the exact process that it had generated itself: an enormous increase in complexity.

There is no way forward in 'more of the old', i.e. no falling back on the hierarchical ordering structure that has been hitherto effective. There is however also no way forward without any orientation providing structure.

This is the dilemma in which our present, highly developed societies are caught. The only way out is only available, when they succeed in enabling their members to create an individual organizing principle that is, however, equally valid for all, and binding. They all need therefore something like an inner compass, its needle pointing in the same direction: to where they shape their life and their living together in the consciousness of their dignity as human beings.

Every civilization reaches at some time a stage of its development, where it cannot go further as it has been used to. The solution for this problem then required, however, lies within – and therewith in the human beings that go through this development through generations – from the beginning onwards innate as biological possibility and potential.

[ ]

In our own constitution, or more precise, in the inner organization and way of working of the human brain there must therefore exist something that not only makes possible, but sometime even urgently necessary, that we human beings develop a concept of our own human dignity...(which) has something to do with the enormous openness and lifelong pliability of the human brain. pp. 67-68

A sufficiently complex brain and a capacity of all to focus on the same.

Two experiences, those of painful failing in the pursuit of one's own view as well as encounters with other human beings and their views, which put one's own ideas and concepts into question, both experiences run like a red thread through the whole history of humanity. As recent as the last century it has become clear that even totalitarian power systems are in the long term incapable of imposing their particular views at the cost of others. Even the terrible attempts - through wars and suppression - to maintain the self-images and world-views that have been developed by those (totalitarian) communities, have in the end failed again. The encounter of human beings and the exchange of their distinct views are apparently not to be suppressed forever.

Never before was this phenomenon that runs through human history so publicly recognizable as now, at the beginning of the 21st century. Firstly a perspective opens itself herewith, that inevitably leads to a decisive question: what does connect us human beings despite our distinctly different origins, experiences and historic contexts. This, too, can only be a view developed by human beings, a view however that human beings share, not despite but because of their mutual differentiation.

No ideology, no religion, no ethical or moral value concept is suitable for this. The only common view that connects human beings in all their differences can only express the experience they have made themselves, the experience of their own dignity. To discover in ourselves our deepest humanity becomes therewith the most important task of the 21st century.

How fortunate, that there are insights and documented facts to show the way, not only out of the sciences of spirit and culture ('humanities'), but also out of natural scientific perspectives.

The for our own self-understanding most important insight says: We human beings are social beings.

[ ]

Human communities are always individualized communities. --- To be able to form such communities it didn't only need a sufficiently complex brain that is as long as possible capable of learning. It also needed the capacity to focus the attention of all members of such a community on what happens for all to see… pp. 83-84

Reducing complexity, avoiding incoherence under the guidance of an overarching concept or idea of what constitutes the human being as a person.

…a very interesting basic principle can be derived from the second law of thermodynamics, that doesn't only determine the way the human brain works, but also how it is structured. By all that goes on up there, it concerns a most possible optimal utilisation of the energy reserves that are supplied by the body in the form of glucose and oxygen, transported to the brain by the blood.

[ ]

Especially interesting and effective is the natural tendency in the brain's working towards reducing complexity…the formation of automatisms and of overarching patterns towards coordinated streamlining of a multitude of single actions and single reactions…

…this makes it then also possible to guide our

attitudes with as little energy as possible.

[ ]

Interestingly, the development of these inner dispositions and attitudes is also guided by an overarching pattern anchored in the brain. This, too, is only being acquired in the course of life…In the widest sense it is a matter of an image or idea of what constitutes the human being as a person. At the same time it also includes what kind of human being one wants to be, whereby one orientates oneself in one's life and one's decisions.

The scientific term for this condition…is coherence. It is a condition, in which everything fits as well and frictionless together as possible. It is then, that the energy consumption required for the maintenance of the internal order of the system in question is the lowest.

When a person does not succeed in developing an inner image of who he wants to be, then he lacks this order providing orientation, and then much of what he thinks and what he does, doesn't fit so well together. It leads then to an increasing incoherence, and this is always accompanied by an increase in energy consumption.

[ ]

In a constantly changing world, the narrowing and limiting of one's own possibilities to perceive, to imagine, to create is…not a long lasting, sustainable solution. Whoever has stayed in the evolution so undifferentiated and hardly specialized as the representatives of our species are, will only be able to survive the continual change of his own life world by constantly developing himself further. To this end a high level of openness and own capacity to change are necessary, and hence a brain capable of lifelong learning has evolved as a distinctive feature of our species.

Gerald Hüther and Uli Hauser
Würde: Was uns Stark Macht – als Einzelne und als Gesellschaft [Dignity: What Makes us Strong – as Individual and as Society]
2018, pp. 93-99
[Translated by Henk Bak]

A final quote with a warning

Arab Nationalist Syria faced three major opposition forces…

> *Its secularism was opposed by political Islam,*
> *its Arab nationalism by Israel and the United States*
> *and its Arab socialism by Wall Street.*
>
> Stephen Gowans
Washington's Long War on Syria
2017, p. 133

Comment:

This final quote comes with a strong warning concerning all of the above:

Even though Gowan's summing up of the challenge faced by Syria neatly addresses a need for a differentiation into cultural/ideological, political and economic domains, this doesn't mean that any of the above offers a method for realizing this differentiation.

Each nation state, each modern democracy would be faced with different but similar challenges, to a greater or lesser extent.

This anthology is not meant to offer solutions or 'blueprints' for how to go about these challenges. Its purpose is to widen and deepen the common 'ground' of our conversations in the hope and confidence, that together they may give us, participants, a sense of direction in which to find responses to these challenges: responses which are both realistic and in line with our ideals and the original impulses out which our world-views have arisen…

For study, reflection and conversation

> *After wandering through a wide and diverse range of texts, it might be worthwhile to rest and reflect on what it means to break with the notion, that lawfulness is determined by legislation alone, i.e. by the only domain in which we, its constituents – as human beings – are equals. The two other domains, in which we - as constituents - are in principle unequal, need to be governed under another lawfulness. The question is then, how to understand in principle the nature of cultural and of economic lawfulness.*
>
> *Using Shin's circle verse of transformation, we might be able to articulate this question in some concrete detail: What kind of protection would the law grant in cultural matters, say education or healing? And how would economic lawfulness protect us as constituents of the economic domain?*

We might keep in mind that, just as is the case with Buddha's eightfold path, this verse is cyclic, so that the 'good law' of the first cycle 'grants protection' on a new level. And just as with the Sharia, in Gazi's understanding, the law is an implicit expression of divine love before this becomes manifested through justice.

Circle Verse of Transformation

Law grants Protection
Protection grants Unfolding
Unfolding grants Strength
Strength grants Encounter
Encounter grants Appraisal
Appraisal grants Deliberation
Deliberation grants Hearing
Hearing grants Justice
Justice grants Love
Love grants Insight
Insight grants Truth
Truth grants Freedom
Freedom grants Peace
Peace grants the Good Law
This is the Seal of the New Reign.

Shin Gwydion Fontalba
2008

7. Anthology – Ceremonies, Rites & Practices

So the counsellor commits himself humbly to his task, entering in the reality that has found form in another human being,
thoughtfully aware of the word: take your shoes from your feet,
for you stand on sacred ground

Jaap van Praag
1953

Introduction

The study that was part of the walking meditation project began as a preparation for the meditation itself and then for the talks and hand-outs. This involved 'reading' in the two meanings of the word: 'making sense of words' on pages in books, etc., and 'gleaning' or selecting texts. In the hand-outs the texts were arranged in a certain order, with captions to show the way through them. These texts ended up as an anthology and their captions as a study: the whole became a book. Within the book the order is reversed, the introductory study is written in hindsight as it were, the anthology is composed in chapters, the first three by way of orientation: dialogue, concepts and the call for renewal, the last three by way of practical application: principles, forms and actual rituals and prayers, of which the meditative walk is the one from which this project started. Central to the book is experience: Implied in the other chapters and in the introductory study – explicit in Chapter 4, where it is considered as an essential element halfway the progression from orientation, which requires a certain standing back, to being 'in here', not 'out there' (Brother David) and then toward practical application, as in paying the 'exceedingly high price for peace' (Brother David) which requires choice and commitment. The standing back allows for a most diverse range of views to be considered and – as in a conversation – an opportunity to dispel apparent conceptual differences and perhaps to transcend the level on which some differences are still real. Choice and commitment enable people and communities to break old forms where they have lost their meaning and are still holding back a next step in development, and where new forms are arising out of new experiences, perceptions, ways of thinking and communicating. Experience is in the moment, now, moment also as in 'momentum', tipping point or turning point, where the 'I' of the individual or the 'WE' of the new collective, moves from contemplation to action.

This final chapter ends where the original project started: with prayer and meditative practice, ritual and ceremony. There are two strands: first a variety of practices for everyday life and special occasions, ending more specifically with the ways we receive, appreciate, consume and express our gratitude for food and the innumerable blessings humanity is receiving from times immemorial and is being enriched with on a daily basis. Then a variety of ways in which we welcome children in this world and accompany those who have left this earth for their 'vast journey in other realms of existence (Shin).

This chapter presents a scattering of practices, more an indication that practices do exist and make sense, than a true representation of what happens. What counts for all selections of texts, counts even more strongly here, where daily life on virtually every place on earth is involved. In institutionalized religions prayer has become more and more a speaking, and to lesser extent a singing practice, where in earlier times and in traditional religions, the whole body is involved, in processions and dances, inclinations and gestures with the hands. In the predominantly Catholic southern region of the Netherlands, I have still experienced and participated in seasonal processions through the countryside to pray for a good crop and give thanks for a good harvest. In Echternach, Luxemburg, a yearly dance procession takes place, in which I participated in the 60's, but which now have become more popular as a spectacle and tourist attraction. As a child and young man I participated in the meditative walk along the '14 Stations of the Cross', mentioned by Henri Nouwen, who makes a strong connection between prayer and action, as a form of 'liturgical renewal'. I quote a passage from the Tanach, describing how King David danced in front of the Ark. The psalms are full of references to trumpets and cymbals in the service of the Highest. Many practices of the East have become popular in the West as well as the practices from indigenous traditions. And there is a growing interest in the whirling dance of the Dervishes. In Victoria where I live and elsewhere in Australia, public events often begin with an acknowledgement of the traditional custodians or owners of the land, and Aboriginal elders are often invited to perform smoking or 'welcome to country' ceremonies, to mark special events. For Reconciliation Prayer Week 1999 I wrote a 'Reconciliation Prayer' that was published in two Aboriginal newsletters. This prayer is based on the structure of the 'Lord's Prayer', a prayer that would be very suitable for many if not all religions, if it had not been identified as Christian. As many of Jeshua's teachings, this one easily transcends the boundaries of one particular faith. It originates in a Jewish prayer and translates meaningfully in a multicultural society of our time. I enclose Rabbi Zalman's all-embracing prayer, traditional, modern, East and West, deeply concerned with our common home: our earth, as well as some prayers for a secular world. Again, there is a wealth to choose from, but these few examples must suffice.

There are some texts on the significance of forgiveness: e.g. that on approaching the altar and remembering that someone has a grudge against you, you are to reconcile first and bring your sacrifice later. This first admonition in the Sermon on the Mount, resonates with Dr Muller's 'Decide to forgive' and the 'Reconciliation Prayer'. The 'Prayer for Peace', usually ascribed to St Francis of Assisi, was actually anonymously published in 1912 in a monthly newsletter called: 'Clochettes'. This newsletter was dedicated to those who service on the altar, including the altar boys who ring the little bells, 'clochettes'. Written in the spirit of St Francis, it was also in line with Jeshua's admonition to forgive first and sacrifice later. And I wonder whether one might extend its meaning by including one's offerings on the altar of public office: public speaking not before one has reconciled with whoever one is in conflict with, would go a long way on the road of peace, not towards peace, because 'peace is the way' (A.J. Muste quoted by Thich Nhat Hanh).

Renewal as an essential and a common concern to all religious and spiritual cultures, can happen in the ways in which children are welcomed and received when they come to this earth with all the gifts of renewal they bring from where they come from. As I found little on this subject in the general, encyclopaedic literature, I resorted to descriptions I found on the internet. It might be inspiring and helpful to realize how different traditions understand, appreciate how children come to us and prepare and care for their reception and welcome.

These descriptions might also draw attention to what is missing: a sense that it is the children who bring renewal. They come with needs, with expectations, with questions and with ways of answering questions and challenges which can be quite revealing, if they are given the space to play them out. It is in play that the new gets a chance to be born and children's play is a learning that embraces the whole spectrum of what is to be learned: a process of integration, that our adult culture is rapidly losing.

Apart from texts that are descriptive of a diversity of approaches, I also made some rather personal choices, of texts that have lived for a long time with me, and reflect something of a much more direct experience within a particular culture: David Mowaljarlai's boyhood memories, the young boy Samuel learning to listen and respond to an inner call, in meditation or prayer, and his mother, Hannah, humiliated because barren, praying to God for the gift of a child, rejoicing when her prayer was answered. But, already – her prayer finished – she "had no longer the same look on her face". I read for the fine, experiential detail wherever I can in the choice of the texts. Her song of praise echoed by Mary's joy, in response Elizabeth's greeting: both Mary and Hannah part of generation after generation of women, praying, aware that one amongst them will be the mother of the anointed One, promised to her people.

Hannah Arendt's concept of "natality", dialogue, spaces (and times) where people are free to speak out of their own selves, as a birthplace of renewal, encapsulates the importance of language in education, the mother tongue, the capacity, even the vocabulary to be able to express a child's inner experiences and spiritual aspirations. Our increasingly "functional" language and reduction of letter writing to "texting" and images to "icons", live storytelling to manufactured video versions etc. deprives children of this essential element in their full development as human beings.

The way Jeshua places a child and children at the centre of the moral space of his teaching, touches me as especially pertinent and urgent in our prevailing culture, which robs children at an ever younger age of their own childhood, making them function in the machinery of an adult world that has lost its bearings. Out of their own resources religions and spiritual cultures urgently need to create sanctuaries for childhood and inspire their members, as parents, educators and responsible adults to slow down the educational machinery, allow children to fully live, experience and enjoy their age, supported by meaningful traditions and encouraging their own explorations. Traditional festivals, holy times like Sabbath and Ramadan, a "radiant month in a darkening world" (Fethullah Gülen) and new forms of retreats (Alain de Botton), seminars, workshops, pilgrimages, including meditative walks offer such space-times for reflection: for speaking out of one's own self and – in dialogue – for becoming sources of renewal. Participating in rituals and festivals, singing, praying, dancing, reliving stories are for children a form of learning that only later needs to become elucidated by formal teaching and intellectual learning which, together with rituals, etc. would remain a lifetime growth process.

Childhood spiritual experiences religious or otherwise: those of David Mowaljarlai, Valentin Tomberg, Jodi, Kirstin, Marilynne Robinson draw attention to the way an adult world makes an imprint on a child's inner life or soul, even for life. In Goethe's "utopian" educational precinct, greeting itself gets spiritual significance, through gestures expressive of respect towards what is above, what is below (not inferior) and what is on one's level (Wilhelm Meister, 1824). Courteous gestures towards the other enhances the dignity of the self.

Many spiritual masters have initiated new forms of education, which honour children as the spiritual beings they are, with the soul, the life and the body they have, rather than as particularly complicated behavioural and intelligent entities, to be programmed to function as parts in the machinery of the "real world". Rabindranath Tagore, Montessori, Steiner, and recently Shin Gwydion Fontalba with a school for "integral learning" in Pauri, near the foothills of the Himalayas, etc.

Gregory Bateson and Rudolf zur Lippe's call for a re-appreciation and re-introduction of an aesthetic, imaginary and poetic dimension in education, would at the same time be a call for a slowing down, allowing children to fully live their age, where their appetite and genius for learning is spontaneous, creative, imaginative and playful. Spatial orientation through the richest variety of physical play is an excellent preparation for formal mathematics, with its sense and search for balance, equations (Steiner); listening to the telling of 'fairy-tales, and more fairy tales' prepares children for becoming a scientist. (Einstein). Teaching writing by dwelling on the different shapes and sounds of letters: 'w' like a wave, water, weave and 's' like snake, serpent, sizzle…, helps children to make the letters their own, rather than foreign tokens, with no connection to their own experience. The 'ideographic space' of Japan and China, as characterized by Fosco Maraini, gives eastern education a rich imaginary scope. Carlyle and Kückelhaus elaborate on the significance of symbol, speech and silence in any spiritual, religious ceremony.

I hope that by these brief indications the texts selected will speak for themselves and that the order in which they follow each other, makes sense. And I trust that they do open a number of new perspectives for a more worthy and adequate reception of children that come to us and for the specific role religious and other spiritual communities need and are able to play in this 'work of progress'. Progress, not by emulating the pace at which education at large is accelerating, but rather by creating a moral, reflective and multidimensional space, where new generations can find meaning and connection with all things beyond, below, above and all around.

I would like to end the sequence of texts with the one theme that for me runs throughout the whole of spiritual culture, religious as well as secular, that of thankfulness or gratitude. It is on the one hand such a deeply human response, that it borders on instinct and on the other hand a most consciously chosen response out of knowledge and understanding, and it is a most noble expression of feeling. I might suggest that gratitude perhaps even more so than fear is at the origin of religious or secular culture: both respond to something awesome and unknown, but gratitude is perhaps closer to an intimation, that 'whatever it addresses is no illusion' (Simone Weil): a real source of life in all its richness. In Christian Morgenstern's 'Washing of the Feet' gratitude intertwines gods and humans, humans, rocks, plants and animals and streams within the Godhead 'to and fro', condensed in a few lines. In Tomberg's 'Duet with St. Francis', the 'Canticle of the Sun' by St Francis himself is expanded to articulate the very many gifts by which humanity is being blessed. It also reads as a comprehensive overview of most if not all what we might have learned on the journey through this book.

Texts

Entering the special solitude of prayer

A peacemaker prays. Prayer is the beginning and the end, the source and the fruit, the core and the content, the basis and the goal of all peacemaking. I say this without apology, because it allows me to go straight to the heart of the matter, which is that peace is a divine gift, a gift we receive in prayer.

In his farewell discourse Jesus said to his apostles: "Peace I leave to you, my own peace I give to you: a peace the world cannot give, this is my gift to you". (John 14:27). When we want to make peace we first of all have to move away from the dwelling places of those who hate peace and enter into the house of him who offers us his peace. Prayer / pp. 25-26

[ ]

The great spiritual tragedy is that many cruel and inhuman acts are committed in the name of serving God. After the atom bomb was successfully exploded above Hiroshima, President Truman wrote: "We thank God that it (the bomb) has come to us...and we pray that he may guide us to use it in his way and for his purposes." Events in Guatemala offer another hideous example. When general Efrain Monte came to power in March of 1982, he presented himself as an ardent follower of Jesus. Seven months later, twenty-six hundred Guatemalan peasants – men, women, and children – had been killed. We cannot assume that those who dropped the bomb or murdered innocent Indians were psychopaths. Most of them were normal men born and raised in Christian families. Prayer / pp. 30-31

[ ]

It is not easy to express the radical change that prayer represents, since for many the word "prayer" is associated with piety: talking to God, thinking about God, attending morning and evening worship, going to Sunday service, saying grace before meals, and many other things. All of these have something to do with prayer, but when I speak about prayer as the basis for peacemaking I speak first of all about moving away from the "dwelling place of those who hate peace" into the house of God. Prayer is the centre of the Christian life...

As I read the Gospels I am struck by how often images connected with a new dwelling place are used. ...John the Evangelist describes Jesus as the Word of God who came into the world and pitched his tent among us. (John 1:14). He also tells us how the first disciples asked Jesus when they first met him, "Teacher, where do you live?" and were invited to stay in his home (John 1:38-39).... We come to see that Jesus not only invites his followers to live with him in the same house, but that he himself is the house. Prayer / pp. 32-33

[ ]

What is the concrete day-to-day implication of this view of prayer? It is that we often have to take time to pray, and recognize prayer as the first and foremost act of resistance against the arms race. ... Entering the special solitude of prayer is a protection against a world of manipulation, competition, rivalry, suspicion, defensiveness, anger, hostility, mutual aggression, destruction and war. It is a witness to the all-embracing, all-healing power of God's love...

Henri Nouwen
Peacework: Prayer, Resistance, Community
2014, p. 44

Entering the secular sacred with prayer

At the end of his life, Jacques Derrida announced that he knelt down beside his bed and prayed every night. His atheistic followers felt bewildered and betrayed. Had they been deceived for so long? Had the master of postmodernism tricked them, and even himself? Some thought that he was losing his marbles and dismissed his prayers as dementia. But Derrida was in full possession of his faculties. He said that as he aged, his childhood Jewish practices came back to him and he embraced them in a new way. After all his exploring Derrida had arrived where he started and knew the place for the first time.

However, Derrida was not embracing any traditional religion so the conservative religious might feel just as bewildered by his prayers. To his dying breath Derrida referred to himself as an atheist, and his prayers were not directed to an atheistic God or personal deity. Derrida was praying to the Unsayable, the Unspeakable, the Unknown: '... the constancy of God in my life is called by other names', he wrote in his essay 'Circumfession: Fifty-Nine periods and Periphrases'. p. 5

[ ]

I think many Australians are following Derrida's trajectory. Many of us grew up with, and later discarded, the religions of our parents or grandparents. They made no sense in a scientific, modern and rational world. But recently there seems to be a change of heart. Many ask: have we thrown out too much?...p. 6

Instead of seeing the sacred as something separate from the ordinary and needing to be celebrated in holy buildings on special days, there is a sense that sacredness is now a dimension of everyday life. It is at this moment in history that the ancient spirituality of Australia speaks to our post-colonial society. Aboriginal culture has never separated the sacred from the ordinary but finds it embedded in the everyday. In fact, the everyday is no longer ordinary if the sacred is present. The horizontal plane is shot through with transcendence. The transcendent doesn't happen elsewhere, apart from the world, but is a dimension of the world. Poets have always known this, as Gerard Manley Hopkins puts it: 'The world is charged with the grandeur of God.' And all of us need to think like poets to bring this awareness into our own lived experience. p. 10

David Tacey in: Jordie Albiston and Kevin Brophy (Editors)'s
Prayers of a Secular World / Introduction: Secular Sacredness
2015

All Inclusive Prayer for Peace

When it is lived well, life is like an interweaving of melodies, not a cacophony of competing claims, each indifferent to the others and each striving for dominance. Once we agree that social harmony based on justice and fairness is our top priority, we can start moving together on the same project, rather than building competing structures ...

Hugh Mackay
The Kindness Revolution
Sydney 2021, pp. 73-74

We - with our world-views in dialogue - open ourselves in awe, gratitude and praise for the unfathomable wisdom and sublime free, intelligence that comes to meet us when we turn ourselves towards the majesty and generosity of the cosmos, to the mystery of life and consciousness. In the presence of this

*enduring Wonder, we open ourselves in confidence and ask for the guidance
and assistance towards a peace that only this Great Life can give us.*

*We pray that the creative generosity which lives and works throughout
our universe, earth and nature, may continue down into our humanity.
We thankfully recognize the harmony in the forms by which the Spirit
functions in soul, life and body. And we pray to be inspired and enabled
in letting such harmony stream into the communities, institutions and
domains that constitute and serve our societies, each with its own specific
task, free from domination: peace in the harmony of a well-tuned society.*

*Let natural prosperity be the leading motive in our economies
guided by a commitment to distributive fairness;*

*Let equal justice for all, be the leading motive in our political
life, established by all-inclusive representation;*

*Let nobility of spirit be the leading motive in all our cultural endeavours, with
creative freedom to pursue our responsibilities, dreams, ideals and visions*

*We pray for a peace full of creative tension, colourful,
with contrasts, light and dark, resonant with dissonances
enlivening harmonies: a peace not without conflicts, but with
the generosity, goodwill and resources to resolve them.*

*We engage and commit all the clarity, purity and strength of our world-
views in our efforts to address and overcome the seemingly intractable
evil of systemic sources of conflicts, wars and destruction.*

*Where divides between races, genders, religions, nations
and between social classes have become entrenched;*

*where a trader- and - producer driven consumerism robs indigenous peoples
of their lands, forests and the secrets of their medicinal plants and deprives
farmers of their land and of the natural productivity of their seed-stock;*

*where we are grossly transgressing the natural boundaries of life, choke
our seas and mine the floor of our oceans, clear-fell and burn our forests,
poison our fields, and drive nations to starvation, famine and food wars:*

*we pray for the grace, insight and strength that enable us to
regret, repent and retreat from the road to destruction.*

Alert and free us from a disembodied artificial world that deprives children and elders of the physical, sensory and emotional experience vital for their early development and lifelong participation in the life of the world, deprives all of us of our capacity to sustain attention and distracts individuals and communities, institutions, governments and public services from the physical, sensory, emotional and intellectual interaction, which would keep us in touch with one another for the wellbeing and sanity of all.

We pray for the capacities to develop and practise the moral imagination, inspired discernment and grounded intuition needed to make peace all-inclusive, alive and lasting.

By the Truth and Source of all Reality, honoured in reverent silence and addressed by many names, we ask and pray with confidence for the peace that the great wisdom and intelligence 'beyond and above all grasp' may grant us.

Henk Bak
Evera, Trentham 2nd of July 2022

The above prayer is intended to follow on from the meditative ritual that introduces the meditative walks, 'World-views in Dialogue' at Evera, Trentham. When we meditate, we generate peace in and around us and may also consider what may constitute the peace we seek or pray for. When we pray, we direct our gratitude, praise, devotion, requests for grace and help to a Higher Being, Power, Consciousness – known or unknown, named or un-named, in religious world-views often, but not always, identified as God, Brahma, Allah

The invasion by Russia into Ukraine on the 24th of February made me search for a prayer to be used for our meditative walk three days later, Sunday the 27th. I felt that not only most religious gatherings would pray that weekend for peace, but also individuals not involved in any religious community as well as humanists.

My work as historian and philosopher, and my involvement with the teachings of Rudolf Steiner, Gideon Fontalba and Shin Gwydion, as well as more than 14 years of meditating for peace had taught me to be rather specific in what would be the kind of peace I would pray for. After many rewritings I refrain from going any further. As part of the way the meditative walk is introduced, it naturally reflects elements of the meditative ritual that precedes it. Having used this draft in its many alterations over the last four months, I found that different elements of the text also resonate with different elements in the world-views represented in the sites visited on my walks.

The Joyousness of Men (Petra White)

> *When we run together I am natively*
> *content as a dog running beside its person.*
> *Gladly I step out into the fresh wind*
> *with my endless legs and swinging arms,*
> *my dog-like pant. He running beside me*
> *is a ball of light in his yellow jacket.*
> *The river runs backward beside us, crinkling*
> *and brown in the dimming air. And on the other side*
> *somebody has a fire going. Our house*
> *is far behind us, we are running*
> *into the night. He sprints in great joy, he splashes*
> *around in his soul like a duck. He waves me forward*
> *and I slip behind. His joy, he throws to me willingly.*
> *Love is running as if nothing can stop it,*
> *to a grave at the end of its own possible time.*
> *It runs and runs and says let's run again.*

Jordie Albiston and Kevin Brophy (Editors)
Prayers of a Secular World
2015, p. 26

Powerful Owl (Maya Ward)

> *To come close to you I must become this:*
> *Dark, weighted silence*
> *Poised, claws empty*
> *Ready for the hunt*
>
>
> *I listen for the noiseless loft of your night feathers*
> *I watch as your greys melt into the dusk*
> *You are a piece of night broken off and coming towards me*
> *And you fly with a loose softness, as quiet as danger*
> *You fly low over my head*
> *And vanish*

I feel you, hovering inside my mind
Now you drop into the dark chasm of my chest
And I know my soul was formed to hold you
My mind was forged in the crucible of you
And my spine is a tree
Where you have perked for thousands of years

I have been awake with you this long night
I have hunted with you in this darkness
And like the swift mouse made limp and bloodied
I am ready to become something other.

Jordie Albiston and Kevin Brophy (Editors)
Prayers of a Secular World
2015, p. 14

The Wind from the Sea

The wind from the sea
The sound of a bird
The taste of the salt on your sweet lips
The quiet of the earth

The stars in the sky
The moon and the clouds
The rise of the child in every heart
The fall of the proud

The wolf in the night
The sun of the dawn
The friend who labours through the night
'til something is born

The smallest of seeds
The greatest of trees
The journey of life from end to end
The wind from the sea.

Sean David Burke
At a 'difficult juncture', what began as poem ended up as prayer and chant
in correspondence with this author

Week 40

Blessing of the kindling

I will kindle my fire this morning
In presence of the holy angels of heaven
God kindle thou I my heart within
A flame of love to my neighbour
To my foe, to my friend, to my kindred all
To the brave, to the knave, to the thrall

Carmina Gadelica in: Olive Brown and Jean Whittaker's
Through the Year with Columba: A Celtic Prayer for Every Week
1997

Prayer for Tolerance

O Thou God of all beings, of all worlds, and of all times,
We pray, that the little differences in our clothes,
In our inadequate languages,
In our ridiculous customs,
In our imperfect laws,
In our illogical opinions,
In our ranks and conditions which are so
disproportionately important to us
And so meaningless to you,
That these variations
That distinguish those atoms that we call men,
One from another,
May not be signals of hatred and persecution!

Voltaire in: Editors of Skylight Paths
Men Pray: Voices of Strength, Faith and Healing, Hope and Courage
2013, p. 69

My relationship with God and the Jewish faith remained a complicated one throughout my life. A defining moment I will never forget was my first trip as a scholar to Auschwitz, where I saw prayer shawls on display. I felt an immense sense of anger at God and at the Jewish men who naively believed that they were going to live and pray in a place where God could not be present. Yet, when I lead groups to the sites of life and death in Poland, in each site I direct the group to recite the Jewish prayers in honor of the dead, Kaddish and El-Maleh Rachamim. Anger and prayer live side by side in my heart. p. 251

Tali Nates In: Menachem Z. Rosensaft (editor)
God Faith & Identity from the Ashes: Reflections of Children and Grandchildren of Holocaust Survivors
2015

That night I addressed a meeting of African Township ministers in Cape Town. I mention this because the opening prayer of one of the ministers had stayed with me over these many years and was a source of strength at a difficult time. He thanked the Lord for His bounty and goodness, for His mercy and His concern for all men. But then he took the liberty of reminding the Lord that some of His subjects were more downtrodden than others, and that it sometimes seemed as though he was not paying attention. The minister then said that if the Lord did not show a little more initiative in leading the black man to salvation, the black man would have to take matters in his own two hands. Amen

Nelson Mandela In: Editors of Skylight Paths
Men Pray: Voices of Strength, Faith and Healing, Hope and Courage
2013, p. 43

The way Jesus says 'I': forgiveness before offering

You have learnt how it was said to our ancestors: You must not kill; and if anyone does kill he must answer for it before the court. But I say this to you: anyone who is angry with his brother will answer for it before the court; if a man calls his brother "Fool" he will answer for it before the Sanhedrin; and if a man calls him "Renegade" he will answer for it in hell fire. So then, if you are bringing your offering to the altar and there remember that your brother has something against you, leave your offering there before the altar, go and be reconciled with your brother first, and then come back and present your offering. Come to terms with your opponent in good time while you are still on the way to court with him, or he may hand you over to the judge and the judge to the officer, and you will be thrown into prison. I tell you solemnly, you will not get out till you paid the last penny.

Sermon on the Mount Matthew 5:21-27

Prayer for Peace

Lord, make me an instrument of your peace.
Where there is hatred, let me bring love.
Where there is offense, let me bring pardon.
Where there is discord, let me bring union.
Where there is error, let me bring truth.
Where there is doubt, let me bring faith.
Where there is despair, let me bring hope.
Where there is darkness, let me bring your light.
Where there is sadness, let me bring joy.
O Master, let me not seek as much
to be consoled as to console,
to be understood as to understand,
to be loved as to love,
for it is in giving that one receives,
it is in self-forgetting that one finds,
it is in pardoning that one is pardoned,
it is in dying that one is raised to eternal life.

Anonymous in: La Clochette
In the spirit of St. Francis of Assisi
1912

DECIDE TO FORGIVE

For resentment is negative
Resentment is poisonous
Resentment diminishes
  and devours the self.
Be the first to forgive
To smile and take the first step
And you will see happiness bloom
On the face of your human
  brother or sister.
Be always the first
Do not wait for others to forgive
For by forgiving
You become the master of fate

The fashioner of life
The doer of miracles.
To forgive is the highest
　most beautiful form of love.
In return you will receive
　untold peace and happiness

Dr. Robert Muller
Long time serving assistant to the General Secretary
of the United Nations

Reconciliation Prayer

Mighty Creator Spirit
We honour You by many names.
You share the universe with us.
Help us share this land with one another.
As sisters and brothers let us
reconnect with the earth who
brings us forth and feeds us.
Through the Spirit of Reconciliation
Let it be done in freedom.

Let us we stand up as individuals
and lift the spirit of our communities,
nourished by your Word
and strengthened by your Love.

Let us join in sorry and in sadness
over what happened in our separation.
Guide us through all the reasons, emotions,
motives - instincts even - that tempt us
and threaten to detract us from
the path together, time and time again.
Amidst misunderstanding and
confusion us be free of evil
and full of goodwill.
Amen.

Henk Bak
Reconciliation Prayer Week Trentham, Australia

18 April 1999/26 January 2016

A memorial service – a statement

On April 9, 1991, a memorial service for Max Frisch was held in St. Peter's Church in Zurich. It began with Karin Pilliod, Frisch's partner, reading out a brief declaration written by the deceased. It stated, amongst other things: "We let our nearest speak, and without an 'amen'. I am grateful to the ministers of St. Peter's church in Zurich...for their permission to place the coffin in the church during our memorial service. The ashes will be strewn somewhere." Two friends spoke. No priest. No blessing. The mourners were made up of intellectuals, most of whom had little time for church and religion. Frisch himself had drawn up the menu for the meal that followed. At the time the ceremony did not strike me as peculiar. However, its form, place, and progression were peculiar. Clearly, Max Frisch, an agnostic who rejected any profession of faith, had sensed the awkwardness of non-religious burial practices and, by his choice of place, publicly declared that the enlightened modern age has failed to find a suitable replacement for a religious way of coping with the final rite de passage which brings life to a close.

One can interpret this gesture as an expression of melancholy over something that has been irretrievably lost. Yet one can also view the ceremony as a paradoxical event which tells us something about secular reason, namely that it is unsettled by the opaqueness of its apparently clarified relation to religion. At the same time, the church, even Zwingli's reformed church, also had to overcome its inhibitions when it allowed this ceremony, given its secular character "without an 'amen'", to take place within its hallowed halls. p.16

Juergen Habermass
An Awareness of What is Missing: Faith and Reason in a Post-Secular Age
2011

The Brush Dance is a Yurok Indian healing ritual where being true to yourself means giving your best to help a person in need.

Being true to yourself is the one and only Yurok Indian law.

Brush Dance
San Rafael
California

Brush Dance is a ceremony held to heal a sick child or to pray for a long, healthy life for the child. The dance is somewhat of a social dance where families and villages come together. In the past, the dance would take place in a home of the child: the roof of the plank house would be removed. Today however, dances take place at specific villages where dance pits still remain. More and more families are participating in dances, thus more dances are taking place throughout the summer. The medicine doctor, her helpers (medicine boy and girl), the child, and dance family begin the dance on a Wednesday. The medicine doctor begins the process much sooner. Actual dancing begins on Thursday night, with two dances. The medicine for the dance continues with dancing resuming Saturday night lasting until late Sunday morning and some say the dance ends before the sun rises above the hills. Other local tribes participate, making up different dance camps. Both females and males dance. Different Tribes take turns hosting dance rounds.

Even if you are not a dancer, every participant has a role at the dance. An overall belief of Yurok people is that you go to the dance with a good heart. This means that you attend with only good thoughts and prayers. You leave all of your anger, meanness, and other bad feelings behind. If you have enemies, you also leave that behind.

www.YurokTribe.org/brush dance

Islam Pilgrimage Hadj to Mecca (Makkah)

I am here because nothing compares to you.
Here I am!
Praise, blessings and the kingdom are yours.
Nothing compares to you.

Labbayk, allahumah, labbayk!
Labbayk, la shareeka laka,
Labbayk!
Innal-hamda, wa n-ni 'mata, laka walmulk.
La shareeka lak.

Bab al Salaam: Gate of Peace

This is your sanctuary.
This is your city.
I am your servant.

Peace is yours.
You are salvation.
Grant us salvation.
And guide us
Through the gate of paradise.

Tawaf: Turning

Allah, I plan to circle your sacred house. Make it easy for me, and accept
My seven circuits in your name.

Under the golden rainspout from the roof of the Ka'ba

On that day
When the only shade is yours.
Take me into your shadow, Lord,
And let me drink
From the Prophet's trough
To quench my thirst forever.

Michael Wolfe, Making the Hadj to Mecca in: Sean O'Reilly and
James O'Reilly's (editors)
Pilgrimage Adventures of the sprit
2000

Praying in dance and gesture

In Sufi dance or "turning", the dervish becomes a doorway through which the Divine and human meet. Receiving energy from God with the right hand turned toward heaven, she returns energy to the earth through her left hand. Praying with our Hands. p. 47

When prayer is not simply petitionary or mental, it involves one's whole being – mind, body and spirit, the conscious and the unconscious. This embodied prayer is expressed by the hands that worship, whether it be the palms pressed together, hands folded and fingers interlocking or opened to the sky and earth.

Among the various parts of the human body, the hands have been regarded as expressive of a vast range of human emotions, from invitation to rejection, grief to anger, generosity to miserliness, benediction to condemnation, possession to power. Hands have been central to healing and blessing, exorcism and magic, religious ritual and worship...

In spite of differences in the doctrines and practices of world religions, embodied prayer plays a central role in all of them. The unity in diversity is explicit in the somatic expressions of faith, symbolized by the hands in prayer, that may further the interreligious dialogues popular today among Buddhists Christians, Muslims, Jews and Hindus.

Afterword by Professor Unno Tattetsu in: John Sweeney's
Praying with our Hands: 21 Practices of Embodied Prayer from the World's Spiritual Traditions
2002, p. 76

...from C.G. Jung, memoir, recalling experiences in Africa

...Every morning at dawn, the people on Mount Egon in East Africa leave their huts and breathe or spit into their hands, stretching them out to the first rays of the sun, as if they were offering either their breath or their spittle....with this act they offer their souls to the mungu...

Not every repetitive conduct is a 'ritual' in the proper sense

I do not think much of the fashion, widespread among sociologists, to apply the very specific concept of ritual to each and every repetitive conduct. It seems, by contrast, that the essential sources of solidarity-providing energies in the rituals described by anthropologists are those ideas and experiences that owe themselves to a very peculiar form of communication. This form distinguishes itself, first, by the absence of a relation to the world in a self-referential communal practice circling around itself. Second, it distinguishes itself by the holistic semantic content of an undifferentiated, or not yet propositionally differentiated, use of different iconic symbols (such as dance and song, pantomime, decorations, body painting, etc.). I would like to maintain that today, only religious congregations, by way of their cultic practices, keep open the access to archaic experiences of this sort. These experiences remain closed to those who are unmusical in religious matters; the likes of us have to content themselves with aesthetic experiences as a highly sublimated substitute. This analogy indeed motivated Peter Weiss to find political hope in an "aesthetics of resistance," that is, in the eye-opening and solidarizing power of an art that "breaks over into life." Even if this hope, inspired by surrealism, has faded in the meantime, there is of course no reason to now count blindly on the motivational powers of religion against the neoliberal desolidarization of society. As we know, these motivational powers are politically highly ambivalent. The democratic constitutional state does not harmonize with every, but only with a non-fundamentalist, religious practice. pp. 8-9

Jürgen Habermas
***A Postsecular World Society?: On the Philosophical Signif-
icance of Postsecular Consciousness and the Multicultural
World Society***
In: The Immanent Frame, Social Science Research Council 2010
URL: mrzine.monthlyreview.org/2010/habermas210310.html

Activism as a ritual – 'aesthetic of resistance'?

On Good Friday we went to Groton to witness for peace (against the Trident, nuclear missiles submarine. H.B.) in front of the administration building of Electric Boat. The leaders of the group asked me to lead the community in the Stations of the Cross. I couldn't resist a smile when I heard that we, people from very different denominations (Baptist, Presbyterian, Lutheran, United Church of Christ, and catholic), would make the Stations of the Cross. As a child I had often made these fourteen stations in church. The commemorate fourteen events between Jesus' being condemned to death by Pontius Pilate and his burial. These events have been vividly portrayed in painting and sculpture...

But as I grew older the Stations of the Cross soon became a pious childhood memory. The Second Vatican Council had so altered my religious consciousness that I, together with most of my fellow Catholics, dropped this devotional practice and focused on official liturgical celebration. Who could have dreamt that twenty years after the Council I would lead an ecumenical group of theology students in the Station of the Cross...in prayerful resistance against impending nuclear holocaust?

[ ]

I have told this personal story (of protest against the Trident submarine, Groton) because it is my way of discovering that resistance is not action in contrast to prayer, but a true form of prayer. After my own, very limited, experience with war resistance I even dare to say that, for those who resist in the name of the living God, resistance is not only prayer but also liturgy. ...The word "liturgy" comes from the Greek phrase 'ergos to lao*', which means "the work of the people." It is the communal work of worship by the people of God.

---

* ergon tou laou

*My Good Friday experience at Groton is only one example of the
many ways in which Christian resisters are reclaiming the peacemaking
power of liturgical celebrations. Traditional feast days, such as the
feast of the Holy Innocents on December 28, or the feast of the
Transfiguration of Christ on August 6, can become radical calls to
conversion for our age. For ours is an age in which children can be
innocent victims of the nuclear bomb, and in which the deadening light
of Hiroshima has replaced the life-giving light of Mount Tabor.*

*As the peace makers movement grows deeper and stronger, more holy
days are becoming peacemaking days. The "Peace Pentecost" celebrated
in the National cathedral in Washington in 1983 and followed by a
day of massive civil disobedience in the Capitol building is another
example of "liturgical renewal". ...As we see the liturgical year
becoming a year of peacemaking we rediscover Advent, Christmas,
Epiphany, Lent, Easter, Pentecost, and many other holy days and seasons
as carrying within themselves a very specific message of peace.*

Henri Nouwen
Peacework: Prayer, Resistance, Community
2014, pp. 87-89

Ritual Language and Symbols: embodiment of the infinite

*Speech is too often not, as the Frenchman defined it, the art of
concealing Thought: but of quite stifling and suspending Thought,
so that there is none to conceal. Speech too is great, but not the
greatest. As the Swiss Inscription says: Sprechen ist silbern,
Schweigen ist golden (Speech is silver, Silence is gold); or as I might
rather express it: Speech is of Time, Silence is of Eternity.*

[ ]

*Is not Shame the soil of all Virtue, of all good manners, and good
morals? Like other plants, Virtue will not grow unless its root be hidden,
buried from the eye of the sun. Let the sun shine on it, nay, do but look
at it privily thyself, the root wither, and no flower will glad thee.*

[ ]

*"Of kin to the so incalculable influences of Concealment, and connected
with still greater things, is the agency of Symbols. In a Symbol there is
concealment and yet revelation: here, therefore, by Silence and by Speech*

acting together, comes a double significance. And if both the Speech be itself high, and the Silence fit and noble, how expressive will their union be! Thus in many painted Device, or simple Seal-emblem, the commonest Truth stands-out to us proclaimed with quite new emphasis."

For it is here that Fantasy with her mystic wonder-hand plays into the small prose domain of Sense, and becomes incorporated therewith. In the Symbol proper, what we can call a Symbol, there is ever, more or less distinctly and directly, some embodiment and revelation of the Infinite; the Infinite is made to blend itself with the Finite, to stand visible, and as it were attainable there. By symbols, accordingly is man guided and commanded, made happy, made wretched. He everywhere finds himself encompassed with Symbols, recognised as such or not recognised: the Universe is but one vast Symbol of God; nay, if thou wilt have it, what is man himself but a Symbol of God; is not all that he does symbolical; a revelation to Sense of the mystic god-given force that is in him; a 'Gospel of Freedom,' which he, the 'Messias of Nature,' preaches, as he can, by act and by word? Not a Hut he builds but is the visible embodiment of a Though: but bears visible record of invisible things; but is, in the transcendental sense, symbolical as well as real.

Thomas Carlyle
Sartor Resartus: The Life and Opinions of Herr Teufels-dröckh / Book III Chapter III Symbols
1836, pp. 216-17

Scriptures and writings – a shared ideographic space.

Writing is a system of signs, intended to organize space and convey meanings.

Because signs have meanings, eyes can scan them with curiosity and love and become docked to them like LEMs to interplanetary ships. A deep relationship is set up in childhood between eyes and signs. An age-long ta-ue*, a transplantation of signs into eyes takes place. At the subconscious level there is a rigorous flourishing in the paddy fields of the mind. Finally eyes are saturated with signs and dictate aesthetic needs to hands. Signs reappear as objects in everyday life, buildings, furniture, posters, toys, hats. There is a continuous, complex flow from sign to eye and back from eye to sign, from eye to world; the taste of an age, a culture, civilization is deeply affected.

Fosco Maraini
Japan: Patterns of Continuity
1972, p. 123

---

* Ta-ue: festive use of symbols, as in the celebration of snow.

The Hidden Way of Language

....The child's mark 'tree' is the tree in its potential rather than as something complete. A mark or sign does not make a thing complete, it makes it possible. And what is possible to begin with or only what is possible first is real.

[ ]

One could say that in hell there are no possibilities – not yet and not any more. The genesis of what is real begins for who-ever begins, who-ever is alive, with the mark or sign as a germ or seed, the rune. He begins at the other side, away from where he has it realised.

To speak less, to draw more. Or- drawing by speaking.

To speak through the mark or sign; speaking making marks.

One should speak through writing; whereby with script is again meant the making of marks.* To this belongs a sign-making, condensed, contracted instrument, a specifically shaped tool. Without a shaped instrument there is no language. The Assyrian wedge-shaped stylus is such tool. The Chinese-Japanese watercolour brush is such an instrument. In this way language finds a solid form and finds its feet on the ground. The technical element is the dough, the dough of existence. For existence to become enjoyable to taste it needs salt. Not too much, otherwise it will be spoilt. A pinch is enough. Such a pinch of salt in the dough of existence is true writing, writing in marks or signs. It is also not necessary that all people are able to write in order for language to remain possible. A rather small circle of writers suffices. The monasteries with their scriptoriums are the keepers and enhancers of language. Not even so much through writing the language of the people, but essentially through writing a language that is not spoken any more: a ritual language. This is a language that begins there where the colloquial communication ends. One says "a dead language". This dead language and - above all the true way of writing it – is in relation to the body of colloquial languages the real thing, like a hormone in an organism: a trace-element that keeps the affairs, the processes of the day in an ordered flow, without containing it or guiding it. In the examples of priest-language, priest-writing in relation to current language, to the body of a people's language one can marvel at the power of what is secret and little.

Hugo Kükelhaus
Das Wort des Johannes

---

* The Latin origin of the English words: 'signify'-'significant' is 'signum facere' = 'making a sign' or a mark. Henk Bak

1953, pp. 150-151
[Translated by Henk Bak]

Holding Hands

Oh, Lord of the Dance,
Four weeks ago
we slow-danced in the kitchen.
I bore most of her weight, but we smiled
as the music reminded us of our first date.
Two weeks ago
she was too weak to get out of bed,
  seldom able to speak.
I stayed with her, holding her hand, speaking softly,
I often hummed her favorite tune –
the one to which we danced.
Four days ago
she slipped away.
I was still holding her hand.
Today,
I need you to hold my hand and my heart.
Both are shaky now –
I need your steady hand and loving heart –
I need you to bear most of my weight in this new dance.

Dr Benjamin Pratt
In: Editors of Skylight Paths'
Men Pray: Voices of Strength, Faith and Healing, Hope and Courage
2013, p. 70

A Passing-On Prayer

When the sunset of this miraculous life arrives
and its twilight shadows fade away,
while dreams of the next begin to dawn
and appear more vividly before the eyes
of your noble consciousness;
May the inner-light essence
of the Buddha
and all the radiant awakened ones
continuously guide you
onwards and upwards

on the evolutionary path of spiritual enlightenment.

Adapted from Tibetan sources by Lama Surya Das in: Editors of
Skylight Paths
Men Pray: Voices of Strength, Faith and Healing, Hope and
Courage
2013

Salat al-Janazah

Ṣalāt al-Janāzah is the Islamic funeral prayer; a part of the Islamic funeral ritual. The prayer is performed in congregation to seek pardon for the deceased and all dead Muslims. The Salat al-Janazah is a collective obligation upon Muslims (fard al-kifāya) i.e., if some Muslims take the responsibility of doing it, the obligation is fulfilled, but if no-one fulfils it, then all Muslims will be accountable.

Description

It is preferable that those praying divide themselves into odd rows with one person as an Imam standing alone in front and while facing in the direction of Qiblah. The body is placed in front of the Imam. If there is more than one body, then these should be put one in front of the other. The spoken part of the prayer involves quietly reciting Al-Fatiha, then praying for God to bestow peace, mercy and blessings upon the Islamic prophet Muhammad, and finally saying two du'as.

Muhammad and his companions explained how the salat should be done, as follows: [1]

1. Having the appropriate neeyat (intention) in your heart, You say the first Takbir while raising your hands, then you fold and hold your hands on your chest in the usual manner, the right hand on the left seek refuge with Allah from the accursed Shayṭan, then you utter Bismillah and recite Al-Fatiha

2. Then you say Takbir and Durood-e-Ibrahimi.

3. Then you say a third Takbir and make du'a for the deceased.

It is narrated that Muhammad said:

"O God, forgive our living and our dead, those who are present among us and those who are absent, our young and our old, our males and our females.

O God, whoever You keep alive, keep him alive in Islam, and whoever You cause to die, cause him to die with faith. O God, do not deprive us of the reward and do not cause us to go astray after this. O God, forgive him and have mercy on him, keep him safe and sound and forgive him, honour his rest and ease his entrance; wash him with water and snow and hail, and cleanse him of sin as a white garment is cleansed of dirt. O God, give him a home better than his home and a family better than his family. O God, admit him to Paradise and protect him from the torment of the grave and the torment of Hell-fire; make his grave spacious and fill it with light."

4. Then a fourth takbir is recited, followed by a short pause, then a final taslim to the right, saying "Assalaamu 'alaykum wa rahmatu-Allah" ("Peace and blessings of God be unto you").

Durood-i-Ibrahimi

One example is Durood-i-Ibrahimi (having a reference to Abraham):

O Allah, let Your Peace come upon Muhammad and the family and followers of Muhammad, as you have brought peace to Ibrahim and his family. Truly, You are Praiseworthy and Glorious. Allah, bless Muhammad and the family and followers of Muhammad, as you have blessed Ibrahim and his family and followers. Truly, You are Praiseworthy and Glorious.

Wikipedia / The Funeral prayer (Islam)
https://en.wikipedia.org/wiki/Funeral_prayer_(Islam)

Meditation addressing the souls leaving the earth 1.

(create an appropriate meditative context in which you might send Love forces, Strength, Goodness, Mildness, Clarity.)

"...And with my sight I turn to you, oh souls, who have entered upon the journey from the Blue Wandering Star – light-filled with earthly knowledge, clothed in strength, merciful – into the world of the lights of the stars, into the realm of the Music of the Spheres, into the World-Being-Word.

Let yourselves be consciously accompanied by the rays of a Sun into the World-Sun- I."

Gideon Fontalba
1982

From a meditation to support souls that have departed from the earth 2:

(Create an appropriate meditative context, in which you might visualize a path that vanishes into the heights, first silver, then golden-diamond. Behold people on this path and encourage them with your thought and love.)

"When you now pass over there, bring with you what you remember and perceive from the earth, what has been during your Earth time, what you received and worked upon.
Be reminded of that, report with open hear
You will receive answers to questions.
You will answer question.
When you pass over, you raise the most precious elements of Earth, of Water, of Air, and of soul experience…
When you come again, bring these answers with you.
Be our true messenger".

Gideon Fontalba
Verses and meditations for accompanying souls
Ash Wednesday 1988

Marriage, conception, birth and education in the Ngarinyin way of life and Wunan (Law).

Prior to the marriage the couple are taken away for a week by an older relation of the promised husband. Here, in the privacy of their own camp, the couple learn how to look after each other's needs under the diligent guidance of their elder. They do not sleep together, but become familiar with each other, learning the essential and intimate nature of each other's personalities and spirits. They hunt together, make camp together, and share stories, all the time noting and appreciating each other's strengths and skills. p. 88

[ ]

Grandmothers coo very softly to the very young as they lift the little ones from their blankets in the early morning light as the fires flares. This is Wuudu Time, when the Morning Star is absorbed in the eagerness of morning light, the time of awakening awareness. As daughter Sun kindles the new day and man kindles the flame of the campfire, awareness is kindled in the children of the tribe.

Hands are warmed over the flames. A grandmother touches a child's eyes with her warmed hands and whispers quietly, intimately "Eeh! You must share .... you must not look around in other people's camps for things you want. Everything is there for you in the Wunan. "She warms her hands again, puts them on the sleepy child's nose and says: "Eeh! You must not sniff around or beg for other people's food .... work hard in your lifetime." Then her hands touch the child's mouth and she exhorts: "Eeh! You must not curse other people. You bring big shame to us when you curse them. They are our brothers and sisters, our aunts and uncles .... they protect you in your place." Finally her hands move to the male child's pubic area for example as she says: "Eeh! You must not look at other womans. You have promise wife in wunan." pp. 50-51

[ ]

Naming and providing language of the world is mostly Women's Business because women are the primary caregivers to the prepubescent young.

Because nature is in essence Wunggud in action, the world is named as a series of actions that, when linked together, generate a whole image or picture. This is the pattern of life or Wunan system, the intricate ecology of sacred relationships. p. 52

Hannah Rachel Bell
Men's Business – Women's Business: The Spiritual Role of Gender in the World's Oldest Culture
1998

"White men think they only have to have sex with women that's all they have to do to have a baby. For Aboriginal people, God puts the baby into the womb.

An Aboriginal man, who has had sex with his wife, goes along the place where he himself was created, where the reflection and image of God is. The Aboriginal man gets his children from the spiritside, not just from himself"

David Mowaljarlai & Jutta Malnic
Yorro Yorro : Aboriginal Creation and the Renewal of Nature : Rock Paintings and Stories from the Australian Kimberley
1993, p. 86

[ ]

David Mowaljarlai: "These things (all the elements of the land: rocks, water courses, waterholes, trees, animals) recognize you. They give their wisdom and their understanding to you when they come close to you" ...It's pulling you."

What is above is mirrored in what is below. Form above – Idea/

*Power below; Wandjina above – his image imprinted below.
Water is both substance (below?) and form (?). Songs are
enacting the relationships between above and below.*

*Something experienced below with some element
of the land announces conception.*

*Place of conception or birth determines your belonging. E.g.
"He is Hibiscus Man and Mountain Man..."*

*Hannah Rachel Bell adds: "The land reflects itself in where
you are born...tree...mountain. The land names us..."*

**An Evening on Australian Spirituality with David Mowaljar-
lai, Michael Leunig, Hannah Rachel Bell**
organized and moderated by David J. Tacey
Melbourne University, 1996
[Notes by Henk Bak]

[ ]

*In the afternoon, when the sun was setting, our grandfather would be
with us again. You know that beautiful colour when the sun is setting?
"You look up at that colour," he would say. With a little wooden stick
he would go tap-tap-tap on your forehead and he would say " Luluai-
luluai-luluai-luluai-luluai..." tap-tap-tap, "Don't be greedy, don't be
selfish, just give the things that you must share with other people. You
must be as beautiful as the sunset." Those were the warnings. Every
sunrise and sunrise. They did this, to all the kids, whether girl or boy.*

David Mowaljarlai & Jutta Malnic
***Yorro Yorro: Everything Standing Up Alive : Public Spirit of
the Kimberley***
1993, p. 105

Maori way of welcoming a child...

*Tikanga (cultural values and beliefs)
The impact of our own cultural values and beliefs has a strong influence
on the way we relate to each other. This can cause complications for
doctors, nurses and midwives as it is particularly important to be aware
of these issues when relating to patients who are often vulnerable.*

*Behaviour and practices that are not consistent with Maori beliefs,
values and concepts, can distress Maori and result in a lack of*

confidence and lack of participation in health care services.

Karakia
Karakia is "Incantation –particularly the ancient rites proper to every important matter in the life of the Maori". Is a "normal" part of Tikanga Maori. Karakia may briefly precede assessment or healing or it may be an integral and ongoing part of the healing process, associated with other rituals like wai tapu (blessed water). Karakia is appropriate in preparation for, during and following birth. Karakia helps whanau:

To be focused
To achieve their goal
To maintain values
To protect everyone

Pregnancy and prenatal care (haputanga)
Pregnancy and prenatal care (haputanga) is a very special time for all. Maori believe that mothers and babies should be comfortable and relaxed throughout the pregnancy and birth. They feel that a baby is fully aware of what is going on in his or her environment and having a mum as calm and relaxed as possible for the entire pregnancy is of great benefit to the baby.

Haputanga is a traditional Maori approach that utilises a combination of gentle belly massage, body alignment and pressure points.

Some benefits of haputanga for the whaea (mother)
It eases discomfort during the pregnancy such as: back pains, strains, muscle aches, bladder and organ discomfort, tiredness and depression and stress relief. It also tends to shorten the length of labour and facilitates an easier birth.

Some benefits of haputanga for the peepi (baby)
It helps keep the baby relaxed and calm, provides more room for the womb to expand so that the baby can move and grow comfortably and aids with keeping the amniotic fluid well balanced.

Nga matua (fathers)
In the Maori culture fathers to be are taught how to do the Maori pregnancy massage and are advised to do it as often as possible, which helps create a more comfortable pregnancy for both whaea (mother) and peepi (baby). Sharing this form of intimacy helps form a close bond between the matua, whaea me te peepi, (father, mother and baby).

Postpartum care for whaea (mums)
Repositioning of internal organs and realignment of the body after
birth by haputanga is thought to help with postpartum depression.

Mothers Matter
https://www.mothersmatter.nz

A secret of Balinese education

Bali has many names, one of them is: 'Last Paradise'. His Excellency Boedidojo, Consul General of the Republic Indonesia, referred to this when he opened the exhibition. Which reminded me of Gregory Bateson's research into the secrets of Balinese education. It must have been around the time of World War II and Bateson wondered whether Balinese culture could offer some hint as to how – in the West – to break the vicious circle of aggression from early childhood on. I don't remember the details of his findings, except that early punishment or retaliation was not one of them. (Mothers would rather tease the little ones into a tantrum and then let the tantrum run its course, just smiling, doing nothing, to stop it.)

Images of war are not absent in Balinese culture. On the contrary. The Ramayana features strongly in story and dance. Part of the secret is perhaps that those images are archetypal, meeting aggressive tendencies halfway in their surge upward from the subconscious depths of instinct and soul. Violence thus experienced virtually, doesn't need to become sensational or real. Aggressive images in fairy tales are archetypal also, not literal. American educational culture tends to ignore this distinction and purge the fairy tales from all those 'scary' images. Bruno Bettleheim, author of 'Uses of Enchantment', passionately opposed this 'emasculation' of fairy tales. By taking the violence out of children's life at an archetypal level, one deprives children of a vital instrument for processing and integrating the violence that lives within themselves: hence the need to experience violence realistically, through sensational, super real images or through acting it out in real life (later on). In Bali children are part of the fabric of life, of family, work, nature, devotion, music, song and dance.

Henk Bak
Review of James Wingate's exhibition of photographs Island of the gods
Melbourne 15 September 2001, Additions 2017

Ceremonies in Bali

Most ceremonies, at the level of the family or of other local temples, cannot take place before a pejati ("notification offering") at the kahyangan tiga. The most important is probably the pura desa, or village temple. Its god, Batara Desa, is usually given the forefront position during the village processions of gods. The desa pekraman (village community) is in reality also the congregation of the pura desa, whatever the other affiliations. It is headed by the bendesa adat.

Much of the ritual work at the village level is shared among the various banjar, for example, more than participate in upacara (ceremonies). One banjar may look after the pura desa for the upcoming festival and another banjar for the one after. Banjars will redistribute the work entrusted to it, via the kelian banjar or neighbourhood headman. All ritual activity will need his involvement before it can take place.

The desa (village) usually has three village temples, the kahyangan tiga, each positioned according to adat (traditional law and custom) and relating to the village's symbolic life: The pura puseh (temple of origin, representing the village founder and also called the navel temple) is located towards Gunung Agung. This is where the important gods of the village and its founders are worshiped; The pura desa (village temple), is located in the center of the village, where meetings of the village assembly and the rituals of fertility are held; the pura dalem (temple of the dead), located toward the ocean, domain of the demons, is where the forces of death are worshiped. Cremation ceremonies take place here and the graveyard, for bodies awaiting cremation is also here. Besides these territorial temples, there is also a temple for each banjar (bedogol or pura banjar), a temple for each subak, and the various temples of the local sub – groups (pura dadia or pura panti), each one having its own calendar of festivals.

All temples of the kahyangan tiga (pura peseh or 'temple of origin', pura desa or 'village temple' and pura dalem or 'temple of the dead') are a vital part of all local rituals.

Every mother knows: the first smile of a child is not a reflex

Incipe, parve puer, risu cognoscere matrem.

Begin, little child, to recognize your mother with a smile.

Quote from Vergilius
In: Prof. Dr. F.J.J. Buytendijk's
De eerste glimlach van een kind
1947
(The first smile of a child) Academische Redevoeringen.(Academic Orations)
Dekker & v.d.Vegt Utrecht – Nijmegen
1961, p. 99

Education: a vision – respect (1824)

The friendly reception from the Three who by and by appeared, at last turned in a general conversation, the substance of which we now present in an abbreviated shape.

"Since you intrust your son to us," said they, "it is fair that we admit you to a closer view of our procedure. Of what is external you have seen much, that does not bear its meaning on its front. What part of this do you chiefly wish to have explained?"

"Dignified, yet singular gestures of salutation I have noticed, the import of which I would gladly learn: with you, doubtless, the exterior has a reference to the interior, and inversely; let me know what the reference is.

"Well-formed, healthy children," replied the Three, "bring much into the world with them: nature has given to each whatever he requires for time and duration; to unfold this is our duty: often it unfolds itself of its own accord. One thing there is, however, which no child brings into the world with him; and yet it is on this one thing that all depends for making man in every point a man. If you can. If you can discover it for yourself, speak it out." Wilhelm thought for a little while, then shook his head.

The Three, after a suitable pause, exclaimed: Reverence! Wilhelm seemed to hesitate. "Reverence!" They cried a second time. All want it, perhaps you yourself.

Three gestures you have seen: and we inculcate a threefold reverence, which, when commingled and formed into one whole, attains its highest force and effect.

The first is reverence for what is above us. That posture, the arms crossed over the breast, the look turned joyfully towards heaven: that is what we have enjoined on young children, requiring from them thereby a testimony that there is a God above, who images and reveals himself in parents, teachers, superiors. Then comes the second: reverence for what is under us. Those hands folded over the back, and, as it were, tied together, that down-turned, smiling look, announce that we are to regard the earth with attention and cheerfulness: from the bounty of the earth we are nourished: the earth affords unutterable joys; but disproportionate sorrows she also brings us. Should one of our children do himself external hurt, blamably or blamelessly; should others hurt him accidentally or purposely; should dead involuntary matter do him hurt; let him well consider it; for such dangers will attend him all his days. But from this posture we delay not to free our pupil, the instance we become convinced that the instruction connected with it has produced sufficient influence on him.

Then, on the contrary, we bid him to gather courage, and turning to his comrades, range himself among with them. Now, at last, he stands forth, frank and bold; not selfishly isolated; only in combination with his equals does he front the world. Further we have nothing to add.

"I see a glimpse of it!" said Wilhelm. "Are not the mass of men so marred and stinted, because they take pleasure only in the element of evil-wishing and evil-speaking? Whoever gives himself to this, soon comes to become indifferent towards God, contemptuous toward the world, spiteful toward his equals.; and the true, genuine, indispensable sentiment of self-estimation corrupts into self-conceit and presumption. Allow me, however," continued he, "to state one difficulty. You say that reverence is not natural to man: now, has not the reverence or fear of rude people for violent convulsions of Nature, or other inexplicable mysteriously-foreboding occurrences, been heretofore regarded as the germ out of which a higher feeling, a purer sentiment, was by degree to be developed?"

"Nature is indeed adequate to fear," replied they; "but to reverence not adequate. Men fear a known or unknown powerful being: the strong seeks to conquer it, the weak to avoid it; both endeavour to get quit of it, and feel themselves happy when for a short season they have put it aside, and their nature has in some degree restored itself to freedom and independence. ...

To fear is easy, but grievous; to reverence is difficult, but satisfactory. Man does not willingly submit himself to reverence; or rather he never so submits himself: it is a higher sense, which must be communicated to his nature; which only in some peculiarly favoured individuals unfolds itself spontaneously, who on this account too have of old been looked upon as saints and gods. Here lies the worth, here lies the business of all true religions; whereof there are likewise only three according to the objects towards which they direct our devotion."

Johann Wolfgang von Goethe, Thomas Carlyle [Translator]
Wilhelm Meister's Apprenticeship
1930, pp. 213-215
[A conversation when visiting an 'educational precinct' in the country ('Pedagogische Provinz')]

King David danced before the Ark of HASHEM

King David was told, "HASHEM has blessed the house of Obed-edom and everything he has because of the Ark of God. "David then went and brought up the Ark of God from the house of Obed-edom to the City of David with joy. Whenever the bearers of the Ark walked six paces, he slaughtered an ox and a fatted ox. David danced with all [his] strength before HASHEM; David was girded in a linen tunic. David and the entire House of Israel Brought up the Ark with loud, joyous sound and the sound of the shofar.

And it happened as the Ark of HASHEM arrived at the City of David, that Michal daughter of Saul peered out the window and saw King David leaping and dancing before HASHEM, and she became contemptuous of him in her heart.

They brought the Ark of HASHEM and set it up in its place, within the tent that David had pitched for it; and David brought up elevation-offerings before HASHEM and peace-offerings.

[ ]

David returned to bless his household. Michal daughter of Saul went out to meet David and said, "How honored was the King of Israel today, who was exposed today in the presence of his servants' maidservants, as one of the boors would be exposed!"

David answered Michal, "In the presence of HASHEM, Who chose me over your father and over his entire house to appoint me as ruler over the people of HASHEM, over Israel – before HASHEM I shall rejoice. And I shall behave even more humbly than this, and I shall be lowly in my eyes; and among the maidservants of whom you spoke – among them I shall be honored!"

Michal daughter of Saul had no child until the day of her death.

(Tanach) Samuel II 6:12-23

Two resonating sounds of praise on receiving a child

"...I am a woman of aggrieved spirit ...and I have poured out my soul before HASHEM...it is out of much grievance and anger that I have spoken until now." Eli then answered and said: "Go in peace, The God of Israel will grant the request you have made of him." She said, "May your maidservant find favor in your eyes." Then the woman went on her way and she ate, and no longer had the same look on her face.

They arose early in the morning and prostrated themselves before HASHEM then they returned and came to their home, to Ramah. Elkanah knew Hannah his wife and HASHEM remembered her. And it happened with the passage of the period of days that Hannah had conceived, and she gave birth to a son. She named him Samuel, for (she said), "requested him from HASHEM."

[ ] She brought him up with her when she weaned him...she brought him to the house of HASHEM in Shiloh, though the child was still tender. They slaughtered a bull, and brought the child to Eli. She said, "Please, my Lord! By your life, my Lord, I am the woman who was standing by you here praying to HAHEM. This is the child that I prayed for; HASHEM granted me my request that I asked of Him. Furthermore, I have dedicated him to HASHEM – all the days that he lives he is dedicated to HASHEM." He then prostrated himself to HASHEM.

Then Hannah prayed and said:

*My heart exults in HASHEM;
my pride has been raised through HASHEM;
my mouth is opened wide against my antagonists,
for I rejoice in my salvation.
[ ]
The bow of the mighty is broken,
while the foundering are girded with strength.
The sated ones are hired out for bread,
while the hungry ones cease to be so;
while the barren woman bears seven,
the one with many children becomes bereft...*

(Tanach) 1 Samuel 1:15-20;24-28; 2: 1-5

Mary set out at that time and went as quickly as she could to a town in the hill country of Judah. She went onto Zecharia's house and greeted Elizabeth. Now as soon as Elizabeth heard Mary's greeting, the child leapt up in her womb and Elizabeth was filled with the Holy Spirit. She gave a loud cry and said, "Of all women you are the most blessed, and blessed is the fruit of your womb. Why should I be honoured with a visit from the mother of my Lord? For the moment your greeting reached my ears, the child in my womb leapt for joy. Yes, blessed is she who believed that the promise made by the Lord would be fulfilled."

And Mary said:

My soul proclaims the greatness of the Lord
And my spirit exults in God my saviour;
Because he has looked upon his lowly handmaid.
Yes, from this day forward all generations will call me blessed, for the Almighty has done great things for me.
[ ]
He has shown the power of his arm,
he has routed the proud of heart,
He has pulled down princes from their thrones and exulted the lowly.
The hungry he has filled with good things, the rich sent empty away.

Gospel of St Luke 1
Alexander Jones [editor]
The Jerusalem Bible
1966, p. 39-53

The birth of every child is important

Whenever I read the stories of Asita and Simeon, I have the wish that every one of us could have been visited by a sage when we were born. The birth of every child is important, no less than the birth of a Buddha. We, too, are a Buddha, a Buddha-to-be, and we continue to be born every minute. We, too, are sons and daughters of God and the children of our parents. We have to take special care of each birth.

I am not sure if I am myself or if I am my brother. Before I came into the world, another boy tried to come before me, but my mother miscarried him. If he had continued to live, I would have another brother. Or perhaps I would have been my brother. Many times as a child, I pondered this.

Expecting parents have to be very careful because they carry with them a baby, one who might become a Buddha or Lord Jesus. They have to be mindful of what they eat, what they drink, what they think, and how they act. The way they take care of their bodies and their feelings affects the well-being of the child within. Our mothers and fathers helped us to come to be and, even now, they continue to give us life.

Our spiritual ancestors have also given birth to us, and they, too, continue to give birth to us. In my country, we say that an authentic teacher has the power to give birth to a disciple... We say that sons and daughters of the Buddha came forth from the mouth of the Buddha, because the Buddha offered them the Dharma, his teachings...

Thich Nhat Hanh
Living Buddha, Living Christ
1995, pp. 46-48

A boy learns to pray

...HASHEM continued to call, "Samuel" a third time, and he arose and went to Eli and said, "Here I am, for you called me." The Eli realized that HASHEM was calling the lad.

Eli said to Samuel, "Go and lie down, and if He calls you, you should say, "Speak, HASHEM, for your servant is listening". Samuel went and lay down in his place. HASHEM came and appeared, and called as the other times, "Samuel, Samuel" and Samuel said, "Speak for your servant is listening."

(Tanach) Samuel 3:8-10

A girl learns to pray:

O Thou most glorious Lord! Make this little maidservant of Thine blessed and happy; cause her to be cherished at the threshold of Thy Oneness, and let her drink deep from the cup of Thy Love so that she may be filled with rapture and ecstasy and diffuse sweet-scented fragrance. Thou art the Mighty and Powerful, and Thou art the All-knowing, the All-seeing.

'Abdu'l-Bahá
Bahá'í Prayers: A Selection of the Prayers
2012, p. 31

Children learn to pray: a Bahá'I parent's account

With regard to the children's prayers, people make their own choice on what they like. With my children they started with

O God, guide me, protect me, make of me a
shining lamp and a brilliant star.

Thou art the Mighty and the Powerful.

'Abdu'l-Bahá
Bahá'í Prayers: A Selection of the Prayers
2012, p. 29

As they got older, they tried,

O my Lord! O my Lord!

I am a child of tender years. Nourish me from the breast of Thy
mercy, train me in the bosom of Thy love, educate me in the school
of Thy guidance and develop me under the shadow of Thy bounty.
Deliver me from darkness, make me a brilliant light; free me from
unhappiness, make me a flower of the rose garden, suffer me to become
as servant of Thy threshold and confer upon me the disposition
and nature of the righteous; make me a cause of bounty to the
human world, and crown my head with diadem of eternal life;

Verily, Thou art the Powerful, the Mighty, the Seer, the HearerI

'Abdu'l-Bahá
Bahá'í Prayers: A Selection of the Prayers
2012, p. 29

If you wanted one for infants, there is the following.

O God! Rear this little babe in the bosom of Thy love, and give
it milk from the breast of Thy Providence. Cultivate this fresh
plant in the rose garden of Thy love and aid it to grow through the
showers of Thy bounty. Make it a child of the kingdom, and lead
it to Thy heavenly realm. Thou art powerful and kind, and Thou
art the Bestower, the Generous, the Lord of surpassing bounty.

'Abdu'l-Bahá
Bahá'í Prayers: A Selection of the Prayers
2012, p. 33

If you wanted one parents can say for children, there is the following.

O Thou kind Lord! These lovely children are the handiwork of the fingers of Thy might and the wondrous signs of Thy greatness. O God! Protect these children, graciously aid them to be educated and enable them to render service to the world of humanity. O God! These children are pearls, cause them to be nurtured within the shell of thy loving-kindness.

Thou are the Bountiful, the All-Loving.

'Abdu'l-Bahá
Bahá'í Prayers: A Selection of the Prayers
2012, p. 28

A child learns to contemplate - evening prayer

*From the head unto the feet
After God's true likeness I am made,
From the heart till in the hands,
God's breath I feel and sense;
When through my mouth I speak,
God's will is my true guide.
When I see God everywhere I look,
In mother, father, all dear people,
In animal and flower,
In tree and rock,
Nothing frightens me;
For everything around me
I have only love.*

No extra teaching. An adult speaks it every evening; bit by bit the child speaks single words, then repeats lines and so learns the whole prayer.

Rudolf Steiner
Wahrspruchworte: Verses and Meditations
1975, pp. 258
[Translated by Henk Bak]

Be like children

An argument started between them about which of them was the greatest. Jesus knew what thoughts were going through their minds, and he took a little child and set him by his side and then said to them, 'Anyone who welcomes this little child in my name welcomes me; and anyone who welcomes me welcomes the one who sent me. For the least among you all, that is the one who is great.'

He said to his disciples, 'Obstacles are sure to come, but alas for the one who provides them! It would be better for him to be thrown into the sea with a millstone put round his neck than that he should lead astray a single one of these little ones, watch your selves!'

Alexander Jones [Editor]
The Jerusalem Bible / Luke 17
1966, pp. 1-2

People even brought little children to him for him to touch them; but when the disciples saw this they turned them away. But Jesus called the children to him and said, 'Let the little children come to me, and do not stop them; for it is to such as these that the Kingdom of God belongs. I tell you solemnly, anyone who does not welcome the kingdom of God like a little child will never enter it.'

Alexander Jones [Editor]
The Jerusalem Bible / Luke 18
1966, pp. 15-17

For Tibetans, bearing a child is an act of conscious intention that involves seven distinct stages - and starts before conception

Exiled from their home in "the land of snows," the Tibetan people – under the leadership of the very popular Dalai Lama – have been sharing more and more of their unique culture with the rest of the world, to the world's great benefit. This article exploring the wisdom of Tibetan childbirth practice is based on Anne Hubbell Maiden and Edie Farwell's forthcoming book Tibetan Birth Wisdom. *Anne is a psychotherapist and social psychologist, and a founder of both the Friends of Children and Parents and of the Conscious Birthing Circle in San Francisco. Edie is a social and cultural anthropologist who founded The Development Collaborative and currently acts as Liaison Director for the Association for Progressive Communications.*

"Conceiving a baby does not mean you create a baby," a Tibetan scholar and friend told me when I was researching Tibetan birth practices. "It is more as if you are calling a being into your womb." In Tibetan Buddhism, the conception of a baby is not a random occurrence. It is much more intentional, often with the being who is going to be born as a baby determining, either consciously or unconsciously, which womb *he or she will enter. Tibetan mothers talk of having dreams when they are first pregnant of inviting someone into a nicely furnished room. This symbolizes to them inviting someone into their womb – a new baby. Often after such a dream a woman will discover she is pregnant.*

Childbirth in Tibetan culture is an especially rich and powerful time. The intention of a spirit or "intermediate being" – the name Tibetans give to one who has died but has not yet been reborn – to take rebirth in a human form is a result of that being's karma. Karma is the causal effect of one's past actions. Thus parents who are conceiving a baby and the intermediate being who will become that baby are drawn together by the circumstances of their previous lives.

Reincarnation is integral to Tibetan Buddhism and virtually all of Tibetan culture. One lives a cycle of life after life, until one has learned what one needs in order to attain enlightenment and be freed from the circle of birth, death and rebirth. Until that time, however, one is born, lives, dies, and according to one's karma, gets born again into a new life. Thus childbirth is part of "beginningless time and boundless space" as one Tibetan lama described it. Rebirth is intentional and for a purpose. That purpose is usually to further understanding of the human condition, help others, or strengthen relationships, such as those with the parents one is born to. A being is able to learn what he or she is intended to learn no matter how long their life is – whether they die in infancy, early in childhood, or even as a fetus due to spontaneous abortion. After experiencing these outcomes, they are born again in another life to learn further. For Tibetan Buddhists the continuing cycles of death and rebirth are as much a part of life as the life itself is.

To help generation after generation of Tibetans progress through this cycle, Tibetans have developed a sophisticated set of beliefs and practices which uses extensive ritual as a way to connect one's present life with one's past lives. Ritual also helps a being move through the birth process into his or her new life.

[ ]

Ritual is present at every stage of the birth process: from before conception through conception and gestation, at the birth itself, in bonding after the birth, and in infancy and early childhood. Tibetan ritual is especially empowering and enriching for the woman. Pregnancy is a time when a Tibetan woman is seen by others as powerful and naturally imbued with access to high spiritual realms. Her husband and family members recognize that this time is special and make sure that she is well cared for, both physically and spiritually. Dreams during pregnancy take on special significance. Rituals surrounding childbirth help women to deliver their babies quickly, easily, and auspiciously.

The seven stages of birth

Pre-Conception. Before conception a woman who knows she wants to have a baby often goes to a holy place to pray, walk around a temple, and do prostrations to statues of Buddha and other Tibetan Buddhist deities. A Tibetan refugee who served as one of our informants now lives in Oakland, California. She had a hard time conceiving a child and so made a pilgrimage to India:

"I went on a pilgrimage to Bodh Gaya," she told us. "Bodh Gaya, you know, is where Buddha attained enlightenment. It is a very holy place where many Tibetans go to make offerings and pray. My two sisters and my friend, Samten, were there with me. Samten asked me if I wanted to have a baby girl.

"She told me what to do to purify myself and prepare to conceive a baby girl. There is a small cave on the other side of a big river at Bodh Gaya," she recounted. "Samten showed me a tree there, and told me to put one hair on it, so then I could pray for whatever I wanted. You have to purify yourself for whatever it is you pray for to come to you. Every morning at five o'clock we would get up and take a walk, and then I would do prostrations for an hour."

Conception. She spent two weeks there, praying, doing prostrations, and circumambulating the temple to purify herself. She told me that she prayed for a baby, stating in her prayers that so many Tibetans had died during China's invasion of Tibet that one of them who wished could be reborn through her. When she told me this story she hugged her toddler daughter, saying, "She is the lucky one. I conceived her soon after I returned home from Bodh Gaya." She felt her pilgrimage had cleansed her and prepared her womb for a baby to enter.

As reincarnation is an integral part of Tibetan Buddhism, often there is a bond, or an understanding, between a parent and the child even before it is born. A woman may have dreams around the time of conception and during pregnancy that let her get to know who her child is and what characteristics the child will have when it comes into the world.

Gestation. During gestation, prayers are made for the health of the baby and the mother and for a quick and easy birth. Lamas are visited to ask for a blessing, offerings are left at the temple, and the woman spends even more time in spiritual activities than she normally would. Particularly complex or symbolic dreams are taken to a lama for interpretation.

In Tibetan medical texts, the development of a fetus is followed week by week. The texts describe not only the physical growth of a fetus, but also when it loses memory of past lives, when consciousness of this life occurs, and when the winds enter to allow the movement of its body.

Birth. When it is time for the birth itself, a series of rituals are enacted that help ease the mother through the delivery. The father, doctor, uncle, or "anyone who has kept his moral obligations" may make nine small indentations on a square of butter and recite a mantra two hundred times over it. The empowerment of the butter is completed by blowing over it. The father then feeds the blessed butter to his wife at the last stages of labor to help her give birth quickly.

The father is present at the birth and helps out where needed, though the midwife or an experienced mother is the primary attendant. The father may recite the "Collection of Mantras" scripture for auspiciousness and for an easy delivery periodically throughout the birth process.

If there is great difficulty at the birth, a lama may be asked to do special prayers at the monastery. The father, or anyone else the family deems appropriate, approaches a rinpoche (the family lama) and makes an offering of money and a white ceremonial scarf, called a kata, for the appropriate ritual to be performed, according to the lama's divination. The spiritual energy created by the ceremony is directed to the mother and baby for an easy birth and good health.

The father may also give the lama butter to bless. During difficult labor, the mother can eat the blessed butter to ease the pain. The comfort of a familiar food that has been blessed relaxes the mother and makes her feel as if a higher power is looking out for her. If labor is strong, the mother may eat a piece of dried fish from the sacred Lake Manasarovar in Tibet. A little bit of the fish is kept on hand in most households and is fed to the mother when her pain increases. The fish from the sacred lake brings blessings and spiritual grace to the woman who takes it, and so eases her mind and helps her relax, allowing the baby to come sooner. This also

*happens commonly when blessed butter is taken. Both taking the fish
and the butter are such standard rituals in Tibetan culture that women
are conditioned to relax and feel safe when they eat them during labor.*

*When contractions become close and intense, the midwife
may give the mother a traditional herbal preparation that
invariably causes the baby to be born soon after.*

*After the birth. Immediately after birth the child begins to breathe. As soon
as its mouth is opened, the symbol Dhih is painted in saffron powder on
the newborn's tongue. Dhih is the seed syllable of Manjusri, the deity of
wisdom. Tibetans do this so the baby will grow to be wise and articulate
– qualities they value highly. In some parts of Tibet, the Dhih is used
to give the child intelligence, long life, and good fortune. In other parts of
Tibet, blessed butter that someone has prayed over is put on the tongue.
It symbolizes good health, longevity, and always having enough to eat.*

*Butter is then put on the tip of the nose. The baby is cleaned with a cloth
and warm water, and wrapped tightly in cotton cloth and wool for warmth.
During this, the baby stays with the mother, and is rarely separated from her.*

*Soon after the birth the mother is given one or two cups
of hot butter to drink to replenish her strength and warm
her. Then she eats soup and drinks Tibetan tea.*

*The placenta is saved until an astrologer indicates the first auspicious day for
the father or another relative to bury it. The placenta can be buried anywhere
as long as no animals can dig it up. The placenta is wrapped in clean cloth
and buried deep in the ground, often with the children of the family assisting.
The place it is buried is not marked by the family, but the process of burying
it symbolizes respect for the placenta which nourished the baby in the womb.*

*The cord is kept in a safe place in the house for about a year.
The mother uses the cord to heal thrush in the baby's mouth by
dipping it in milk, tea, or water and rubbing it over the sore.*

*Bonding. Traditionally, a family with a newborn spends a few quiet
days alone before visitors are welcomed. These days are a special time
for the family to be all together, to bond closely with the new baby
and to enact cleansing rituals and prayers for the baby's health.*

On the third day (for a boy) or the fourth day (for a girl), a big welcoming ceremony is held for the newborn. Relatives, friends, and neighbors come to the family's house bringing gifts and blessings to the new infant. The traditional view is that coming earlier may bring bad luck for the child or the parents and could cause the baby to lose its tenuous hold on life.

During the first quiet days, the baby lies next to the mother as both rest. The father is kept busy helping with all the extra chores that need to be done: watching the other children; washing diapers; making special meat broth, chicken soup, tsampa or roasted barley flour, and butter tea for the mother; and heating water for her, as she is not allowed to touch cold water for the first month after birth. Doing so, it is thought, may later cause her harm.

To ensure that a child has the best chance of developing her capacities to their full potential, elaborate rituals are performed to protect the infant and to facilitate growth. Offerings are made to the deities and protectors, butter lamps are lit, and prayers chanted in the house to honor the newborn and to mark the baby's integration into this world. These rituals begin to carve the baby's niche in the patterns of relationship she will have both to her family and to the deities.

My friend Dorje told me how a couple of days after his daughter's birth he went to a high lama to receive a name for her. He visited the lama that his family regularly consults for ceremonies and special needs. Dorje prostrated three times in front of the lama and made a small offering of money wrapped in a kata, or ceremonial scarf. The lama blessed the scarf and returned it to Dorje, placing it gently around his bowed neck.

Then the lama asked, "Is the baby a boy or a girl?" "A girl," Dorje answered proudly. The lama, sitting upright, concentrated his full energies on the new baby. After a few minutes he raised his cupped hands to his mouth and blew his blessing on the knotted protection cord he held. Handing the cord to Dorje, he said, "This is for your daughter, Dolma Tsering."

Respectfully bowing to the lama as he accepted the protection cord to pin on his daughter's shirt, Dorje hurried home with the blessed string to tell his family the name their daughter had received. The validation of a name gives the baby another strong hold on this life that she is just beginning.

Receiving her name from a lama further bonds Dolma Tsering with the realm of deities and the spiritual dimension of her Tibetan heritage and indicates that she has a place and role to fulfill during this lifetime. The parents' request for a name from a lama represents their acceptance of the greater force of which both they and the baby are a part. Even Tibetans in the United States will have a relative or close friend go to the Dalai Lama in India, or another high lama, to have a name sent for their child.

On the day of the welcoming ceremony, Dorje and Lhamo rose early to enact rituals of purification and welcome. First they lit butter lamps and made offerings to the deities and protectors. Then, using a special bottle of water obtained that morning from the lama, Dolma Tsering was cleansed of any impurities associated with the birth. Her grandmother blessed the water by receiving it in her cupped hands from Dorje, and pouring it into Lhamo's palm. After Lhamo drank a little of the water, she wiped her palm on her head and then on Dolma Tsering's. In this way, not only was Dolma Tsering cleansed, she was also bound yet deeper to the traditional ways.

With the first visitor's arrival, which marked the end of the family's time alone, Dorje prepared incense and a small container of milk. Giving a short prayer for Dolma Tsering, his brother lit the incense and sprinkled milk around the room, thereby cleansing the house and initiating Dolma Tsering's welcoming ceremony.

Friends and family welcomed the new baby by presenting a kata, the blessing scarf, to Dolma Tsering, who lay peering up out of her mother's lap. (Visitors usually don't touch a newborn right away; they wait until the child is a month or so old and strong enough not to pick up any illnesses from them.) Throughout the day they came, bringing small presents and good wishes to celebrate Dolma Tsering's arrival into both the family and the community. Thermoses filled with butter tea flowed liberally, and trays of freshly fried Tibetan cookies were passed. After a while, Dorje brought out dishes of rice mixed with raisins and butter. Each guest took a handful, some to eat and some to throw into the sky for the child's auspicious life. The rice symbolizes both protection for the young baby and the harvest of nine months of pregnancy.

This welcoming ceremony marks the beginning of the baby's relationship with most of the people to whom she will be closest as the years go on, thus establishing both her right to receive their care and love throughout her life, as well as cementing her responsibility to care for and love all of them as she grows older.

Infancy. After the birth, clothes are made and new blankets and wraps *are given to the infant. Although young mothers outside of Tibet today share baby clothes and blankets with one another, traditionally it was believed to be inauspicious to dress a new baby in used clothes. Before the birth, a mother, grandmother or other relative would cut out cloth for new baby clothes — but could not sew the clothes to completion. To do so could also have been inauspicious and might have brought harm to the baby. Only after the baby was safely born and gave signs of being strong and healthy would the new clothes be finished.*

Throughout infancy, a baby is incorporated into the daily rhythm of the family, usually on the back of the mother when she goes to make prayers and offerings, and as she goes about her routine.

If a baby becomes sick, special rituals are enacted for curing. One ritual used to cleanse sickness from a baby's body is to give barley flour dough, or tsampa, to the mother and then to the baby and have the baby squeeze it in her two fists. The dough is then rolled all over the baby's body to pick up any negativity or toxicity. The tsampa is taken and cast away with effigies in the likeness of the offending spirits, made by a lama from dough. The dough becomes food for the effigy so that the effigy can feel that it has had enough to eat and therefore has no interest in bothering the baby further.

Childhood. Much of a young child's acculturation is done naturally through the child's participation in everyday family life. Children are taught to enter the prayer room with respect, to bring their hands together in prayer, and to prostrate before the statues and paintings of the deities. Children can be heard singing mantra to themselves or with other children from an early age. Games are played both inside and outside the house, and older children care for and watch after the younger children.

By participating in her parents' activities, a child easily and naturally learns the values of her family and of her culture. In these days, as Tibetans struggle to keep their culture alive in the midst of genocide, destruction, and dispersal, it is especially important that cultural values be passed from one generation to another. Enacting the traditional rituals, particularly around the powerful time of childbirth, is an effective and enriching way to do this.

Edie Farwell and Anne Hubbell Maiden
***The Wisdom of Tibetan Childbirth in: Birth, Sex & Death
(IC#31)***
1992, p. 26

Catholic Church the Baptismal Ceremony

Most priests are willing to go through the ceremony with you beforehand if you are a bit unsure of what is involved.

Sign of the Cross
Usually when you enter the church the priest will trace the cross on the forehead of your baby and invite the parents and godparents to do the same. The cross is a reminder of the love of Christ who gave his life for his friends.

The tracing of a cross on the forehead of the person being baptised is an invisible 'branding' that says 'you belong to Christ'.

Baptismal Promises
You will gather around the baptismal font - a large bowl, usually of stone or marble or glass holding the waters of baptism. Usually the mother holds the child. The celebrant asks the parents what they want for the child. You reply, 'Baptism.' Then you make the baptismal promises on behalf of your child.

These promises are based on the Apostles Creed.

Anointing
The celebrant anoints your baby with oil on the forehead and on the chest. He anoints the baby with the Oil of Baptism (Catechumens) and with the Oil of Chrism. The Oil of Baptism is olive oil. It relates to the days when athletes used to rub oil into their bodies before events to strengthen them and make their skin more supple. It symbolises strengthening for the struggles of life ahead.

The Oil of Chrism is a combination of olive oil and balsam. It symbolises the sealing with the gifts of the Holy Spirit.

Baptism with Water
The priest pours water over the head of your baby (or immerses the baby in the water) and says "I baptise you in the name of the Father and of the Son and of the Holy Spirit."

The water is a sign of cleansing. The water symbolically washes the person being baptised of all sin.

It is also a sign of life. Without water nothing can grow. It is a sign of the new spiritual life into which the baptised person is entering.

Candle
As a sign of the new life a candle will be lit, usually from the Easter Candle which symbolises the light of Christ.

Usually the father of the child or a godparent will stand by the child and hold this candle.

You might ask the priest beforehand whether it is the custom in your parish for the parents to bring their own baptismal candle or whether the parish provides them. If you provide the candle, you can choose either to buy a baptismal candle or to decorate one yourself.

White Garment
Your child is given a white garment as a sign of being clothed in Christ.

Your family might have a Christening gown that you want to use or a shawl. If you want to use this, then let the priest know beforehand.

You might like to use a baptismal gown, either a white stole, a white scapular or a white bib - perhaps one that you have made and bearing the sign of a cross. The white garment is a symbol of purity and innocence.

From the Internet

The splendour of recurrent existence

The immersion in water can be understood literally, as in many religious rituals where water is the purifying element, or as I see it, we become the water. Like dolphins who returned to the sea after millions of years, we can return to our inner sea; where the dissolution of boundaries, structure, and form leads to a greater whole where life-sustaining nutrients are once again absorbed and one now is filled with the splendour of recurring existence.

Emilie Conrad
Life on Land: The Story of Continuum, the World-Renowned Self-Discovery and Movement Method
2007, pp. 246-247

Promoting human dignity the most fundamental way of promoting peace

Mother Theresa once said: *"In these twenty years of work among the people, I have come more and more to realise that it is being unwanted that is the worst disease that a human being can ever experience."* She *believes that the worst disease today is not leprosy or tuberculosis, but rather the feeling of being unwanted, uncared for and deserted by everybody.*

It was precisely people in this plight, the poorest of the poor, who were the very first to find warmth and shelter with Mother Theresa. Her intention was to ensure that they enjoyed the feeling of being received and recognised as people with their own human dignity and the right to respect.

Mother Theresa works in the world as she finds it, in the slums of Calcutta and other towns and cities. But she makes no distinction between poor and rich persons, between poor and rich countries. Politics have never been her concern, but economic, social and political work with the same aims are in complete harmony with her own life's work.

[ ]

There would be no better way of describing the intentions that have motivated the decision of the Norwegian Nobel Committee than the comment of the World bank president, Robert Macnamara, when he declared: "Mother Theresa deserves the Nobel's Peace Prize because she promotes peace in the most fundamental manner, by her confirmation of the inviolability of human dignity." pp. 227-8

[ ]

"And today the greatest means, the greatest destroyer of peace is abortion. And we who are standing here – our parents wanted us. We would not be here if our parents would do that to us.

Our children, we want them, we love them. But what of the other millions. Many people are very, very concerned with the children of India, with the children of Africa where quite a number die, maybe of malnutrition, of hunger and so on, but millions are dying deliberately by the will of the mother. And this is what is the greatest destroyer of peace today…

[ ]

I will tell you something terrifying. We are fighting abortion by adoption. We have saved thousands of lives. We have sent word to all the clinics, to the hospitals, police stations: 'Please don't destroy the child; we will take the child'...And we have a tremendous demand for families who have no children, that is the blessing of God for us. And also, we are doing another thing which is very beautiful. We are teaching our beggars, our leprosy patients, our slum dwellers, our people in the street, natural family planning.

And in Calcutta alone in six years – it is all in Calcutta – we have had 61,273 babies less from families who would have had them because they practice this natural way of abstaining, of self-control, out of love for each other. We teach them the temperature method which is very beautiful, very simple. And our poor people understand. And you know what they have told me? "Our family is healthy, our family is united, and we can have a baby whenever we want". From the Nobel Lecture / pp.232-233

Kathryn Spink
For the Brotherhood of Man under the Fatherhood of God:
Mother Theresa of Calcutta, her Missionaries of Charity and
her Co-Workers.
1981

Muslim birth rites for welcoming a child.

The Muslim call to prayer or adhaan ("God is great, there is no God but Allah. Muhammad is the messenger of Allah. Come to prayer.") are the first words a newborn Muslim baby should hear. They are whispered into the right ear of the child by his or her father.

The baby's first taste should be something sweet, so parents may chew a piece of date and rub the juice along the baby's gums. It was a practice carried out by the Prophet Muhammad and is believed to help tiny digestive systems to kick in.

There are a number of events that take place on or after the seventh day.

After seven days the baby's head is shaved (a tradition also carried out by Hindus). This is to show that the child is the servant of Allah. Although Hindus may take the baby's hair to India and scatter it in the holy river Ganges, Muslims weigh it and give the equivalent weight in silver to charity.

Ideally, Muslim baby boys are circumcised when they are seven days old although it can take place any time before puberty. It is also tradition to choose a name for the baby on the seventh day.

The aqeeqah is also traditionally carried out on the seventh day. This is a celebration which involves the slaughter of sheep. Sheep are sacrificed (in Britain the meat is ordered at the butchers) and the meat is distributed to relatives and neighbours and also given to the poor.

Birth and the Basque

I see two vistas across a Spanish countryside. The first is roughly criss-crossed by layered, low walls of field stones which create many tiny plots of green. The other is home to a circle of stone houses surrounded by spacious growing fields and trees.

In the first vista the land has been divided among progeny of large families over generations, until the walled sections appear too small for cultivation. In the second, a Basque settlement, custom has it that younger children leave home to explore the world while the first-born cares for the land.

Among the mystical Basque, conception is a sacred act, and men and women wait to marry until they have come to maturity in their thirties or forties. Traditional Basque who practice the old pre-Christian ways (now 15% or less of the modern population) marry only when they plan to have children.

Within this group, marriage is both a sacred union and a working partnership between the extended family cooperative and the land. Both parts of the family come together with the whole village to share food, dances, songs, and tributes all day and through the night. Then the husband or wife goes to the home place of whoever is older.

Human life is given great value, as are strength, integrity, honesty, balance, and self-sufficiency. Boys and girls grow up with strong family ties and same-sex friendship groups, which last throughout their lives. Around the circle of houses, each neighbor to the left, when called upon, is helper and healer.

For the Basque, family comes first, and home is sacred. In Basque mystical practice, birth is an event celebrated by the whole extended family. Thus birthing provides continued and sustained family bonding, and the young learn of birth in a sacred family context. Birth is also highly valued as practice for facing what is new, including the ultimate new experience, which is death. Death in its time is seen as a return to the natural beginning of things.

Edie Farwell and Anne Hubbell Maiden
The Wisdom of Tibetan Childbirth in: Birth, Sex & Death
(IC#31)
1992, p. 26

[This sidebar was based on observation in the Pyrenees and talks with Angeles Arrien, an anthropologist at the California Institute of Integral Studies with a specialty in Basque folklore]

Hindu rituals (sanskars) begin before a child is born.

Hindus believe that it is the responsibility of each individual to continue the Hindu race and therefore soon after a couple are married, a prayer called Garbhadana (conception) is recited for fulfillment of one's parental obligations.

During the third month of pregnancy the ceremony of Punsavana (foetus protection) is performed. This is done for the strong physical growth of the foetus.

The Simantonnyana is performed during the seventh month. This is the equivalent of a baby shower and means 'satisfying the craving of the pregnant mother'. Prayers are offered for the mother and child with emphasis on healthy mental development of the unborn child. Hindus believe that mental state of a pregnant woman affects the unborn child.

Once the child enters the world, Jatakarma is performed to welcome the child into the family, by putting some honey in the child's mouth and whispering the name of God in the child's ear.

Other rituals include a naming ceremony (Namakarna), the Nishkarmana (the child's first trip out) and the Annaprasana, (the child's first taste of solid food).

The ear-piercing ceremony (Karnavedha) and first haircut (Mundan) ceremonies are also considered highly significant. These sacraments are performed on both the sexes. Hindus believe that the piercing of a hole in the lower lobes of the ear have benefits of acupuncture.

Head shaving is connected to the removal of impurities.

When the child reaches school-going age, the Upanayana (sacred thread) ceremony is performed. The three strands of the sacred thread represent the three vows (to respect the knowledge, the parents and the society) taken before the start of formal education. Although Hindu scriptures explain the rituals, it is possible that Hindu rituals and rites will differ according to particular castes and regions.

Hindu Baby Rights
https://www.bbc.co.uk/religion/religions/hinduism/ritesrituals/
baby.shtml
2009

From a meditation addressing the souls who are approaching the earth:

(Create an appropriate meditative context in which you might send Life-Light, Clarity, Mildness, Goodness, Strength.)

...And with my sight I turn to you, oh Souls, who have entered upon the journey to the Blue Wandering Star – strength-filled with spirit-will, clothed in light, full of blessing. Let yourselves be consciously accompanied by awakened human beings on earth, who hear the harmonious unison of worlds in the flame of their heart knowingly, lovingly and wakefully guarded, in work as in life.

Gideon Fontalba
Verses and Meditations for Accompanying Souls
Ash Wednesday, 1988

Prayer

God, our children are Yours.
May happen on their life's journey
what happens with the eggs
in the nest of the dove:
they are being turned over and shaken
many times,
but never do they fall to the ground.
So, too, are our children
In your hand, always.

From Angola

Love my children

O stars, animals and trees
Love my children, for they are your kin.
even if they 've flown far from me,
I can trust you wth their destiny.

To me you were always kind and only kind.
Love them after my body dies.
Winter, Spring, Summer, Fall, rivers and groves,
Please love my children for they are all of you.

Eagles rising, Eagles flying
in: Les Endrei's
Tales from the Present
2014, pp. 123-124

Welcoming Children as Expression of Human Dignity

Children bring precious abilities and strengths with them in your earthly life. In their lively young way they can give new ideas and wise inspirations to the family and society.

The basic dignity of the children is extended in the charter of the Movement for Human Dignity in such a way, that they are not only regarded as young people needing protection, but are seriously honoured as important carriers of life and ideas.

Because children are those people who will responsibly take charge of the future of earth and mankind, it is clear that parents, teachers, researchers and politicians together have to provide the best possible development of the children.

Essential for this task is that the concerns, opinions, the new undistorted ideas of children and the ways in which they want to design and shape things, will also be taken up in cultural practice and eventually in the ways of everyday life!

1. Children are messengers of joy, light and love. They radiate a holy life- magic that sweetly moves the heart and awakens a gentle attraction. Many small children are able to instantly win you over and when – in that moment of affection - you look with awe into the deep and open eyes, you might receive a greeting from heaven, from very close and from very far simultaneously. How precious is such a moment.

2. Children come to earth with abilities and powers. And when they enter in a good family or community, where healthy, harmonious, dynamic life-circumstances and loving mutual dedication really exist, they rapidly show what beautiful gifts they have brought. If we open the space and the way for their development and engage ourselves with them in a joyful learn-play

activity, we all will win and adults will perceive how they themselves learn and are taught anew by the children. Children need above all the living presence of the parents. Joyful dedication and the experience that the parents truly love each other!
The fundamental dignity of children has to be so extended that children are not only honoured as young people who need to be protected, but also respected and heard as important carriers of new life on earth and as free contributors of ideas.
In their consciousness holy, pure, germs of a non-earthly wisdom are alive. Many adults are in their soul-life already permeated with and to a degree heavily burdened by the human complications caused by the culture of this world. If they ridicule the messages of the children and shove those aside as childish nonsense or suppress them with reserved strictness, then earthly humanity cannot longer receive spiritual youth-forces and must decay.
The young people will become sad and annoyed, rightfully they rebel or become deeply depressed.
Youthful strength declines. Love takes hold only lightly and connections are fleeting. Sterility, low levels of conception and ageing of the population are often signs that the messages of the children and the nobility of young people are not understood.

3. True dedication to the children according to divine and natural laws takes time!

Parents, FREE RELATIVES, carers, teachers, they all need time for the children and young people.
They also need time for themselves to be able to fulfil their task in balance and with joy.
It is their task to receive the young human beings, who are not from this world with its busy doings, warm-heartedly and friendly, meaning here: friend-worthy. To give the children opportunities for an inspiring development and let them become strong and radiant in all areas. The earthly young person who comes from the spiritual world needs on the one side strength and courage and on the other side joy and love. Otherwise his/her full being cannot full-heartedly grow. The young earth citizen is then not able to fully realise what he might have had to bring as perhaps important and even decisive work for earthly humanity.
Many things have to change in society to make it possible to fulfil the demands of the healthy human intelligence and of the intelligent love-filled heart.
Every human being contributes to this when he/she works on him/herself in order to come to a natural noble dignity, obtained through a meaningful life!

Shin Gwydion Fontalba
Kempten Germany January 2010

Prayer and meditation- the breath and heartbeat of the soul

...just a breathing and the beating of the heart are an expression of the breath of life in the waking and sleeping conditions of the body, so may conscious thinking and conceptualization be compared to the breath and heartbeat of the spirit. Similarly prayer and meditation are the breath and heartbeat of the soul, the breath of life in the human being's higher self (atma in Hindu philosophy), above and beyond which God himself exists as its source and origin.

Valentin Tomberg
Covenant of the Heart: Meditations of a Christian Hermeticist on the Mysteries of Tradition
1992, pp. 245-6

Food is Brahman

*Bhirigu went to his father, Varuna,
And asked respectfully: "What is Brahman?"*

*Varuna replied: "First learn about food,
Breath, eye, ear, speech, and mind; then seek to know
That from which these are born, by which they live,
For which they search, and to which they return.
That is Brahman."*

*Bhirigu meditated and found that food
Is Brahman. From food are born all creatures
By food they grow, and to food they return.*

From the Taittriya Upanishad Part III, in: Alice Peck's
Bread, Body, Spirit: Finding the Sacred in Food
2008

If there is any word that should characterize the life of peacemakers, it is "gratitude". True peacemakers are grateful persons, persons who constantly recognize and celebrate the peace of God within and among them. This might at first sound sentimental, but those who have lived through periods of true pain and agony know the mystery of gratitude... To say thanks in the face of a nuclear holocaust threatening our planet with extinction of all human life may seem ridiculous. But when we realize that Christ also suffered this nuclear agony and anguish and overcame it on the cross, then our gratitude can even be deeper and stronger.

When we try to face the demons of violence and destruction, we quickly feel powerless. This experience of powerlessness easily leads to an inner rage and when this becomes a lasting emotion it settles within us as resentment. Resentment is the opposite of gratitude. It is the mood of a hardened heart that no longer waits for anything new and has accepted death as a fatality that cannot be escaped. Resentment is thus a sign of our having lost faith in the One who is the light. pp. 115-16

[ ]

...the community of peacemakers is a Eucharistic community. The word "eucharist" means gratitude. Wherever peacemakers speak and act, their words and actions announce the "good grace" (eu = good, charis = grace) of God.

Henri Nouwen
Peacework: Prayer, Resistance, Community
2014, p. 118

The Washing of the Feet

I thank you silent rock
and gently bow before you:
through you I live as plant.
I thank you field and forest
and deeply bow before you:
through you as animal I stand.
I thank you plant and animal and rock
and deeply bow in awe before you:
you three enable me to be.
We are thanking dear child of man
and deeply bow in awe before you:
through your being we exist.
Gratitude streams to and fro
in all the Godhead, one and many:
in gratitude all being is entwined.

Christian Mogenstern
Die Fusswashung
1973, p. 169
[Translated by Henk Bak]

Food as Sacrament

It has become clear to me that the concept of food itself is key to the transformation of our ecological crisis.

Unless our human species can open itself to the contemplation of food as a holy mystery through which we eat ourselves into existence, then the meaning of existence will continue to elude us. Our present cultural experience of food has degenerated into food as fuel, for supplying the energy of our insatiable search for that which will fill the hungers of our soul.

When we understand that food is not a metaphor for spiritual nourishment, but is itself spiritual, then we eat food with a spiritual attitude and taste and are nourished by the divine directly.

[ ]

As our culture shrinks in its inner life and rages in violence between individuals and groups, and against the whole of nature, we might do well to reflect on the meaning of food. I do not believe, that we are doomed to the inevitability of "engineering" food into a state of eternal shelf life, or that we must use our deadly nuclear inventions to irradiate our food for its immortality. These compulsive tendencies can be changed.

[ ]

By opening afresh the sacramental dimension of food, I hope to open the meaning of Eucharist and Gospel, so that we learn again to treat creation "knowingly, lovingly, skillfully, reverently"...as a sacrament.

Sister Miriam Therese MacGillis
Director of Genesis Farm, a biodynamic farm, founded and farmed
by the Dominican Congregation, Caldwell New Jersey
In: Alice Peck
Bread, Body, Spirit: Finding the Sacred in Food
2008, pp. 8-10

Are they Kosher?

As you can see, the concept of kosher has to do with both the individual and the universe. Helping to take care of the business of the universe begins with taking care of ourselves. The Jewish tradition is very clear about this. Each of us is part of the whole, and we matter. We are therefore obliged to treat the temples of our bodies with the respect, gratitude, and even awe they deserve.

> *Once we have learned to care for ourselves – as individuals. As families, as groups, as an entire species of human beings – we establish our organic connection with the will of God. This organic connection is neither abstract nor supernatural. It is based on a functional response to the ongoing processes of the universe. To rediscover these processes, all we have to do is open our hearts and eyes. If there is any great heresy, it is making ourselves opaque to the world.*

Rabbi Zalman M. Schachter-Shalomi
In: Alice Peck
Bread, Body, Spirit: Finding the Sacred in Food
2008, p.35

Sun spiritualizes earth

> *Sun spiritualizes earth*
> *Earth embodies sun –*
> *This is grain.*
> *Earth ensouled by human being*
> *Sun embodied by human being –*
> *This is bread.*
> *Earth-transforming sun*
> *Sun-embodying earth –*
> *This human being may become.*

Gideon Fontalba
Ein Brot (One Bread)
p. 106

Bread

> *A piece of bread contains a cloud. Without a cloud, the wheat cannot grow. So when you eat the piece of bread, you eat the cloud, you eat the sunshine, you eat the minerals, time, space, everything.*

Thich Nhat Hanh in: Jon Sweeney's
Praying with Our Hands: 21 Practices of Embodied Prayer from the World's Spiritual Traditions
2002, p. 49

This plate of food

This plate of food,

so fragrant and appetizing,

also contains much suffering.

Thich Nhat Hanh in: Alice Peck's
Bread, Body, Spirit: Finding the Sacred in Food
2008

The Blossom gives Way to the Fruit

Passing, passing
The blossom gives way to the fruit,
Both are necessary.
One passes into another.
Bread exists to be broken
To sustain its purpose,
The grape on the vine
Is wine in the making,
Crush it and it comes alive.

Jalal ad-Din ar-Rumi in : Alice Peck's
Bread, Body, Spirit: Finding the Sacred in Food
2008

Wandering Nourishment

Truth in the hands,
Wisdom in the eyes,
Strength in the word that creates,
Love in life that streams,
Thus, as wandering nourishment you serve!

Gideon Fontalba
Ein Brot (One Bread)
p. 114
[Provisionally translated by Henk Bak]

Source of Time and Space

Avinu Malkainu!
From infinity draw down to us The great renewal!
Attune us to Your intent,
So that Wisdom, Your daughter
Flow into our awareness,
To awaken us to see ahead,
So we help instead of harm.

May devices we make and use,
Be sparing and protecting Your creation.
Help us to set right what we have debased,
To heal what we have made ill,
To care for and restore what we have injured.
Bless our Earth, our home
And show us all
How to care for her
So we might live Your promise,
Given to our forebears
"To live heavenly days
Right here on this Earth."
May all the beings,
You have fashioned,
Become aware that it is You
Who has given them being.
May we realize that You shaped our lives,
And may each one, who breathes
Join with others who breathe
In the delight of shared knowing,
Of the great breath.
Assist us in learning
How to partner,
With family, neighbours,
And friends.
Aid us in dissolving old enmities;
May we come to honor,
Even in those whom we fear,
Your image and form,
Your light Dwelling In their hearts.
May we soon see the day, when
When Your House will be indeed,
A House of Prayer
For All Peoples,
Named and celebrated
In every tongue and speech.
On that day You will be one
And one with all cosmic Life
Amen!

Rabbi Zalman Schachter-Shalomi

The Emerging Cosmology
[An Excerpt from an Unpublished Manuscript the Emerging Cosmology]

Am I too deaf to hear...
Am I too deaf to hear
the singing of the Nightingale
am I too blind to see
the colours of the spring
the rising of the Sun
and the glorious rainbow
Am I too blind to see
the coming of the
Kingdom of God?

I am too dumb to see
the breaking of the drought
Am I unaware
that we are standing
at the end of the desert
am I not aware
that we are standing at the Gate
of the City of God?

Les Endrei
Poems for the Planet
2018, p. 117

Our Mother Prayer

Our Mother, thou who art in the darkness of the underworld,
May the holiness of thy name shine anew in our remembering,
May the breath of thy awakening kingdom warm the hearts of all
who wander homeless,
May the resurrection of thy will renew eternal faith even unto the
depths of physical substance.
Receive this day the living memory of thee from human hearts,
Who implore thee to forgive the sin of forgetting thee,
And are ready to fight against temptation in this world
which has led thee to existence in darkness,
That through the deed of the Son the immeasurable pain of the
Father be stilled,
By the liberation of all beings from the tragedy of thy withdrawal.
For thine is the homeland, and the boundless wisdom, and the

all-merciful grace, for all and everything in the circle of all. Amen.

Valentin Tomberg, Christmas 1940 in: Robert Powell:
The Most Holy Trinosophia and the New Revelation of Divine
Feminine
2000, pp. 42-43

Orientation

Before presenting a poetic 'thank you' that includes virtually everything that has been theme or motive of the dialogue imagined for this book, I want to clarify a theme that thus far has not been part of the dialogue: known under many names, gods, deva's, angels, messengers, spirits, jinn. Many religious and nonreligious accounts of the cosmos include spiritual realms above and below the kingdoms of our world. As soon as academia including academic theology, lifts its embargo on these matters, an articulate dialogue on these realms should be possible. Till then, Rudolf Steiner's insight in the nature of these beings may count as the most authorative source on this subject from a Western point of view. In his 'Meditations on the Tarot' Valentin Tomberg has elaborated also extensively on the Judaic esoteric tradition on this subject. In the following song of gratitude Tomberg uses the names as they appear in the Christian church liturgy. As those names have become unclear and meaningless even for many Christians themselves, I include the names Rudolf Steiner has given to them.

Duet with Brother Franciscus

Brother Franciscus, in your days on earth,
you have praised and thanked
Sun, Water, Fire and Death,
as it was becoming for your wakeful eye and wakeful heart.

Would you not now join in with me,
so that we together sing a song of gratitude
for all and for everything in this great, wonderful world?
I begin, and you join in.

We thank You, Eternal Giver of all gifts,
for the wonderful all-embracing gift,
that includes and makes possible all other gifts.

We thank You for the gift of Being

*We thank You, Enlightener of all brightness,
for the wonderful gift of clear consciousness,
that enlightens us with clarity, determination and purity.
We thank You for the gift of consciousness.*

*We thank You, Grounder of all that there is to be fathomed,
for the wonderful gift of pure thinking,
that streams into us with crystal-clear transparency and
connects yesterday and tomorrow, the above and the below
with a silver thread (or glass pearl thread).
We thank You for the gift of thinking.*

*We thank You, Warm Heart of the world,
for the wonderful gift of warm feeling,
that fills us with unutterable melodies
and erects thrones in the heart for Queen Beauty.
We thank You for the gift of feeling.*

*We thank You, lightning Primal Source of all daring endeavour,
for the wonderful gift of the fiery will,
which has adorned the world with
heroes, builders and achievers.
We thank You for the gift of will.*

*We thank You, Who values and preserves
the greatest and the smallest,
for the wonderful gift of memory,
that weaves the wonderful fabric in colours, brilliance and tone,
which we stretch out over the pillars of time.
We thank You for the gift of memory.*

*We thank You, Who heralds and promises
inexpressible sacred mysteries;*

for the wonderful gift of de word,
through which we live and work together as brothers and sisters
and celebrate our community in giving and taking.
We thank You for the gift of the word.

We thank You, Shaper of what is fleeting,
for the wonderful gift of the body,
that gives us the face and the wonderful senses,
the arms and legs for working and wandering.
We thank You for the gift of the body.

We thank You, Deepest Ground of all that is solid and reliable,
for the wonderful gift of the stable earth,
which under our feet provides us
with a foundation for our building, dwelling and wandering.
We thank You for the gift of the earth.

We thank You, Wellspring of all life,
for the wonderful gift of nature,
that surrounds us in earth, in water and air
with the wealth of stones, plants, fish, animals and birds.
We thank You for the gift of nature.

We thank You, Guardian of Eternity,
for the wonderful gift of the heavens,
that into our lives let stream
sun-gold, moon-silver and star-sounds.
We thank You for the gift of the heavens.

We thank You, Gracious Father in heaven,
for the wonderful gift of culture,
in whose temple the sisters science, art and religion
bring day and night their offerings to You.
We thank You for the gift of culture.

We thank You, Breathing Spirit of giving fullness
for the wonderful gift of inspiration,
out of which prayers, songs, poetry, images
and temples out stone and thought arise.
We thank You for the gift of inspiration.

We Thank You, Guide of transformative unfolding of beings,
for the wonderful gift of transformation,
through which righteous ones, prophets, saints,
wise ones and your servants arise
and shine as stars in the heavens of eternal being.
We thank You for the gift of transformation.

We thank You, primordial image of individuality
for the wonderful gift of Your true likeness,
in which the human face lights up,
the Angels shine, the Archangels flash as lightning,
the Archai thunder,
the Powers - Spirits of Form - shape, the Virtues - Spirits of Movement - rule,
the Dominions - Spirits of Wisom - elevate,
the Thrones - Spirits of Will - shake, the Cherubim - Spirits of Harmony - appear
and the Seraphim - Spirits of Fire and Love - realise their being.
We thank You for the gift of the true likeness.

And we thank You, Treasurer of what has not yet become,
for the holy gift of hopeful expectation,
that keeps us awake and prepared in faith, hope and love
for the new in what is becoming of the future.
We thank You for the gift of hopeful expectation.

Valentin Tomberg, Muelheim 1947
From the German, Eine Biografie von Elisabeth Heckmann und Michael French:
Valentin Tomberg, Leben. Band 1.2 1944-1973
2005, pp 143-145
[Translated by Henk Bak, with the names within hyphens added for clarity: they were given by Rudolf Steiner. Tomberg himself considered Steiner the 20th century authority on Angels in the Christian tradition]

Epilogue

What begins as dialogue may end up as living form, without ceasing to continue as dialogue. Just as the contours of fruit-fly or human being arise as embryos out of fluid beginnings.

Fruit-flies grow fast and are therefore often chosen for tests relating to evolutionary development. Humans grow slower and adolescents mercifully stop growing and can concentrate the rest of their lives on developing their full potential. Trees grow tall and don't overtake their measure. But a book? If I am not careful and if there are not planes to catch, in which the book should travel in printed form, I would find myself coming up with new ideas, insights, possible additions or new topics. Overwhelmed by the thought, I suddenly realize, that in every passage, text or chapter of this book, a reader might get some idea, some insight or the urge to add something to that point. I also realise, that a dialogue on paper or screen allows for lengthier contributions than a dialogue in the form of a conversation would tolerate. In conversation contributions need to be relatively short, as the conversation needs to flow. But the lengthy written contributions may serve to remind us, that a brief contribution might be the fruit of lengthy consideration and deep reflection.

These thoughts help me to let go. And I hope that this book will find its way to anyone interested as well as teachers and parents, educators and senior students, to preachers, pastoral carers, religious or secular and to intercultural/interfaith groups. Even though the book is obviously based on scholarly work, it is intended to break through to the world of everyday life, where a lay person needs to become competent in dealing with experts, where ignorance is often the root of violent conflict and where the adult world often appears to have failed its educational responsibility towards the younger and newest generation...

At the end of my notes on the selection of texts (Chapter 4), I had come to realize, that the writing and composing of this book had become part of my life, and the dialogue part of my life's story. Composing it with dialogue in mind and introducing sections with introductions, orientations and captions meant, that I engaged repeatedly with all the texts and learned to treat them as proxy partners in the dialogue itself. Quite a few have been interrelated for me for a long time. One example: In the '60's Jürgen Habermas introduced me to the Husserl's notion of 'intersubjectivity' − in the 50's my history of philosophy lecturer, Adelard Epping had explained to us, Husserl's method of 'epochè': withholding judgement, let phenomena 'speak' for themselves, place your statements 'in between brackets', much later did I come across

S.T. Coleridge's way of 'suspending disbelief' and in the 90's I learned about Jacques Derrida's 'deconstruction' in literary criticism: interpreting a text by paying attention to its constituent parts, without pulling the text apart (analysis). What he was looking for he summed up in one word: 'ringing', 'resonance' (in French: 'glas').

A voice, a musical instrument needs resonance to ring true, to touch a listener somewhere in his or her being…My piano teacher, Willem Hielkema, began his first lesson by showing me, at sixteen, how a sequence of 'levers' transfers my touch to the strings the piano a string instrument to make the instrument resonate and sing! Music and resonance seem to be integral to most spiritual, religious and cultural traditions. May be 'resonance' has guided me all along when composing and writing this book. I certainly hope so.

And I would be grateful for your patience, even if you might have to read something twice or more, just as I am grateful to God, to our teacher Shin, to the people around me and beyond, for making it possible for me make this journey happen.

Henk Bak
Evera, Trentham
8th of April 2019

Acknowledgements

At the end of this work my sense of gratitude filled my imagination with a great gathering in a grand amphitheatre: all the people I mention in this book are there, the ones I quote and the ones that guided me along and are somewhere behind the experiences and ideas that have contributed to its inception and development. Friends and strangers, players on the world stage and fellow travellers on the different roads of life and work.

In my imagination, I stood on the stage, alone, a stage of which I am told that if I drop a pin, one would hear its sound in the furthest and highest gallery, the 'gods' or – in Dutch – the 'angels gallery'. Angels or gods are certainly part of my imagined audience, as they have been my real guides as well. In the face of such enormous audience my thank-you will sound like nothing, less than a pin –drop, but I hope it is heard by all…For all your contributions, ephemeral, enduring and every shade of meaning and importance in between: a heartfelt thank you!

One by one I invite some out of the audience whom I remember, recognize, to join me on the stage for a special acknowledgement: first of all the unknown soldier, mentioned in chapter 4, who on a Christmas morning, 1944 in wartime The Hague offered us bread and thereby offered me a lesson for life. Then the ones who kindly gave me permission to quote from their work: the poet Les Laci, the theologians John Dupuche and Charles Sherlock, my friends Rebecca Maxwell and Lisaruth Webster. My friends Sean Burke and Dr Dzavid Haverick not only allowed me to quote from their work, but also contributed: Dzavid by suggesting the inclusion of the 'Golden Rule' in its subtitle and Sean Burke by thoroughly proofreading an early draft and improving the text by asking pertinent questions. Caroline Goode, also an early proof-reader, encouraged me when I wondered: do I make sense? and helped with questions as well as with the setup of the bibliography which is still a work in progress.

This is the place to mention friends who walked with me in the early stages of the project, especially Margaret and Maree Crutch, and Rosemary Ward who was the one who encouraged me to go public with it; the reverend Laurie McIntyre who asked me, could he walk with me and after the walk donated a tree to the Christian site of the walk; reverend Ken Parker who brought the Castlemaine Interfaith Group along, and Brigid O'Carroll-Walsh (1944-2019) who did the same with the Interfaith Group of Ballarat, with her partner Ian taking photos. I would also like to thank Andrew Stranieri and Megan Young for supporting this project by buying the printed draft

During my life as a student, teacher and convener of interfaith conversations and meditations for world-peace, I have been pulled along by other peoples' discoveries and readings. In a conversation after a peace meditation here in Trentham, Ian McBean suggested Paul Hawken's 'Blessed Unrest' to me, whilst on another occasion, Judith Weatherhead put me on to Margaret Somerville's 'The Ethical Imagination'. In another setting, a little group studying and discussing the 'philosophy of current affairs', as I liked to call it, Judith Couch drew our attention to Andrea Nye's 'PhilosOphia', on the three most significant philosophers of the 20 Century: Rosa Luxemburg, Simone Weil and Hannah Arendt. I was familiar with Simone Weil and had quoted her already, but Andrea Nye's elaborations on Hannah Arendt's have been a welcome enrichment to this book. She also drew our attention to "Ethics under Fire – challenges for the Australian Army", edited by Tom Frame and Albert Palazzo, which brought a new perspective to the section on the virtues in chapter 5.

Having gathered all those contributors on my imaginary stage, I realize that I had let the image itself slip. My large audience was gone and I just got a glimpse of a new audience coming in: readers of the few copies that are around. I hope that by putting the manuscript on the internet more people will have the benefit of this project, which has given me so many new insights, new experiences and energy in doing this.

Meanwhile I want to acknowledge those whose support and encouragement reach far beyond the genesis of this book alone. Again too many to mention. The way my parents, Jan Bak en Zus Baard taught me reverence, honesty and self-worth. How their families, uncles and aunts from both sides widened my experiences and views in the areas of music, visual arts and language. A widening that was greatly extended and deepened by virtually all the teachers, lectores, professors I have had. My late wife and life's companion and teacher Helma Overmars (1934 - 1964 – 2014) and our foster-son Michael and children Tineke and Tao. Michael by extending our experience to include Africa and the developing world. Tineke and Tao by extending our educational and spiritual horizon to include Steiner Education and the whole range of the Anthroposophical Movement, especially Stefan Lubienski who introduced us to Valentin Tomberg whose work has been extensively quoted in this book.

It was Helma who ventured out to widen her already thorough grounding in the humanities, to her training and practice as a nurse, her conventional medical training and a wide range of therapeutic modalities, as well as the spiritual grounding which came with Rudolf Steiners work and then Gideon Fontalba and Shin Gwydion, who have brought the work of spiritual masters like Rudolf Steiner, Sri Aurobindo, Rabinath Tagore, Peter Deunov and Omraam Michael Aivanhov up to the new level of understanding and action that humanity and the earth are dearly needing in our time. I thank Shin Gwydiion Fontalba (1948-2022) and his secretary Joannes Schmid especially for their encouragement, and Shin for his permission to use many of his texts for this publication, including His 'Circular verse of transformation' Anthology Ch2 and Anthology Ch5 section D: 'From Fire Being to Light Being'.

Michael through his intensive work with mentally and physically disabled people and his active interest in the political and social-economic developments in his native Tanzania; Tao through his PhD research into the development of educational initiatives for more humane, less rationalist, slower and more joyful ways of education; and Tineke through her ongoing involvement in the healing profession and spiritual developments of our time: all three keep me up to date. Tineke also regularly updates the website henkbak.com. The website itself gives an insight in the wider context out of this project has arisen.

Archie Patel provided invaluable assistance in making this text available for publication, designing the layouts and the wonderful cover. Her expertise and appreciation of the work of nature and architectural space has been much appreciated.

Finally I remember and thank the two new friends, who - shortly after Helma had left – entered my life on her birthday, 10 December 2014, to look at our garden and land: Alison (Ali) O'Brien and Ron White. Ali was interested to work in the garden, Ron was interested in the Interfaith Meditative Walk project. After walking for three hours Ron told me to write a book. I was reluctant but he persisted and this manuscript is the result. Both Ali and Ron participated in the walk several times. They both made and make me feel that I make sense: Ron in his eighties like me, Ali in her twenties. Every now and then Ali comes and stays here at Evera. Once she said on arrival: "wait till I have read the book" meaning, that I should not call myself a 'dinosaur' because I still work with books, not the internet. Two years ago Ron had to have a brain tumour removed. He recovered so well that he took it upon himself to proof-read, correct the manuscript and made helpful suggestions for improvement, which I happily followed. At his last visit Ron read out the last text: Tomberg's duet with St Francis, stanza for stanza. The cancer returned and Ron passed away on the 1st of July, aged 84. It is to his memory I dedicate this book – in gratitude.

Even though I would like to generously take responsibility for all the errors that may show up in the book, it lies in the nature of an anthology, that the chosen texts speak for themselves and that here my responsibility is limited to their selection, not their content. Many of those texts are in the public domain, have their copyright expired or fall within the length of legally permitted quotation. Where possible, texts have their source acknowledged in the anthologies themselves. An extended bibliography is available on henkbak.com. Copyright for the translations rest with this author.

www.ingramcontent.com/pod-product-compliance
Lightning Source LLC
Chambersburg PA
CBHW031359290426
44110CB00011B/207